Globalization or Regionalization
of the European Car Industry?

Globalization or Regionalization of the European Car Industry?

Edited by

Michel Freyssenet
Department of Sociology, National Scientific Research Centre (CNRS), Paris

Koichi Shimizu
Faculty of Economics, University of Okayama

Giuseppe Volpato
Faculty of Economics, University of Ca' Foscari, Venice

in association with

GERPISA

Réseau International
International Network
Groupe d'Étude et de Recherche Permanent sur l'Industrie et les Salariés de l'Automobile
Permanent Group for the Study of the Automobile Industry and its Employees
École des Hautes Etudes en Sciences Sociales, Paris, Université d'Évry-Val d'Essonne

First published 2003 by
PALGRAVE MACMILLAN
Houndmills, Basingstoke, Hampshire RG21 6XS and
175 Fifth Avenue, New York, N.Y. 10010
Companies and representatives throughout the world

PALGRAVE MACMILLAN is the global academic imprint of the Palgrave
Macmillan division of St. Martin's Press, LLC and of Palgrave Macmillan Ltd.
Macmillan® is a registered trademark in the United States, United Kingdom
and other countries. Palgrave is a registered trademark in the European
Union and other countries.

ISBN 1–4039–0581–9

This book is printed on paper suitable for recycling and made from fully
managed and sustained forest sources.

A catalogue record for this book is available from the British Library.

Library of Congress Cataloging-in-Publication Data
Globalization or regionalization of the European car industry?/edited by
Michel Freyssenet, Koichi Shimizu, Giuseppe Volpato.
    p. cm.
    Includes bibliographical references and index.
    ISBN 1–4039–0581–9
    1. Automobile industry and trade—Europe. 2. Globalization—Economic aspects.
    I. Freyssenet, Michel. II. Shimizu, Koichi. III. Volpato, Giuseppe.
HD9710.E82 G58 2003
338.4'7629222'094—dc21   2002030791

10   9   8   7   6   5   4   3   2   1
12   11   10   09   08   07   06   05   04   03

Printed and bound in Great Britain by
Antony Rowe Ltd, Chippenham and Eastbourne

Contents

List of Tables

List of Figures

List of Appendix Tables

List of Abbreviations

AEU	Amalgamated Engineering Union
AGVs	automated guided vehicles
AMC	American Motors Corporation
AMIA	Asociación Mexicana de la Industria Automotriz
ASEAN	Association of South East Asian Nations
BBC	brand to brand complementation
BCG	Boston Consulting Group
BFA	Bertrand-Faure
BL	British Leyland
BLMC	British Leyland Motor Corporation
BMW	Bayerische Motoren Werke
BNP	Banque Nationale de Paris
CAT	Compagnie d'affrètement et de transport
CBU	completely built up
CCFA	Comité des Constructeurs Français d'Automobiles (French Chamber of Automobile Builders)
CEEC	Central Europe and Eastern Countries
CEO	chief executive officer
CGT	Confédération Générale du Travail (France)
CKD	completely knocked down
CNUCED	Conférence des Nations Unies sur le Commerce et le Développement (UNCTAD: United Nations Conference on Trade and Developement)
COFACE	Compagnie Française d'Assurances pour le Commerce Extérieur
COFAL	Financial Company for Latin America
COO	chief operational officer
COS	Chrysler's operating system
DATAR	Délégation à l'Aménagement du Territoire et à Régionalisation (France)
DB	Daimler-Benz
DC	DaimlerChrysler
DFIs	direct foreign investments
DM	Deutsche Mark
DRG	Democratic Republic of Germany
EAC	Executive Automotive Committee
EC	European Commission
ECC	European Community Committee

ECIA	Équipement et Composants pour l'Industrie Automobile (subsidiary of PSA)
EIU	Economist Intelligence Unit
EU	European Union
F.A.S.A.	Fiat Auto South Africa
FASA	Fabrication de Automobiles, Sociedad Anonima
FDI	foreign direct investment
FIEV	Fédération des Industries d'Equipements pour Véhicules (French professional organization of car industry suppliers)
FF	French Franc
FRG	Federal Republic of Germany
FT	Financial Times
4WD	four-wheel drive
GAAP	General Accepted Accounting Principles
GATT	General Agreement on Tariffs and Trade
GDR	German Democratic Republic
GERPISA	Groupe d'Études et de Recherche sur l'Industrie et les Salariés de l'Automobile (Permanent group for the study of the automobile industry and its employees)
GM	General Motors
ICDP	International Car Distribution Programme
IGM	Industriegewerkschaft Metall
ILO	International Labour Organization
IMF	International Monetary Fund
IPO	Initial Public Offering
KD	knocked down
Mercosur/ Mercosul	Common Market of South American countries
MIT	Massachusetts Institute of Technology
MITI	Ministry of International Trade and Industry
MVMA	Motor Vehicle Manufacturing Association
n.a.	not available
NAFTA	North America Free Trade Agreement
NICs	newly industrialized countries
NIEs	newly industrializing economics
OEM	original equipment manufacturing
OICA	Organisation Internationale des Constructeurs d'Automobiles
QC	quality control
R&D	research and development
RNUR	Régie Nationale des Usines Renault
ROCE	return on capital employment
RVI	Renault Véhicules Industriels
RVs	recreational vehicles

SKD	semi-knocked down
SOFASA	Sociedad de Fabrication de Automotores
SUVs	sport utility vehicles
TKM	Toyota Kirloskar Motor
UAW	United Automobile Workers
UETs	Unités Élémentaires de Travail
UK	United Kingdom
UNCTAD	United Nations Conference on Trade and Development
USA	United States of America
USSR	Union of Soviet Socialist Republics
USTR	United States Trade Representative
UTE	elementary technology units
UV	utility vehicles
VEC	Volvo Europe Cars
VP	vice-president
VW	Volkswagen
WTO	World Trade Organization

Foreword

Over the next few decades, will 'lean production', and a generalized deregulation of trade have become the norms for the international environment in which firms and political and economic spaces will be operating?

The GERPISA Group, a French-based permanent research network devoted to the study of the automobile industry and its labour force, has been transformed into an international network of researchers whose backgrounds cover a wide range of social sciences (economics, business, history, sociology, geography and political science). Between 1993 and 1996 the Group carried out an initial international programme entitled 'The Emergence of New Industrial Models', a project in which it examined whether existing industrial models were in effect starting to converge towards the principles of 'lean production' – as had been theorized by the MIT's IMVP (International Motor Vehicle Programme) team. By focusing on what was happening in the automobile industry, the GERPISA Group's work was able to demonstrate the great diversity, and divergence, of the trajectories that firms have been following in recent times. Examples have been the wide spectrum of product policies; of productive organizations and labour relations; and the hybridization of production systems in the new spaces towards which firms have been expanding. There is no 'one best way' today – there never has been, and there probably never will be. In fact, the first GERPISA research project made it possible to identify and characterize not one, but three industrial models, all of which have been in operation since the 1970s: the Toyotaist model, the Hondian model, and the Sloanian model (epitomized today by Volkswagen, not GM). The reasoning behind this conclusion is presented and discussed in the four collective books produced by the four working groups, which represent different elements of the integrated project: Freyssenet, M., Mair, A., Shimizu, K. and Volpato, G. (eds), *One Best Way? Trajectories and Industrial Models of the World's Automobile Producers* (Oxford/New York: Oxford University Press, 1998); Boyer, R., Charron, E., Jürgens, U. and Tolliday, S. (eds), *Between Imitation and Innovation: The Transfer and Hybridization of Productive Models in the International Automobile Industry* (Oxford/New York: Oxford University Press, 1998); Durand, J. P., Stewart, P. and Castillo, J. J. (eds), *Teamwork in the Automobile Industry: Radical Change or Passing Fashion?* (London: Macmillan, 1999); and Lung, Y., Chanaron, J. J., Fujimoto, T. and Raff, D. (eds), *Coping with Variety: Flexible Productive Systems for Product Variety in the Auto Industry* (Aldershot: Ashgate, 1999).

This made it possible to construct theories to explain the processes that had led to this multiplicity of models. Companies follow different profit strategies – their attempts to increase their profitability cause them to favour certain policy combinations over others (for example, volume and diversity, quality, innovation and flexibility, the permanent reduction of costs, volumes and so on). However, in order to be efficient, all these strategies have to fit in with the environments in which they are to be applied – especially with respect to the modes of income growth and distribution that are being practised in the spaces under consideration. Moreover, to form a 'productive model', born out of an 'enterprise–government compromise' between the main parties (that is, the shareholders, management, unions, workforce, and suppliers), the strategies need to be implemented coherently. This analytical framework is presented in Boyer, R. and Freyssenet, M., *The Productive Models: The Conditions of Profitability* (London/New York: Palgrave, 2002).

Between 1997 and 1999, GERPISA carried out a second international programme, entitled 'The Automobile Industry between Globalization and Regionalization'. This project tested the thesis that globalization is an imperative for corporate profitability; and that it is the inevitable consequence of the deregulation of trade in the aforementioned 'new' spaces. This was the logical extension of the first programme, given that 'lean production' was the most suitable model for markets that are variable and diversified, and ostensibly moving towards a single global standard. Firms are establishing themselves across the whole of the planet; new industrialized nations are emerging as a result of their having opened up to international trade; and, more recently, certain automakers have been at the heart of some mega-mergers. All these events have supported the thesis of globalization, a process that is supposedly galvanized by the fact that companies, in their efforts to benefit from economies of scale, and from improved cost structures, are always increasing their organizational integration, and doing this on an ever-greater geographical scale. The commercial opening of the new spaces, which some expect to create a homogenization of demand, is also deemed to contribute to this process.

A previous study (Humphrey, J., Leclerc, Y. and Salerno, M. S. (eds), *Global Strategies and Local Realities: The Auto Industry in Emerging Markets* (London: Macmillan; New York: St. Martin's Press, 2000)) constituted a first attempt to put this hypothesis to the test, and it did so by focusing on the situation in the emerging countries. The main objective was to scrutinize a concept that is being presented nowadays as if it were self-explanatory: economic globalization. The authors who have collaborated had all emphasized the diversity of the productive and spatial configurations that can be observed in the emerging countries.

The present publication aims to carry out a systematic description and analysis of the trajectories of internationalization that are being followed by the various types of firms involved in the European automobile industry (manufacturers, suppliers and dealers). A companion book looks at the American and Asian automobile industries from the same perspective

(Freyssenet, M., Shimizu, K. and Volpato, G. (eds), *Globalization or Regionalization of the American and Asian Car Industry?* London/New York: Palgrave, 2003). Another book (Carillo, J., Lung, Y. and van Tulder, R. (eds), *Cars, Carriers of Regionalism*) analyses the process of regionalization of the auto industry in different areas of the world. These studies identify and characterize the different processes of periodic re-heterogenization, and the conditions that are necessary if firms, and spaces, are to be successful. Moreover, within this perspective, they will be particularly keen to analyse the steps that are being taken in order that firms' and areas' trajectories can be adjusted and hybridized – actions which in all probability will require considerable strategic and organizational inventiveness. A recent book from the second GERPISA programme particularly examines the form and the character of the internationalization of employment relationships in the automobile industry (Charron, E. and Stewart, P. (eds), *Work and Employment Relations in the Automobile Industry*, London/New York: Palgrave, 2003).

GERPISA's books are not only the result of the work done by their contributors, and by the editors who have assembled and organized them. Through their participation in international meetings, and in the annual symposiums, the members of the programme's international steering committee and the other members of the network have contributed in various degrees to the discussions, and to the general thought process. In addition, the books would have never seen the light of day had it not been for GERPISA's administrative staff, who take care of the tasks that are part of the daily life of an international network. We thank them all.

MICHEL FREYSSENET
YANNICK LUNG
Scientific co-ordinators of the GERPISA programme
'The Automobile Industry between Globalization and Regionalization'

Notes on the Contributors

Leonardo Buzzavo is a Senior Lecturer at Ca' Foscari University, Venice, Italy. His research fields are marketing and strategy. His most recent publication is Buzzavo, L. (2000) 'Rethinking Used Cars', In Whiteman, J., Tongue, A. and Jones, D. (eds), *Fulfilling the Promise: What Future for Franchised Car Distribution?* (*The ICDP Review*, International Car Distribution Programme, Solihull).

Andrea Eckardt teaches at the Institute of Sociology, Friedrich-Alexander University, Erlangen, Nuremberg, Germany. Her research topics are industrial relations, the global automotive industry, production and working systems. Her most recent publications are Eckardt, A., Köhler, H.-D. and Pries, L. (1999) (eds), *Global Players in lokalen Bindungen – Unternehmensglobalisierung in soziologischer Perspektive* (Berlin: Sigma, 2001).

Michel Freyssenet is Research Director in Sociology at the National Scientific Research Centre (CNRS), in Paris, France. He is co-founder and co-director of the GERPISA international network (michel.freyssenet@gerpisa.univevry.fr). He is working on the division of labour, productive models, employment relationships and the concept of work. His latest book in English is Boyer, R. and Freyssenet, M., *The Productive Models: The Conditions of Profitability* (London/New York: Palgrave, 2002).

Bruno Jetin is Associate Professor in Economics at the Centre d'économie de Université de Paris Nord (CEPN, CNRS, jetin@seg.univ-paris13.fr), France, where he specializes in International Finance topics such as currency transaction tax and capital controls. He is a member of the Steering Committee of the GERPISA. His most recent publications are: 'The Historical Evolution of Product Variety in the Automobile Industry: An International Comparative Study', in Lung, Y. *et al.* (eds), *Coping with Variety* (Aldershot: Ashgate, 1999), and 'The Tobin Tax and the Regulation of Capital Movements', with Suzanne de Brunhoff, in Bello, W. *et al.* (eds), *Global Finance* (London: Zed Books, 2000).

Matthias Klemm teaches at the Institute of Sociology, Friedrich-Alexander University Erlangen, Nuremberg, Germany. His research project is communication in multicultural companies – the case Volkswagen-Skoda. His research topics are: the sociology of culture, knowledge and organization. His most recent publication is: Heyder, T. and Klemm, M., 'Einige Daten zur Entwicklung des Automobilismus', in Schmidt, G. (ed.), *Technik und Gesellschaft. Jahrbuch 10: Automobil und Autombilismus* (Frankfurt/Main, New York: Campus, 1999).

Holm-Detlev Köhler is Professor of Sociology at the University of Oviedo, Spain (hkohler@correo.uniovi.es). His main research topics are comparative industrial relations, and local and regional development. His most recent publication is 'Netzwerksteuerung und/oder Konzernkontrolle? Die Automobilkonzerne im Internationalisierungsprozeß', in Sydow, J. and Windeler, A. (eds), *Steuerung von Netzwerken. Konzepte und Praktiken* (Opladen/ Wiesbaden: Westdeutscher Verlag, 2000).

Lydie Laigle, Doctor of Economy, is a Senior Researcher at CSTB (Centre Scientifique et Technique du Bâtiment) in Paris, France. She has carried out studies on changes in the organization and geographical location of supplier networks in Europe for French Ministries and the European Commission. She has participated in programmes dedicated to ICT and Internet applications for housing and cities. Her most recent English publication about the automobile industry is 'Co-operative Buyer–Supplier Relationships in Development Projects in the Car Industry', in Lundin, R. A. and Midler, Ch. (eds), *Projects as Arenas for Renewal and Learning Processes* (Kluwer Academic Publishers, 1998).

Jean-Louis Loubet is Professor of History at the University of Evry, France. His main research field is the French automobile industry. His most recent publication in English is *Road Book: Renault 1898–2001* (Boulogne: ETAI, 2001).

Ludger Pries is Professor of the Department of Social Science of Ruhr-Universität Bochum, Germany, Chair of the Sociology of Organizations and Participation Studies (SOAPS). His research fields are the comparative sociology of work, organizations and migration. His most recent book in English is *New Transnational Social Spaces: International Migration and Transnational Companies* (London: Routledge, 2001).

Koichi Shimizu, Doctor of Economics from Paris IX, is Professor of the Faculty of Economics, University of Okayama, Japan. He is a member of the Steering Committee of the GERPISA. His research topics are studies on the evolutionary theory of the firm, labour relations in the Japanese and French automobile industries, and Toyota. His most recent publication in English is Freyssenet, M., Mair, A., Shimizu, K. and Volpato, G. (eds), *One Best Way? Trajectories and Industrial Models of the World's Automobile Producers* (Oxford/New York: Oxford University Press, 1998).

Giuseppe Volpato is Dean of the Faculty of Economics at Ca' Foscari University, Venice, Italy, and Professor of Management and Business Strategy (volpato@unive.it). He is a member of the Steering Committee of the

GERPISA. His main research interests include industrial economics, strategic management, the management of innovation, and the theory of the firm. A number of theoretical and empirical studies have been carried out in these fields. As a result many national and international contributions have been published. His most recent publication in English is Lung, Y. and Volpato, G. (eds), 'Reconfiguring the Auto Industry', *International Journal of Automotive Technology and Management*, vol. 2, no. 1, 2002.

1

Introduction: The Diversity of Internationalization Strategies and Trajectories of Automobile Sector Firms

Michel Freyssenet, Koichi Shimizu and Giuseppe Volpato

For most observers, the globalization of firms is under way and irreversible. In accordance with their descriptive and analytical orientation, GERPISA contributors to this book question this common affirmation relating to the internationalization trajectories of automobile sector companies – builders, suppliers and distributors – over forty years. They show the diversity of ways and forms of internationalization, the reversibility of these processes observed in the past, the restrictive conditions of profitability in overseas operations, and the prevalence of regionalization in spite of globalization attempts since the early 1990s. For this reason, the automobile firms' trajectories are grouped and analysed by their region of origin. This book considers Europe. A companion book looks at the American and Asian automobile industry (Freyssenet, M., Shimizu, K. and Volpato, G. (eds), *Globalization or Regionalization of the American and Asian Automobile Industry?*). In the conclusion, we propose to understand the diversity of the forms of internationalization, their success or their failure, considering the differences in the companies' profit strategies and the variable relevance of these strategies according to the evolutionary regional context. To aid understanding of the rest of this book, we introduce here the different forms of internationalization observed in the automobile industry since its beginning.

The relevance of the internationalization process in the automobile industry

The internationalization of the automotive industry is a typical feature of the establishment of the first automakers who, as soon as they were able to offer products with enough competitiveness and reliability to domestic customers, tested their luck in foreign markets, searching for the scale economies that were necessary to gain a strong position in an industry in which manufacturing investments were undoubtedly high (Bardou *et al.*, 1977; Bonnafos

1

et al., 1983; Volpato, 1983; Laux, 1992; Chanaron and Lung, 1995). But a quick thought about the history of the industry and a glimpse to the current structure of the automobile supply chain show clearly how the past forms of internationalization differ from those currently being developed. To a certain extent we could say that the history of internationalization in the automotive industry is the history of the automotive industry *tout court*, given the extraordinary role that such a phenomenon has always played, both in defining the type of competitive confrontation between automakers, and in the evolution of growth and consolidation strategies by automakers and their suppliers.

Such a statement aims at underlining the two-edged nature of the phenomenon of internationalization in the automotive industry, on the one hand always the same, but on the other always different compared to what had developed in previous years, because of the changes in automobile demand across the various markets, to the degree of maturity of the competitive challenge among industry players, to the evolution of product and manufacturing process technologies, and to the opening of the various national economies to exchanges and multilateral agreements.[1] Hence if one wants internationalization, as a concept both descriptive and interpretative of some of the most relevant aspects of the automotive supply chain, to have some hermeneutic meaning, it must be storicized – in other words applied to a given historical time and described in the aspects that derive from it, with respect to any automaker.

The multiplicity of forms of internationalization

It is commonly agreed to divide the internationalization process into stages, representing the stages of progress in the manufacturing and marketing organization of industrial firms on a multinational scale. In this introduction it is worth listing, briefly, the various roles of the internationalization process which at the beginning were measured by the amount of direct foreign investment:

- The export of completely-built-up vehicles (CBU). It is important to note that, contrary to popular belief, this first stage represented an important international involvement as well, since it implied the establishment of a decentralized marketing organization, a network of dealers and service agents, a system of parts warehouses, a logistics organization for their shipment to end customers, and finally marketing and promotion activities, with a multi-year time-frame. All this implies relevant investments, often higher than those required by small manufacturing and assembly plants. The failure of some European automakers in entering the North American market, as well as of some North American firms entering Europe through various historical stages, including the most recent ones, stems from the complexity of problems that arise even during the first step of the internationalization process, and from the difficulties shown by firms in adapting their marketing and product strategies, carried out successfully in the domestic market, to the needs of foreign markets.

- The assembly abroad of semi-knocked down vehicles (SKD), that is, vehicles partially assembled which require further operations, mainly with respect to the coupling of internal parts to the external body. It is a frequent solution in the first stages of the internationalization process, but is currently seldom applied outside small-volume manufacturing of vehicles.
- The assembly abroad of completely knocked down vehicles (CKD), that is, the complete assembly of vehicles whose individual parts are imported from abroad.
- The assembly of CKD vehicles through component parts partially manufactured in the same country and partially imported.
- The assembly of CKD vehicles starting from components wholly manufactured in the country where assembly takes place. A further development of such a stage consists of the organization of product export flows by the foreign country where assembly takes place towards more export markets (or even return exports to the country where the automobile company is based).

New forms of internationalization

However, at the beginning of the 1990s it became evident that these forms of internationalization, believed to be the most typical and relevant within the strategies adopted by automakers, albeit important, were not exhaustive, since they all revolved around a single parameter: the one based upon the degree of manufacturing integration achieved by automakers in the country at which the end product was directed. Such integration was minimal when there was the export of complete vehicles, but it was at a maximum with the local manufacturing of parts and final assembly. With the change in industry equilibria that took place mainly in the 1990s, it became evident that internationalization is a fact that presents a range of forms which cannot in the main be related to the degree of manufacturing integration. It encompasses a growing set of features which tend to play a higher role relating mainly to organizational, financial and decision-making aspects (Boyer *et al.*, 1998; Carrillo *et al.*, forthcoming; Freyssenet and Lung, forthcoming).

The forms of internationalization referring to organizational aspects can be defined by an automaker along a continuum between two extremes: at one end is an internationalization based upon a high standardization of the various organizational and decision-making forms of activities located abroad, involving a replication of procedures adopted in the mother company, and at the other end an eclectic organization inspired by localism, where in each individual market the organizational criteria are driven by the specific traits of the foreign situation.

Financial aspects are manifold. They range from less invasive forms of financial internationalization characterized by the forms of acquisition and the source of borrowed capital, to stronger forms that can affect the degree of international dispersion of capital, mainly in cases in which foreign placements of stocks are not acquired by individual investors, only interested in returns on the specific investment, but by other companies in the industry which exchange stocks in order to strengthen the range of agreements that are played mainly on the industrial front. Then comes the most relevant form of financial internationalization, in which an automobile company holds a major stake in a foreign automaker that it becomes the economic subject of reference, inspiring manufacturing and marketing strategies.

Also, decision-making aspects can be framed according to the various forms of internationalization. With the growth in forms of internationalization that has already been described, the possibility of co-ordinating tightly the policies adopted by individual makers controlled by an automobile company acquires a specific meaning.[2] In the past, both because of the complexity of the phenomena and the absence of communication media that were adequate to deal with and solve problems, the decision-making internationalization was limited. But now, thanks also to the innovation potential offered by the newest systems of information and communication technology (ICT), the possibility of developing competitive strategies on a world-wide scale appears as hard a goal as it is necessary (at least as an end objective) for all its implications, and currently it is pursued more and more firmly by all automakers, albeit following different paths and with different priorities. In this case as well, the forms of globalization of decision-making choices can develop in relation to set areas of application. By limiting ourselves to the analysis of the forms that currently involve automakers to a great extent, we must mention at least two specific areas: the design of shared platforms, and system integration and modularization.

The design of shared platforms

The search for scale and scope economies by suppliers can be exploited adequately only with forms of further product standardization by automakers. However, it is now evident that the 'simple' forms of internationalization based on the offer of an identical model for a range of markets (world car) turned out to be a failure. This result emerged through the difficulties encountered in transferring products within the most advanced markets in the Triad (USA, Western Europe, Japan), but the inadequate standardization of models will be exacerbated as emerging markets consolidate (Eastern Europe, Latin America, China, India and so on).[3] Therefore, automakers are experimenting with new forms of standardization, more refined and complex, yet only partial, as they aim to use common parts without the standardization of models, which must maintain margins of customization, both related to the various national markets, and to the specific needs of the individual end customer.[4]

Such a process moves along the design of 'common platforms' capable of using a relevant number of common sub-systems, but leaving the freedom to develop the body and other elements more readily visible to the customer according to forms that are differentiated for individual markets. It is a key move, in order to obtain considerable cost advantages. It is also hard and complex. No automaker can declare it to have been achieved in a satisfactory way, but all of them, without exception, are moving towards it, aware that only in such a way will they manage to solve the current contradiction between the advantage of expendable variety on the marketing side, and standardization linked to low-cost and high-quality manufacturing.

System integration and modularization

Another key element of the strategic reorganization of the automotive supply chain is the design of the vehicle by parts or systems, and the modularization of assembly. These are different features, which must be considered separately, but they share some common aspects. Vehicle design by systems that are integrated internally stems from the fact that the vehicle can be described as a set of functional groups, each of which is charged with carrying out different tasks: the production of moving energy and its transmission to the wheels (engine and powertrain); the braking system; the vehicle driving system; the control system; and the exhaust system. In the past, such systems had, from the design standpoint, a low degree of internal integration since they were made from single mechanical elements which could be designed with modest levels of interdependence. Currently, all these functional systems have a very high degree of integration because their operation is governed by electronics. In substance, each functional system is no longer the mechanical sum of many different parts, but represents an integrated complex that can be designed in an optimal way only through a unitary direction, carried out by a supplier acting as system integrator.[5] On the other hand, the phenomenon of modularization does not refer to the design of the individual component parts of a functional system, but focuses on its assembly and on the testing activities to be carried out at the stage that comes immediately before the transfer on to the vehicle assembly line. The module is therefore a macro-component, made up of many parts, which it is possible and economically attractive to assemble and test outside the vehicle's final assembly line, in order to increase its simplicity and speed. In some cases, therefore, it can happen that a functional system is a module, as in the case of the powertrain of the exhaust emission system, but in other cases this may not occur. For example, the vehicle lighting system or the driving system clearly represent functional systems, but their complexity and their extension over a set of vehicle parts prevent their pre-assembly as modules (Sako and Warburton, 1999).

All these new forms of design and co-ordination of activities are intrinsically linked to the phenomenon of internationalization, since on the one hand the possibility of fully exploiting the synergies deriving from these strategies lies in the development of a wide-ranging internationalization process, and on the other hand because the continuing tension between the acquisition of competences necessary to develop these highly complex projects, and the constant compression of costs, implies the selection both of partners with highly sophisticated technologies in the most advanced industrial areas, and of partners featuring low manufacturing costs in the emerging areas.

The destabilizing aspect of the globalization process

The globalization process under way is a sign of a response to a situation of strong competitive tension, but it has become in turn a case of further destabilization depending on the variety of strategies adopted by some automakers, which are obviously characterized by different evolutionary trajectories (path dependency) and by different profit strategies.[6] In such a sense, the policy of globalization that had initially acted as a 'response' strategy to the tensions triggered by the competitive challenge is becoming, within the complex system of interdependencies in the international automotive supply chain, the triggering factor for further initiatives by companies which see themselves threatened by recent transformations.

The chapters that follow describe in a rich and detailed way the variety of internationalization models developed by the main automakers in different markets. While directing the reader to them for a full appreciation of the pros and cons of the various strategies, it is, however, worth underlining here two phenomena that are both relevant and general: on the one hand, the fast and to some extent astonishing exchanging of competitive positions which again marks a strong, diverging trend for the individual automakers (hence the sustainability of different profit strategies), and on the other hand a sort of convergence by individual automakers in an attempt to reduce strongly their vertical integration.[7]

With respect to the exchanging of competitive positions, it is very significant that a considerable number of automakers who over the recent years did show a marked level of activity, mainly through policies of acquisitions, mergers and equity alliances (such as DaimlerChrysler, Ford and GM–Fiat), are undergoing a time of difficulty, whereas many observers, and financial consulting companies in particular, expected them to make a strong recovery. An exception within this picture is the Renault–Nissan group, the one that was credited with the hardest and most complex task. On the other hand, the highest profitability spot is held by the PSA group, which in the recent past was criticized for an excessively static attitude linked to the refusal to pursue a more marked policy of internationalization.

Instead, the traits of relative uniformity in the strategies of automakers relate to the forms of division of labour within the supply chain. All the main players in the industry are developing a further programme of reduction of their manufacturing borders, in order to transfer to first-tier suppliers not only the responsibility of development of product and process innovations, but also final assembly activities. Even Toyota, notably the automaker less inclined towards this, seems to have adopted a more open position.[8]

Clearly, such policy is based upon the belief that automakers are capable of maintaining, also in the sharing of activities and responsibilities, necessary know-how in order to integrate the contribution of suppliers into a product that is adequate for consumer needs and featuring a brand image strong enough to sustain an adequate premium price compared to the policies of direct market entry by component manufacturers. Once again the automotive industry appears likely to feature novelty and surprises.

Notes

1 On the reorganization of the automobile industry which took place after the oil shocks of the 1970s, see Freyssenet *et al.* (1998).
2 We hereby refer to the concept of globalization in the meaning defined by Porter (1986), according to whom an industry can be defined as global if there are competitive advantages deriving from the integration of activities on a world-wide scale.
3 On the NICs' automotive industry see, in particular, Humphrey *et al.* (2000).
4 For an analysis of the evolution of variety strategies developed over time by automobile companies, see the set of essays in Lung *et al.* (1999). On the concept of world car and of common platforms, see Camuffo and Volpato (1997), and Volpato and Stocchetti (2000).
5 The key characteristic of a system integrator is the undertaking of the responsibility for the execution of most relevant technical tasks in the product/system chain, and the co-ordination of the chain's technical and operational performance over time.
6 The original instability appears mainly to be generated by the fact that the development of the motorization process for the newly industrialized countries (NICs) is still insufficient to fully utilize the excess of production capacity accumulated by all automakers.
7 On the singularity of 'productive models' pursued by the various automobile companies, and on the links between their 'profit strategies', see the analysis in Boyer and Freyssenet (2000, 2002) and the conclusion (Chapter 11).
8 On Toyota's trajectory and its recent changes, see, in particular, Shimizu (1999).

References

Bardou, J.-P., Chanaron, J.-J. and Fridenson, P. (1977) *La révolution automobile*, Paris: Albin Michel.

Bonnafos, G., Chanaron, J.-J. and Mautort, L. (1983) *L'industrie automobile*, Paris: La Découverte.

Boyer, R. and Freyssenet, M. (2000, 2002) *Les modèles productifs*, Paris: La Découverte (2000); English revised edition: *The Productive Models: The Conditions of Profitability*, London/New York: Palgrave (2002).

Boyer, R., Charron, E., Jürgens, U. and Tolliday, S. (eds) (1998) *Between Imitation and Innovation: The Transfer and Hybridization of Productive Models in the International Automotive Industry*, Oxford/New York: Oxford University Press.

Camuffo, A. and Volpato, G. (1997) *Nuove forme di integrazione operativa: Il caso della componentistica automobilistica*, Milan: F. Angeli.

Carillo, J., Lung, Y. and Van Tulder, R. (eds) *Cars, Carrier of Regionalism*, (forthcoming).

Chanaron, J.-J. and Lung, Y. (1995) *Économie de l'automobile*, Paris: La Découverte.

Freyssenet, M. and Lung, Y. (forthcoming) 'Multinational Car Firms' Regional Strategies', in Carillo, J., Lung, Y. and van Tulder, R. (eds) *Cars, Carrier of Regionalism*.

Freyssenet, M., Mair, A., Shimizu, K. and Volpato, G. (eds) (1998) *One Best Way? Trajectories and Industrial Models of the World's Automobile Producers*, Oxford/New York: Oxford University Press.

Freyssenet, M., Shimizu, K. and Volpato, G. (eds) (2003) *Globalization or Regionalization of the American and Asian Car Industry?*, London/New York: Palgrave.

Humphrey, J., Lecler, Y. and Salerno, S. (eds) (2000) *Global Strategies and Local Realities: The Auto Industry in Emerging Market*, London: Macmillan.

Laux, J. M. (1992) *The European Automobile Industry*, New York: Twayne.

Lung, Y., Chanaron, J.-J., Fujimoto, T. and Raff, D. (eds) (1999) *Coping with Variety: Flexible Productive Systems for Product Variety in the Auto Industry*, Aldershot: Ashgate.

Porter, M. E. (ed.) (1986) *Competition in Global Industries*, Boston, Mass.: Harvard Business School Press.

Sako, M. and Warburton, M. (1999) *Modularization and Outsourcing Project*, IMVP Annual Forum, Boston, 6–7 October, Cambridge, Mass.: MIT.

Shimizu, K. (1999) *Le toyotisme*, Paris, La Découverte.

Volpato, G. (1983) *L'industria automobilistica internazionale*, Padua: Cedam.

Volpato, G. and Stocchetti, A. (2000) 'Managing Information Flows in Supplier–Customer Relationships: Issues, Methods and Emerging Problems', in Freyssenet, M. and Lung, Y. (eds), *The World that Changed the Machine: The Future of the Auto Industry for the 21st Century*, Proceedings of 8th GERPISA International Colloquium, Paris (CD ROM).

2
The Internationalization of European Automobile Firms: A Statistical Comparison with American and Asian Companies

Bruno Jetin

Introduction: internationalization, a necessary but risky adventure

The internationalization of the automobile industry is a phenomenon that goes back a long way. Most automobile firms have tried to move into the international theatre within a few years of beginning operations, first of all through export activities and later by establishing overseas production facilities. However, internationalization has taken on a new dimension in the context of economic globalization. The reinforcement of free trade, the new rights guaranteeing the mobility of productive and financial capital, and the intensification of competition in the firms' market of origin – all these factors have induced companies to try to use internationalization as a solution to the structural problems they face.

In the developed countries, the slowdown in growth, rising inequalities, the predominance of a product replacement type of demand, and even demographic trends, have combined to make it harder to produce and sell an ever-greater volume of motor vehicles.

The profitability constraint has also become more severe. To better anticipate or adapt to demand (and to the increased number of environmental and safety-related standards), the new models that are being launched are increasingly differentiated. However, this has led to a rise in investment outlays at a time when greater competition squeezes profit margins, causing shareholders to demand higher remuneration.

The solution to these problems can no longer be found within a national market that exists in isolation. Conversely, by making sales in as many markets as possible, some of the aforementioned constraints can be loosened.

Growth rates in the 'three poles of the Triad' (North America, Japan and the European Union) became uncoupled to a greater degree during the 1990s than during the 1970s and 1980s. Renewed growth in the United States between 1991 and 2000 enabled certain Japanese and European firms to make substantial profits, which in certain cases supplemented the profits (or offset the losses) they were making in their domestic markets.

The so-called 'emerging' countries experienced rapid growth up to 1997. For the first time since the 1970s, the emerging markets' enormous potential translated into high real demand. Firms that were ready for this scenario were able to make a lot of money in these parts of the world.

To take advantage of these overseas profit opportunities without reviving protectionist tendencies (and to satisfy demand to a maximum extent while minimizing costs), most automakers were forced to manufacture in the same places as they were making their sales. This created a veritable investment race (notably in the so-called 'emerging' countries). This drive could be meaningful at the individual firm level, but at a global level it translated into a further increase in the excessive production capacities from which the automobile sector was already suffering.

According to certain estimates (PriceWaterhouseCoopers, 1999), production capacities grew by 17 million units between 1990 and 1997, the equivalent of an additional North American market. This can be explained by the rapid growth of automobile demand from the 'emerging' countries up to 1997, and from the North American market up to 2000. But what remained of this legacy once economic crises struck the emerging countries (1997–8) and growth slowed down in the developed countries (2001)?

Calculated at a global level, unused production capacities were estimated to be 30% in 1990 and 39% in 1999 (PricewaterhouseCoopers, 1999; Economist Intelligence Unit, 2000). However, this average covers significant geographic variations: 40% in Asia in 1998 (PricewaterhouseCoopers, 1999), 56% in Brazil in 1999 (Financial Times Auto Survey, June 2000) and 65% in Argentina in 1999 (Ward's Automotive Yearbook, 2000). At first glance, it would appear that firms that are present throughout the world's regions are best able to absorb those demand shocks that can engender major financial losses. However, firms with a low level of geographic diversification can also suffer greatly in such situations, and even go bankrupt. When a fallback in growth also affects the firm's country of origin, which often remains its main market, doubts can be raised about the viability of its overseas operations. As such, the late 2000 decline in American growth immediately led to the closure of a number of American automakers' overseas plants as they tried to restore profits as soon as possible so as to regain shareholder confidence.

Internationalization increases firms' vulnerability to cyclical fluctuations in growth. For this reason it is at best a positive strategy for a few firms, and certainly not for all. It is from this perspective that the present chapter will try to develop a quantitative analysis of firms' internationalization. We shall be attempting to answer two fundamental questions:

1. What are firms' current levels of internationalization? Is there really such a thing as a 'global' firm?
2. How do international activities contribute to firms' profits (or losses)?

Although quantitative analysis cannot in and of itself answer these questions, it nevertheless constitutes a good starting point and can be supplemented by the qualitative analysis offered in other chapters of this book.

At a methodological level, this quantitative analysis will exploit systematically long-term data that firms have published in their financial reports. Some will argue that this data is inconsistent because it is subject to the firms' desire to publish information that is reliable within accounting and legislative frameworks that can vary over time and from one country to another. Nevertheless, and despite the difficulty of achieving total precision, we still feel that our findings correspond to the known characteristics of the firms under study and to the events that have affected them.

In addition, this quantitative investigation will be based on the following hypotheses:

1. It will be postulated that multinational firms are not 'footloose'; rather, that they are dependent upon their territory of origin, which provides them with economic and institutional support. This territory might be the firm's country of origin but it can also be the region, even if the process of regional integration varies greatly from one continent to another. Depending on the particular example, internationalization will be defined as all the activities situated outside a firm's country or region of origin.
2. Multinational automobile firms are to be considered as industrial and financial groups in addition to their vehicle-making activities. This is indeed the relevant level of analysis for studying all of a firm's financial flows and sources of profit, rather than their physical production of passenger vehicles alone. Whereas in most firms, passenger vehicles and commercial vehicles represent 80% to 90% of (external) revenues, there are significant exceptions. As an example, passenger vehicles and commercial vehicles only accounted for 55% of the Fiat Group's revenues in 1997–9. The 'motorcycle' branch accounted for 14% of Honda and Suzuki's revenues in 1995–9. Services represented 18.5% of Ford's revenues in 1996–8.

Given these hypotheses, the present chapter will be organized in the following manner: the first section, 'the inventory', is an inventory intended to present the level of concentration that characterizes the world's automobile industry. We shall then measure the extent of firms' commercial internationalization, and subsequently their level of productive and financial internationalization. We shall conclude this first section with a presentation of two synthetic indexes. The second section focuses on the contributions that overseas activities make to firms' world-wide profits (or losses). In particular, we shall look at American, Japanese and French firms.[1]

The inventory

A sector's degree of internationalization is a multi-faceted phenomenon. Just using a criterion such as assets held abroad in 1998 (calculated in absolute terms), we find no less than nine automobile firms among the world's twenty-five leading multinationals (UNCTAD, 2000). Automobile firms also lead the tables in areas such as foreign sales volumes (in absolute terms) and number of overseas staff members. This is because they are among the world's largest multinational firms. If we analyse overseas business as a proportion of total activities by combining several criteria (as per the UNCTAD index's transnational logic), we can see that there has been a substantial rise in the automobile industry's degree of internationalization.[2] In 1990, the transnationality index was 35.8%, far behind the 51.1% average (all sectors combined) for the world's 100 leading multinational firms. By 1998, the automobile industry's transnationality index had risen sharply, reaching 49% and approaching the average index value of 53.9%. This was still behind the values for industries such as the media (86.7%), food and drink (74.3%), pharmaceuticals (64.3%), chemicals (58.5%) – and even oil (52.7%) (UNCTAD, 2000). But it is clear that the automobile industry has been experiencing a recent acceleration in its internationalization levels, thus raising questions about the existence of qualitative changes in its supply structure and forms of competition.

The constitution of a space of global competition

The automobile industry was not left untouched by the wave of mergers/acquisitions and partnerships that affected all industrial activities and services during the late 1990s. This led to a rapid rise in concentration, a development portrayed in Table 2.1, with its analysis of changes in the output of the world's twenty largest firms between 1985 and 1999.

We see that, in 1985, three firms manufactured more than 4 million units, representing 42.2% of world output.[3] By 1999, six firms were producing more than 4 million units, and controlling 65.1% of global production.[4]

In 1985, two firms made between 2 and 3 million units, representing 11.6% of world output.[5] By 1999, four firms were in this situation, representing 17.3% of world output.[6] Eight firms produced between 1 and 2 million units, representing 27.8% of 1985 totals.[7] By 1999 this was down to four firms, representing 9.3% of world output.[8] Finally, seven firms were producing between 400,000 and 700,000 units in 1985, representing 9.3% of world output.[9] Six firms fit into this category fourteen years later, only accounting for 4.3% of global production.[10]

This concentration trend, which has accelerated with the process of globalization, raises questions about the very nature of the automobile industry.

Table 2.1 Changes in level of concentration of world automobile industry, 1985–99

Production volume (millions of units)	Number of firms		Percentage of world output	
	1985	1999	1985	1999
4 –9	3	6	42.2	65.1
2–3	2	4	11.6	17.3
1–2	8	4	27.8	9.3
< 1	7	6	9.3	4.3
Total	20	20	90.9	96.0

Sources: Calculated using data from the Comité des Constructeurs Français d'Automobiles (CCFA) (1999), and the Motor Vehicle Manufacturing Association (MVMA) (1985).

Has this sector become a 'global industry', with the meaning that M. Porter lends to this term (Porter, 1986) – that is, an industry where not only are domestic markets so integrated that they form a unified market at the global level, but where firms themselves have integrated their activities world-wide, leading to the constitution of a global oligopoly? If this is the case, the six firms that produce more than 4 million units enjoy a crucial competitive advantage thanks to the economies of scale and scope they can obtain across the world – and thanks to the global integration of their innovation activities. However, the failure of those firms who have attempted to market 'world cars' and the difficulties that have been encountered during attempts to integrate the engineering departments of the many subsidiaries located across the world's continents demonstrates that, while competition has indeed become global, the automobile firms themselves are not globally integrated companies.

As such, our six leaders do not comprise a new and definitively established global oligopoly, inasmuch as they still have to transform their relatively larger size into a real competitive advantage, notably by sharing platforms and by commonalizing components on a global scale. Yet recent experience shows that only a small percentage of mergers/acquisitions in fact succeed (The Economist, 1999). In the automobile industry, there have been a number of recent failures, casting doubts on the inevitability and sustainability of a global oligopoly made up of five or six automakers (Lung, 2000). The smaller firms, especially those that refuse to participate in this concentration trend, are not irremediably condemned.

The concept of a global oligopoly must not therefore be defined as a 'supply structure' that has been established once and for all. Instead, it should be defined as a 'space of industrial rivalry' (Chesnais, 1994), which 'is bordered by a type of interdependency relationship that creates linkages between the small number of large groups within a particular industry who have succeeded in acquiring and maintaining the status of someone who can compete effectively at the global level'. This is an 'area of intense competition' born out of mutual invasion strategies, 'but also out of inter-group collaboration' (Friedman, 1983). The oligopoly is global in nature because of these competition-based relationships, even if its industrial foundations are not global (in fact, they are usually regional).

This definition seems to us to be very useful for analysing the automobile firms' current stage of internationalization, inasmuch as commercial internationalization is generally more advanced than productive internationalization.

This is what we shall try to verify by analysing three forms of internationalization on the basis of five quantitative criteria. The proportion of total revenues realized outside of the country of origin comprise an indicator we shall call 'commercial revenues'.[11] This makes it possible to measure the firms' degree of commercial internationalization. The proportion of revenues 'produced' by subsidiaries located outside the country of origin, called 'production revenues', and the proportion of complete vehicle production carried out outside the country of origin, are factors that will help us to measure productive internationalization.[12]

Commercial internationalization is the automobile firms' most advanced form

UNCTAD studies (2000) have demonstrated that commercial internationalization has only developed in recent times. In 1993, the top 100 MNEs (multinational enterprises), all sectors of activity combined, still relied for 57% of their business on their national market. Nevertheless, commercial internationalization has been growing rapidly and represents the vanguard of the internationalization process. Foreign markets reached a proportion of 52% in 1997–8. According to the same sources, the automobile sector, with 57.2%, is clearly above average for all sectors and thus appears, at a commercial level, to be one of the world's most internationalized industries.[13]

This analysis could be enhanced by incorporating an even greater number of firms, their national origins, and the diversity of the commercial strategies they have adopted. Our own sample, comprised of twenty-one firms, satisfies this objective by offering a more comprehensive vision of the automobile industry (albeit one that remains incomplete).[14] In 1995–9, the American firms analysed in Table 2.2 realized an average 51.3%[15] of their total sales outside their country of origin. Note the American firms' low level of internationalization (average of 24.5%) – far behind the Japanese (57%) and above all the European (72.5%), averages. For this latter sub-set, the domestic market is no longer the main market.

American firms' low level of commercial internationalization is surprising, given that ever since the early twentieth century, GM and Ford, the world's top two automakers, have been running the world's largest overseas operations (in absolute terms), primarily in Europe. It is also surprising, given that

Table 2.2 Comparison of degree of internationalization of automobile firms, 1995–9, as percentage of total, and synthetical index

Firms	Degree of internationalization of automobile firms, 1995–9					Synthetical index internationalization	
	Commercial revenues	Productive revenues	Production	Workforce	Total assets	Global	UNCTAD
American firms							
Chrysler (95–97)	13.1	n.d.	37.7	17.0	14.8	20.7	15.0
Ford (95–97)	34.2	n.d.	46.0	48.2	26.0	38.6	36.1
Navistar (96–98)	8.8	n.d.	27.3	11.0	8.6	13.7	9.5
GM (95–96)	30.4	n.d.	45.1	32.8	26.9	33.8	30.0
Paccar (96–99)	36.2	n.d.	33.6	n.d.	49.3	n.d.	n.d.
Average (1)	**27.4**	**n.d.**	**38.0**	**30.7**	**27.7**	**28.7**	**25.2**
Average (2)	**32.3**	**n.d.**	**45.6**	**40.5**	**26.5**	**36.2**	**33.1**
European firms							
BMW (95–99)	72.0	n.d.	49.1	41.1	61.7	56.0	58.3
Daimler-Benz (95–97)	61.1	47.5	46.7	23.4	38.0	42.3	40.8
DaimlerChrysler (95–97)	81.3	n.d.	77.0	47.5	73.4	69.8	67.4
Fiat Auto (95–99)	58.9	n.d.	41.2	34.1	41.7	44.0	44.9
Fiat Group (95–99)	62.7	38.4	41.2	39.7	45.3	47.2	49.2
PSA (95–99)	60.7	50.8	22.9	24.3	39.3	36.8	41.4
Renault (95–99)	58.2	45.7	27.2	30.8	48.5	41.2	45.8
Scania (95–99)	90.0	n.d.	74.0	50.4	n.d.	n.d.	n.d.
VW (95–99)	64.6	35.6	53.2	47.0	58.3	55.8	56.6
Volvo (95–99)	90.4	n.d.	68.1	43.5	n.d.	n.d.	*n.d.*
Average (3)	**72.5**	**34.1**	**51.6**	**40.5**	**54.4**	**51.1**	**53.1**
Average (4)	**62.9**	**44.0**	**45.1**	**37.5**	**53.8**	**50.6**	**52.4**

16

Table 2.2 continued

Firms	Degree of internationalization of automobile firms, 1995–9					Synthetical index internationalization	
	Commercial revenues	Productive revenues	Production	Workforce	Total assets	Global	UNCTAD
Japanese firms							
Honda (95–99)	69.2	64.9	46.9	73.2	53.6	60.7	65.3
Isuzu (96–99)	59.7	35.6	41.8	55.5	10.6	41.9	41.9
Mazda (95–99)	60.6	36.8	17.9	24.0	16.9	29.9	33.8
Mitsubishi (95–99)	52.5	32.9	29.8	29.7	30.4	35.6	37.5
Nissan (95–99)	56.0	51.6	39.7	71.0	37.6	51.1	54.9
Subaru (95–99)	52.1	39.2	16.6	34.7	25.9	32.3	37.6
Suzuki (95–99)	50.7	22.7	36.8	n.d.	18.1	n.d.	n.d.
Toyota (95–99)	53.5	43.3	31.0	59.8	42.9	46.8	52.1
Average (5)	56.8	40.9	31.2	48.7	29.5	42.7	46.2

Notes: The Global Synthetical Index is an average of Commercial Revenues, Production, Total Assets, and Workforce Indexes. The UNCTAD's Synthetical Index is an average of Commercial Revenues, Workforce and Total Assets Indexes. Average (1) is calculated with all American firms. Average (2) is calculated with Ford and GM only. Average (3) is calculated with all European firms except Fiat Auto and Daimler-Benz. Average (4) relates to BMW, DaimlerChrysler, Fiat Auto, PSA, Renault and VW. Chrysler's and Daimler-Benz's results are given for information. Average (5) is calculated with all Japanese firms. Italic figures are for 1995–8 only. Total assets for the Fiat and VW groups are estimations. VW's productive revenues are 1995–7 only.

Navistar is the world's second leading maker of commercial vehicles. The extremely large size of the North American market is one natural reason for this paradoxical result, but it does not explain everything. General Electric, which in 1998 was the world's leading multinational (in terms of total assets), makes 28.6% of its total sales overseas, a percentage comparable to GM and Ford – yet at the same time overseas sales represented 56.8% of IBM's total sales in 1998 (UNCTAD, 2000). In addition, we could have expected American firms to take greater advantage than their colleagues of their large size in order to develop their commercial presence across the world.

It remains that GM's and Ford's repeated efforts to homogenize their global product range are hampered by the still highly heterogeneous nature of the preferences shown in the demand that emanates from different areas of the world, both for passenger vehicles and commercial vehicles. This hampers an otherwise very real chance to share components and achieve economies of scale. For example, light truck volumes in North America are higher than the volumes achieved with the infamous 'world cars'. American firms have therefore been forced to market products that are specific to each continent, reducing their opportunity in their internationalization efforts to leverage the size advantage they have acquired in the American market, and thereby leaving themselves more exposed to foreign competition. This explains the highly stable geographical spread of North American firms' commercial revenues, with a predominant proportion of total sales having been realized in the North American and European markets.

In 1970–9, North America accounted for 71% of Ford's commercial revenues, Europe 23%, and South America and Asia/Africa/Pacific around 3%, respectively.[16] Twenty years on, this breakdown has remained practically identical, despite globalization.[17] GM's experience is comparable, except for the fact that it involved an even greater initial dependency on the North American market (84.2% of the firm's commercial revenues) between 1971 and 1979. Europe only accounted for 10.3% at that time, and the rest of the world 5.5%. In 1990–9, this was rebalanced in favour of Europe (19.2%), with NAFTA's share dropping to 75.4%. The rest of the world's share of GM's total sales remained identical, with around 3% for South America and 3% for Asia/Africa/Pacific.

GM and Ford thus present a similarly bipolar geographic spread, with a great deal of focus on developed Western countries. The two firms have been unable to develop their market share in South America (despite the US government's very strong influence in this region), and even less so in Japan and the rest of Asia, despite the fact this latter region experienced the world's fastest rate of growth over the period of time in question.

Diametrically opposed to the American example, European firms feature a very high degree of commercial internationalization (with an average [3] of 72.5%; see Table 2.2). This can be explained partially by the smaller size of European national markets. From the outset, local automakers were forced to engage in export activities so as to discover the additional volumes they need to achieve economies of scale abroad (and particularly in their neighbouring countries). This is particularly true for Swedish firms which, faced with a very narrow domestic market, realize 90% of their total sales outside Sweden, unlike American and Japanese commercial vehicle manufacturers, who feature a very low degree of internationalization.[18] Even outside this particular sub-set of firms, European generalist automakers' degree of internationalization remains high, with nearly 63% of sales being made outside the country of origin (cf. average [4]). As such, the European market has become a natural battleground for competition, much like the entity that NAFTA has created in North America. Proof lies in the European market's preponderant position (between 67% and 93%) in the geographic spread of European firms' commercial revenues (see Table 2.3). Only DaimlerChrysler is an exception to this rule, with the European market now representing only about 33% of the firm's commercial revenues (67% before the acquisition of Chrysler). Note that Europe's share has been shrinking for most firms (notably Volvo), something that is explained by the decision to increase sales in the world's other regions in order to benefit from growth in the new markets, and to reduce dependency on Europe. In this respect, European firms have been pursuing highly differentiated commercial diversification strategies, as shown by Table 2.4.

Table 2.3   Europe's share (including country of origin) in European firms' commercial revenue, as percentage of world sales

Years	BMW	DaimlerChrysler	Fiat Group	PSA	Renault	Scania	VW	Volvo
1990–9	n.a.	66.9	79.8	92.8	86.0	71.1	76.8	60.0
1995–9	67.6	35.4	76.0	93.4	85.0	74.8	74.2	58.0
1999	64.4	33.3	79.5	93.7	83.2	82.9	74.0	55.2

Note: For DaimlerChrysler, the periods are 1990–6, 1997–9 and 1999. For Volvo, 1991–9, with passenger cars being excluded; n.a. = not available.

Sources: Our own calculations with data from the companies' financial reports.

Table 2.4   Breakdown of European firms' commercial revenue outside Europe, 1995–9, as percentage of world sales

Regions	BMW	DaimlerChrysler	Fiat Group	PSA	Renault	Scania	VW	Volvo
North America	18.0	49.9	6.8	n.a.	10.0	n.a.	10.4	27.3
South America	n.a.	8.5	11.8	n.a.	n.a.	15.7	9.8	6.0
Asia/Pacific	9.2	3.7	n.a.	n.a.	3.5	4.5	4.1	5.9

Note: For DaimlerChrysler, the period is 1997–9; n.a. = not available. The total does not equal 100% because of other countries not included in this table.

Sources: Our own calculations with data from the financial reports of the companies.

Although a geographic breakdown does not enable any distinction to be made between the three poles of the Triad and the developing countries, note that only Volvo and the three German firms have been able to build a significant commercial presence in the Triad's second pole – that is, in North America.[19] In this respect, the Japanese firms are far ahead. Fiat is an interesting example inasmuch as it owes its North American presence not to its automobile assembly activities in the strictest sense of the term, but to its other group subsidiaries. Another special case is Daimler-Benz, which between 1990 and 1997 realized in North America nearly 23% of its world sales, and more than doubled its sales in this continent after the creation of DaimlerChrysler. As is the case for American firms, European firms' commercial revenues in Asia (and *a fortiori* in Japan) remain less than 5% of their total sales, except for premium brands such as BMW (9.2%) and Mercedes-Benz (9.7% over 1990–6).

Outside the Triad, European firms differ from American and Japanese firms because of their significant presence in South America, particularly in Mercosur. Fiat and Scania are the most active in this market. Mercosur represents an even greater percentage of Fiat's automobile activities, accounting for 20.7% of Fiat Auto's total world sales in 1995–8. South America constitutes the most accessible rapid development zone for those European firms that are seeking to reduce their dependency on the European market. PSA, which set itself an objective of making 25% of its total sales outside Europe by 2003, has reinforced its presence in Mercosur. Renault has announced a target of 40% of sales outside Europe by 2010, with Mercosur supposed to become the firm's second largest market (after Europe) in 2005.

We should emphasize that European firms' generally high level of internationalization in fact hides a major regional phenomenon. Like GM and Ford, most European firms realize around 25% of total sales outside their region of origin (Europe or North America), thanks to a strong presence in a second continent. However, they are often even more geographically diversified than their American counterparts, possessing a significant presence (around 10%) in a third zone (South America or Asia).

Finally, most Japanese firms are even more geographically diversified, although the proportion of commercial revenues realized abroad is on average lower than for European firms (see Table 2.5). Japanese firms are noteworthy because they have the highest commercial presence in a second Triad pole (North America) and a significant commercial presence in a third pole (Europe). With the exception of Mitsubishi and Suzuki, all realize at least a third of their total sales in North America. For Honda this percentage is 50%, higher even than its sales in Japan. This is the only example of this sort aside from DaimlerChrysler, which is a less straightforward situation.

The big Japanese firms realize at least 10% of their total sales in Europe. It is also the case of Toyota, following its establishment of production facilities in France. As a result of this commercial diversification, Japanese firms would appear to be the least dependent on their region of origin. Although

Table 2.5   Breakdown of Japanese firms' commercial revenues, 1997–9, as percentage of world sales

Regions	Honda	Isuzu	Mazda	Mitsubishi	Nissan	Subaru	Suzuki	Toyota
North America	50.1	35.4	31.9	21.9	33.3	43.6	12.6	36.6
Europe	12.0	n.a.	17.5	14.3	15.4	7.5	21.0	9.0
Asia/Pacific	(28.38)	46.8	(37.51)	51.1	(41.49)	(44.49)	59.9	(42.54)

Notes: n.a. = not available. Japan is included in the Asia/Pacific zone. The numbers in brackets are estimations based on the following principles: the minimum corresponds to Japan's share, the maximum to Japan's share plus the share of countries from the rest of the world (Asia, South America, Pacific, etc.).

Sources: Own calculations with data from the companies' financial reports.

available statistics remain somewhat imprecise, we know that Suzuki alone (mainly because of its successes in Japan and India in the mini-car niche) depends on the Asian market for around 60% of its business, a figure that is nevertheless lower than the region of origin's significance for American or European firms' commercial revenues.

In conclusion, the findings confirm that the automobile industry is not entirely globalized, since no firm sells a balanced proportion of its total output in all three poles of the Triad. However, if firms do reach the targets they have set, within ten years there should be an increase in the percentage of commercial revenues realized outside their region of origin.[20] American and European firms want to reinforce their commercial presence in Asia, and specifically in Japan.[21] Japanese firms are trying to develop sales in Europe. As competition is particularly strong in the three poles of the 'Triad', it is likely that only a few firms will be able to realize a significant proportion (that is, 20%) of total sales in each of the three continents. Hence their strong interest in emerging countries, where the potential for market growth makes it easier for a firm to gain a foothold.

Although the productive internationalization of the automobile industry has increased, it still remains limited in scope

Productive internationalization can first of all be analysed in physical terms by measuring the percentage of total output realized outside a country of origin, and then outside a region of origin. These first two findings will be supplemented by value analysis that compares total sales by zone of commercialization with turnover by production zone in order to evaluate the respective importance and role of commercial and productive internationalization.

Automobile firms' production outside their country of origin rose sharply during the 1990s. From an average of 27% in 1990–4, it reached 40.6% in 1995–9.[22] As such, the automobile industry has not been globalized from a production perspective, with the national framework continuing to exert a crucial influence on productive organization, employment relations and relations with the state. But even though productive internationalization continues to rise at the same pace, most firms will be producing at least 50% of their total output overseas over the course of the coming decade. Figure 2.1 shows how firms were positioned in 1995–9. Fifty per cent of all firms realized outside their country of origin an output that was superior or equal to 40% of their world production. Only five out of twenty firms, all European, featured an overseas production superior or equal to 50%. This category includes Volvo and Scania, who were forced to behave in this manner by the narrowness of their country of origin. There were also two firms whose presence in this leading group can be explained by their acquisition of a foreign competitor: BMW, which bought Rover in 1994 and resold it in 2000;[23] and DaimlerChrysler, after Daimler-Benz bought Chrysler in 1997. With the exception of these special cases, VW appears to be the only integrated generalist firm whose production outside its country of origin (56%) is ten points higher than Honda, Ford and GM.

This vision of an already significant yet rapidly rising productive internationalization should be fine-tuned through the incorporation of a regional dimension. As shown in Figure 2.2, which covers 1996–9, a much lower percentage of total production is being realized outside firms' region of origin.[24] This indicates that firms are more regionalized than globalized. Fifty per cent of all firms feature production outside their region of origin that is superior or equal to 19.6%, with average extra-regional output reaching

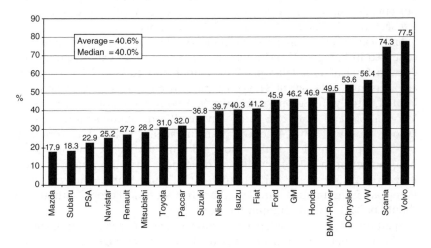

Figure 2.1 Production share outside the country of origin, 1995–9, percentages
Source: Own calculation from data of the CCFA.

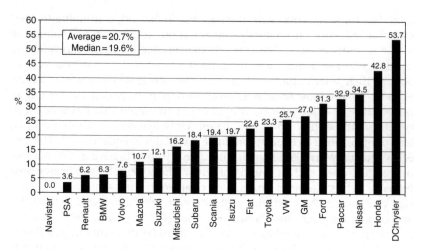

Figure 2.2   Production share outside the region of origin, 1996–9, percentages
Source: Own calculation with data from the CCFA.

20.7%, a very low figure. Only DaimlerChrysler (54%) and Honda (43%) distinguish themselves from the pack with outcomes that are more than twice the overall average. Apart from the special case of DaimlerChrysler, Honda has gone the furthest towards productive internationalization. However, Honda's extra-regional production is spread very unevenly: 37.6% in NAFTA versus only 4.8% in Europe. Nissan, which manufactures 34.5% of its output outside Asia/Pacific/Africa, features a more balanced spread of productive facilities: 20.6% in NAFTA and 13.7% in Europe.

American firms' extra-regional production is just as unbalanced and concentrated in Europe. Of GM's output, 25.2%, out of an extra-regional production total of 27% takes place in 'Europe and Turkey'.[25] For Ford, the amounts are 25.2% out of 31.3% (Paccar's extra-regional production being located entirely in 'Europe and Turkey'). Among the European firms, only VW (25.7%) and Fiat (22.6%) do any significant manufacturing outside Europe, mostly in South America. VW manufactures 12.8% of its world output in South America, while also producing in NAFTA (6.9%) and in Asia/Pacific/Africa (5.9%). Fiat is very dependent on South America, where it realizes 20.5% of its world output. Apart from Scania, the remaining European firms manufacture less than 10% outside Europe, although it should be said that the amount has been rising.

Apart from Toyota, most Japanese firms are characterized by extra-regional production that is inferior or equal to the overall average (20.7%). Apart from Suzuki, they all have in common the fact that they basically do zero manufacturing in South America and produce less than 6% in Europe.

Japanese NAFTA zone output ranges from 11% (Mazda, Mitsubishi) to 19% (Toyota, Isuzu and Subaru). Production in the 'Asia/Pacific/Africa' zone can be quite significant (Mitsubishi 15%, Isuzu 22%, Suzuki 28%).

In conclusion, we are a long way away from the often conjectured generalization that global firms have been carrying out manufacturing operations in all three poles of the 'Triad'. In its current shape, international production focuses on the region of origin. At best, foreign plants have been built in a second pole of the 'Triad' for American and Japanese firms and some European firms; and in emerging countries for other European firms. If this concentration trend continues into the first decade of the twenty-first century – that is, if it turns out to be a durable phenomenon, we might witness the creation of firms who do manufacture in all three poles of the Triad.[26] However, given the difficulty of transforming such groupings into profitably integrated firms, it is much more likely that productive internationalization will follow a slower and more modest path involving a steady increase in existing firms' production capacities outside their continent of origin.

We have seen that productive internationalization is already significant outside of firms' countries of origin, but that it remains limited to the regional framework. This, in turn, provides a glimpse of an incipient regional division of labour within which subsidiaries from the country of origin can play a key role as an export base destined to supplement the regional subsidiary network. A value analysis that distinguishes between commercial revenues and production revenues will help us to delve further into this phenomenon.

More specifically, the difference between commercial and production revenues, as presented in Table 2.2, helps us to calculate how important exports are to each firm's total sales.[27] When overseas sales are greater than overseas production (the sales realized by each production facility), exports coming out of a firm's country of origin automatically explains the difference.

We can then break these export flows down by main geographic zones to evaluate the regional phenomenon's significance.

The results are combined in Table 2.6, which presents a geographical breakdown of exportable surpluses by firms and by era.[28] Note that the country of origin's subsidiaries almost always show an exportable surplus that can be added to local production by foreign subsidiaries, which are generally net importers. With respect to European firms, note also that VW and Fiat, the most internationalized companies in terms of the number of vehicles produced abroad, nevertheless generate much lower revenues per overseas production facility (36% and 38.4%, respectively – see Table 2.2). They must therefore be exporting a high percentage of goods and services (27.3% and 24.2%, respectively – see Table 2.6). It would appear that overseas investments generate a flow of exports from a country of origin. We infer from this that overseas production is marked by a low level of local content. German and Italian subsidiaries satisfy demand from their respective countries but

Table 2.6 Breakdown of exports from the country of origin destined for foreign subsidiaries, as percentage of commercial revenue

Firms	Exports (+) and imports (−)				
	Country of origin	Europe	North America	Other countries	Total abroad
VW (95–97)	27.3	−19.0	−4.8	−3.5	−27.3
Fiat (95–99)	24.2	−18.7	n.a.	−5.5	−24.2
PSA (95–99)	10.6	−4.9	n.a.	−5.7	−10.6
Renault (95–98)	11.3	−5.5	n.a.	−5.8	−11.3
Honda (97–99)	3.8	−0.3	0.4	−3.8	−3.8
Nissan (97–99)	4.0	−0.2	2.5	−6.4	−4.1
Toyota (97–99)	8.6	−0.4	−2.5	−5.5	−8.4
Isuzu (97–99)	22.6	n.a.	−0.8	−21.9	−22.7
Mazda (97–99)	20.5	−7.3	−3.7	−9.4	−20.4
Mitsubishi (97–99)	17.5	−3.9	−2.4	−11.2	−17.5
Subaru (97–99)	15.0	−7.5	−3.2	−4.3	−15.0
Suzuki (98–99)	21.2	−6.5	n.a.	−14.7	−21.2

Notes: For each geographical zone, the difference between productive revenues and commercial revenues has been calculated. Whenever data is not available (n.a.), it is included in the category 'other countries'. Fiat is the Fiat Group.

Sources: Our own calculations from the financial reports.

also serve as an export base, essentially for exports towards other European countries (and to a much lesser extent, to subsidiaries on other continents where the firms have established operations).

In percentage terms, French firms achieve much higher revenues from overseas production facilities (45.6% for Renault, 50.1% for PSA). Above all, they are twice as high as one would expect, given the foreign manufacturing in which they engage (measured in physical terms). In this sense, Renault and PSA are more internationalized than VW and Fiat. Unsurprisingly, their exportable surplus is twice as low (10.6% for PSA and 11.3% for Renault). It is also relatively equally balanced between their other European subsidiaries and the units they run in other continents (see Table 2.6). French firms' foreign subsidiaries are therefore much less dependent on the goods and services that their parent company subsidiaries export than is the case for VW and Fiat.[29]

The Japanese firms are divided into two groups. On the one hand there is Honda and Nissan, whose revenues per production facility are very similar to their overseas commercial revenues (see Table 2.2). This explains why exports from Japanese subsidiaries only represent around 4%, the lowest figure in our sample – a confirmation that the two firms have been able to set up autonomous productive bases outside their region of origin. Honda and Nissan's Japanese exports are for the most part destined for the 'other countries' (including Asia) that also receive goods and services from North America (this latter zone featuring a slight trade surplus, whereas trade with Europe is more or less in equilibrium). The other firms (Isuzu, Mazda, Mitsubishi, Subaru and Suzuki) realize overseas sales of below 40% (see Table 2.2) and depend more traditionally on their Japanese subsidiaries for exports to the world's other regions (see Table 2.6). Such exports are for the most part to Asia (that is, the 'other countries' category) and to a lesser extent to Europe, where this sub-set is still running a small and sometimes non-existent productive base. Toyota is in an intermediate position, as it only exports 8.6% of the total revenues of its Japanese subsidiaries in 'other countries' and North America.

In sum, these figures confirm that commercial internationalization no longer plays anything more than a minor role for the big firms, even if it still plays a significant role for the 'small' ones. It complements productive internationalization in the region of origin, and to a lesser extent it supports the presence of firms in other continents.

Finally, this overview of corporate internationalization confirms that most firms remain rooted in the country that is crucial to their business. Although all firms have developed a commercial and productive presence in their region of origin, this is only really crucial for European firms and for certain Japanese companies (Isuzu, Mitsubishi and Suzuki). The drive to establish operations in a second region can vary greatly, accounting on average for anywhere between a fifth and a third of firms' total activities (with very few exceptions – for example, Honda and DaimlerChrysler). The result is that firms' global profits continue to be highly influenced by their national context, with the international environment allowing firms to smooth out fluctuations in their national markets, and to create additional profit opportunities. This is what we shall be analysing in detail in the following section.

Internationalization, a source of profit and of loss

International expansion is usually viewed as something that is indispensable for a firm's survival. Yet international activities are not always profitable, and can even be a source of substantial loss. Conversely, foreign profits can sometimes offset the losses made in a firm's country of origin, particularly when the economic situation is desynchronized from one continent to the other. In order to verify the contribution of foreign profits to total profits, we have defined a contribution indicator based on the total profits realized by domestic and foreign activities. This is expressed as a percentage (refer to the methodological explanations contained in the Appendix on p. 46).[30]

Changes in American firms' international profits

Ford and GM setup overseas facilities from the early twentieth century onwards, first in Europe and then throughout the world. The data we have been able to gather begins after the Second World War and covers the two firms' net world profits (see Figures 2.3 and 2.4). We can see that, for GM and Ford, international profits made a positive but small contribution to world profits during all of the post-war boom years and up to the early 1970s. Most profits were realized in domestic activities, which represented an average of 80% of the two firms' world profits – foreign activities thus only contributing an average of 20%. Then, starting with the first generalized world recession (1974–5), the two firms' paths began to diverge.

Ford was shaken deeply in its domestic market by this first recession, but was able to offset lower profits in North America with profits drawn from its foreign activities, which at the time represented more than half of its world profits. On the other hand, during the second global recession (1979–81), North America's preponderance in the firm's total revenues was reflected in Ford's problems in finding sufficient foreign profits (which were also in decline) to offset the losses made by its American subsidiaries. The end result was that it was no longer possible to avoid an overall loss. Renewed growth in North America from 1983 onwards re-established the hierarchy that had characterized the 1950s and 1960s (with around 80% of profits being made in North America and 20% overseas), but this was temporary. During the third global

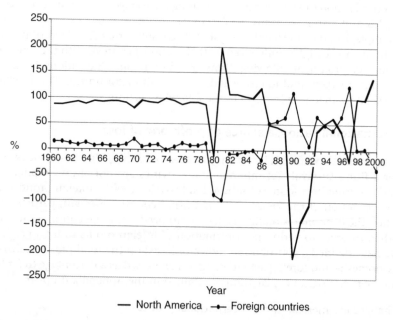

Figure 2.3 North America's and foreign countries' contribution to GM's global net profit, 1960–2000

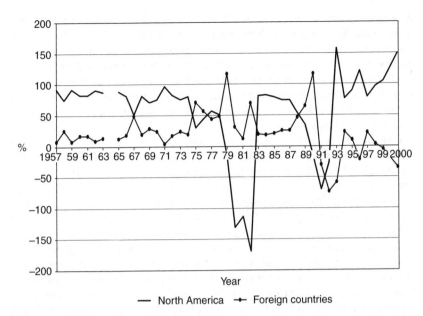

Figure 2.4 North America's and foreign countries' contribution to Ford's global net profit, 1957–2000

recession (1991–2 in North America; 1992–3 in Europe) overseas subsidiaries made substantial losses, exacerbating losses in North America. Subsequently, and during the entire 1990s, profits from abroad could no longer offer any significant and/or durable contribution to world profits, nearly 100% of which would come from North America. This change can be explained by the long duration of North American growth (March 1992–December 2000) but also by the fact that Ford was unable to adapt to a period of slow growth in Europe (1990–7). Yet it was in Europe that most of the firm's overseas profits were being determined, accounting for 24% of Ford's total sales. From 1990 to 2000, European subsidiaries had five years in the red, totalling $3.5 billion in losses – versus six years in the black, totalling $639 million.

Ford's foreign profits outside of Europe were nothing to write home about. The firm had been making significant profits in South America in the late 1970s, when the Brazilian market was nearing its first apex. It then lost money throughout the 'lost decade' of the 1980s. Later on, Ford did not really derive maximum benefits from the Mercosur rise (1990–7), and ran loss-making operations from 1995 onwards. It reached a nadir of $642 million in 1996, with the firm subsequently having to take the full brunt of the 1998–9 Mercosur crisis. In comparison, Asian subsidiaries turned out to be much more profitable and were hardly affected by the Asian crisis (1997 a loss of $33 billion, returning to profit in 1998). But Asian profits did not in general suffice to offset South

American losses. From 1990 to 2000, the whole of South America and Asia/Pacific/Africa recorded three years in the black, totalling $116 million, versus eight years in the red, totalling $1.6 billion. Instead of offsetting European losses, losses in the developing countries compounded them.

Above and beyond temporary vicissitudes, there is also a structural problem. It is surprising that the main and almost sole profit source of the world's second leading automaker, whose internationalization goes back a long way, is its domestic market.

GM has to a certain extent had the opposite experience. Its North American subsidiaries overcame the second global recession better than did its foreign subsidiaries. In 1981, GM's North American contribution to world profits was about 200%, more than offsetting the negative contribution of its loss-making overseas operations (around 100%). This allowed GM to record an overall profit. During the 1980s, earnings from foreign subsidiaries (which were mediocre at first) improved up to 1987, reaching and then surpassing 50% of world profits. At the same time, profits from North American subsidiaries trended downwards. Profits from foreign subsidiaries helped GM partially to absorb the shock of the 1992 recession in North America, accounting for 100% of world profits in 1997 (before collapsing in 1998–9). As was the case with Ford, these changes were mainly a reflection of the European subsidiaries' behaviour. It is specifically because of European losses that overseas activities made an overall negative contribution to GM's world profits in 1979–82, and it is thanks to Europe's positive contribution that GM was able to limit the impact of American losses in the early 1990s. South America and Asia/Pacific/Africa made a marginal but almost always positive contribution during the 1970s and 1980s. South America's contribution rose after 1992, with a jump of more than 150% in 1997, a year when South America was the only region where GM recorded net profits. This shows that GM (unlike Ford) was able to take full advantage of South America's return to growth after the 'lost decade' of the 1980s. However, the 1997 Asian crisis, which led to the region making a negative contribution equivalent to 50% of world profits, soon had a knock-on effect in South America, whose contribution became negative in 1998. The speed with which this crisis spread, characteristic of financial globalization, demonstrates the fragility of the profit opportunities that emerging countries offer to multinational firms. Even more surprising is Europe's mediocre profit contribution. Throughout the 1990s this had remained below 30%, and it continued to decline in 1998, despite Europe's return to growth. This is another sign of the structural difficulty of satisfying European demand.

In sum, the results have been more positive for GM than for Ford. Foreign subsidiaries played a positive role in profitability terms during the 1980s–1990s, a period of decline for GM in North America. Renewed growth in this region during the 1990s meant that US profits superseded foreign profits from 1998/9. In 1990–2000, GM accumulated around $18 billion of profits in North America versus nearly $13 billion of losses. Overseas it accumulated nearly $14.4 billion of profits versus $883 million of losses. Internationalization has indeed been very profitable.

Japanese firms' international profits[31]

In recent years, the Japanese economy has been characterized by the strong rise of the yen versus the dollar in 1986–7, and then, during the 1990s, by the country's entry into a period of slow growth triggered by the 1991 bursting of the financial bubble (and followed by recessions in 1993, and above all in 1998). In 1998–9, new vehicle sales in Japan fell below the 4 million unit threshold for the first time since 1984, and production levels dropped back to their level of twenty years before. Against this backdrop of Japanese economic crisis, foreign markets represented a crucial source of profit.

From this perspective, Japanese automakers can be divided into two categories. On the one hand there is a sub-set with Toyota (from 1982–99) and Honda (from 1972–99), who were profitable the whole time (whether profits came from Japan or from abroad), and who were not really affected by the recent macroeconomic shocks. Suzuki is also part of this sub-set, even though its profitability is less clear-cut. Inversely, there is a sub-set with Nissan, Mitsubishi and Mazda, whose internationalization strategies ended in failure (inasmuch as overseas activities almost always recorded losses that were difficult to offset against domestic profits). Subaru is in an intermediate position, having recently succeeded in rebuilding an overseas activity that had long been a loss-maker.

Toyota is a paragon of regularity (see Figure 2.5), with profits from domestic activities varying between 70% and 90% of total profits, leaving overseas profits to make a contribution of 10–30%. Toyota thus remains highly dependent on its country of origin in profit terms, but is one of the few firms to have a regular flow of profits from abroad. These foreign profits stem almost entirely from North America, with Europe and 'other countries' contributing nothing at all, and sometimes even a negative amount. Over 1997–2000, foreign contributions to Toyota's operating profits reached 21.6%, including 21.5% for North America – 0.7% for Europe and 0.8% for other countries.

On the other hand, Honda (see Figure 2.6) experienced a period of great instability. Except for 1981–5, when net profits from Japan were increased by a factor of 2.4 (at the same time that foreign profits were growing slowly), net Japanese and overseas profits evolved in a similar and closely correlated manner, but with hierarchical modifications from one year to the next.[32] This led to a strongly oscillating contribution to domestic and foreign profits, rotating around an average value of 53% for foreign profits versus 47% for Japanese profits in 1990–9. Honda is one of the few firms where foreign profits tend to represent more than 50% of world profits. This is the highest value found in our sample, confirming the highly internationalized

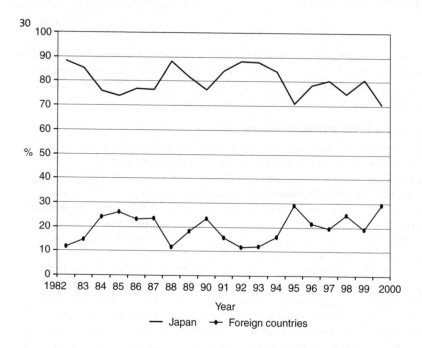

Figure 2.5 Japan's and foreign countries' contribution to Toyota's global net profit, 1982–2000

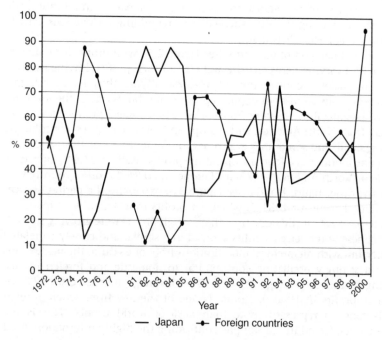

Figure 2.6 Japan's and foreign countries' contribution to Honda's global net profit, 1972–2000

character of this particular firm. With respect to operating profits, foreign profits accounted for as much as 60% of world profits on average in 1994–2000, and as much as 63% in 1997–2000, because of substantial profits in North America (where Honda makes 50% of its total sales). North America made a contribution of 57.5% against 8% for the 'other countries', and there was a loss of −2.3% in Europe, where the euro's weakness against the pound, yen and dollar weighed heavily on profitability. According to Honda's managers, the unfavourable impact of the euro's weakness should be offset in the future by internal productive flexibility (known as the 'Takai' system) in factories in Great Britain, making it possible to manufacture different models using one and the same production line.[33] Instead of making a small passenger car aimed at the continental European market, where profit margins that were at best mediocre have been wiped out by the pound's strength against the euro, the British subsidiary might choose to manufacture SUVs with their higher profit margins, and then to export them to the United States where there is strong demand (the dollar also being strong against the pound). The room to manoeuvre is limited, however, and Honda was unable to avoid losing money in Europe in 2000.

These European losses are going to weigh more and more heavily on profitability, since the slowdown in North American growth means that profits in North America will no longer be enough to offset deficits elsewhere. Honda's extreme dependency on North America might actually turn into a weakness.

Suzuki (see Figure 2.7) is characterized by a successful internationalization strategy with the exception of two interludes: 1982, when heavy foreign losses were offset by higher profits in Japan; and then briefly in 1988–9, when overseas activities made a negative contribution to profits. All in all, foreign profits contributed positively and regularly to world profits, reaching 22% on average between 1983–9, and 60% over 1990–9 (this being the record among Japanese automakers). In terms of operating profits, the foreign contribution was more modest (16.7% over 1997–9) but more geographically diversified, with 9.7% emanating from Europe and 7% from North America and Asia.

The other Japanese automakers are characterized by the mediocre contributions of foreign profits, and even by the magnitude of overseas losses.

Subaru (see Figure 2.8) recorded negative contributions from net overseas profits up to 1995. This is mainly because of an inappropriate product offer in the United States combined with a rising yen.[34] Foreign losses were difficult to offset with (lower) profits in Japan, especially during the early 1990s domestic crisis. As a result, Subaru recorded a net world loss over 1987–94. It was finally able to recover, with overseas profits making a contribution of 40% (and national profits a contribution of 60%) over 1995–9. Subaru was not affected by the Asian crisis of 1997–8, as Asia accounted for only a small percentage of its sales. More surprising is the fact that it was not harmed by the Japanese recession of 1998. A geographical breakdown of the firm's

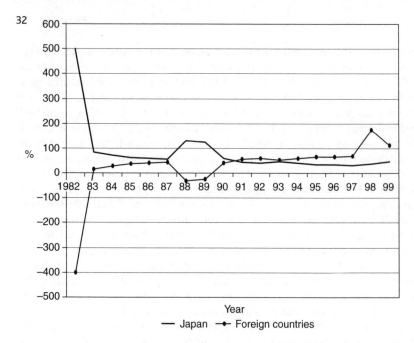

Figure 2.7 Japan's and foreign countries' contribution to Suzuki's global net profit, 1982–99

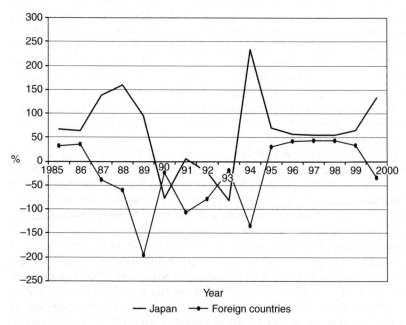

Figure 2.8 Japan's and foreign countries' contribution to Subaru's global net profit, 1985–2000

operating profits again highlights Japanese firms' significant dependency on the North American market for foreign profits: over 1997–9, North America's contribution was 29.5%, versus a total foreign contribution to world profits of 30.5% (Europe and the rest of the world thus representing only 1%).

The example of Mitsubishi (see Figure 2.9) is much less clear-cut. Overseas activities made only a modestly positive contribution (13%) to the firm's net world profits in 1989–93, and then made a negative contribution (−224.5%) in 1994–9. This could no longer be offset by the positive contribution (+124.5%) of the net profits realized in Japan, leading to a negative world income (−100%) over the recent period.[35] Mitsubishi was hard hit by the Asian crisis[36] and subsequently by the recession in Japan. Nevertheless, from 1998 onwards the firm's overseas activities were again in the black thanks to strong growth in the North American market. The 1997–2000 geographical breakdown and operating profits shows a negative contribution from Japan (−1858.3%) that was offset by a foreign contribution of 1958.3%. However, this performance can only be explained by an excellent performance in North America (2988%) and to a lesser extent in other countries (30.1%), offsetting European losses (−1061.1%).

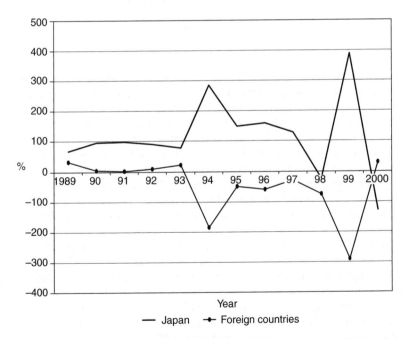

Figure 2.9 Japan's and foreign countries' contribution to Mitsubishi's global net profit, 1989–2000

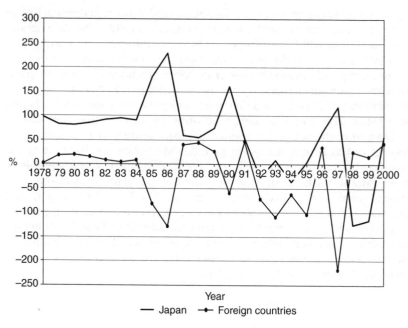

Figure 2.10   Japan's and foreign countries' contribution to Nissan's global net profit, 1978–2000

Nissan and Mazda are characterized by the almost systematically negative contribution of their foreign subsidiaries. For Nissan, the late 1970s and early 1980s were marked by foreign earnings' positive but modest contribution (12%) to world profits (see Figure 2.10), with domestic profits accounting for between 90% and 100% of this total. The situation did, however, take a turn for the worse in the 1980s, and deteriorated even further in 1992–5, when foreign losses could no longer offset domestic activities that had been hit hard by the Japanese economic crisis. The 1997 Asian crisis had an even greater impact on Nissan's foreign activities, although Japanese operations were profitable that year. From 1998 onwards, foreign profits (mostly the result of good performances in the American market) were able to offset losses in the Japanese market, albeit only partially. This improvement continued into 2000, when Nissan's Japanese activities started to make money again. A geographical breakdown of operating profits again reveals a dependency on the North American market, which made a contribution of 36.9% to Nissan's global operating profits over 1997–2000, against a total foreign contribution of 37.7%. Europe was again a source of losses (−5.6%), and the rest of the world made a modest contribution (2%).

Mazda (see Figure 2.11) shows a similar story. Overseas operations made a modest contribution to profits (12%) between 1983 and 1989, but almost

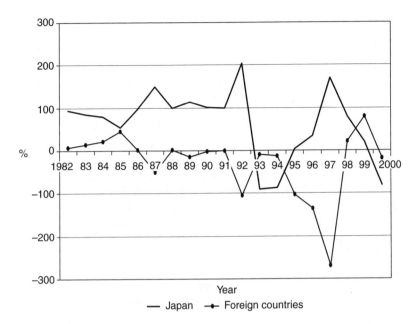

Figure 2.11 Japan's and foreign countries' contribution to Mazda's global net profit, 1982–2000

none over the period 1990–2. From 1993 onwards, they became more and more negative. The domestic profits that used to offset mediocre foreign earnings could no longer stave off the losses, given that Mazda was also a victim of the Japanese economic crisis. Despite a 1995–7 rationalization-driven recovery in Japanese profits, Mazda (like Mitsubishi) was particular hard hit by the 1997–8 Asian crisis. In addition, Mazda is very sensitive to exchange-rate fluctuations, as it depends on exports more than any other Japanese automaker (exporting more than 60% of its domestic Japanese production, versus 50% for Toyota and 40% for Honda). It is expensive to manufacture in Japan; moreover, these exports are being sent to countries with currencies that tend to be weak. As a result, net earnings in Japan plummeted from +30.5 billion yen in 1998 to −127.6 billion yen in 2000, whereas net foreign profits (which had recovered to reach 21 billion yen in 1999) fell back again to −27.6 billion yen in 2000 as a result of the rise in the yen.

The geographical breakdown of operating profits over this period (1997–2000) shows modest overseas contributions (3.1%) thanks to Europe (6.8%) and other countries (1.5%) and despite losses in North America (−5.2%). Mazda is the only Japanese firm that was unable to benefit from North America's long period of growth to offset the losses it was making in the Japanese and Asian markets.

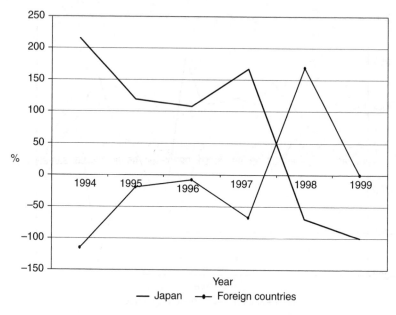

Figure 2.12 Japan's and foreign countries' contribution to Isuzu's global net profit, 1994–9

Isuzu provides us with a final example of relatively unsuccessful internationalization. A commercial vehicle and SUV maker, the firm suffered the full impact of the slowdown in Japanese growth and above all of the 1998–9 recession (see Figure 2.12), during which time net losses reached 104 billion yen. Overseas subsidiaries made a negative contribution to net global profits from 1994 to 1997, offset Japanese profits in 1998, and made a zero contribution in 1999. A geographical breakdown of operating profits shows that over a very short period of time (1998–9), North America and the rest of the world's contributions to foreign profits (5.1% and 2.7%, respectively) were small and in any event insufficient to balance out Japanese losses.

Changes in European firms' international profits[37]

European firms can be divided into two categories. On the one hand, French firms remained highly dependent upon Europe until the late 1990s, but, on the other, Fiat, VW and Scania experienced an earlier and more successful internationalization outside Europe.

For Renault, foreign profit contribution over 1982–8 was almost always positive (see Figure 2.13). From 1982 to 1989 the average contribution of foreign profits was +59.6%, while domestic French contribution was negative (−159.6%). From 1990 to 1998, with the foreign contribution remaining at

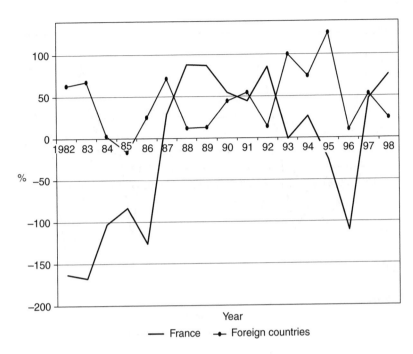

Figure 2.13 France's and foreign countries' contribution to Renault's operating profit, 1982–98

54.8%, a positive French contribution of 45.2% enhanced overall operating profits. Moreover, foreign profits played an important counter-cyclical role during periods of recession in France (1982–4 and 1992–5). However, this role was limited by the fact that Renault's foreign profits were primarily European in origin: 43.8% out of total foreign profits of 54.8% over 1990–8. As such, it was the gap (or uncoupling) between French and European growth that allowed European profits to offset French losses. Finally, the overseas subsidiaries' ability to absorb potential French losses was hampered by the fact that Renault's centre of gravity was still in France at the time. In 1987–8, foreign profits remained surprisingly stable, revolving around an average value of 1.7 billion French francs, whereas French subsidiaries' profits fluctuated wildly around an average value of 2.5 billion French francs.

With PSA, as was the case with Renault, after the 1979–85 crisis years, foreign profits almost always made a positive contribution to the company's world profits. During the era of economic recovery (1985 to 1999), they accounted for 36.1% of PSA's overall earnings, against a contribution of 63.1% from French profits (much lower than for Renault). In addition, PSA's geographic diversification was almost entirely limited to Europe, meaning that foreign profits were basically tantamount to European profits

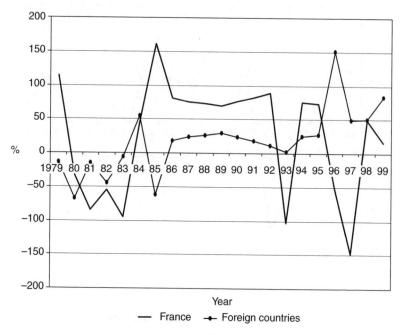

Figure 2.14 France's and foreign countries' contribution to PSA's operating profit, 1979–99

(see Figure 2.14). This dependency on Europe, which became a handicap once European growth began to slow, also turned out to be an advantage when European growth accelerated, allowing PSA to avoid the negative effects of the emerging countries' crisis. This explains why PSA's foreign profits rose continually after 1993, enabling it both to offset partially French losses in 1996–7 and to enjoy much higher world profits in 1998–9. However, such a favourable set of circumstances does not happen all that often, and the rest of the world's marginal but negative contribution to global profits (−2% in 1985–99) represents a structural weakness (one that could, however, be overcome if PSA reinforces its presence in South America and Asia).

The Fiat Group's operating profits are also highly dependent on Europe, despite the geographical diversification efforts Fiat has undertaken. Over 1995–2000, European operating profits represented 66.2% of world operating profits versus 33.8% outside Europe (including 18% for Mercosur, 16.7% in North America and −1.1% in other countries). This limited diversification by the Fiat Group turned out to be very useful for overcoming the 1996 European recession (see Figure 2.15). A drop in operating profits from 2,500 billion lire in 1995 to around 1,000 billion in 1996 was offset by continued strong operating profits outside Europe (staying slightly above 1,000 billion lire; that is,

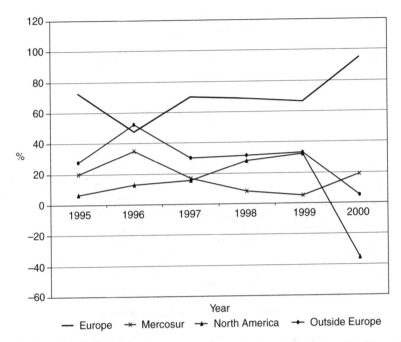

Figure 2.15 Europe's, Mercosur's and North America's contribution to Fiat Group's operating profit, 1995–2000

around 500 million euros). However, the 1997 Asian crisis and its 1998 contagion to Mercosur highlighted the fragility of this result. In 1998–9, operating profits outside Europe were divided in half and their contribution to world profits fell back to 30% (and then to 5% in 2000). These developments are explained by the collapse in North American profits, which had risen between 1995 and 1999, ultimately accounting for 32.5% of the Fiat Group's world operating profits – previously, North American profits had been able to offset a drop in earnings in Mercosur and in the other countries. As for Fiat Auto, the foreign profits' fragility has been aggravated by the absence of any profits in North America, and by the fact that activities are concentrated in Europe and South America. Note that Fiat Auto suffers from chronic mediocre profitability in Europe.[38] Although Fiat Auto's large profits during the Mercosur automobile market's growth phase (1994–7) made it possible to remedy this shortcoming, the 1998–9 Mercosur crisis exacerbated for Fiat Auto the effects of its insufficient European profitability. As a result, Fiat Auto made an operating loss in 1998 and 1999, and only turned a small profit in 2000 thanks to the cost savings generated by its new partnership with GM. Between 1998 and 2000, the only profit sources were the group's

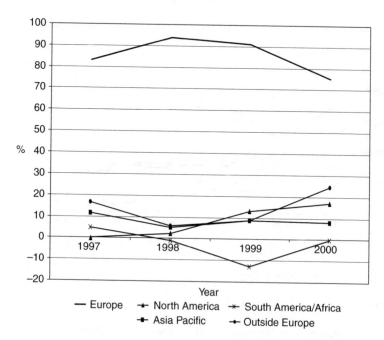

Figure 2.16 Europe's and other geographical areas' contribution to VW's operating profit, 1997–2000

non-automobile business, underlying the usefulness of the Fiat Group's industrial and geographic diversification, as well as Fiat Auto's difficulty in sustaining a successful long-term emerging country internationalization drive (even as European heartland profits were coming under attack).

VW is a special case among European firms. Since 1970, VW has only experienced operating or net losses for the briefest of periods, during the three global recessions of 1974–5, 1981–2 and 1993. Since then, VW has broken all earnings records, moving from a 1993 operating loss of −1.6 billion DM to a 2000 operating profit of 6.7 billion DM, and from a net loss of −1.9 billion DM to a net profit of 4 billion DM. VW increased its internationalization efforts in Europe and across the world during this period yet was not too severely hurt by the 1997–9 emerging countries' crisis. Over 1997–2000, VW's European operating profits represented 85.6% of its global operating profits.[39] The remaining 14.4% included 16.9% in North America, −2.4% in the 'South America and Africa zone', and finally 7.8% in Asia/Pacific. As demonstrated in Figure 2.16, VW's significant geographic diversification allowed it to overcome lower Asian earnings and losses in South America/Africa through a constant rise in North American profits (because of the success of the

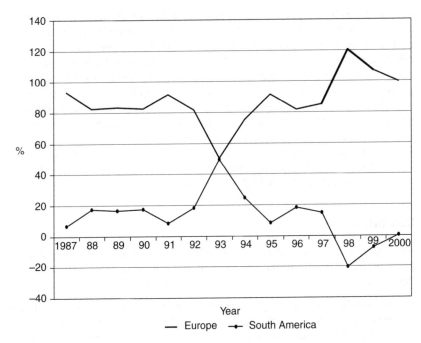

Figure 2.17 Europe's and South America's contribution to Scania's operating profit, 1987–2000

New Beetle, reinforced by the weakness of the euro versus the dollar), which jumped from 0.3% of world profits to nearly 17% in 2000. In 1999, for example, losses of 710 million DM were offset by North American profits of 727 million DM. In addition, VW is one of the few firms to have made major profits in Asia/Pacific (2 billion DM over 1997–2000) without having suffered any losses, even during the worst of the Asian crisis. Of course, our period of study is short, although it does cover a crucial time in the late 1990s crisis in the emerging countries (and in Japan). Still, our example does at least contain an example of successful internationalization, at least in profitability terms (as with Toyota and Honda).

Finally, Scania is another example of a successful internationalization (see Figure 2.17). A commercial vehicle specialist since 1991, like most capital goods producers Scania is very sensitive to fluctuations in growth rates (since this sector tends to anticipate and accentuate recession and recovery phenomena).

Moreover, the only Scania facilities outside Europe, where it realized around 16% of its production revenues in 1995–9, are found in Mercosur, a market characterized by great instability throughout the 1990s. In fact, Scania's global operating profits dropped from 3 billion to 1 billion kroners between 1989 and 1993, rose to 5 billion in 1994, suffered from the effects of the 1996 European recession, and finally recovered in 1997-9. In studying geographic contributions to Scania's global profits, note that despite the highly unstable nature of the market, the firm did not experience any losses in 1987-97, either in Europe or Mercosur. Europe accounted for around 82% of its world profits, and Mercosur the remaining 18%. In 1993, Mercosur profits, which, because of the general recovery in South America had just doubled their 1992 levels, helped Scania to cope with the recession that was just breaking out in Europe. They eventually accounted for 50% of Scania's world profits. Inversely, the 1998-9 Mercosur crisis created losses for Scania that reached 20% in 1998, but which were largely offset by higher earnings in Europe.

Conclusion

Although the information at our disposal was neither exhaustive nor homogeneous for all the automakers, the following lessons can nevertheless be derived from our analysis of levels of internationalization:

1. Automobile firms, perhaps with the exception of Honda, are not global firms. Commercial internationalization is by far the most advanced with Japanese (57%) and European (73%) firms, but for the Americans (24.5%) the focus of activity remains the domestic market. The large size of the American market does not explain all of this, given that the European market now accounts for equivalent volumes (around 20 million units per year). Productive internationalization outside a firm's country of origin remains below 45% on average, according to our production revenue criterion. Moreover, according to our overseas production criterion, it only surpasses 50% in Europe.[40] Capital internationalization is even less developed – foreign assets only represent 30% or less of American or Japanese firms' total assets (although this number does rise to 54% for European firms). Table 2.7 provides a synthetic vision of the various forms of internationalization by means of a synthetic global index which adds the proportion of overseas production to the synthetic UNCTAD index we have shown for comparative purposes.[41] Globally, we find that the average level of internationalization is 43.2%, and 50% of all firms feature a level of internationalization of more than 41.5%. Only five out of sixteen firms feature an internationalization of more than 50%, regardless of the index being used. This includes three European and two Japanese firms that are not necessary the largest ones in terms of their overall production volumes. These firms also have in common the fact that they market least a quarter of their revenues and manufacture at least a quarter of their output outside their region of origin.[42] Toyota and the Fiat Group, with a global index of around 47% and UNCTAD index

Table 2.7 Ranking of firms according to the synthetical indexes

Firms	Global	UNCTAD
DaimlerChrysler (97–99)	69.8	67.4
Honda (95–99)	60.7	65.3
BMW (95–99)	56.0	58.3
VW (95–99)	55.8	56.6
Nissan (95–99)	51.1	54.9
Fiat Group (95–99)	47.2	49.2
Toyota (95–99)	46.8	52.1
Isuzu (96–99)	41.9	41.9
Renault (95–99)	41.2	45.8
Ford (95–97)	38.6	36.1
PSA (95–99)	36.8	41.4
Mitsubishi (95–99)	35.6	37.5
GM (95–96)	33.8	30.0
Subaru (95–99)	32.3	37.6
Mazda (95–99)	29.9	33.8
Navistar (96–98)	13.7	9.5
Average	**43.2**	**44.8**
Median	**41.5**	**43.9**

Sources: Our own calculations from the data in financial reports. For methodology, see Table 2.2.

values of 52% and 49%, respectively, are very close to this leading group, and they present similar characteristics. But we cannot call the seven most internationalized firms 'global firms'. Instead, they should be called multi-regional firms, given that they run at least one major facility on another continent (Honda, Toyota, Nissan, DaimlerChrysler), or else several significant but smaller facilities in different continents (VW). The new merger/acquisition or partnership projects, which can be based on capital stakes being taken with or without a controlling participation, presuppose that the internationalization trend will continue, but that this will sometimes take the shape of original forms that will make it more difficult to identify the exact perimeter of the new entities being created.[43] The profitability of this new stage of internationalization also raises a number of issues, especially since it has been shown that those firms that are the most internationalized are not necessary the most profitable.

2. We do note that few firms have succeeded in transforming foreign operations, all regions combined, into a durable source of profit. Among the American firms, and unlike Ford, GM (despite the fact that it has long been described as a leader in decline) was able to achieve this not only during the long post-war period of high growth but also over the course of two decades (1980–2000) of slow and unstable growth. In Japan, since the 1980s, only Toyota, Honda and Suzuki were able to achieve this.

Table 2.8   Number of loss-making years, 1990–9, by geographic zone

Firms	Overseas	Country of origin	World
Toyota	0	0	0
Honda	0	0	0
Suzuki	0	0	0
VW	Probably 0	1	1
Renault (1990–8)	0	3	1
PSA	0	3	2
GM	0	4	3
Scania	2	0	0
Isuzu (1994–9)	5	2	1
Ford	5	3	2
Subaru	5	3	4
Mitsubishi	6	1	1
Nissan	6	4	7
Mazda	7	2	5

Sources: Our own calculations from financial reports.

All the other Japanese firms' performances were either mediocre (Subaru, Isuzu) or even negative (Mazda, Mitsubishi, Nissan). In Europe, French firms have only been making a profit on their foreign operations since 1986. Scania (and probably VW) had similar results. Table 2.8 provides a synthesized view of this result for 1990–9, a period covering an entire cycle of growth in North America, a period of slow growth and then recovery in Europe,[44] and the beginning of an extended period of stagnation in Japan. Seven out of thirteen firms did not make any foreign losses at all over this decade, including three Japanese, three Europeans and one American. These are firms for whom internationalization has generally developed into an additional competitive advantage. The three Japanese firms present the particularity of not having suffered any losses in their original market, in spite of the Japanese economic crisis and the country's weaker automobile market. In Europe, only VW has achieved a similar performance. French firms and GM only lost money in their domestic markets, and this was offset occasionally by foreign profits. Scania is close to this first group – the Mercosur crisis caused it to lose money for two years in its number two market, yet it did not record any overall losses, coming out ahead both in its original market and globally. This initial category is followed by a group of firms (almost all of whom are Japanese) that lost money during at least half of the 1990s, something that cannot be explained solely by short-term fluctuations. For these firms, internationalization has represented a handicap that has often compounded a precarious national situation.

Ultimately, we know that there is no clear and linear relationship between levels of internationalization and profitability. Honda, VW, and to a lesser extent Toyota, are members of a category comprised of the world's most internationalized firms (using a classification derived from synthetic indexes), but Renault and PSA are not really members of this group (given their average level of internationalization), and GM even less so.[45] Similarly, within the group of those firms for whom internationalization has been the least successful, we find relatively less-internationalized firms such as Mazda, Mitsubishi and Subaru, as well as a firm that is highly internationalized (Nissan). A firm can fail as a result of insufficient internationalization (for example, Mazda) or else because of its high but inappropriate degree of internationalization (for example, Nissan). In the same vein, a firm can obtain profits from abroad because it has a low level of internationalization (PSA) – or else its higher level of internationalization can expose it to greater possibilities of loss (Fiat Auto). Internationalization is truly a risky business, and not always a source of advantage. More than the actual level of internationalization, it is the quality of this status, its appropriateness to the firm's specific resources, to the competitive environment and to the characteristics of market demand that leads to success or to failure – an observation that raises questions about the organizational characteristics of those firms that have been the most successful.

3. The three firms (Toyota, Honda and VW) whose productive models have turned out to be the most relevant and coherent (Boyer and Freyssenet, 2002) are among the most internationalized firms of all (Honda and VW) or are at least belong to the upper tier in this category (Toyota). These are firms where internationalization has become a durable source of profit. Should we consider this to be a confirmation that their respective productive models, built within a national framework, have been reinforced by the international situation post-1974? The figures sustain this thesis but do not prove it. Indeed, when these firms internationalize, their national productive model undergoes an inevitable hybridization that can vary depending on the region in which the firms have set up facilities. This hybridization affects their initial 'profit strategy' and 'company government compromise' – these being the two preconditions for a firm's profitability. Will Honda be able to pursue its 'innovation–flexibility' strategy in those regions where it has set up operations, or is it going to change strategy? How can we be certain that the successes that these firms have achieved abroad are the consequence of an original productive model? Might they not be a hybrid variant that is quite distinct from the original model? To answer these questions, we need a specific in-depth analysis of firms' internationalization trajectories – something that can be found in the later chapters of this book.

Translated by Alan Sitkin

Appendix

Sources

National and world production data of automobile firms are taken from: *L'industrie automobile française*, by 'Le Répertoire Mondial des activités de production et d'assemblage des véhicules automobiles', CCFA, 2, rue de Presbourg, 75008, Paris, France (www.ccfa.fr). All other data are taken from the financial reports published by firms every year.

Contribution index to world profit

We have tried to determine whether the national or foreign profit contributed to increasing or decreasing world profit, or to reducing or worsening world loss. To do so, we have divided the foreign profit or loss by the absolute value of the world profit or loss. We have done the same with the national profit or loss. We can therefore take into account all possible cases.

Two examples:

1. If the national and foreign profits are worth 50 each, world profit is worth 100, and the contribution of national and foreign profit is 50%.
2. If national profit is worth 50, and a foreign loss worth -70 is registered, there is a world loss of -20. The contribution of national profit is 50 divided by the absolute value of -20, (equal to 20), which gives a positive contribution of 250%. The negative contribution of the foreign loss is -70 divided by 20, which gives -350%. Finally, the sum of the contribution of the national profit (250%) and that of the foreign loss (-350%) gives a negative balance of -100%, pointing to the fact that the firm has suffered a world loss. The national profit has contributed to reduce this world loss; and the foreign loss has contributed to worsen it.

We can also imagine the case of a world profit resulting from a foreign profit despite a national loss, and so on.

Notes

1   Unfortunately, we do not have access to sufficient information on Fiat or the German firms.
2   The transnationality index is calculated as an average of three relationships: foreign assets versus total assets; foreign sales versus total sales; and foreign staff versus total staff (cf. UNCTAD, 1999).
3   GM, Ford, Toyota/Daihatsu/Hino.
4   GM (Isuzu included), Ford (Mazda included), Toyota/Daihatsu/Hino, DaimlerChrysler, Renault/Nissan, VW.
5   Nissan and VW.
6   Fiat, PSA, Honda, Mitsubishi.
7   Chrysler, Renault, PSA, UAZ, Fiat, Honda, Mazda, Mitsubishi.
8   Suzuki-Maruti, Hyundai-Kia-Asia, Daewoo-Ssangyong, Avtovaz.

9 Suzuki, Daimler-Benz, Isuzu, Subaru, British Leyland, Volvo, BMW.

10 Avtovaz, Subaru, Volvo, Proton, Gaz, ChinaFirst.

11 The 'commercial revenues' indicator allows us to break world sales down into their components (all products combined) by place of sale, regardless of where the product was manufactured. A product can be sold in a given foreign country after having been made in the firm's country of origin or in another country.

12 The 'production revenues' indicator allows us to break global sales down into their components (all products combined) by the location where the firm's subsidiaries have set up operations. One product can be manufactured by an overseas subsidiary of the firm and sold in the same country, or in another country.

13 These are personal calculations based on the fifteen automobile firms that appear among the 100 leading multinationals comprising the UNCTAD sample.

14 Korean firms were not included because of the insufficiency and unreliability of relevant statistical information. The same applies to Russian, Chinese and Indian firms. Often smaller than average, these firms are barely internationalized and their future as independent concerns remains in question, particularly in South Korea.

15 This number can be obtained from the average of (1), (3), and (5) (see Table 2.2).

16 During the 1970s, North America was limited to the United States and Canada. Since the creation of NAFTA, Ford includes Mexico in North America.

17 In 1990–9, 69.8% for NAFTA, 23.7% for Europe and 6.5% for the rest of the world, including around 3% in South America and 3.5% in Asia/Africa/Pacific (*Sources*: Personal calculations based on financial statements).

18 Like Paccar and Navistar (see Table 2.2), and especially the Japanese commercial vehicle makers. Hino, Japan's top automaker, made only 12% of its total sales overseas in 1998–9.

19 Fiat's example shows the usefulness of industrial diversification, as 6.8% of the group's revenues in North America are not made by Fiat Auto, the group's passenger car subsidiary, but by other units within the group.

20 French firms, for example, make 25% of their total sales outside Europe.

21 By the year 2010, GM wants to realize 10% of its total sales in Japan.

22 If we include the Korean firms, overseas production reached an average of 24% in 1990–4, and 36.3% in 1995–9.

23 As a result, BMW's percentage of overseas production dropped sharply below 50% in 2000.

24 Here we are defining the term 'region' in the broadest sense of the term. For American firms, this means NAFTA plus South America. For European firms, it is the European Union (EU) plus other countries in Europe (including Turkey). For Japanese firms, it means the other countries in Asia, plus Oceania and Africa.

25 That is, outside NAFTA and South America.

26 Here we could mention the 'Renault/Nissan' grouping, linked to the 'Volvo/RVI/Mack/Nissan Diesel' grouping; 'DaimlerChrysler/Mitsubishi'; and other groupings such as 'VW/Scania' and 'GM/Fiat' (or even the take-over of Navistar by Hino).

27 Sales by zone of production is a measurement that includes all the products (complete passenger vehicles, commercial vehicles where applicable, motorcycles, motors, spare parts) that are used in all the business lines (automobiles, other manufacturing activities, services).

28 The periods that Tables 2.2 and 2.6 cover in terms of commercial revenues and production revenues are different from the ones referred to here, since information on breakdown by geographic zone has only been available since

1997 for Japanese firms (with VW and Renault no longer providing this information from 1997 and 1998 onwards). Generally speaking, this has a minimal impact on the exportable surpluses (commercial revenues – production revenues) we have calculated.

29   The revenues 'produced' by foreign subsidiaries (see Tables 2.2 and 2.6) modify the hierarchy of productive internationalization (when measured by overseas production and calculated in physical terms). This applies mainly to European firms. Several reasons explain this phenomenon: the nature of the product range that is being manufactured; the average purchasing power in each operational zone; the foreign production's rate of integration; variations in exchange rates and so on. There is not enough room in the present chapter to do justice to all of these considerations.

30   For the American and Japanese firms, we can make use of long series of net profit statistics. For European firms, we have series of varying lengths covering operating profits. These two measurements of profit are clearly not the same. The point, however, is not to compare them, but instead to study, with the help of our indicator, overseas contributions to profits.

31   To analyse Japanese firms' world profits, we dispose of two sources of information. On the one hand, we have net consolidated world-wide earnings, and net unconsolidated earnings (reflecting changes in Japan itself). To calculate net foreign earnings, we subtract net unconsolidated earnings from net consolidated earnings. Using these two time series we calculate an indicator of contributions by net national and foreign profits to net world profits. This is, of course, a rough assessment, but it is an accurate one that is particularly useful in analysing long-term trends. In addition, we can break operating profits down by geographic zone from around 1995–6 onwards. By definition, operating profits are a truer reflection of a firm's productive activities – but our information is more recent. Net profits, which include financial income and charges, tax, and extraordinary income and costs, reflect a firm's final earnings. We have tried to combine the two sets of information. The only numbers represented in a graphic form are changes in net profits.

32   The sharp drop in Honda's net earnings in Japan are explained by an exceptional domestic loss of 109.4 million yen.

33   Reuters interview with M. Davies, General Manager Honda UK, 21.12.00 (http:/just-auto.com/features).

34   US sales reached a peak of 183,000 units in 1986 and fell to a low of 100,000 in 1995, before going back up to 172,000 in 2000 thanks to a rejuvenated product range.

35   In 2000, Mitsubishi's sales in Japan suffered as a result of a scandal involving the recall of faulty vehicles. Passenger car and truck sales fell by 8.6%, and mini-car sales by 7%.

36   Its subsidiary in Thailand suffered a loss of 43.7 billion yen (around $350 million) because of the impact of the baht devaluation on dollar-linked debt (and because of the collapse of the local market).

37   Operating profit is the only geographical zone information available on European firms. Renault and PSA stopped publishing this data in 1998. Fiat and VW started to publish it in 1995 and 1997. Volvo does not publish it at all.

38   Despite major productive modernization initiatives during the 1990s, Fiat Auto is still handicapped by its specialization (70% of the firm's sales) in a small-car sector that is typified by weak profit margins. The firm does not achieve sufficient economies of scale compared to its European rivals. Turnover was increased by a factor of 1.8 between 1990 and 2000, but operating profits never got back the level they reached in the late 1980s.

39 To break the VW Group's pre-tax operating profits down on a geographical basis, we have used the following method (based on the segment analysis contained within the company's annual report): (i) we only use gross profits for manufacturing activities, thus excluding financial activities; and (ii) we consider that each marque (VW, Audi, Skoda, SEAT, Rolls-Royce/Bentley) made its profits in Europe, with the world's 'other regions' being presented as such in the report.

40 If we exclude firms specializing in commercial vehicle production, overseas manufacturing represents around 45% of world output for European and American firms, but only 31% for Japanese firms (see averages (2), (4), and (5) in Table 2.2).

41 We have sometimes supplemented the UNCTAD calculations, for example by incorporating Honda Motor's number of overseas staff members. Where information is lacking on assets or staffing, we did not calculate the UNCTAD index, unlike the UNCTAD itself, which calculates this index even when it only disposes of two out of the three necessary pieces of information.

42 Apart from BMW, which has an extra-European production of only 6.3% BMW's 2000 divorce from Rover does not seem to have undermined the group's level of internationalization. Quite the contrary, in fact: it diminishes Europe's role. BMW has continued to stress its internationalization drive in North America, the proportion of total assets located in this region rising from 23.7% in 1999 to 30.3% in 2000.

43 For example, there was no ambiguity during the DaimlerChrysler merger, given how long the illusion of a 'merger among equals' lasted. Less straightforward was the take-over of Mitsubishi by DaimlerChrysler and of Nissan by Renault. Although there is no ambiguity with respect to the leading role played by DaimlerChrysler and by Renault in these operations, the new groupings do not (yet?) constitute jointly operating firms, and may never reach this stage. The Fiat/GM agreement (not to mention the increased number of *ad hoc* partnership arrangements) raises the same types of issue.

44 This is the only period where available information allows a comparison of the greatest number of firms.

45 We have not been able to calculate the synthesized index for Scania and Suzuki, since one of the necessary pieces of information is not available. Based on three elements out of four, Scania's overall synthesized index value is 71.5%, and Suzuki's 35.2%.

References

Boyer, R. and Freyssenet, M. (2002) *The Productive Models: The Conditions of Profitability*, London/New York: Palgrave.

Chesnais, F. (1994) *La Mondialisation du capital*, Paris: Syros.

Economist, The (1999) 'How to Make Mergers Work?', *The Economist*, 9 January.

Economist Intelligence Unit (2000) *The Automotive Industries of Asia-Pacific: Prospects for ASEAN and the Emerging Markets to 2005*.

Financial Times Auto Survey (2000) 'Brazil: Sights Set to Give Exports Needed Boost' (website: www.ftsurveys/industry/sccc0a.htm).

Friedman, J. (1983) *Oligopoly Theory*, Cambridge University Press.

Lung, Y. (2000) 'Towards a Worldwide Oligoly in the Automobile Industry?', *La Lettre du GERPISA*, no. 143, June (website: www.gerpisa.univ-evry.fr).

Ohmae, K. (1985) *Triad Power*, New York: The Free Press.

Porter, M. (1986) *Competition in Global Industries*, Boston, Mass.: Harvard Business School Press.

PricewaterhouseCoopers (1999) *Global Automotive Industry Review 1998*.

UNCTAD (1998) *World Investment Report: Trends and Determinants*, New York/Geneva: United Nations.

UNCTAD (1999) *World Investment Report: Foreign Direct Investment and the Challenge of Development*, New York/Geneva: United Nations.

UNCTAD (2000) *World Investment Report: Cross-Border Mergers and Acquisitions and Development*, New York/Geneva: United Nations.

Ward's Automotive Yearbook (2000).

3
Volkswagen: Accelerating from a Multinational to a Transnational Automobile Company

Ludger Pries

Volkswagen as a German-based international player

At the beginning of the 1990s Volkswagen was the only German automaker with a considerable level of international production activity. Although BMW and Daimler-Benz, the other two of the German 'Big Three' car assemblers, sold more than half of their overall car production outside Germany in 1990, BMW realized less than 4% of its production outside Germany (mainly CKD assembly in South Africa), and Daimler-Benz had no passenger vehicle production facilities abroad at all at that time. In 1990, the Volkswagen consortium (consisting of the brands Volkswagen, Audi and SEAT at that time) sold exactly two-thirds and produced 40% of all units outside Germany.

The structure of the internationalization of the German automakers that prevailed until the end of the 1980s was characterized by Ulrich Jürgens as follows: 'Daimler-Benz is still exclusively a German company in the area of car production; it only has international production sites in the area of trucks and commercial vehicles. BMW and Porsche, finally, are the firms which are most closely limited to Germany in their production and work force' (Jürgens, 1992). He described the Volkswagen consortium as 'the only German automobile company that pursued an internationalization strategy with regard to its production system' and as a 'European oriented corporation'. This definition of Volkswagen would be quite adequate to describe the situation up to the beginning of the 1990s – but does it also hold for the last decade? In a more recent analysis, Jürgens distinguished three periods in the development of Volkswagen's industrial model, separated from each other by 'periods of internal crisis, indecision, trial-and-error approaches, and accompanying internal controversies and uncertainty, which were of extended length: from around 1968 until 1974 in the first case, and from around 1988 until 1994 in the second' (Jürgens, 1998). One important question is: What came after this period of uncertainty in the later 1990s?

This chapter analyses the development of the Volkswagen consortium during the 1990s.[1] The main argument is that Volkswagen changed its business model and production system as well as its internationalization strategy during this decade. After a small crisis until 1993/4, during the second half of the 1990s Volkswagen – as well as BMW and Daimler-Benz – played a very active and successful role in the international automobile industry. The take-over of Rover by BMW in 1994 was an attempt of 'going global', the Daimler–Chrysler merger in 1998 and the competition between Volkswagen and BMW to buy Rolls-Royce at the same time are the most visible expressions, and the tip of the iceberg for this new dynamic internationalization of the German Big Three.

It is argued that Volkswagen's crisis of 1993/4 reflects only a transition period towards a new and successful consortium profile, where major changes in the three dimensions of corporate governance and profit strategies, of product structure and market strategies and of production systems at plant and headquarters level coincided with important shifts in the internationalization profile. In short, Volkswagen's internationalization profile changed from that of a multinational to a transnational company. Meanwhile, in multinational companies, *all three dimensions* are structured mainly by a multiplicity of local logics, in transnational companies they are modelled increasingly by a global or at least by a pluri-local logic. This differentiation of multinational and transnational companies combines aspects of the spatial structure of co-ordination and control (Porter, 1986), of the configuration of values, capacities, knowledge and functions (Bartlett and Ghoshal, 1989), and of the overall spatial division of all productive functions of the value chain (Ruigrok and van Tulder, 1995).

At the beginning of the 1990s, BMW and Daimler-Benz were completely German-centred companies concerning their corporate governance and profit strategies, their product structure and their production systems. Being highly internationalized with respect to their market strategies, both companies could be described as distribution orientated multinational companies. Volkswagen, on the other hand, could be characterized as a production orientated multinational company. During the 1990s, Daimler-Benz began to internationalize, mainly its corporate governance structure (merger with Chrysler) and its production system (new production sites in a number of countries), while BMW experienced a failure with its engagement in Rover and returned to be a highly German-centred and distribution-orientated multinational company.

Taking into account the different dimensions of corporate governance and profit strategies, of product structure and market strategies, and of production systems, it is possible to characterize the internationalization dynamics of the companies more clearly. The argument will be put forward that Volkswagen started the 1990s as a production orientated multinational company, but took significant steps towards becoming a transnational company operating globally at the levels of market strategies and production systems, but remaining strongly a German-centred company in relation to its corporate governance and profit strategies. First, a brief description of the internationalization history of Volkswagen is offered. Second, some important changes to Volkswagen's internationalization profile during the 1990s are presented. And finally, some concluding remarks are made.

Volkswagen as a genuine international company

After the Second World War and the corresponding debacle of the Volkswagen factory after war production for the Nazi regime (from 1939 until 1945, Volkswagen produced only about 600 civil cars) the plant in Wolfsburg was administrated by the Allies until 1947. From the very beginning of post-war production a considerable share of the total production of Beetles and Bullys was exported. Even in 1947, 1656 (or 20% of the total of 8382 cars) were sent abroad. In 1949, the Allies handed over the company to German state ownership (as Volkswagenwerk GmbH). In the same year, the first two Beetles were exported to the USA, beginning thereby the success of the Beetle in the biggest auto market in the world. After the 1950s, Volkswagen opened overseas plants in a considerable number of countries, mainly in the Third World. Therefore Volkswagen has to be considered as an internationally active company from its beginnings.

To understand the characteristics of the new internationalization period of the 1990s it is worth summarizing briefly the preceding period. The identification of distinctive development phases depends on the topics of interest and of the applied criteria – which frequently are not mentioned explicitly. Focusing on economic development, industrial relations and the 'regulation mode', some authors differentiate one phase up to the crisis in 1966, a phase of recuperation up to the end of the 1970s, a third phase of decrease from 1980 to 1983, a fourth phase of renewed expansion from 1984 to 1991, a fifth phase of crisis and adjustments in 1993/4, and a sixth phase of dynamic growth (Wellhöner, 1996; Haipeter, 2000). Analysing the 'industrial model', Jürgens distinguished the aforementioned three periods, first up to the crisis and adjustment of 1967–73, second up to the crisis and structural change of 1988–93, and third beginning from the mid-1990s (Jürgens, 1998).

As far as this chapter concentrates on the internationalization profile of Volkswagen in the context of the overall consortium profile, the main concerns are on the specific structures and strategies of the geographic-spatial distribution of resources, functions, competencies and power between the headquarters and plants. This spatial configuration of resources, functions, competencies and power between headquarters and plants refers to the already mentioned three dimensions of corporate governance and profit strategies, of product structure and market strategies, and of production

Table 3.1 Three phases of Volkswagen's internationalization profile

Resources, functions, competencies and power to define	Distribution-orientated multinational company (1940s–1967/9)	Production-orientated multinational company (1967/9–1990/2)	Globally operating transnational company (since 1990/2)
Corporate governance and profit strategies	centre–periphery configuration	centre–periphery configuration with centralization	globalized centralism and intra-organizational competition
Product structure and market strategies	centre–periphery configuration	centre–periphery configuration	globalized platforms with regionally specified car bodies
Production systems	centre–periphery configuration	world-wide production networking	global learning and transfer of general production principles

systems. Based on these concepts, three phases of Volkswagen's internationalization profile can be distinguished, as indicated in Table 3.1.

During the first phase (1940s to 1967–9) Volkswagen operated as a distribution-orientated multinational company. World-wide distribution was organized with independent general import partners or by direct Volkswagen dependencies, for example, in Canada, the USA and France. Assembly and production facilities were opened in countries such as Brazil, Mexico, South Africa and Australia, where national regulations hindered free market access. In this context, new and highly integrated production facilities with press shop and stamping, body shop, painting, sub-assembly and final assembly were constructed in the 1950s in Anchietta, Brazil, and in the 1960s in Puebla, Mexico. These plants represented the dominant internationalization strategy of the consortium during this period: with old and used tools and machines (for example, discarded stamps from Germany) the factories produced older models (the old Beetle and Combi), mainly for the protected national markets, and local plant management was relatively autonomous (Doleschal, 1987; Wellhöner, 1996; Pries, 1999). The main strategic aims of the distribution-orientated multinational company were to secure access to potentially large markets and to use cheap labour in work-intensive Fordistic production lines. There was a very clear technological hierarchy of products and production systems, and a definitive division of labour between the core plants at the centre and the peripheral overseas plants. For managers, it was a kind of punishment and a career disadvantage to be sent for years to an overseas plant.

During the second period of its internationalization trajectory (1967–9 to 1990–2), Volkswagen can be labelled as a production-orientated multinational company. The centre–periphery figure was stable regarding corporate governance and profit strategies and product structure and market strategies (with a tendency towards a centralization of profit strategies), and considerable efforts were made in the field of world-wide production networking (the so-called *Verbundproduktion*). Similar cars were assembled in a wide range of world-wide distributed plants. In spite of the clear polarization of old products in the peripheral plants and new ones in the central plants, all parts of the company were redefined in a transnational division of labour. Nevertheless, a strong hierarchy of products and production technologies between core and peripheral plants remained. Whereas the latter had functioned exclusively for local market access during the first period, they were now integrated increasingly into a global division of production. Through increased production capacity and economies of scale, a growing share of auto parts were produced in places other than where the assembly took place. For instance, the Volkswagen plant in Puebla, Mexico produced millions of body parts and rear axles for export to Germany and other Volkswagen plants from 1974 to 1991; it exported CKDs to Volkswagen's Nigerian assembly plant in 1984–5; and it produced millions of doors, chassis parts and engines to the Westmoreland, USA, plant from 1984 until the closure of that assembly facility in 1988–9.

World-wide production networking continued, with vertically highly integrated production in the Volkswagen consortium producing more than 50% of added value. During this first phase, the peripheral plants were just passive, less productive 'dependencies' serving protected markets and to a great extent not connected to the production flows in the centre, but during the second period the main peripheral plants took on an important role in the overall transnational division of labour inside the company. Concerning product structure and marketing strategies, the basic centre–periphery position was maintained: the peripheral plants produced and sold old-fashioned models (like the old Beetle or the first generation of the Golf) or even produced their own locally developed products as for example in Brazil with the BX-series models, Gol, Voyage, Parati and Saveiro (see Eckardt *et al.*, 1998, 2000).

In general, the 'modernity gap' of models produced in the periphery compared with those produced at the centre narrowed slowly during this phase, but still remained tangible. For example, the Shanghai plant produced an older, Santana model, while in Germany and Belgium a newer one was being assembled; the Volkswagen de México plant manufactured the Golf A2 model while in Germany the next generation of Golf A3 had already been assembled. Peripheral plants like those in Brazil, Mexico and South America became more important; besides providing access to a protected market and to cheap labour, these factories entered increasingly into transnational productive networks and macro-regional market strategies (such as using Mexico as an export base for the USA and Canada, when the Westmoreland factory of Volkswagen USA was closed in 1988). In terms of the internationalization profile of the overall consortium, these tendencies were precursors of the third period.

The internationalization trajectory of Volkswagen in the 1990s

During the 1980s–1990s, Volkswagen began to change more and more from being a simple multinational company to become a globally operating transnational company. The traditional centre–periphery configuration began to become less significant, although Volkswagen is – as will be shown – far from turning into a rootless global company. The internationalization profile changed qualitatively by integrating new foreign companies and brands, and by reorganizing the overall corporate governance structures. Concerning product structure and market strategies as well as the production systems, there was no longer a fixed and defined hierarchy between a 'centre' and a 'periphery'. On the contrary, the company began to globalize the search for the best places and best practices. An important mechanism was diffusing the notion – not necessarily of concrete mechanisms – of intra-organizational competition between plants, independently of their former central or peripheral location, for products and production quotas. Core strategic competencies such as design, research and development (R&D) or construction remain in the central plants, but spatially diffused to a greater extent than before. Recently opened new plants or strongly restructured old ones are considered as technical, organizational and social laboratories in the development of new production systems and best practice principles. The strategic function of each plant is to maximize the exploitation of all local idiosyncrasies and to optimize intra-consortium competition and learning processes.

In this overall setting, the 1990s are characterized by fundamental changes in all three dimensions discussed above, leading to a general shift in the internationalization profile. The argument is that innovations in these different dimensions and levels were not only additive but cumulative, thus reinforcing one another. Therefore, it is possible to speak of an 'acceleration spiral'. Important elements of these transformations will be described in more detail below. To get a general idea of their scope and quality, a comparison with the situation of Japanese automobile companies during the 1980s is useful. The wave of Japanese car plants that were opened, mainly in the USA and the United Kingdom, during the 1980s happened largely because of the highly competitive Japanese production system of lean production. High export rates and a corresponding high favourable balance of trade led to political pressure on Japanese automakers to bring production facilities and jobs to the regions of sale, namely the two other Triad regions, the USA and the EU.

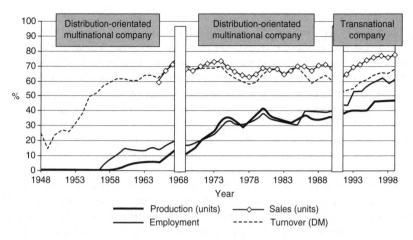

Figure 3.1 The three internationalization phases of the Volkswagen consortium: share of foreign production, sales, turnover and employment, 1948–98

Source: Annual reports, Volkswagen.

In contrast to this, the transnationalization push of the German automakers, and in particular of Volkswagen in the 1990s, started from a situation of fragility and disadvantage. Compared with Japanese and US companies, the German Big Three – Volkswagen, Daimler-Benz and BMW – had serious productivity problems detected not only by the MIT study (Womack *et al.*, 1990), but also by international benchmarking realized by the firms themselves (Springer, 1999). Although well aware of this situation at the end of the 1980s, German automakers enjoyed a short but quite artificial recovery period resulting from German unification up to 1992. Meanwhile, and taking advantage of this 'breathing period', all three companies initiated a twofold offensive of company restructuring and internationalization. In sum, the Japanese internationalization push of the 1980s was based on a position of high international competitiveness, whereas the German internationalization push of the 1990s started from an unfavourable situation of multifaceted crisis.

But the internationalization push of the 1990s was not only an increase in vehicle exporting, but a general shift in the internationalization profile. Important indicators for the changing spatial distribution of productive resources and functions are the shares of units produced and sold, of employment and of turnover in Germany and abroad (see Figure 3.1). Taking into account the portion of turnover (in DM) and of sales (in vehicle units) realized outside Germany as a share of the total turnover and sales of the Volkswagen consortium (that is, Audi, SEAT, Skoda, Volkswagen cars and Volkswagen trucks) Figure 3.1 reveals a long tradition and high level of international activities. Since the 1950s roughly two-thirds of sales and turnover of Volkswagen were realized outside Germany. The two corresponding lines only have one significant peak in 1967–8 (foreign sales compensated the relatively and even absolutely decreasing sales in Germany caused by the first severe post-war economic crisis) and one significant breakdown in 1991–2 (indicating the enormous demand push caused by German unification). These two extremes indicate the turning point from one period to another.

But these shifts from one internationalization dynamic to another become clearer when comparing sales and turnover with production (in vehicle units) and employment (in people employed directly by one of the Volkswagen consortium's companies). Whereas during the first period of Volkswagen as a distribution-orientated multinational company, foreign production and employment were very low compared to sales and turnover, this began to change during the second phase of Volkswagen as a production-orientated multinational company: foreign shares of employment and production rose to 30–40% of the total. During the third phase – Volkswagen as a transnational company – this share of vehicles produced abroad and employment outside Germany went up significantly, to 60% and 50%, respectively. The growing distance between the two lines indicates the increasing labour productivity of the formerly peripheral plants. At the same time, foreign sales and turnover showed a new upward dynamic. The opening gap between sales in units and turnover in DM is considerable, but needs careful interpretation. Turnover per sold unit abroad decreases relatively, which reflects currency shifts (devaluation of the DM in relation to the US$ and the corresponding US$-bound currencies, as in Mexico and Brazil) as well as market opening in former peripheral countries (which caused prices to go down relatively; see also the transnationality index in ILO, 2000).

The three periods of Volkswagen's internationalization trajectory coincide with the findings of Jürgens (1998) concerning the industrial model. However, two additional remarks are necessary. First, the internationalization push of the 1990s is not primarily a Europeanization, as indicated by Jürgens (1992) for the beginnings of that decade. During the 1990s the share of Volkswagen cars produced in Europe fell from 85% to 70.5%, when the production portion in America and Africa rose from 14% to 19%, and Asia expanded from 1% to 10.5%. Taking into account that the European part also includes the dynamic expansion in Eastern Europe, the significant *relative* decrease of production in Western Europe remains even clearer. Although Volkswagen developed a lot of new activities in Eastern Europe (in Poland, Slovenian Republic, Czech Republic and Hungary) during the 1990s, the increasing production shares, mainly of South America and China (see the appendices at the end of this chapter) indicate a qualitative shift towards a globally operating and transnational company.

The second point to mention concerning Jürgens' analysis deals with the general judgement of the success and stability of Volkswagen's consortium profile in the 1990s. Compared with the relatively pessimistic view of Jürgens (1992, 1998) the Volkswagen consortium – and its industrial model – did quite well throughout the decade. When Jürgens suggested that 'the strike of 1995 could turn out to be an early sign of a weakening of the very foundations of this model' (1998), viewed with hindsight this insinuation has not been verified. Obviously, there are some structural problems in the overall profile of the Volkswagen group – which will be described below – but in general the internationalization trajectory of the 1990s was combined successfully with qualitative shifts in all three dimensions under discussion.

Corporate governance and profit strategies

The success discussed above is mainly a result of Volkswagen's special corporate governance and profit strategies. Volkswagen maintained itself as a strongly Germany-rooted consortium controlled by shareholders as well as by strong groups of stakeholders. Although the federal state began to sell its 4.8 million shares (only to private buyers and in small packages) after 1988, the state of Lower Saxonia kept its shares of about a fifth of the corporate capital. The specific 'Volkswagen law' of 1960, which prohibits the concentration of shares in the hands of private institutional shareholders, stayed in force despite rising criticism, often neoliberally inspired. This has led to an embeddedness of the Volkswagen consortium in national and micro-regional networks of interest and power groups. The corporate governance structure of Volkswagen is traditional and stayed truly corporatist during the 1990s, in the sense that capital, labour and the state played important roles each having, if not equal, then at least a similar weight (Workers' Council, 2000).

Volkswagen's trajectory during the 1990s reveals the importance of this 'corporatistic corporate governance', even for its internationalization profile. When, in 1992, a successor to CEO Karl Hahn was discussed, Daniel Goeudevert, as the friendly and communicative 'best-seller' with an ecological marketing approach, was at first considered to be the favourite candidate in Wolfsburg. But in the face of growing sales and at the same time decreasing profits – a sign of productivity and efficiency weaknesses – the supervisory board elected Ferdinand Piëch in April 1992 and designated him Hahn's successor from January 1993. Piëch opted for a relative successful reorganization of the Audi brand focusing on product innovation and process optimization. This was an important aspect for the president of the IG Metall union, Franz Steinkühler, and the president of the Workers' Council, Klaus Volkert, both powerful members of the supervisory board of Volkswagen. The workers and employees, with their representatives, were mainly interested in a long-term competitive company with a typically German product approach to technology and quality – and therefore supported Piëch against Goeudevert.

With Piëch as the new strong chairman, raised to power by the triadic support of capital, labour and the state, the Volkswagen consortium maintained the characteristics of its 'corporatistic corporate governance' during the 1990s. From an international perspective, this is probably one of the most interesting aspects of the Volkswagen case. In a decade of strongly growing international competition and a neoliberal 'shareholder value' bias in general, Volkswagen not only survived, but was successful with a completely different corporate governance model. Nevertheless, there were important processes of overall consortium restructuring during the decade. Product innovation and brand differentiation and development were probably the most important of these.

Product structure and market strategies

The incorporation of SEAT (Spain) in 1986 represents the beginning of brand differentiation and a new type of internationalization of production for the Volkswagen consortium. The acquisition of Skoda (Czech Republic) in 1991 was the second step, and then in 1998 the brands Bentley, Bugatti and Lamborghini (additionally, Rolls-Royce until 2003) were bought. By 1995, Volkswagen Nutzfahrzeuge (trucks) was already separated from the Volkswagen Pkw (cars) brand. In particular, Audi and Volkswagen Cars were developed as premium brands in their segments. At the end of the 1990s, Volkswagen presented itself as a complex consortium focused on the 'core competencies' of car and truck production with a defined brand strategy and a global presence in the most important world automobile regions. There was a certain regional focus of the SEAT brand towards South European countries and of Skoda towards Eastern Europe, but at the same time Skoda, for instance, aims at price and quality orientated buyers in Germany.

In the international automobile industry as a whole, the Volkswagen consortium was probably the most successful in differentiating brands with specific car models and image, on the one hand, and homogenizing platforms, on the other hand. Platform strategies are nothing completely new to Volkswagen. The very first and successful models of the old Beetle and the Combi were built on the same platform. During the 1970s, the new Golf and the Audi 50 were based on the same A1 platform. But for the engineer Piëch, platform homogenization was one of the most important issues during the 1990s. The aim was to reduce the overall scope of car models to only four platforms. At the end of the decade the body chassis, axles, engines, gearbox and powertrain, gearshift, tank and air conditioning system were very similar in the A4 platform models VW Golf, VW Bora, VW New Beetle, Audi A3, Audi TT, SEAT Toledo and Skoda Octavia (*Auto-Zeitung*, January 1999).

Even if further platform unification remains a complex task – in 1999 there were still seventeen basic platforms in the Volkswagen consortium – and only about 10% to 20% of the overall car parts are homogenous at platform level, it seems that this is the most promising strategy for combining economies of scale with economies of scope. At the same time, this strategy presses towards stronger ties and real global co-operation of all organizational units with regard to product structures and market strategies. Volkswagen of Brazil will no longer develop and produce its own car models, but produce a regionally adapted part of the consortium's model range and perhaps adapt new 'hats' to the standardized platforms. Realizing platform strategies in the very different plants all over the world requires a certain homogenization of production technologies, of organization and of skill requirements (see below). Therefore, on the one hand, platform strategies are a precondition for a real transnationalization of consortium structures and strategies, but on the other, platform strategies *reinforce* transnationalization in all the important dimensions under discussion.

Concerning its internationalization trajectory, the Volkswagen consortium followed a 'double strategy' of buying existing foreign brands and internationalizing its VW and Audi brands. With regard to the latter, Volkswagen Cars has traditionally been an internationally orientated and known brand. After its foundation as an independent brand in 1995, Volkswagen Trucks began internationalization, mainly with the Resende plant in Brazil. In this country 52,911 light and heavy trucks were sold in 1999, representing, with more than a quarter of total sales of the VW Trucks brand, the most important foreign market. During the 1990s, the Audi brand experienced an internationalization push as well, with the North American region being the most important foreign market for Audi (with 12% – or 72,757 – units sold, out of a total of 635,343 units in 1999). The internationalization of Volkswagen Cars and Audi cannot be seen only in the growing shares of foreign sales, but also in qualitative new production activities.

Production systems

Understanding production systems as specific configuration of technologies, organization and work in a given factory, platform strategies do not only determine but actually motivate the homogenization of production systems in certain aspects,. The traditional centre–periphery duality (new versus old products and production technologies; high versus low production quality and productivity) could not be sustained. Therefore, the *outcomes* of production systems in terms of productivity, flexibility and quality have to be similar in all plants all over the world that are included in the networks of global production. Concerning the differentiation–homogenization and the adaptation–application problems of production systems (Pries, 2000), our findings suggest a certain hierarchy of local embeddedness of technologies, organization and work. As in the analogy of the concentric circles of an onion, production technologies tend to become similar in all plants of Volkswagen all over the world. At the other extreme, work (qualification structures, recruitment and employment systems, individual and collective rules and mechanisms for vertical and horizontal mobility, industrial and labour relations) was and remains most influenced and structured by local factors (labour law, labour markets, socio-cultural norms and so on), and organization as the specific way of dividing and integrating the working process holds an intermediate position.

Based on qualitative case studies and visits to five overseas plants and comparisons with German plants, we found substantial elements leading us to conclude that, during the 1990s, production systems in the overall consortium became more similar regarding their benchmarks and production technologies, but they remain quite different with respect to their work systems (Eckardt *et al.*, 2000). Some quantitative data indicate the qualitative shift in the international profile of Volkswagen's productive resources. In the last four years of the decade alone (1995–9) the Volkswagen consortium expanded from a total of thirty-five to forty-seven production and assembly sites all over the world.[2] The majority of plants were 'one brand plants' (such as two Skoda, three Audi, and twelve Volkswagen plants in 1999), but there were also a lot of mixed plants, where cars of more than one brand were produced (for example, Cheshire (Great Britain), Martorel (Spain), Brussels (Belgium), Poznan (Poland), Curitiba (Brazil), Pacheco (Argentina), Uitenhage (South Africa), Kvasiny (Czech Republic) and Changchun (China) in 1999, and the Wolfsburg (Germany) plant in 1995 as well). Comparing only the changes of models produced by plants between 1995 and 1999 reveals the high international productive flexibility of the Volkswagen consortium. Concerning production, sales and employment, the weight of the Volkswagen Cars brand in relation to the other car brands (Audi, SEAT, Skoda) went down during the 1990s, but it still represented two-thirds of production, sales and employment (Haipeter, 2000).

Meanwhile, international division of labour between plants during the 1980s concentrated on the North American region (between the Mexican Puebla and the US Westmoreland plants) and on the West European region (between plants in Germany, Belgium and Spain). During the 1990s, transnationalization strengthened world-wide production networking, and platform strategy was an important element in this. The twenty-five most important and defining parts of the body chassis of the A4 platform are produced exclusively for world-wide assembly in the headquarters (Wolfsburg) plant. This means that about a thousand or more equal pieces a day with identical measurements and quality are produced. This global platform strategy also means that equal quality standards in production, for instance concerning measurements in the body shop, or paint colours, are necessary in all integrated plants. Through this, interchangeability of components and the assembly of pluri-locally produced parts in one plant are possible. The qualitative shift from a centre–periphery configuration of an international division of labour towards a transnational production networking becomes clearer, taking the example of the New Beetle and its production in Puebla (Mexico).

The qualitative shift from the old Buggy to the New Beetle: Volkswagen's Puebla plant

During the 1980s the Mexican plant in Puebla produced a wide range of Volkswagen cars and different product generations. The old 'Buggy' and the different variants of the old Combi – at consortium level and viewed by current international standards as old-fashioned models – were sold mainly in Mexico, and only a small proportion of the Golf/Jetta (models A1 and A2) were exported, mainly to the USA. Even in 1991, the old Buggy and the Combi model represented about half of the overall production of 209,000 units. Contrary to the declared market strategy the export of Golf and Jetta models towards the USA and Canada remained insignificant during the 1980s, and the share of the overall Volkswagen consortium in the US car market was less than 1% (Schreiber, 1998). Until the end of the 1980s, the Puebla plant was very important as a component and engine supplier for the assembly plant in Westmoreland, USA (which was closed in 1988/9). In sum, the Mexican Volkswagen factory was part of an international division of labour at consortium level, but this division of labour assigned a clearly subordinate position to the Puebla plant. Volkswagen worked as a production-orientated multinational company, but the division of labour in the sense of the geographic–spatial distribution of resources, functions, competencies and power between headquarters and plants followed a centre–periphery scheme.

This situation began to change dramatically during the 1990s. In 1991 the headquarters assigned the Mexican plant to be the strategic export base of the Golf/Vento A3 for the US market, and made efforts to change the failed strategy of the previous decade. Facing the liberalization of auto markets in the Mexico–USA–Canada region through the NAFTA agreement – which came into operation on 1 January 1994 – and the internationalization strategies of BMW (initiating construction of its Spartanburg, South Carolina, plant in 1993) and Daimler-Benz (starting construction of its plant in Tuscaloosa, Alabama, in 1994) the Volkswagen consortium felt the need for qualitative shifts. During the model change of the Golf and Jetta (from A2 to A3), a one-month labour dispute stopped nearly all activities in August 1992 and led to a 'model change' of the work organization and industrial relations system. In 1993 the future of the Puebla plant was between being demoted to a third-level assembly plant or promotion to a top-level production facility. Nearly half of the top managers were fired or replaced, and working groups were established by force. Productivity and quality increased in the new A3 models.

But the qualitative divide came with the decision to produce the New Beetle in Puebla. After strong intra-company competition and campaigns (in 1995 more than one million signatures in favour of New Beetle production in Puebla were collected), in September 1995 the Mexican plant was defined as the first world-wide and tentatively exclusive producer of the New Beetle. This car was defined as the keystone in Volkswagen's market strategy to restore its presence in the USA, reviving the image and nostalgia of the old Buggy and combining it with a high-tech fun car for a market niche. Based on the A4 platform, a completely new 'hat' was designed, mainly in Volkswagen's

California studios, and developed at the German headquarters in Wolfsburg. In 1996 the New Beetle group grew in size to include more than thirty managers and technicians. A third of them went from Mexico to Wolfsburg to develop the project and prepare for production in Puebla. In the Mexican plant, more than 200 technicians were trained in the Vocational Training Centre in 1997. Pre- and Zero-Series Production began in Autumn 1997, and in December of that same year normal production began. Average daily output increased to more than 600 units in 1998, and more than 107,000 New Beetles were produced that year. The destination of 70% of total production was the US–Canadian market, 20% for the European market and just 10% to satisfy Mexican demand. In 1999, more than 160,000 New Beetles produced in Puebla represented a share of about 40% of Volkswagen's Mexican production, with the Golf and Jetta A3 and A4 models making up another half, and the old Buggy less than a tenth of total production in Puebla.

This marked a qualitative shift in product structure and market strategies during less than ten years. But during the same period the production system changed dramatically as well. After the labour conflict of 1992, a system of working groups was imposed unilaterally in almost all production areas. The payment system changed to a productivity-orientated evaluation within nine months. Management offered higher wages and regular rises in exchange for a high quality and productivity commitment from the workers. The union politics and structure changed as well, from a culture of confrontation and distrust towards a model of productivity consent and commitment. During the last five years of the decade, systems of quality management, of visual management, and of workers' participation in product and process improvement were developed and refined. Hierarchy levels were reduced, information flows were accelerated, and new forms of inter-disciplinary and inter-hierarchical team working and management were developed.

These changes in the production system led to increased productivity and production quality. In 1999, the Puebla plant produced 410,061 cars with less than 16,000 employees. Compared to 1990, this indicates a gross productivity growth from an average of 6.75 cars per employee per year to an average of about 25.6 cars per employee per year. The export share was more than two-thirds of total production, and only about 36,500 old Beetles (8.9% of total production) were produced in 1999. Of course, these numbers reflect not only productivity gains, but also, for example, changing structures of procurement, namely a massive outsourcing and subcontracting of productive and service activities (Müller-Neuhof, 1994; Kilper and Pries, 1999). But they actually also indicate the qualitative and really dramatic changes that occurred in Volkswagen's Puebla plant during the 1990s – in terms of product structure and market strategy as well as in the production system. At the same time, the changing plant profile of the Puebla factory indicates the general shifts in Volkswagen's overall consortium profile and internationalization strategy.

Conclusion

Although Volkswagen was a highly multinational company during all of the second half of the twentieth century, the decade of the 1990s was crucial for a general shift towards a transnational internationalization profile. Foreign production gained relative importance. Old brown-field factories (as in Puebla (Mexico) or Anchietta (Brazil)) have been restructured fundamentally, and new assembly facilities opened (from the Czech Republic, Poland, Hungary and Portugal to Malaysia, Indonesia, Taiwan, the Philippines and China). But not only the *quantity* of foreign production activities changed dramatically; the quality of the geographic distribution of resources, functions and competencies also altered. The consortium began to shift from the traditional division of labour between centre and periphery towards a more homogenized and centralized product structure and more regionalized market strategies. Concerning the production system, a certain convergence at the level of production technologies and some elements of organization could be observed, but there remain strong differences in relation to work and labour relations.

Compared with the internationalization of Japanese automobile companies during the 1980s, the transnationalization push of the Volkswagen company in the 1990s is a dialectic process of company restructuring and company internationalization. The search for new production systems and higher productivity, on the one hand, and the expansion into new markets and production sites, on the other, are two mutually accelerating processes in the change from a multinational company towards a transnational company (see also ILO, 2000). This transnationalization process continues. Theoretically, it could end in a completely globalized company as an economically, culturally and politically 'uprooted' and 'unbound' cosmopolitan business network acting in all of the most important world regions. But this option is not very likely, because of the particular corporate structure and capital strategy of the company.

Volkswagen is deeply embedded in the economic, political and social structure of the Lower Saxonian state. In the very precise German system of corporate governance with workers' participation at company level (workers' council) and strong union participation on the supervisory board, the Volkswagen case is unique. It is very interesting that despite – or perhaps because? – of these aspects Volkswagen was quite successful during the 1990s.

Nevertheless, there remain some structural problems for the future. In the name of equal opportunities the European Union could probably put into question the specific Volkswagen Law. This could challenge the corporate governance fundamentally – if there is no new and now European special arrangement in the case of Volkswagen. A second structural problem deals with the contradiction and combination of platform strategy and brand differentiation. In the short term there were advantages in combining economies of scale with economies of scope. But in the longer term it could be difficult to maintain brand differences and images if people increasingly gain awareness that all the brands use the same platforms and parts. A third problem relates to the centralization of strategic decisions and control on the one hand, and the need for decentralized, more autonomous and eth-nocentric structures. Piëch is a very strong and authoritarian CEO who has been able to maintain and control the consortium centrally – but who and what comes after him? The development of Volkswagen during the first decade of the twenty-first century will be at least as interesting as during the last decade of the twentieth.

Statistical Appendix: Volkswagen

Table A3.1 Volkswagen production and employment by regions, 1990 and 2000

Regions	1990				2000				Growth 1990–2000	
	Production	Share	Employment	Share	Production	Share	Employment	Share	Production	Employment
Europe	2,525,103	82.09	195,755	75.80	3,770,386	73.12	252,653	78.16	49.32	29.06
North America*	192,587	6.26	20,196	7.82	425,703	8.26	16,800	5.20	121.04	−16.82
South America/Africa**	339,908	11.05	39,309	15.22	628,235	12.18	36,782	11.38	84.83	−6.43
Asia/Pacific	18,537	0.60	2,994	1.16	332,131	6.44	17,003	5.26	1691.72	467.90
Total	3,076,135	100.00	258,254	100.00	5,156,455	100.00	323,238	100.00	67.63	25.16

Notes
* Only the Volkswagen de México plant in Puebla.
** Includes Autolatina, a Ford–Volkswagen joint venture that existed from 1986 to 1995.

Sources: Annual reports and other company documents.

Table A3.2   World-wide production sites, Volkswagen Consortium, 2001

Company name and plants	Employees	Products
Germany	**155,749**	
Volkswagen AG	*111,334*	
Wolfsburg	50,360	Golf, Golf-Variant, Bora, Bora-Variant, Lupo, Lupo 3L, components
Kassel	15,418	Gearboxes, aggregates, components, spare parts store, Gießerei, zentrale Ersatzteilversorgung
Hannover	15,072	Transporter and Caravelle, Volkswagen LT2, VW T4, Gießerei, components
Emden	9,740	Passat, Passat-Variant
Salzgitter	7,284	Engines, components, engine assembly
Braunschweig	6,691	Tools and machinery, components
Audi AG	*40,634*	
Ingolstadt	30,540	Audi A3, Audi A4, Audi A4 Avant, Audi TT, Audi S3, Audi RS4, Audi S4, bodyshell, engines
Neckarsulm	12,875	Audi A6, Audi A6 Avant, Audi A8, Audi S6, Audi S8, Audi A2, all-road quattro
Volkswagen Sachsen GmbH	*6,700*	
Mosel	5,945	Golf A4, Passat
Chemnitz	824	Engines, engine assembly
Belgium		
Volkswagen Bruxelles S.A.	6,986	Golf, Seat Toledo S5, Seat Leon
Great Britain	**3,052**	
Rolls-Royce and Bentley Motor Cars Ltd, Crewe, Cheshire	2,614	Rolls-Royce Silver Seraph, Bentley Arnage, Bentley Arnage Red Label, Bentley Arnage Green Label, Bentley Continental R, Bentley Continental T, Bentley Azure, Bentley Continental SC, Rolls-Royce Corniche, Rolls-Royce Parkward
Cosworth Technology Ltd	*738*	
Northampton	300	Headquarters, research and development engines + powertrain, Motoren- und Fahrzeugwerkstatt, Motorprüfstände
Wellingborough	160	Produktion von Zylinderköpfen und Motorblöcken
Worcester	278	2 Aluminiumgießereien, Herstellung von Zylinderköpfe und Motorblöcken

Table A3.2 continued

Company name and plants	Employees	Products
Spain	**21,814**	
SEAT S.A.	*21,814*	
Barcelona	3,068	Headquarters, Preßwerk
Martorel	11,561	Arosa, Cordoba, Cordoba Variant, Ibiza, Inca, Leon, VW Caddy, Polo Classic, Polo Variant, Toledo, engines, central spare parts store
Gearbox del Prat, Prat	1,350	Gearboxes for SEAT and Volkswagen, Getriebe, Gießerei, Preßwerk
Volkswagen Navarra S.A., Pamplona	5,097	VW Polo, engine assembly
Portugal		
AutoEuropa-Automóveis, Lda Palmela	4,000	Sharan, SEAT Alhambra, Ford Galaxy
Poland	**3,438**	
Volkswagen-Poznan Sp.zo.o.	2,614	Audi A6, Audi A6 Variant, Skoda Felicia, Felicia Combi, Felicia Pick-up, Octavia, Octavia Combi, VW Bora, Caddy, Passat, Passat Variant, Polo, LT2, T4
Volkswagen Motor Polska, Sp.zo.o./Polkovice	824	Engines
Czech Republic	**24,549**	
SKODA Auto a.s.	*24,549*	
Mladá Boleslav	21,848	Fabia, Felicia, Felicia Combi, Octavia, Octavia Combi, engines, engine assembly
Vrchlabi	1,388	Skoda Felicia, Skoda Felicia Combi, Skoda Fun, Skoda Octavia 4*4, Skoda Octavia, Skoda Octavia L + K, Skoda Octavia Combi, Skoda Octavia L + K Combi, Pick up
Kvasiny	1,313	Skoda Pickup, Skoda Vanplus, VW Caddy Pick-up
Slovenian Republic		
Volkswagen Slovakia, a.s./Bratislava	7,390	VW Bora 4Motion, Bora Variant 4Motion, Golf, Golf 4Motion, Golf Variant 4Motion, Polo GP, gearboxes, components
Hungary		
Audi Hungária Motor Kft., Györ	4,809	Audi TT coupe, Audi TT Roadster, engines

Table A3.2   continued

Company name and plants	Employees	Products
Italy		
Automobili Lamborghini S.p.A., Sant' Agata Bolognese	414	Diablo GT 2WD, Diablo Roadster 4WD, Diablo SV, Diablo VT 4WD, Diablo GTR 2WD, engine assembly
Bosnia-Herzegovina		
Volkswagen-Sarajevo d.o.o.	108	Skoda Felicia
Peoples' Republic of China	**16,478**	
Shanghai Volkswagen Automotive Company Ltd, Shanghai	10,387	Santana 2000, Santana, engines, engine components
FAW-Volkswagen Automotive Company Ltd, Changchun	6,091	Audi 200, VW Jetta, VW Jetta Facelift, engines, engine components, engine assembly
South Africa		
Volkswagen of South Africa (Pty) Ltd, Uitenhage	5,321	Audi A4, Audi A4 Avant, VW Citi-Golf, Golf, Pick-up, Polo Classic, Polo Playa, Kombi T3, Jetta A4, engines
USA		
Cosworth Technology Inc., Novi-Michigan	231	Power train systems, Motorendiagnose
Mexico		
Volkswagen de México S.A. Puebla	15,977	New Beetle, Golf Cabriolet, Jetta A4, Käfer, engines
Brazil	**28,621**	
Volkswagen do Brasil Ltda.	*28,621*	
Anchieta	17,000	Gol, Saveiro, Santana, Quantum, Kombi T4, engines, Gießerei
Taubaté	6,300	Gol, Parati
Curitiba	3,000	Audi A3, Golf A4
Resende	1,795	VW Bus, VW LKW
Sao Carlos	526	Engines
Argentina	**3,531**	
Volkswagen Argentina S.A.	*3,531*	
Buenos Aires	2,262	SEAT Inca, VW Caddy, Gol, Polo Classic
Córdoba	1,269	Gearboxes, engines, components, engine assembly, Fahrwerkteile, Getriebe
Israel		
Dead Sea Magnesium Ltd/S'dom	404	Magnesium

Table A3.2 continued

Company name and plants	Employees	Products
Independent Assembly Companies		
Germany		
Karmann		Audi Cabriolet, Golf Cabriolet
Westfalia		Multivan, California
Indonesia		
PT Garuda Mataram Motor Company		Audi A4, Volkswagen Caravelle
Malaysia		
Auto Dunja Snd. Bhd.		Audi A4, Audi A6
Philippines		
Proton Philipinas Co.		VW Polo Classic, Audi A4
Taiwan		
Chinchun Motor Co.		VW T4

Source: Elaborated based on Volkswagen 2000, and www.volkswagen.de, January 2002.

Notes

1 It is based mainly on a research project carried out at the Institute of Sociology, University of Erlangen-Nürnberg and sponsored by the German Association for Scientific Research (DFG). Andrea Eckardt, Holm-Detlev Köhler and Ludger Pries formed the core of the research team in its first phase (1997–9); Ludger Pries and Christian Sandig were responsible for the second phase (1999–2001); Gert Schmidt and Rainer Trinczek co-operated in discussion and field work; Thilo Heyder, Matthias Klemm and Sylvia Korell participated as research assistants. I thank Christian Sandig for his critical reading of a draft version of this chapter.

2 Five (in 1995) resp. six (in 1999) of these were independent assembly facilities; see, for this and the following, Table A3.2 in the statistical appendix and Eckardt *et al.*, 2000.

References

Bartlett, C. and Ghoshal, S. (1989) *Managing across Borders: The Transnational Solution*, London: Century Business.

Doleschal, R. (1987) *Automobilproduktion und Industriearbeiter in Brasilien*, Saarbrücken/Fort Lauderdale.

Eckardt, A., Köhler, H.-D. and Pries, L. (1998) The Internationalization Trajectories of the 'German Big Three', in M. Freyssenet and Y. Lung (eds), *The New Spaces in the World Automobile Industry*, Proceedings of Sixth International Colloquium of GERPISA, Paris: GERPISA.

Eckardt, A., Köhler, H.-D. and Pries, L. (2000) *Auf dem Weg zu global operierenden Konzernen? Fallstudien zu den Internationalisierungsverläufen deutscher Automobilkonzerne in den 90er Jahren* (Report to the German Association for Scientific Research), Erlangen: IPRAS.

Haipeter, T. (2000) *Mitbestimmung bei VW: Neue Chancen für die betriebliche Interessenvertretung?*, Münster: Verlag Westfälisches Dampfboot.

ILO (International Labour Organization) (2000) *The Social and Labour Impact of Globalizaiton in the Manufacture of Transport Equipment*, Geneva: ILO.

Jürgens, U. (1992) 'Internationalization Strategies of Japanese and German Automobile Companies', in T. Shigeyoshi, N. Altmann, and H. Demes (eds), *New Impacts on Industrial Relations*, Monographien aus dem Deutschen Institut für Japanstudien der Philipp-Franz-von-Siebold-Stiftung. München: Deutsches Institut für Japanstudien.

Jürgens, U. (1998) 'The Development of Volkswagen's Industrial Model 1967–1995', in M. Freyssenet, A. Mair, K. Shimizu and G. Volpato (eds.) *One Best Way? Trajectories and Industrial Models of the World's Automobile Producers*, Oxford/New York: Oxford University Press.

Kilper, H. and Pries, L. (eds) (1999) *Die Globalisierung der deutschen Automobilindustrie. Herausforderungen für Wirtschaft und Politik*, Munich/Mering: Rainer Hampp Verlag.

Müller-Neuhof, K. (1994) 'Die Unternehmensstrategie von Volkswagen de México in bezug auf die Nordamerikanische Freihandelszone' (MA thesis), Berlin: Free University of Berlin.

Porter, M. A. (1986) 'Competition in Global Industrie: a Conceptual Framework', in M. A. Porter (ed.), *Competition in Global Industries*, Boston: Harvard Business School.

Pries, L. (1999) *Auf dem Weg zu global operierenden Konzernen? BMW, Daimler-Benz und Volkswagen – Die Drei Großen der deutschen Automobilindustrie*, München/Mering: Rainer Hampp Verlag.

Pries, L. (2000) 'Emerging Production Systems in the Transnationalization of German Carmakers: Adaptation, Application or Innovation?' (paper under revision).

Ruigrok, W. and van Tulder, R. (1995) *The Logic of International Restructuring*, London/New York: Routledge.

Schreiber, G. (1998) *Eine Geschichte ohne Ende: Volkswagen de México*, Puebla: Volkswagen de México.

Springer, R. (1999) 'The End of New Production Concepts? Rationalization and Labour Policy in the German Auto Industry', *Economic and Industrial Democracy*, vol. 20.

Volkswagen (2000) *Ideen, die bewegen. Volkswagen*, Wolfsburg: Volkswagen AG.

Wellhöner, V. (1996) *'Wirtschaftswunder' Weltmarkt. Westdeutscher Fordismus – Der Fall Volkswagen*, Münster: Verlag Westfälisches Dampfboot.

Womack, J. P., Jones, D. T. and Ross, D. (1990) *The Machine that Changed the World*, New York: HarperCollins.

Workers' Council (Gesamt- und Konzernbetriebsrat der Volkswagen AG) (2000) *Mitbestimmung bei Volkswagen*, Wolfsburg: Volkswagen AG.

4
The DaimlerChrysler Deal: A Nice Marriage or a Nightmare?

Holm-Detlev Köhler

On 6 May 1998 the 'gamma-project', one of the best guarded secrets in industrial history, took off. A new star was born through the merger of the Mercedes star and the Pentastar, the first 'world company' and similar attributes were awarded. The protagonists of the merger, Jürgen Schrempp (Daimler-Benz) and Robert Eaton (Chrysler) spoke of the birth of the leading twenty-first-century automotive company, and *The Economist* (9 May 1998) wrote: 'Once it was the Japanese who turned the world's car industry upside down. Now it is the Germans.' Leaving aside all immediate exaggerations, the merger of these two famous companies rang alarm bells all over the automobile world, acting as a starting signal for a new wave of mergers and alliances.

Before analysing the merger, the chapter starts from the company situation in the 1960s/1970s, outlining the different strategies in the context of the shared or unique problems during the 1980s, and the transformation of strategy and organization since the beginning 1990s that finally led to the merger situation. The conclusions are made on some conceptual issues and the future perspectives of the new company.

The Daimler-Benz story[1]

The origins of Daimler-Benz lead to the beginning of the automobile, invented by the German engineers Gottlieb Daimler, Carl Benz and Wilhelm Maybach in the 1880s. In 1902, the 'Mercedes' brand name was patented, and from the 1920s on, when Benz & Cie and the Daimler Motor Company were merged, there is a continuity of some core elements of the Daimler-Benz complex. Since then, the shareholder interests have been controlled by the Deutsche Bank, who also worked as a central pillar of the industrial complex bridging the company interests with politics, a tradition not interrupted by the Nazi regime (Gregor, 1997; Appel and Hein, 1998).[2] The internationalization of the commercial vehicle business had some precedents before the Second World War, and took off immediately afterwards, while the passenger car division followed the German export model until the 1990s, abstaining from any foreign direct investment. The post-war development of Daimler-Benz can be divided into three phases (Töpfer, 1998), as follows.

1946–85: German export model

Immediately after the end of the war, Daimler-Benz, which had been a major pillar of the German war industry, exploiting thousands of Jewish, Polish and Russian forced workers, took up car production again for the allied forces. A few years later, the internationalization of the commercial vehicle business started to focus on South and North America and some Asian countries. During the following decades, an expansive growth and acquisition strategy (Hanomag, Henschel, MAN, Steyr-Puch (Austria), Freightliner (USA) and FAMSA (Mexico)) made DB a leading global player in the truck and bus markets. In 1978, the foreign turnover of the group exceeded the domestic figure for the first time.

The passenger car division followed a completely different path. With the selling off of Auto Union to Volkswagen (the germ of Audi) in 1964, the segmental (premium class) and territorial (Stuttgart region in the south-west of Germany) concentration was confirmed. The Mercedes brand became a synonym for high price/high quality premium cars exported to the main markets all over the world. Under the favourable conditions of growing markets and incomes at home and an undervalued DM, the Mercedes brand wrote one of the success stories of the German post-war miracle, establishing itself as an internationally recognized, upper-class, high-quality producer. The internationalization of production facilities had been limited to some small CKD joint ventures with local partners (South Africa, 1966; Indonesia, 1971; Steyr-Daimler-Puch, Austria, 1979).

1985–95: integrated technology corporation

After the second oil shock in 1978/9 and the rise of ecological and growth-critical social movements, a new corporate vision emerged at the DB head-quarters. To balance the risks of the car business the company wanted to diversify its activities towards new potential growth sectors such as financial services, electronics and aerospace. Several companies were purchased in the end of the 1980s: AEG (consumer electronics), MTU (engines), Dornier, Fokker and MBB (aerospace, armaments); the Interservices AG (Debis) was founded; and the automotive divisions (passenger cars and commercial vehicles) were converted into an autonomous company (Mercedes-Benz AG).

After few years the new concept turned out to be a disaster, and Daimler-Benz moved into the deepest crisis in its history (Schweer, 1995). All the new activities and subsidiary companies made deficits, the aerospace and armaments industries were shrinking and the synergies could not be realized. When, in 1992/3, the crisis reached the core business passenger cars, which had maintained the deficit divisions so long, the time for radical change had come. The impact of the international exchange rate movements, new competitors and the opening productivity gap threatened the heart of the company.

The catalyst for the introduction of a new globalization and re-engineering strategy came with the end of the artificial unification boom, when the German car industry in general (and Mercedes-Benz in particular) became aware abruptly of the end of their German export model strategy (Schumann, 1997a). In this situation, all German car producers faced a series of serious challenges: economic difficulties after the unification boom; shrinking growth expectations in their traditional European markets as well as in their export market segments; a productivity gap became evident; the poor presence in the new emerging automobile markets in Asia and Latin America; and the growing niche segments.

1995–8: restructuring and globalization

When Jürgen Schrempp became chief executive chairman in May 1995, one of his first jobs was the promulgation of a new strategic concept with the following five principles (Töpfer, 1998; Daimler-Benz Annual Report, 1996):

(i) *stop the bleeding*: the resources of the group to be concentrated on core competencies and high-value-added activities;

(ii) *shareholder value orientation and direct leadership*: the ROCE (Return on Capital Employment) index became the orientation mark for all businesses, with a minimum rate of 12%. A ranking for all divisions and cost centres and direct control of all business units by the executive board was introduced;

(iii) *strategic reorientation*: the unification of the guiding principles and indicators, the dynamization of the planning processes, flatter hierarchies, project organization to be the starting measures for a new corporate identity suitable for a future leading global player;

(iv) *new management culture*: the creation of a renewed management with value orientation and performance-based reward systems would be the human resources element of the corporate restructuring; new management development programmes and a 'corporate university' were created for this purpose; and

(v) *globalization*: the globalization of the core businesses by foreign direct investment, strategic alliances and acquisitions/mergers complete the radical corporate restructuring.

The automotive business moved again to the centre of the group, and Mercedes-Benz AG was reintegrated in the corporate structure of the Daimler-Benz group. AEG and Fokker were closed down or sold; thus the former thirty-five business divisions were reduced to twenty-three between 1994 and 1998. Overall, the company was centralized under the guidelines of a core competencies concept and a centre philosophy. The hierarchies and business divisions were reduced, the reporting and communication channels shortened, the headquarters staff numbers reduced, competencies bundled, and the company passed through a dynamic concentration and recentralization process. At the same time the cost centre principle was implemented in order to facilitate direct control and to promote an 'entrepreneur' culture among the plant managers. The conflict between the decentralization and recentralization tendencies of these restructuring strategies tends increasingly towards the latter, because of the needs of an integrative steering leadership during the expansive globalization phase, and some disadvantages during the decentralization period, such as non-cooperative lock-in behaviour among the centre heads.

In the passenger car division, the company pursued a globalization and rationalization strategy with four main elements: conversion into a producer of all types of cars, (re-)opening of the US market and emerging markets; becoming a global player; and productivity and process improvement.

'Since 1993 Mercedes-Benz turns … from a premium car specialist into an exclusive seller of high-value vehicles in several market segments' (Mercedes-Benz Annual Report, 1996). In 1998, the small city vehicle Smart Compact Car, co-developed with the Swiss clock producer Swatch, was launched. Together with the new A Class, this model aims at the lower volume segments. Niche markets are to be supplied by the M Class (All Activity Vehicle) and the SLK roadster, and the super-luxury segment with its own high-value model revitalizing the old Maybach brand. Up to that time, Mercedes had relied on its own self-developed new models in new segments and its new greenfield plants in the USA and Brazil. The merger added a completely new speed and dynamic to this process (see Table 4.1).

As Mercedes, like all the other German automakers, considers the US market to be the most important and competitive automobile market in the world, it tried to strengthen its position in that country, and in 1994 decided to establish a greenfield plant in Tuscaloosa, located far away from the traditional automotive regions, in the south-east of the USA. With regard to Mercosul, Mercedes has set up a new plant for the production of the A Class in Juiz de Fora, Brazil (opened in 1999), again distant from the main automotive region (ABC–São Paulo). The model is produced in parallel in the Brazilian plant and the German Rastatt plant.

With regard to the other emerging markets, mainly in Asia, Mercedes-Benz adopted completely knocked down (CKD) assembly as the main market access strategy. Mercedes assembles C, E and S Models in Vietnam, Mexico, Indonesia, India and South Africa to meet local and regional demand, often compelled politically into a joint venture framework with a local partner by the national automotive regimes. The growing relevance of the South East Asian region for assembly also indicates a focus for future global production strategy.

The pre-merger period was full of activities leaving the traditional German export model behind: building up production facilities (Tuscaloosa, Juiz de Fora, Hambach) and CKD assembly plants abroad, internationalizing the management (expat programmes, corporate university), looking for transnational alliances, and adopting a new 'global player' image (from 'made in Germany' to 'made by Mercedes-Benz') (see Figures 4.1 and 4.2).

Besides the 'product' and the 'globalization' offensive, the Daimler-Benz report from 1995 announced two more strategic offensives: the 'learning' offensive and the 'productivity' offensive. The new foreign, union-free greenfield plants were not only market openers and new model producers but also laboratories for new production processes with very lean designs, flat hierarchies, teamwork and modular supplier organizations. The abovementioned new corporate philosophy was implemented in a process that transformed the organizational dynamic of the firm.

Diverging from its competitor BMW (Eckardt and Köhler, 1999), Mercedes stopped high-tech attempts at flexible assembly lines and multi-product processes in favour of the 'solitary factory' (one factory – one model – one production line) concept, producing one model with reduced variations and high volumes in specialized production facilities for entire continental or global markets. This facilitates economies of scale and process standardization, and lowers complexity and technological vulnerability. Platform or similar commonization strategies, however, are denied as being incompatible with the individualized high-quality policy of Mercedes. The reduction of vertical integration through outsourcing combined with the global co-ordination of purchasing activities and the early integration of system suppliers in product development are other 'lean production' elements put in place by Daimler-Benz in the 1990s. The home-based brownfield plants have been put under multiple and continuous pressure in order to improve performance and profit rates. The palpable result of these efforts in 1999 were 40,000 fewer employees in the German automotive division and an increase in productivity.

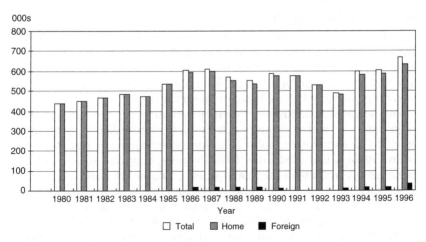

Figure 4.1 Domestic and foreign production of Cars Mercedes-Benz, 1980–96

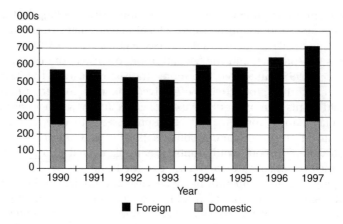

Figure 4.2   Domestic and foreign sales of Cars Mercedes-Benz, 1990–7

The Chrysler story

The Chrysler trajectory is much more turbulent than the Daimler-Benz story, and passed through several existential crises: 'In a broad sense, Chrysler's leaders reinvented the company each time economic conditions forced change' (Belzowski, 1998). The original invention occurred in the 1920s, when the Maxwell Motor Co. persuaded the former GM executive manager, Walter Chrysler, to become president of the later renamed company. Until the 1960s, the Chrysler Corp. expanded with typical American full-sized, powerful models (Dodge, Plymouth) and light trucks. The company trajectory from the 1960s to the merger can be divided into three stages.

1958–78: the Fordist model

The end of the 1950s/beginning of the 1960s brought the first serious crisis, with a sales decline, financial problems and outdated models. Under the leadership of Lynn Townsend the first reinvention took place, establishing a Fordist model with high vertical integration, Taylorist employment and adversarial labour relations, based on unskilled labour.

Chrysler tried to follow the internationalization steps of GM and Ford, acquiring major stakes in the French Simca, the British Rootes, the Spanish truck maker Barreiros and some Latin-American companies, and at the end of the 1960s it had production facilities in eighteen countries. In 1971 it began co-operation with the new Japanese producer Mitsubishi.

Another 'follow-my-leader' strategy consisted in efforts to enter the growing small car market, but it lacked sufficient money for its own development projects, so relied on Mitsubishi and Simca. When the oil-shock 1970s shifted the demand to fuel-efficient small cars, Chrysler had only one model to offer – the Dodge Colt – an import from Mitsubishi. Increasing public involvement in the USA, manifested in the Safety and Clean Air Acts (1970, 1975) forced the company into further research and development spending, thus aggravating its financial difficulties even more.

This costly and widely failing globalization, and the lack of innovative product developments – particularly for the American home market – were at the root of the structural problems the company faced in the 1970s. So the oil shocks caught the company offguard, leading it to virtual bankruptcy in 1980.

1980–91: the first reinvention

Chrysler chairman, John Riccardo, hired the former Ford executive, Lee A. Iacocca, to navigate the company out of the deepest crisis it ever faced. He first had to organize a stakeholder movement (banks, suppliers, UAW, dealers) in order to convince the government to give a loan guarantee of $1.5 billion (Belzowski, 1998). Chrysler laid off 75,000 workers and closed twenty-one plants (1978–82), launching the new front-wheel-drive K cars (Plymouth Reliant and Dodge Aries) as the first recovery measures. The downsizing lowered fixed costs and the break-even point, the outsourcing offered new options for supplier relations, and Chrysler built the foundation for recovery as a smaller company, earning money with less volume and market shares.

But the real second reinvention of Chrysler emerged from an idea to develop a family/utility vehicle that had as much room as a van but drove like a car. 'The minivan completely changed the way that American consumers viewed light trucks, and led Chrysler to change the way it defined its vehicle market mix' (Belzowski, 1998). After a recovery in sales in 1983, Chrysler launched the new minivans in 1984 (Dodge Caravan, Plymouth Voyager) and enjoyed a high-speed upgrading of all its main economic data. Neither GM, nor Ford, nor even the Japanese were able to react fast enough, and this fast-growing market was dominated by Chrysler for the rest of the decade.

In parallel to its later merger ally, Chrysler started a diversification adventure in 1985 investing its recently earned money in non-automotive companies such as Gulfstream Aerospace (1985), Electrospace Systems (1987) and several financial services companies, reorganizing itself into a holding with four subsidiaries. After the turbulent years, Chrysler wanted to be independent of automobile up and downs. On the other hand, it purchased stakes in some niche-market car producers such as the Italians Maserati and Lamborghini, and the Jeep brand-holder American Motors Corporation (AMC): 'The result was that Chrysler now had seven distinct car lines (only one fewer than GM), with weak product development and marketing to support them, as well as further huge fixed costs to maintain assembly plants' (Belzowski, 1998).

At the end of the 1980s, the Chrysler story took a new turn, in part because of the hiring of Robert Lutz as product development manager. A major study of Honda was undertaken which led to two innovations: long-term quality and customer orientation; and the cross-functional team concept. The influence of the recently opened joint-venture plant with Mitsubishi and Diamond-Star Motors in Illinois, supported the implementation of elements of the Honda system. But before the new structure could produce palpable results a new financial crisis and sales decline from 1988–91 urged a second reinvention.

1992–8: the second reinvention

Emergency credit, the sale of re-purchased shares (at a much lower price), the Mitsubishi and Maserati equities, and the non-automotive businesses allowed the company to survive until the launch of the new L/H models in 1992. This reinvention was not so much based on products but rather on processes (Belzowski, 1998) and the reconcentration on core competencies. Five cross-functional platform teams were installed: the L/H team (Intrepid/ Concorde/Vision), the Z/J team (Jeep Grand Cherokee), the pick-up truck team (Ram), the new compact team (Cirrus/Stratus) and the new sub-compact team (Neon) were created and proved extraordinary successful in the complete overhaul of the product segment in a short time.

The 1990s converted the Chrysler trajectory in an impressive success story (Womack and Jones, 1994). From 1994 to 1997, Chrysler beat one historical record after another, with several models being elected as 'cars of the year'. Forbes crowned it the 'company of the year' in 1996, Bob Eaton was named 'executive of the year' by Automotive Industries, former Chrysler chief executive Robert Lutz sold the success story entitled 'The Seven Laws of Business that Made Chrysler the World's Hottest Car Company' and so on. The 'Chrysler Operating System', its purchasing and product development organization, and its manufacturer–supplier relations became models for a new hybrid system of American Toyotaism. Labour relations, which had been the worst of the Big Three from the 1950s to the 1980s (Belzowski, 1998) improved through corporatist agreements with local authorities regarding investment and participation in re-engineering measures. Nevertheless, the frequent crises and the internationalization deficits of the company had planted the idea of a partner in the minds of the Chrysler executives.

Encouraged by its success story, Chrysler began timid attempts at re-internationalization, opening distribution networks in several European countries (the Netherlands, Belgium, Germany), the Asia Pacific Headquarters in Singapore, investing $100 million in its Japanese dealer network, and starting overseas production in Austria (1994). In the Mercosul, a joint venture engine plant (Campo Largo) and two assembly plants (Campo Largo and Córdoba) were built.

The merger

The protagonists of the merger, Schrempp and Eaton, spoke of a 'marriage-made-in-heaven', while others compared it with the match of Prince Charles and Lady Diana – a German aristocratic noble brand asking for the hand of a beauty bride from the New World (Schneider, 2001). With the re-meeting of Chrysler and Mitsubishi under the Mercedes wing, an eternal flirt was added to the marriage. The immediate merger process can be dated between August 1997, when Daimler-Benz definitely opted for Chrysler, and discarded other possible partners such as Ford or Renault, and the end of 1999, when the Post-Merger Integration Council was dissolved and Robert Eaton announced his retirement. Daimler-Benz and Chrysler shared some development constraints, which made them think of being partners for several years. These constraints refer to the specific profit strategies in their internationalization processes. Neither Daimler-Benz (DB) nor Chrysler had the volume (by model or platform) as a source of profit and were moving in stagnant traditional markets – DB in Europe and Chrysler in North America, with evident difficulties in the past in opening new foreign markets. The interest in the merger can be located in the acceleration of the ambitious 'globalization strategy' in the case of Daimler-Benz, and the assurance and consolidation of the risky 'innovation and flexibility strategy' in the case of Chrysler (Freyssenet *et al.* 1998). The latter is particularly risky, because innovation does not necessarily guarantee success but requires continuous investment. New market strata permit profit gains with little competition, but they are easy to miss and quite short-lived. The geographical implantation, the product range and the brand images offer a nearly ideal complementary picture with a minimum of overlapping. But this means at the same time that the brands cannot be merged.

Further globalization and cost-cutting via synergies, know-how transfer and mutual learning were the middle-term goals of the merger. Both companies are still facing the task of entering their respective markets (Chrysler failed several times in Europe, and Daimler-Benz started its first timid recovery of the lost North American market after the opening of the Tuscaloosa M Class plant) and the emerging Asian markets, where the joint ventures and alliances have so far not achieved their objectives.

The synergies will not be so much in production but in opening markets, in purchasing, and in research and development competencies. This interesting attempt consists of combining the Chrysler strategy of permanent innovation and the Daimler-Benz strategy of high-tech quality to gain technology and innovation leadership in a variety of markets. The global sourcing permits a stronger bargaining position in supplier relations, obtaining lower prices, particulary for high-volume standard components. The most interesting, and most worrying for competitors, is the synergy potential for areas of research, development and design. Here, both companies were leaders in some segments and can therefore mutually reinforce their positions.

The 'post-merger integration process' was organized by ninety-eight project teams, co-ordinated by twelve monitors and supervised by the 'post-merger integration co-ordination team' (see Figure 4.3). Besides the set of issues necessary for the management of an automotive company there

Table 4.1 Product range, DaimlerChrysler, 1999

	Mini/City	Small compact	Compact	Middle	Upper middle	Coupé	Cabriolet	Roadster	Combi	Luxury	Sport utility	Minivan	Pick-up	Commercial	Bus
Daimler-Benz	Smart	A Class	B Class (planned)	C Class	E Class	CLK Coupé	CLK Cabri SL	SLK	T Models	S Class Maybach (planned)	G Class M Class	V Class		Mercedes, Freightliner, Sterling Unimog	Mercedes, Setra
Chrysler			Chrysler-Neon	Chrysler Stratus	Chrysler 300 M	Chrysler Sebring	Chrysler Stratus Convertible, Chrysler Viper			Chrysler LHS	Jeep Wrangler, Grand Cherokee	Chrysler Voyager	Dodge Ram		

Source: http://www.daimlerchrysler.com

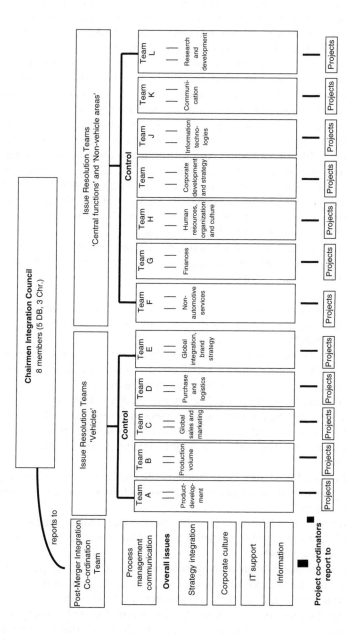

Figure 4.3 The post-merger organizational structure of DaimlerChrysler, 1998–9

Note: About 100 projects with 782 sub-projects.

Source: Wirtschaftswoche, 19/6.5.1999.

were also 'non-automotive councils' set up to deal with the integration of non-automotive Daimler-Benz activities such as DaimlerChrysler Aerospace (former DASA) and DaimlerChrysler Services (Debis) in a joint organizational structure. Last, but not least, there was a special team set up to deal with cross-functional cultural problems, to avoid possible cultural incompatibilities.

After fifteen months of integration activities, the post-merger integration co-ordination team was disbanded and the executive board was reduced from fifteen to twelve members in order to create a 'lean' and efficient leadership. Behind this restructuring, however, there are strong micropolitical and personal battles, and American fears about German dominance seem to be confirmed, particularly by the dismissal of the strongest Chrysler manager, Thomas Stallkamp. Stallkamp and Cunningham (both sales executive) were the most prominent members of a long list of Chrysler top managers to leave DC (for example, former vice-president, Dennis Pawley; two board member – for communication, Steven J. Harris and for finances, Rex Franson; production managers Samuel Rushwin and Chris Theodore), some of them going to competitors such as GM or Ford.

In order to highlight the initial steps and outcomes of the post-merger integration process, some significant integration measures undertaken during the first year are listed below:

- The financial services were integrated into DaimlerChrysler Services AG (Debis), creating the fourth largest non-banking financial service company in the world.
- The European production of the Grand Cherokee and the M Class were united in the Steyr-Daimler-Puch plant in Graz, specializing in off-road models. The two very different models are assembled in the same factory and partly on the same line by the same workers, who have to change tools, welding programmes and operations with the models. Also, the logistics (component supply from the USA) is unified. So Graz is, at the time of writing, the most far-reaching experiment in the synergies of production.
- A 'benchmark book' has been implemented in order to continually identify potential improvements in the production system over all the company plants.
- A 'brand bible' ('Guidelines for DaimlerChrysler Brand Management') has been designed as a guide to integrating the sales and marketing divisions without mixing brands.
- R&D activities offers huge synergy potential, and Daimler in particular wants to use the merger to reinforce its leading R&D position in the sector even more. One of the first measures was to concentrate electro-engine development in the USA and fuel-cell technology in Germany. The drive-train for the fuel-cell engines will be developed by the 'Californian Fuel Cell Partnership', a strategic alliance between DC and Ford, Shell, Texaco, Ballard (fuel cell producer) and ARCO (energy producer).

- Economies of scale: the merger offers large economies of scale in components that do not influence the product/brand identity and in global volume sourcing. The diesel engines, for example, for the Grand Cherokee, will be provided by Stuttgart, and Auburn Hills will receive 200,000 gearboxes from Germany.
- Cultural integration plays a prominent role in the merger process, with the protagonists being aware that the long story of merger failures has its roots in inter-cultural problems.[3] Apart from the corporate university as the central integration project for the future management generation there are several exchange projects already ongoing, such as the expert workshops for Mercedes models in Auburn Hills and Chrysler models in Stuttgart, funds for an exchange programme for employees' children and so on. In 2001, the LEAD (leadership evaluation and development) system was implemented, to standardize executive assessment and development throughout the Group world-wide.
- In 2000, the new company reinforced the provisionally deferred Asian strategy, paying US$2.1 billion for a controlling minority stake in Japan's Mitsubishi Motors (34%) and US$428 million for Korea's Hyundai (10%), both at the time in deep crisis, creating the world's third biggest auto group in terms of sales and units sold. Mitsubishi provides access to the Asian market, offers great synergy potential with Smart and his former partner Chrysler, and has the small-car expertise that DaimlerChrysler needs to satisfy the 2008 deadline for more fuel-efficient cars in Europe.[4] Another interesting aspect of these acquisitions is the long-lasting alliance tradition between Mitsubishi and Hyundai, with the latter using Mitsubishi production licences, and its engines in some models.

Three groups can turn the deal to immediate advantage. First, the chief executive managers of both companies created new bonus and remuneration systems for themselves.[5] Second, the American shareholders received a windfall via two extra dividends, and third, about 800 investment banks all over the world were included in the financial management of the operation.

There is another interesting winner, which could give rise to conflict, particularly in North America. Stephen Yokich, president of the United Automobile Workers' Union (UAW), occupies one union seat on the supervisory board of DaimlerChrysler because the new company will legally be German for tax reasons. The American unionists aspire to adopt German social conditions and co-determination benefits – including union representation in the Mercedes non-union plant in Tuscaloosa – so the German unionist may argue for some compensation as a result of the merger, as the managers multiplied/Americanized their income. The relations between the UAW, the German metal union IGM (Industriegewerkschaft Metall) and the Canadian Auto Workers' Union (CAW), however, are far from friendly for several, long-standing reasons, and close co-operation seems even more difficult than between German and American managers.

The results of four years of integration

After some months of optimistic global company rhetoric amid favourable car business prospects, some dark clouds began to appear around the two merged stars. Not all of the problems are caused by the merger, but the complicated integration process makes problem management even more difficult.

The main pressure comes from the stock market, where the share price fell from US$108 (January 1999) to less than US$40 (January 2001, the level maintained since then) – less than DB or Chrysler shares before the merger. Even record benefits in the first merger year could not convince stock investors, who are very sensitive to the performance of the company divisions. Some shareholders and board members even think of selling their shares in the American brand (*Reuters*, 28 November 2000; *AP*, 15 January 2001; *Der Spiegel*, 4 June 2000; *DPA* 7 February 2001).

The second problem stems from Chrysler, which in 2001 showed several signs of a need for another reinvention. Since the middle of 2000, Chrysler has faced growing losses and reducing market shares. In a shrinking US market[6] dominated by low margins and discount battles, the Chrysler deficits in model ranges and international presence become obvious.[7] The minivan strategy with its huge profit margins is running out of steam, the competitors have caught up, and Chrysler has failed once again to enter the European market with the Neon model. The DC board cancelled plans to develop a Chrysler passenger vehicle for the European market in favour of a successor model of the Mercedes A Class, in question before for its low profit margins in spite of good sales (*Automotive News*, 17 July 2000). But times have changed and the reinvention has to be managed by a mainly German board and in the context of some strong anti-German feelings.[8]

The third problem was created by the Japanese acquisition. The strategic advantages in having access to Asian markets and small-car technologies only count in the longer term, but the massive debt, record losses, overcapacities, high procurement costs, the scandal about the cover-up of defects (which forced president Katsuhiko Kawasoe to resign in September 2000), and so on are urgent problems to be solved. Similar things may be said of the Hyundai deal, where DC acquired a 10% stake. At the beginning of 2001, DC increased the stake to 38% and sent a fourth board member to control the Mitsubishi restructuring programme and improve quality control. The Brazilian Renault manager Carlos Ghosn ('*le* cost-killer'), who restructured Nissan after the take-over in 1999, serves as a model.

The fourth, and perhaps most delicate, problem is the continuous management struggle with two main aspects: a take-over by the Daimler-Benz team, and a loss of experienced top managers. With Robert Eaton, Thomas Stallkamp, Theodor Cunningham, James Holden and Thomas Gale, the whole Chrysler senior management team departed and at the time of writing Chrysler is managed by the two Schrempp confidants, Dieter Zetsche and Wolfgang Bernhard. Many other American top managers have left the firm, some of them going to direct competitors Ford (Samuel Rushwin, Chris Theodore) and GM (Steven Harris, Robert Lutz) (see Table 4.2). The new Chrysler head, Zetsche, however, has tried to reverse the steady drain of American senior managers by hiring top executives from Ford and GM, such as marketing managers James Schroer and George Murphy (Ford) and production officer Thomas LaSorda (GM). At the same time, four DaimlerChrysler representatives took their place on the Mitsubishi board to manage its crisis and restructuring programme. But not only Americans left the company – German top managers like Heiner Tropitzsch and Manfred Remmel left, and the former BMW chair Bernd Pischetsrieder, knowing both companies very well, preferred to go to VW-SEAT rather than to DaimlerChrysler. So there has been a simultaneous process of increasing need for top managerial qualities and the eviction of experienced top managers.

So the recently globalized company is facing the new millennium in a very delicate situation with a fragile organizational structure, internal cultural conflicts, a managerial crisis, shrinking economic prospects in the main markets, fading share prices and the crisis of two important divisions. The German management team, strengthened by good Mercedes

Table 4.2 The DiamlerChrysler management board

1998	2002
Jürgen E. Schrempp, Robert Eaton: Chairmen	Jürgen E. Schrempp: Chairman
Prof. Jürgen Hubbert: Mercedes-Benz Passenger Cars and Smart	Prof. Jürgen Hubbert: Mercedes-Benz Passenger Cars and Smart
Thomas Stallkamp: Chrysler Group	Dr Dieter Zetsche: Chrysler Group
Kurt Lauck: Commercial Vehicles	Dr Eckhard Cordes: Commercial Vehicles
Dr Manfred Gentz: Finance and Control	Dr Manfred Gentz: Finance and Control
Dr Manfred Bischoff: Aerospace and Industrial Businesses (DASA)	Dr Manfred Bischoff: Aerospace and Industrial Businesses (DASA), Mitsubishi board member
Gary C. Valade: Global Procurement and Supply	Gary C. Valade: Global Procurement and Supply
Thomas W. Sidlik: Procurement and Supply, Chrysler Group and Jeep Operations	Thomas W. Sidlik: Procurement and Supply, Chrysler Group and Jeep Operations, Hyundai board member
Prof. Klaus-Dieter Vöhringer: Research and Technology	Prof. Klaus-Dieter Vöhringer: Research and Technology
Heiner Tropitzsch: Human Resources and Labour Relations Director	Günther Fleig: Human Resources and Labour Relations Director
Dr Klaus Mangold: Services (Debis)	Dr Klaus Mangold: Services
Thomas C. Gale: Product Development, Design, Chrysler Group and Passenger Car Operations	

Table 4.2   continued

1998	2002
Eckhard Corde: Group strategy	Deputy Members of the Board of Management
James P. Holden: Chrysler dealer relations	Dr Wolfgang Bernhard: Chief Operating Officer (COO) Chrysler Group
Dr Dieter Zetsche: Mercedes-Benz dealer relations	Rüdiger Grube: Corporate development
Theodor Cunningham: South America	

Source: http://www.daimlerchrysler.com

performance, has to manage the Chrysler and Mitsubishi crisis in very hostile conditions and to look for new shareholder value strategies. The standard reaction (which seems to have been adopted by the Schrempp team) would be to impose a radical cost-cutting and 'Germanization' programme and to enter the 'new economy' where the short-term stock movement takes place.

The company's strategy at the beginning of the new millennium

The company's strategy can be resumed using the following elements (Annual Reports, 2000 and 2001): E-business, technological leadership, cost-cutting and a concentration on automotive business. Schrempp announced big efforts in B2B (business-to-business) and B2C (business-to-consumer) E-commerce, perhaps not so much to achieve advantages in supplier and customer relations but rather to restore investor confidence. In October 2000, DCX NET-Holding was created in order to cover all DaimlerChrysler E-business activities from B2B procurement to B2C sales and marketing, and telematics online vehicle and fleet management systems. DC participates in the world's largest E-marketplace Covisint (together with GM, Ford, and Renault-Nissan) for the common global purchasing of goods and services.

The development of new materials (Composite Concept Vehicle, light-weight thermoplastics), fuel-cell technology, electronic operation systems ('the car without a steering wheel or pedals') and so on confirm the classical Mercedes strategy of technological leadership through high R&D investment and development partnerships with suppliers and high-tech companies.

Several thousand jobs at Mitsubishi and Chrysler and in some plants have fallen victim to the recent recovery plans. The Chrysler 'turnaround plan' 2001–3 provides for job cuts of approximately 20% (19,000 hourly and 6,800 salaried employees) in the North American facilities and several plant closures (just-auto.com, 29 January 2001). Component sharing,[9] dealer and sales integration and global cross-brand sourcing to reduce by 15% the cost of bought-in parts are some complementary cost-cutting policies. Mitsubishi planned to reduce output by a fifth, with the loss of 9,500 jobs (*The Economist*, 3 March 2001). Whereas Mitsubishi is aware of the need for a restructuring programme, the North American Auto Workers' Union could create serious problems. The UAW used the record year 1999 to sign a job security agreement until 2003 that makes lay-offs very expensive and compels the management to set up early retirement and voluntary leavers' incentives programmes. A second anti-cost-cutting front is made up of suppliers: 70% of the largest 100 suppliers, among them very important ones such as Dana and Bosch, rejected in January 2001 the DC demand for a 5% price cut (*Reuters*, 22 February 2001; 26 April 2001; *Handelsblatt*, 15 January 2001). Since 2001, the commercial brands in Europe (Mercedes, EVO) and North America (Freightliner) have also suffered sales crises and made recovery plans. Not only has this crisis shuttled brands, but in addition the administration of the different headquarters are being made the objects of ambitious job-cutting and cost-cutting drives (*Der Spiegel*, 8 July 2000).

After the sell-out of the telephone division DEBITEL, the information technology services division Debis Systemhaus (to German Telekom), the rail systems division Adtranz (to the Canadian group Bombardier), the automotive electronics unit Temic (to Continental) and the folding of DaimlerChrysler Aerospace (Dasa) unit into European group EADS (European Aeronautic Defence and Space Company), the emerging company structure will be reduced to four vehicle divisions (luxury, compact, minivan/offroad and commercial vehicles). The automotive business (including financial services) accounted for over 90% of total revenues in 2000. This concentration on core competencies will accelerate the company integration of all brands and allow a leaner organizational structure where the released management resources can be used for emergency rescue teams abroad (as when the former head of Adtranz, Rolf Eckrodt, was sent to Mitsubishi, or the former chief of the tuning division, Wolfgang Bernhard, to Chrysler).

To carry out this strategy and to co-ordinate the four automotive divisions, a new power centre for the Group was created in February 2001 in the form of the (exclusively German) Executive Automotive Committee (EAC) (see Figure 4.4).

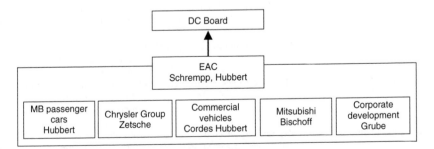

Figure 4.4 The Executive Automotive Committee (EAC)

Work organization and labour policy

To deal with labour politics requires a particular justification in the modern academic community, thus the DaimlerChrysler story is full of evidence that labour hardly matters. In fact, Chrysler is considered, even by Mercedes managers, as highly productive but Mercedes remains the company flagship and gains high profits whereas Chrysler is suffering losses and putting in place restructuring programmes. So the highly productive plants of Chrysler are under pressure from new targets to accelerate quality levels and productivity while the workers of the less productive Mercedes plants are not put under stress (see Figure 4.5). Labour politics, against the general rhetoric of management, MIT studies and the mass media, is not so much a determinant of company performance but rather the conditions of thousands of working people.[10]

At the beginning of the 1990s, Mercedes Benz stated a productivity gap of about 30% in comparison to Japanese car manufacturers, and in some areas such as gearbox and engine production even higher (*Industriemagazin*, March 1996). Against this background, a 'Germanized' version of the Toyota production model was thought to be the ideal way of organizing the production process. The Mercedes plants in Germany became prominent examples for the search for a 'third way between Sweden and Japan', a 'specific German version of adaptation to lean production' (Schumann, 1997a) consisting of a combination of workplace democracy, job enrichment and productivity improvement. Social scientists labelled this concept 'structurally innovative'

Table 4.3   Ideal types of teamwork

Elements	Structurally conservative	Structurally innovative
Scope of direct production tasks	Small; short tact times, discrete definition of work elements	Enlarged; enriched; long tact times, rotation
Amount of indirect tasks	Small, specialists for indirect production tasks	Integrated in the team
Degree of self-organization	Low; decisions made by supervisors and team leaders, production goals come from the engineering department	High; workplace organization made by the team, production goals result of bargaining processes
Team leader	Member of hierarchy, imposed	Elected team co-ordinator without disciplinary functions
Team meetings	Time and topics determined	Element of self-organization and mutual learning; empowerment of production workers
Continuous improvement	Experts and selected employees, focused on productivity	Team based, inclusion of working conditions

or self-organized against the 'structurally conservative' or Taylorized work organization (Kuhlmann, 1998; Kuhlmann and Schumann, 1997). These two concepts competed against each other within the company (Springer, 1997b) (see Table 4.3).

An illustrative example of the struggle for a humanized version of lean production is the German Rastatt plant. Before its opening in July 1992, a special commission of the company works council and the management elaborated a new model for work organization, with the following elements (Fischer *et al.*, 1996): flexible body-suspension to avoid overhead and stooped operations; reduction of the assembly line by improving the previous assemblies in boxes; lengthening of cycle-times up to twelve minutes on the assembly line; teamwork with the integration of indirect tasks, team-meetings during regular working time; elected team moderators; and 'training islands' (*Lerninseln*) for continuous training in production areas.

The aim was to reach productivity and flexibility goals through motivation and participation, improving at the same time the working conditions and skills of the assembly workforce. The first years were full of economic difficulties and pressures, and in order to assure the production of the new A Class in Rastatt in 1994, the works council had to accept the return of the whole assembly-line production to neo-Taylorist practices with short cycle-times, overhead operations and the separate organization of maintenance and quality control. However, before the innovative work organization could be tested it was abandoned in favour of an expert-led new centralist rationalization concept.

The changes took place under the label 'New Labour Policy' (Springer, 1997a,b; Schumann, 1997a). To implement this the management used internal competition among the plants, benchmarking as well as the threat of shifting production to other plants ('whip-sawing') – mainly to Tuscaloosa (USA) (M Class), Juiz de Fora (Brazil) (A Class) and Hambach (France) (Smart). The French plant, located near the German frontier, challenges directly German social standards as its pay level and taxes are considerably lower, and the number of working hours per year higher than in comparable German plants. Thus the German employees had to make concessions and accept a restructuring of their traditional working time regime, the reduction of recreation times, of payments and supplements, and the introduction of a profit-related remuneration system as well as an individual control system for absenteeism (Mercedes-Koordination, 1997).

The main result, however, was that the implicit employee pact 'more participation for more productivity' did not work. The productivity figures and pressures mobilized by the neo-Taylorist players against the participative humanization actors turned out to be the stronger. The New Labour Policy was converted into a neo-Taylorist/Toyotist strategy where planning, design and optimization were given back to the experts inside and outside (consultants) the company, and where the work process is standardized into repetitive, short-cycled operations (Springer, 1999a; Fischer *et al.*, 1996). The Mercedes reality revealed the participation element of the 'Lean System' as a myth.

Recent trends point to a (at least temporary) defeat of the 'structural inno-vative' attempt against a neo-Taylorist version of Toyotaism. Whereas at the beginning of the 1990s, the DB managers still had their own references, par-ticularly the Rastatt plant, at the time of writing, the reference models are Opel Eisenach and Ford Saarlouis for Europe, and some American–Japanese transplants. The new foreign 'greenfield plants' in Tuscaloosa and Juiz de Fora are explicit laboratories for a new company-wide production system – at least some sort of general framework – combining the main Toyotaist principles with the premium quality claim of Mercedes. Standardization, repeatability, process stability and predictability are the key terms defining the goals for the production system labelled 'widened Taylorism', 'group based Taylorism' or 'self-directed Taylorism' by prominent protagonists (Eckardt *et al.*, 2000). Centralization and top-down implementation charac-terize the 'New Labour Policy' encouraged by the experiences and difficul-ties of former decentralization attempts.

Why did the participative, socially innovative concept lose the battle against the neo-Taylorist, conservative model? There are two answers, one standard and one political. The standard answers of the company represen-tatives just state the superiority in productivity and efficiency. There is some internal opposition to this official position stressing the long-term benefits of the participative approach against the short-term shareholder-value view. The basic argument of this internal opposition is the danger of losing the competitive advantage of the German high-skill/high-quality production by sub-utilization of the knowledge and skills of the workforce.

For the political answer, following our theoretical 'micropolitical' approach (Köhler, 2001), the standard answer is nothing other than an offensive strategy in the struggle for power and control within an industrial complex.

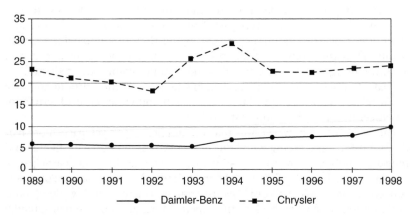

Figure 4.5 Productivity development of Daimler-Benz and Chrysler (vehicles/ employees), 1989–98

Source: Company reports.

The success of a labour policy strategy is not the result of an evolutionary selection process or of 'best practice' winners of productivity benchmarks, but the temporary and unstable consequence of power relations. The neo-Taylorist party in the game mobilized more and stronger resources inside and around the company, and therefore achieved better performance figures.

What impact does the Chrysler merger have on this game? Our still tentative impression is that it will strengthen the winners in this political game even more. The 'Chrysler Operating System' (COS) – frequently labelled 'Toyota à la Chrysler' – in manufacturing, new models of supplier value chain management and time to market improvements in product development characterize recent gains in company re-engineering. The 'learning-from-the-Japanese' process started late, although Chrysler was the first American Big Three company to sign an alliance with a Japanese partner (Mitsubishi in 1971). The turning point was the agreement, with the UAW and the local authorities, of the temporary closure of the Jefferson Avenue Plant in Detroit. The redesigned and reopened plant employed fewer workers to produce more cars of higher quality, dropped the number of job classifications from ninety-eight to ten, and implemented teamwork, a six-day week and flexible worker employment, among other features.

The figures of the new 'lean' Jefferson North Assembly Plant, the model of the COS, are quite impressive for the German production managers. The daily production of the 4,500 Chrysler workers is nearly double the output of the 4,000 workers in the modern West German Rastatt plant. 'We want to learn lean production from Chrysler… We know that they make more cars with fewer people', a Mercedes production manager told us, and the first results can already be seen. Following former chairman Robert Eaton, the adoption of Chrysler processes in the Mercedes E Class production enabled Mercedes to cut three hours off assembly labour (*FT*, 31 August 1999). The fact that Chrysler already has a common, standardized, high-productivity production system, whereas the Daimler-Benz plants still have their specific models and traditions, supports this impression. There will eventually be attempts, whether successful or not remains to be seen, to elaborate a unique DC-operating system based on the Chrysler model. The Austrian DC plant, where the four-wheel models of both brands are assembled, may be the first door-opener for the COS in Europe. On the other hand, the recent Chrysler crisis could be a strong argument for the operations system opponents (with the German works councils at the forefront) to defend German high-skill working conditions.

Conflicts and structural problems in further integration and internationalization

Labour relations

The hope to compensate rationalization and synergy effects through sales increase and avoid major lay-offs turned out to be a bubble of rhetoric, and the Chrysler restructuring could be only a starting point in a long series of labour conflicts. The aim of a new 'Toyotist' operating system indicates a painful future, particularly for the German brownfield employees and their unions, already suffering a lot during recent restructuring measures. The German highly-skilled workers might be squeezed, but probably will not surrender without resistance. The good Mercedes performance could strengthen them, recovering lost battlegrounds. On the other side, the UAW unionists might feel encouraged at recovering bargaining power and claiming German social conditions and union rights, thus ending nearly two decades of concession bargaining.

Quality production against 'Toyotaism'

The productivity difference between Chrysler and Mercedes is to some extent grounded in the high quality and customer approach of Mercedes cars, which require interruptions in the assembly line process for high-tech operations – for example, the wiring of the S Class premium model. These sophisticated assembly operations are incompatible with the 'Chrysler Operation System' and there will be micropolitical struggles between 'Toyotaists' and 'high-quality advocates' in the company, an issue located at the heart of both brands. After two years of Chrysler high-productivity propaganda, with American managers blaming the Germans, the wind has changed, the Americans gone, and the Mercedes high-profit managers are increasingly unwilling to finance Chrysler, Mitsubishi, Hyundai and Freightliner losses.

Management remuneration

American managers earn several times more than their European counterparts; Robert Eaton, for example, earned more than the whole DC board put together, thus a complete 'Americanization' would be very expensive and difficult to justify. Thus far, the income level of about 1,500 German top managers has been elevated by bonus systems and 'stock appreciation rights' (a form of virtual assets), a measure ridiculed by the recent share price losses. This is not a mere management problem but undermines the legitimacy in the workers' minds of future cost-cutting programmes.

Shareholder value orientation against long-term firm strategies

The different profit rates and shareholder value orientation of the sub-companies cannot be equalized in the short run. Chrysler made high profits, paid high dividends, but risks bankruptcy situations. Although Daimler chairman Schrempp increased the shareholder value orientation in the company before the merger, raising the return on capital from 5.8% to 10.2% (1998) it is doubtful if the high American dividend expectations can be maintained in the long run. On the other hand, the shareholder value pressure for immediate radical interventions, as in the Chrysler crisis at the time of writing may jeopardize long-run business strategies.

Inter-managerial conflicts

The numerous resignations of US top-managers and some DB colleagues will probably continue with the implementation of flat hierarchies, administrative integration/synergy measures and so on. Every restructuring and downsizing operation leads to power struggles between top managers, concepts and cultural traditions, and the 'Germanization' debate of US analysts and shareholders is only one of a long list of possible management clashes. The performance disparity between the brands and divisions adds further conflict potential. In some areas, the group may lose important management competencies and know-how to rivals.

With the seeping down of the integration to middle management levels, real blockade coalitions and powerful conservative status defence groups may be formed, able to sabotage important merger aims. Particularly in the huge brownfield areas of Detroit and Stuttgart, the fear of job losses, investment reduction in favour of new greenfield sites and the continuous pressure can lead to worker–manager resistance coalitions.

Economies of scope against brand separation

The search for synergy potentials leads to an increasing commonization and cross-brand integration in marketing, services, controlling, sales and so on, undermining the brand and image separation objectives. This problem, in addition, meets the general problem of future brand strategies such as the controversial Smart project or the risky 'Java' strategy of Chrysler in Europe.

Decentralization against recentralization

This has been a structural problem at Daimler-Benz during the whole restructuring process, which may become critical in the post-merger integration process. On the one hand, there is a need for decentralization, self-reliant plant leaders and centre heads, but on the other these impede smooth co-operation and co-ordination, transparency and, above all, run counter the central goal of a company-wide rationalization strategy – for example, the elaboration of a new 'DaimlerChrysler Operation System'.

Conclusion

Managing plurality seems to be the big challenge for the automobile managers at the beginning of the new millennium. At the same time, different management structures bring different institutional conditions for decision-making (for example, the number and weight of actors participating, fighting and putting forward their ideas and resources), what will decisively affect the outcomes with regard to the applied profit strategy.

There cannot be 'one best way' for internationalization because there are a lot of contradictory options and strategic combinations from which to choose, and because the context is changing continually, and strategies are blamed for being inefficient which, under different conditions, would be the opposite. Another aspect is the timing. Investment in Brazil at the beginning of the 1990s would have been a good strategic decision, but nobody did so. At the end of the decade a dozen new producers tried to enter a market surrounded by great uncertainties and constraints.

Reality and theory point to a plurality of internationalization trajectories, the coexistence of different successful steps, and failed projects inside one company and across the different companies and places. The accelerated internationalization of the German late-comer Daimler-Benz drove the company to a simultaneous application of different forms of internationalization: mergers (DaimlerChrysler), acquisitions (Mitsubishi, Hyundai), concentration on core competencies/selling out, joint ventures (Micro Compact Car, Egyptian German Automotive Company, Yaxing-Benz Ltd, China), CKD assembly (Mercedes-Benz Tianguistenco, Mexico; several commercial vehicle plants), transplants (Tuscaloosa, USA; Juiz de Fora, Brazil) and multiple forms of alliances in limited areas. These internationalization strategies are complemented by the development of new models (Mercedes M Class, Smart, A Class, SLK Roadster, Maybach) aiming at new markets and places. In all the different strategic options, thus far there have been failures and successes and there is no reason to think that this will change. The merger with Chrysler opens up new horizons for the internationalization strategies of both partners with many new possibilities and speeded-up processes, but also with new obstacles and traps.

Statistical appendix: DaimlerChrysler

Table A4.1   Operating profit, 1998–2001 (in millions US$)

	1998	1999	2000	2001
Operating profit	8,593	11,012	9,752	1,318
Operating profit*	8,583	10,316	5,213	1,345
Net profit*	5,221	6,230	3,480	730
Earnings per share*	5.58$	6.21$	3.47$	0.73$
By segments				
Mercedes-Benz P.C. & Smart	1.99	2.70	2.87	2.96
Chrysler Group	4.25	5.19	0.53	−2.18
Commercial vehicles	0.95	1.06	1.15	0.51
Services	0.39	1.02	0.64	0.21
Aerospace	0.62	0.73	0.45	0.09
Other	−0.15	−0.22	−0.28	−0.28

Note: * Adjusted, excluding one-time effects.

Table A4.2   Revenues, 1998–2001 (in millions US$)

	1998	1999	2000	2001
Total revenues	131,782	149,985	162,384	152,873
By regions				
Germany	24,918	28,393	25,988	23,157
EU excl. Germany	20,072	21,567	24,360	22,483
USA	65,300	78,104	84,503	81,132
NAFTA excl. USA				12,040
By segments				
Mercedes-Benz P.C. & Smart	32,587	38,100	43,700	43,705
Chrysler Group	56,412	64,085	68,372[1]	63,483
Commercial vehicles	23,162	26,695	29,804	28,572
Services	11,410	12,932	17,526	16,851[2]
Aerospace	8,770	9,191		
Rail systems	1,658	3,562		
Automotive electronics	754	890		
MTU/diesel engines	921	959		
Other activities			10,615	4,507

Notes
1. The increase is largely attributable to the strength of the US$ against the DM.
2. Decrease attributable to the sale of Debis Systemhaus.

Table A4.3   Employees, 1998–2001

	1998	1999	2000	2001
Total	441,502	466,938	416,501	372,470
By regions				
Germany	228,000	241,233	196,861	191,158
USA	137,000	123,928	123,633	104,871
NAFTA				133,214
Rest of the world	66,000	101,777		48,098
By segments				
Mercedes-Benz P.C. & Smart	95,158	99,459	100,893	102,223
Chrysler Group	126,816	129,395	121,027	104,057
MB commercial vehicles	89,711	90,082	101,027	96,644
MB Sales & Marketing	31,280	34,133	36,857	38,733
Services	20,211	26,240	9,589*	9,712
Aerospace	45,858	46,107		
Other business units		34,297		
Headquarters/other	32,581	7,225		
Other activities			47,108	21,101

Note: * Decrease attributable to the sale of Temic.

Table A4.4 Sales, 1998–2001

	1998	1999	2000	2001
Total vehicles	4,506,200	4,835,000	4,749,100	4,478,400
Mercedes-Benz P.C. & Smart	922,800	1,080,000	1,155,000	1,229,700
Chrysler Group	3,093,700	3,200,000	3,045,200	2,755,900
Commercial vehicles	489,700	555,000	548,950	492,850

Table A4.5 DaimlerChrysler data by branches and regions, end 2001

	Number of sites		Revenue (millions US$)	Employees
	Production	Sales & service		
Germany				
MB pass. cars & Smart	4			70,442
Chrysler Group				
Comm. vehicles	12			67,554
Automotive sales				
Services		3	2,054	1,797
Other activities		2	2,487	7,839
Europe				
MB pass. cars & Smart	8		29,894	93,807
Chrysler Group	2		3,785	2,261
Comm. vehicles	17		15,313	63,080
Automotive sales		5.012		35,293
Services		95	4,768	3,817
Other activities	2	3	2,221	16,898
NAFTA				
MB pass. cars & Smart	1		11,891	2,111
Chrysler Group	41		58,210	101,027
Comm. vehicles	19		9,463	18,615
Automotive sales		5.522		2,200
Services		48	11,596	5,231
Other activities	2	1	2,012	4,030
South America (excl. Mexico)				
MB pass. cars & Smart	1		347	1,508
Chrysler Group	2		725	748
Comm. vehicles	2		1,456	12,024
Automotive sales		691		
Services		9	212	305
Other activities	2	1	72	
Asia				
MB pass. cars & Smart	3		4,236	347
Chrysler Group	2		443	16
Comm. vehicles	2		1,170	1,496
Automotive sales		1.054		511
Services		3	109	76
Other activities		2	167	173

Table A4.5 continued

	Number of sites		Revenue (millions US$)	Employees
	Production	Sales & service		
Africa				
MB pass. cars & Smart	1		776	4,450
Chrysler Group	1		168	5
Comm. vehicles	2		774	898
Automotive sales		210		
Services		3	71	151
Other activities			20	
Australia/Oceania				
MB pass. cars & Smart			561	
Chrysler Group			152	
Comm. vehicles			396	531
Automotive sales		343		729
Services		2	95	132
Other activities			15	

Source: http://www.daimlerchrysler.com

Notes

1 This chapter is mainly the result of a research project the author carried out together with Andrea Eckardt and Ludger Pries at the University of Erlangen-Nürnberg (Eckardt *et al.*, 2000).

2 The term 'industrial complex' refers to Ruigrok and van Tulders' concept of the international restructuring of firm networks (Ruigrok and van Tulder, 1995; van Tulder, 1999; Köhler, 1999c).

3 Board member, Jürgen Hubbert: 'We have a clear understanding: one company, one vision, one chairman, two cultures' (*The Economist*, 29 July 2000).

4 The German automobile producers made a voluntary agreement with the government to reduce the average fuel consumption of their model range to 5.8 litres until 2008, an agreement with certain difficulties for high-class producers such as Mercedes-Benz.

5 Robert Eaton himself, because of his share options forming part of the American Top-Manager remuneration system, increased his personal fortune by about US$70 million through the merger (Schneider, 2001).

6 The recession in the North American automobile market was essentially a crisis of the Big Three in their home market, while Japanese and German automobile makers have gained market shares since 1997.

7 The exit of leading Chrysler managers may not be so much a result of German dominance but rather the will to avoid a crisis when the Stallkamp team criticized the Germans for its low profits and deficit businesses like Smart and Adtranz.

8 These anti-German feelings had already marked the protests against the merger at the decisive Chrysler shareholder meeting where a small group reproached Eaton about selling out one of the most traditional American companies to a German firm that had been involved in Nazi business during the Second World War. While the legendary 'Willy-Jeep' represented the US Army's contribution to the liberation of

Europe from fascism, Hitler used a Mercedes Cabriolet, and now the latter has taken over the former. At the end of 2000, some of these critics formed a group around the 83-year-old billionaire Kirk Kerkorian, the biggest single Chrysler shareholder, and presented a lawsuit of about US$8 million against Schrempp, claming that he deceived the shareholders. The merger was not a 'merger of equals' but a take-over by the Germans, converting Chrysler into a mere division. On the other hand, some German stockholders are demanding the spin-off of Chrysler because of the crisis and damage to their image similar to the disastrous BMW–Rover deal. A group of small shareholders presented a demand to prove the share values at the merger exchange date, suspecting that Chrysler shares had been overvalued at the expense of the Daimler-Benz shareholders.

9   The company will reduce the number of different gearboxes, engines and axles by about 39% until 2007 (FT Germany, 30 October 2000; DPA-AFX, 26 February 2001) and Chrysler will be put back on its feet by Mercedes and Mitsubishi parts in its models. While Mercedes managers are against the use of cheap Chrysler components in their models in order to protect the jealously-guarded Mercedes premium image, Mitsubishi and Chrysler (and perhaps Hyundai) will even share platforms and models (AP and DPA, 11 December 2000; just-auto.com, 29 January 2001; DPA-AFX 26 February 2001) and co-operate in the development of future models (DPA, 27 January 2001). The total group number of twenty-nine platforms will be halved in the next decade (Reuters, 28 February 2001). The new Chrysler CEO Bernhard is even considering of converting Chrysler from a mass to a premium brand by upgrading its models with Mercedes components (DPA, 9 January 2002).

10   The most productive and flexible car plant in Europe, Nissan Sunderland, is making losses because of the strong pound against the euro. It receives a £40 million aid grant from the British government to boost the factory's chances of securing a £203 million contract to build the next generation Micra, beating off French competition from a Renault factory in Flins. The Sunderland employees are working seven days a week on a flexible shift system, whereas the French plant respects the 35-hour ceiling.

References

Appel, H. and Hein, C. (1998) *Der DaimlerChrysler Deal*, Stuttgart: DVA.

Bahnmüller, R. (1996) 'Konsens perdu?', in R. Bahnmüller and R. Salm (eds), *Intelligenter, nicht härter arbeiten?*, Hamburg.

Belzowski, B.M. (1998) 'Reinventing Chrysler', in M. Freyssenet, A. Mair, K. Shimizu and G. Volpato (eds) (1998) *One Best Way? Trajectories and Industrial Models of the World's Automobile Producers*, London/New York: Oxford University Press.

Büchtemann, C. and Kuhlmann, U.-W. (1996) 'Internationalisierungsstrategien deutscher Unternehmen: Am Beispiel von Mercedes-Benz', in P. Meil (ed.), *Globalisierung industrieller Produktion. Strategien und Strukturen, Ergebnisse des Expertenkreises 'Zukunftsstrategien' Band II*, Frankfurt: Campus Verlag.

Dicken, P., Forsgren, M. and Malmberg, A. (1994) 'The Local Embeddedness of Transnational Corporations', in A. Amin and N. Thrift (eds), *Globalization, Institutions, and Regional Development in Europe*, Oxford: Oxford University Press.

Durand, J.-P., Stewart, P. and Castillo, J.J. (eds) (1999) *Teamwork in the Automobile Industry*, London: Macmillan.

Eckardt, A. and Köhler, H.-D. (1999) 'The Internationalization of Premium Car Producers: The Case of BMW/Rover and Mercedes/DaimlerChrysler', in M. Freyssenet and Y. Lung (eds), *Internationalization: Confrontation of Automobile Firms Trajectories and Spaces*, Proceedings of Seventh GERPISA International Colloquium, 18–20 June, Paris.

Eckardt, A., Köhler, H.-D. and Pries, L. (eds) (1999) *Global Players in lokalen Bindungen*, Berlin: Sigma.

Eckardt, A., Köhler, H.-D. and Pries, L. (2000) *Auf dem Weg zu global operierenden Konzeren?*, Erlangen: IPRAS.

Fischer, K., Zinnert, U. and Streeb, G. (1996) 'Rastatt – Mythos und Realität', in R. Bahnmüller and R. Salm (eds) *Intelligenter, nicht härter arbeiten?*, Hamburg.

Freyssenet, M., Mair, A., Shimizu, K. and Volpato, G. (eds) (1998) *One Best Way? Trajectories and Industrial Models of the World's Automobile Producers*, London/New York: Oxford University Press.

Gregor, N. (1997) *Stern und Hakenkreuz – Daimler Benz im Dritten Reich*, Berlin: Propyläen.

Köhler, H.-D. (1999a) 'The Daimler–Chrysler Deal', *La Lettre du Gerpisa*, no. 129.

Köhler, H.-D. (1999b) 'Auf dem Weg zum Netzwerkunternehmen?', *Industrielle Beziehungen*, vol. 6, no. 1.

Köhler, H.-D. (1999c) 'Netzwerksteuerung und/oder Konzernkontrolle. Die Automobilkonzerne im Internationalisierungsprozeß', in J. Sydow and A. Windeler (eds), *Steuerung von Netzwerken*, Berlin.

Köhler, H.-D. (2000) 'La fusión Daimler-Chrysler: ¿un matrimonio feliz o una pesadilla?', *Revista Asturiana de Economía*, no. 18.

Köhler, H.-D. (2001) 'The TNC as a Transnational Political Complex. Research Questions Stemming from the DaimlerChrysler and BMW–Rover Deals', in Y. Lung (ed.), *Reconfiguring the Auto Industry: Merger and Acquisition, Alliances, and Exit*, Proceedings of the Ninth GERPISA International Colloquium, Paris.

Kuhlmann, M. (1998) 'Arbeitspolitische Alternativen in der Automobilindustrie', in Werner Fricke (ed.), *Innovationen in Technik, Wissenschaft und Gesellschaft*, Bonn: Friedrich Ebert Foundation.

Kuhlmann, M. and Schumann, M. (1997) 'Patterns of Work Organization in the German Automobile Industry', in K. Shimokawa, U. Jürgens and T. Fujimoto (eds), *Transforming Automobile Assembly*, Berlin: Springer.

Lutz, R. (1998) *The Seven Laws of Business that Made Chrysler the World's Hottest Car Company*, New York: John Wiley.

Mercedes-Koordination express-Redaktion, Hg. (1997) *Werktage werden schlechter*, Offenbach.

Ortmann, G. (1991) 'Unternehmensstrategien und Informationstechniken', *Zeitschrift für Betriebswirtschaftliche Forschung*, 11/1991.

Ortmann, G. (1995) *Formen der Produktion*, Opladen.

Ortmann, G. (1998) 'Mikropolitik', in Heinrich, Schulz zur Wiesch.

Ortmann, G., Sydow, J. and Türk, K. (eds) (1997) *Theorien der Organization*, Opladen.

Powell, W. W. (1991) 'Expanding the Scope of Institutional Analysis', in W. W. Powell and P. J. DiMaggio (eds), *The New Institutionalism in Organizational Analysis*, Chicago: University of Chicago Press.

Riehle, W. (1996) 'Globalisierung als unternehmerischer Entwicklungsprozeß', in U. Steger (ed.), *Globalisierung der Wirtschaft*, Berlin: Springer Verlag.

Ruigrok, W. and van Tulder, R. (1995) *The Logic of International Restructuring*, London/New York: Routledge.

Schneider, P. (2001) 'Sieg der Sterne', *Die Zeit*, no. 36.

Schumann, M. (1996) 'Gruppenarbeit und Zukunft der Industriearbeit in Deutschland', in L. Kissler (ed.), *Toyotismus in Europa. Schlanke Produktion und Gruppenarbeit in der deutschen und französischen Automobilindustrie'*, Frankfurt/ New York: Campus Verlag.

Schumann, M. (1997a) 'Die deutsche Automobilindustrie im Umbruch', *WSI-Mitteilungen*, 4/97, vol. 5.

Schumann, M. (1997b) 'Frißt die Shareholder-Value Ökonomie die moderne Arbeit?', *Die Frankfurter Rundschau*, 18 November.

Schumann, M. and Gerst, D. (1996) 'Innovative Arbeitspolitik – ein Fallbeispiel. Gruppenarbeit in der Mercedes-Benz AG', *SOFI-Mitteilungen*, no. 24.

Schumann, M., Baethge-Kinsky, V., Kuhlmann, M., Kurz, C. and Neumann, U. (1994) 'Zwischen neuen Produktionskonzepten und lean production', *SOFI-Mitteilungen*, no. 21.

Schweer, D. (1995) *Daimler-Benz. Innenansichten eines Imperiums*, Düsseldorf.

Shimokawa, K., Jürgens, U. and Fujimoto, T. (eds) (1997) *Transforming Automobile Assembly*, Berlin: Springer.

Springer, R. (1997a) 'Rationalization also Involves Workers – Teamwork in the Mercedes-Benz Lean Concept', in K. Shimokawa, U. Jürgens and T. Fujimoto (eds), *Transforming Automobile Assembly*, Berlin: Springer.

Springer, R. (1997b) 'Arbeitsorganization in der Fahrzeugmontage', in E. Frieling, H. Martin and F. Tikal (eds), *Neue Ansätze für innovative Produktionsprozesse*, Kassel: Kassel University Press.

Springer, R. (1998) 'Arbeiten wie die Japaner? Zur Zukunft des Automobilmontage-Standorts Deutschland', in W. Fricke (ed.), *Innovationen in Technik, Wissenschaft und Gesellschaft*, Bonn.

Springer, R. (1999a) 'The End of New Production Concepts? Rationalization and Labour Policy in the German Auto Industry', *Economic and Industrial Democracy*, vol. 20.

Springer, R. (1999b) *Rückkehr zum Taylorismus?*, Frankfurt/New York.

Töpfer, A. (1998) *Die Restrukturierung des Daimler-Benz Konzerns 1995–1997*, Neuwied.

van Tulder, R. (1999) 'Rival Internationalization Trajectories', in A. Eckardt, H.-D. Köhler and L. Pries (eds) (1999), *Global Players in lokalen Bindungen*, Berlin: Sigma.

Womack, J. P. and Jones, D. T. (1994) 'From Lean Production to the Lean Enterprise', *Harvard Business Review*, vol. 72.

Womack, J. P. and Jones, D. T. (1997) *Auf dem Weg zum perfekten Unternehmen* (Lean Thinking), Frankfurt/New York.

Womack, J. P., Jones, D. T. and Roos, D. (1990) *The Machine that Changed the World*, New York: HarperCollins.

5
Renault: Globalization, But For What Purpose?

Michel Freyssenet

In the late 1990s, Renault took the decision to become a global firm. It acquired Nissan, Dacia and Samsung one after the other, as well as setting up its own operations in two new countries (Brazil and Russia).

This was not Renault's first attempt to escape the confines of Western Europe – being, in fact, the fourth time that the French automaker had tried to do this since the Second World War. Earlier efforts had either failed, or else involved operations that were a long way away from achieving the expected outcomes. In certain instances they had even caused serious problems for the firm. Is it possible that the lessons we can derive from these earlier episodes will help us to understand and evaluate recent internationalization-related decision-making? Did Renault absolutely have to internationalize in order to remain durably profitable and independent? Which problems will the alliance between Renault and Nissan have to overcome if it is to be successful?

We try to answer these questions by analysing Renault's stop-and-go internationalization trajectory in the light of the fundamental preconditions for automobile firms' profitability, such as they were defined during the 1993–6 GERPISA research programme entitled 'The Emergence of New Industrial Models' (Freyssenet, 1998a; Boyer and Freyssenet, 2000a,b). There are two preconditions that need to be met: the 'profit strategy' the firm pursues must be relevant to the 'growth modes' of the countries in which it is operating; and the means to implement this profit strategy (product policy, productive organization and employment relationship) must be coherent and acceptable over the long run to all the parties concerned, through the development of a 'company governance compromise'.

Renault has gone through six phases since the Second World War, alternating between a renewed focus on Western Europe and other initiatives involving the establishment of commercial and industrial operations in the world's other regions. In the decade following the Allied victory in the Second World War, Renault emphasized its domestic market, abandoning its older foreign operations or allowing them to become dormant. From 1955 onwards it set itself the target of exporting 50% of its total output. Renault's initial commercial success in the United States was as dramatic as its subsequent demise, following which it withdrew to Western Europe for a period of twenty years. It was during this time that the company signed a number of agreements (and set up operations) in the 'new' automobile countries as well as in Central and Eastern Europe – a region where there was a commitment to import substitution or counter-trade policies. It again tried to enter the United States in the late 1970s/early 1980s, this time by taking control of a local manufacturer, American Motors. Once again, the initiative was a failure, and Renault retreated to Europe for a second time, this time preparing for the future through an alliance (and later through a planned merger) with Volvo, which was solidly established in the North American market. The Swedish automaker's shareholders eventually refused its offer, and Renault was again prevented from becoming a 'big exporter'. After returning to financial health during the 1990s, the company's first reaction was to try to move into Brazil and Russia, before jumping at the opportunity to take advantage of the weakness of some Japanese, Romanian and Korea automakers to acquire firms in these countries. By 2001 it was present, either directly or indirectly, in all the world's markets. In the words of one of its executives, it was trying to build up global policies (and an organization to match) within the framework of its alliance with Nissan.

The prioritization of the domestic market after a brief export phase: 1945–54

Like all the countries that were so badly damaged during the Second World War, France emphasized investment over consumption during the following decade. The purpose was to rebuild the nation's infrastructure and relaunch its basic industries. The growth mode at the time was 'shortage and investment-orientated' in nature (Boyer and Freyssenet, 2000a).

Nationalized and renamed the *Régie Nationale des Usines Renault* (RNUR), Renault's mission was the topic of heated political discussion. Given people's priorities at the time (and prevailing attitudes towards nationalization), it was no surprise that certain members of the French government, particularly ministers from the Communist Party, wanted Renault to create an association with the Berliet Company with the aim of manufacturing light and heavy commercial vehicles, thereby making an immediate contribution to the national recovery programme.

The RNUR did indeed become a presence in the light and heavy commercial vehicle market, but its first CEO, Pierre Lefaucheux, stressed that its mission was also to service anyone who was interested in purchasing an automobile, a product that had previously been restricted to the better-off segments of society. Cars were to become accessible to as many people as possible. Private-sector companies had been unable to achieve this goal, and did not expect to be able to do so in the near future. As such, it was up to a nationalized company to run the risk of starting production of large series of 'people's cars'. From then onwards, the 'nationalization war' intersected with the 'war for a people's car' (Fridenson, 1979).

Pierre Lefaucheux emphasized export activities during his first three years, thus satisfying the wishes of successive governments, who were all seeking to obtain the foreign currency that France needed so urgently. Moreover, he too was able to use some of these funds to purchase, notably in the United States, the special machine tools necessary for large-series production runs. Once Renault's factories had been equipped to a sufficient level, he reorientated sales towards the domestic market (Freyssenet, 1979, 1984).[1]

Although Renault was aware of the importance of having a presence in the export markets, this was not a priority for the company. The battle for a 4CV (4HP) car and the recent nationalization dominated Renault's domestic preoccupations, both commercially and politically. The RNUR had to show that it was capable of manufacturing its 4CV in large series, and that this car could be sold on the French market at an attractive price and under the same constraints as a private-sector company – that is, without subsidies and while paying a normal return to shareholders.[2] As such, it simply could not disperse its financial resources. For a long time, lack of capital would be a factor in Renault's management.

However, from its ancestor, the *Société de Louis Renault*, the RNUR had inherited dealer networks in Northern Europe, sales subsidiaries in the United States, Spain, Italy and the French Union (which included France, its colonies and its protectorates), and two assembly plants, one at Haren in Belgium and the other at Acton in the UK.

Even after having assumed this heritage, however from 1949 onwards the general export market actions that the RNUR could take had to stay well within the boundaries of certain very explicit restrictions. Renault was not allowed to keep any of the capital resources it acquired, which at the time were indispensable to the French nation; it had to repatriate any foreign currency it received immediately; and the networks it had inherited were to be supplied whenever possible with an express stipulation that payment be made without delay. Assembly operations only restarted in Belgium (1948) and in the United Kingdom (1950) with the most basic and the least costly resources.[3] In those countries, which were mounting their own industrialization drives or trying to restrict currency outflows by forcing foreign firms to produce locally, Renault preferred to sign manufacturing and distribution licences with domestic companies, providing parts that could not be produced on site and offering whatever technical assistance was necessary. This policy brought in complementary resources (royalties plus the immediate payments for parts and machines) without needing any capital outlays. By 1954, Renault had signed six agreements of this type – in Europe (Ireland, Spain), South America (Mexico), Asia (Japan), Oceania (Australia) and Africa

(South Africa).[4] The third and final reason why the company had to look outside metropolitan France was that all the French governments of the time were trying to get the country's national automakers to set up operations throughout the French Union. Renault was therefore 'forced' to become involved in this type of business. In fact, to all intents and purpose it was the only automaker really to do so. Nevertheless, none of these projects ever really materialized in the end (Loubet, 1995).

The battle for the 4CV car was won both politically and commercially. Even if the vast majority of wage-earners in France were still unable to access motor vehicles, the country's independent professionals (and soon its top-earning employees) could do so. Note that the virtuous circle that would later be termed 'Fordist' implies a distribution of national income in the form of a generalized increase in household purchasing power. However, this was not yet the case in France.[5]

Export as an indispensable factor in Renault's new 'volume and diversity' profit strategy: 1956–60

With the exception of the United Kingdom, during the 1950s European countries adopted the 'co-ordinated and moderately hierarchical' mode of national income distribution that the United States had invented a decade earlier. However, countries continued to vary in terms of the motors they used to drive growth: domestic consumption for some (notably France and Italy), export for others (Federal Republic of Germany, Belgium and the Netherlands, in particular). The constitution of a 'common market' within the framework of European construction seemed at the time to be a way of achieving the critical size that was essential for sustaining growth.[6] At the same time, France continued to be tied up in colonial conflicts that were mobilizing significant resources to the detriment of domestic consumption.

Pierre Dreyfus, put in charge of the RNUR in 1955 after the accidental death of Pierre Lefaucheux, immediately began to try to build up what we would now call a 'company governance compromise' in an effort to clarify Renault's strategic orientations, and to render them coherent with one another. Renault was the first company in France to guarantee a regular increase in its employees' purchasing power, and to offer a third week of paid holiday. It did this in exchange for a union commitment to try out all arbitration possibilities before going on strike, and not to oppose new production methods.[7] As for the choice of a 'profit strategy', there were two alternatives. The first was to wager everything on 'volume' by specializing in one or two bottom-of-the-range models (as suggested by the success of the 4CV), thus imitating Volkswagen's profitable efforts along these lines. The second was to opt for a strategy that would be based on volume and diversity at the same time. This could be achieved through the development of a complete product range in which models would share a number of common elements, as General Motors had been doing to good effect. Against the opinion of many engineers who stood in favour of the first solution, Pierre Dreyfus chose the second one, which materialized through the steady rise of Renault's products up the quality scale in a way that matched the development of its clientele's level of income. The general hierarchy of incomes was relatively flat, something that allowed for a 'volume and diversity' strategy inasmuch as this ensured that it was commercially and socially acceptable to sell for different prices cars that shared a number of components. Pierre Dreyfus considered this to be the most promising of all strategies. He felt that this was confirmed by the domination of General Motors, which had 'invented' this strategy and designed a new productive model in order to implement it. This productive model was named the Sloanian model, after Alfred Sloan, who developed it and later theorized it when he became chief executive officer (CEO) and then president of General Motors – the American firm that was the embodiment of the one best way for a new era.

None the less, the strategy could only be viable for a French automaker if it were as export-orientated as it was domestic-orientated. The size of the French population and competition from the three other national automakers limited any possibility of achieving economies of scale. Renault only exported 25.9% of its total output in 1954 – but Pierre Dreyfus set a target of 50% by the end of the decade (Dreyfus, 1977). Licensing agreements were no longer enough. The RNUR had to invest both in its international sales network and in new industrial operations. Yet Renault still lacked capital – hence its systematic search for alliances that would enable it to share its costs.[8]

Dreyfus negotiated to no avail with Fiat, Volkswagen and Mercedes, trying to put together future collaborative arrangements (Loubet, 1995). In 1958 he did, however, succeed in signing an agreement with Alfa Romeo, owned by IRI, the Italian state holding company. The two firms committed to marketing each other's cars in their respective countries. Furthermore, Alfa Romeo, which had surplus capacity at the time, made its Milan and Naples plants available for the assembly of the Renault Dauphine (Freyssenet, 1979). Note that Renault also maintained its Haren plant in Belgium because of a lack of capacity in France, even though the planned elimination of customs duties within the Common Market should logically have led to this facility's eventual closure. The effects of the Common Market were soon felt, with its member states accounting for a proportion of Renault's total exports in Western Europe that rose from 48% in 1957 to 53.3% in 1960.

Despite a sudden and temporary increase in sales in Great Britain, Renault decided to close its Acton plant in 1960. The return cost of locally produced vehicles had become higher than the cost of imported vehicles, even after the payment of duties and taxes. Moreover, industrial relations in the UK had been deteriorating rapidly (Ramirez, 1994). In 1958, Renault changed its assembler in Ireland but never passed the 1,000-vehicle mark. In Spain, there was a modest but steady growth in output, which had reached 9,900 units by 1960. The most remarkable result of this period involved the local assembler, FASA, which, to the surprise of the people at Renault, showed itself capable of quickly reaching the 90% local contents ratio that was a requirement under Spanish law (Charron, 1985).

Outside Europe, Renault moved to renew certain licensing agreements (Australia and South Africa) but not others (Japan and Mexico). It signed new contracts in Israel (1956), the Philippines (1959) and New Zealand (1960). Its Brazilian and Argentinian operations remained a novelty, for two reasons: because they were located in a region that Renault had previously left untouched; and because they involved the RNUR taking a financial stake in local assemblers and betting on a development of the domestic market.

It remains that Renault would have never beaten the export production target it had set itself (reaching a score of 61.6% in 1959) had it been not been for a sudden and unexpected breakthrough on the American market. From fewer than 5,000 units in 1956, sales rose to 91,000 units in 1959 (*Automotive News*, 1996), nearly 20% of Renault's total output. The 1958 recession in the United States induced customers there to move to cars that were cheaper to purchase and to use. Renault's sales prices were such that its new cars were just as accessible as used cars on the American market. Compact cars rose from 12% of all sales in 1958 to 25% in 1961 (Volpato, 1983). Although Renault's senior management was surprised and hesitant at the beginning, it soon made a commitment to this adventure, eventually convincing itself that no real harm could come of it in a market where Volkswagen had been so successful.[9] In fact, the unthinkable did eventually occur, and in 1959 the French automaker sold more passenger cars in the USA than its German rival. Renault ultimately founded its own ocean transport company, CAT, to ship its Dauphines from the Flins plant in France and the Haren plant in Belgium to Florida and California.

Renault tried to diversify its product offer as an extension of this initial drive. It had abandoned the idea of shipping its upscale estate car, the Domaine, and was not yet offering the Estafette small van – these being two types of vehicles that were in full expansion in the United States. As a result, it made a (successful) proposal to Peugeot to market different versions of the latter company's 403 (Loubet, 1995). It also had a two-door convertible especially designed for the American market: the Caravelle, derived from the Dauphine. However, by the time this model could be delivered, the situation had changed completely.

The balloon was punctured as quickly as it had been inflated. Renault's sales in the USA fell by 33% in 1960, 50% in 1961 and 67% in 1962 (*Automotive News*, 1996). The same thing happened to all of the other foreign marques (Austin, Fiat, Peugeot, Simca, Triumph and Volvo) including the American automakers' European subsidiaries (Ford UK, Vauxhall and Opel) – with the notable exception of Volkswagen, which continued its steady rise. Reasons for this downturn included the vigorous response of the

Big Three American automakers (who launched their own compact cars in late 1959), and above all the economic upturn in 1962, which reorientated demand towards larger automobiles. Nevertheless, the only reason the changes had this effect was because of the errors that the foreign automakers had been making. Volkswagen's continued rapid rise constituted a meaningful counter-example.[10]

The sudden downturn was a financial debacle for Renault, which was more interested in satisfying its dealers' demands in full, whatever the cost, than in taking the time to verify their sales forecasts, financial solvency and equipment levels. By so doing, it helped to create a situation in which stocks of cars and spare parts were allowed to build up beyond all reason. Inventories of unsold new vehicles sat around for so long on company parking lots that it sometimes had to undertake costly repairs to fix external paint jobs, or tyres or rubber joints that were worn out from constant exposure to the sun. The Dauphine's relative inability to cope with driving conditions in the USA meant that Renault had to underwrite exorbitant guarantees. The car's resale prices collapsed eventually, and with finance companies refusing to pre-finance customer purchases, many resellers went out of business. Others, under the threat of losing their dealership agreements with the American marques, reneged on their contracts. Even the heavens got involved, with Renault once having to repatriate nearly 5,000 cars that had been damaged by a cyclone in Houston and by a tidal wave in New York. To make matters worse, American authorities refused to authorize the Estafette 'small van' once it was launched, alleging that when it was fully loaded it was not quick enough for American freeways. Around 1,000 units had to be sent back to France. Finally, instead of returning its unsold stock to Europe, Renault organized a fire sale at prices below its own return costs. This was the nail in the coffin of its brand image. Renault took fifteen months to get rid of this stock, even in a market that had already been in a recovery phase for a few years. In the end, American Motors Corp. (AMC), which had been approached regarding the possibility of marketing Renault cars (or even assembling them locally) turned the offer down (Picard, 1976; Dreyfus, 1977; Freyssenet, 1979, 1984; Loubet, 1995).

During the first months of 1960 the production rate for the Dauphine and its derivatives alone had reached 2,000 units/day, including 500 for the United States. Subsequently, however, the RNUR had to resign itself to a lower level of output. The working week was cut from 48 to 45 hours for the 50% of all workers who were on hourly pay; 950 temporary workers were not re-hired; and above all 3,000 jobs were eliminated, two-thirds through outright dismissals.[11] This was a big shock for Renault. It undermined the company's internal governance compromise with its unions, and gave new arguments and energy to those who had been opposed to its nationalization. Moreover, these losses denied Renault precious capital that it desperately needed in order to develop its product range and operations overseas.

Success of Renault's 'volume and diversity' strategy in those countries where it could be viable: 1961–73

Added to the developments discussed above was the fact that the international environment was worsening. Just as American automakers had reacted vigorously to European competitors' penetration of their domestic market, in 1960 the American administration quickly responded to the creation of the European Common Market by reopening negotiations on the GATT. After some hard bargaining, it succeeded in reducing the differences between the various levels of customs duties that the Treaty's signatories could charge one another. Above all, it negotiated the possibility that foreign companies could participate (and conceivably take majority stakes) in firms hailing from other member countries. As such, Renault, like the other European automakers, not only had to cope with the progressive disappearance of customs duties between the six Common Market countries but also with an 'American offensive'. Countries seeking to increase their industrialization levels via import substitution policies thus became increasingly important for the RNUR.

Renault had a very bad year in 1961. The bottom-of-the-range replacement for the 4CV, the R4, was not ready yet, even though the French domestic market was starting to grow again after three years of semi-stagnation. Lower sales in France thus compounded lower global volumes, with Renault's world-wide production dropped by a whopping 27.6%. Thankfully, the R4 was an immediate success once it came out in late 1961. With French national automobile demand rising at the same time (exceeding the one million unit mark in 1963) Renault had to re-hire people immediately after finishing its staff restructuring programme! France rose from 38.4% of the RNUR's total sales in 1959 to 62.3% in 1963.

To protect itself against an American offensive and to maintain its market share in Europe, Renault tried to reinforce its alliance with Alfa Romeo, suggesting a global merger between the two firms' sales networks, as well as a jointly designed new vehicle. Instead, the two companies broke up in 1963. As is always the case in these situations, the divorce was caused by many different factors. In any event, and regardless of the circumstances, the alliance between these two automakers was undermined by the fact that they were pursuing incompatible profit strategies. Unsurprisingly, they were unable to overcome the problems inherent to trying to sell within one and the same network vehicles designed for the widest possible public alongside vehicles whose main function is to provide their owners with social distinctiveness.

In the end, it was within the French national framework that Renault was to develop its European alliances and mergers. In 1966, Peugeot and Renault created an association that was based in France, and whose official objectives were the realization of economies of scale through the design and manufacture (internally or on a sub-contracted basis) of shared parts and sub-systems, with each party continuing to develop its own model ranges and target different clienteles through distinct networks – except abroad, where joint commercial assistance was planned. Peugeot had rallied the 'volume and diversity' strategy in the mid-1960s, a precondition for the success of this association inasmuch as economies of scale only became feasible once the two firms had decided to pursue the same product policy. The association potentially turned Peugeot-Renault into the world's fifth largest group. Many activities were carried out within a short period of time in an effort to share costs (sourcing, design, shared registration of patents, joint manufacturing initiatives intended to saturate productive capacities, joint ventures and so on). The two partners tried to involve other European automakers in their endeavour, but only Volvo accepted, taking a stake in 1971 in one joint venture (*La Française de Mécanique*) to co-finance the design and production of a V6 engine. Moreover, international co-operation between Peugeot and Renault became almost systematic after the association was founded (Freyssenet, 1979, 1998b).

Even though it did not particularly lead to the creation of trans-European firms, the Common Market (which grew from six to nine members after Denmark, Ireland and the UK joined in 1971) caused a remarkable interpenetration of markets in the automobile world.[12] Renault benefited greatly from this, with its exports to the six Common Market countries growing by a factor of eleven between 1958 and 1972, while sales in France and the rest of the world rose only by factors of 2.5 and 2.7, respectively. During the same period, Common Market sales rose from 14.5% of Renault's exports to 38.8%. Ultimately, we can say the company's profit strategy was appropriate and efficient in those countries that featured a similar type of national income distribution and which shared the same conception of the automobile. But what about those countries that practised import substitution or counter-trade?

At the time, the optimistic view was that these countries' modes of growth (often 'inegalitarian and rent orientated' in South America or 'shortage and investment orientated' in the Communist countries) would converge with the one model that had already demonstrated its efficiency by enabling a widespread redistribution to the general population of productivity or competitiveness-related gains – namely, they were expected to converge with a mode of growth that was 'co-ordinated and consumer-orientated'. No one expected the shift to occur immediately, but everyone hoped that the system would be making a clear move in this direction. With this in mind, Renault established facilities in many new countries: Algeria in 1961, Ivory Coast and Madagascar in 1962, Portugal and Venezuela in 1963, Chile in 1964, Tunisia, Uruguay and Costa Rica in 1965, Bulgaria in 1966, Morocco and Peru in 1967, Romania, Malaysia and Singapore in 1968, Yugoslavia in 1969, and Columbia and Turkey in 1971. To fund these international operations, it created a financial structure that was located in Switzerland.

It remains that by 1973 none of the countries in which Renault was present had succeeded (or had even tried) to set up a 'co-ordinated and moderately hierarchized' national income distribution system – with the exception of Spain. Indeed, it was in Spain that Renault experienced its only success. By 1973, Renault's local production in Spain had reached 173,000 vehicles, accounting for a quarter of all national demand. The suitability of the Spanish market's structure to Renault's product offer (based as it was on volume and diversity, and on the workforce's acceptance of polyvalent work forms) was not the only factor driving this success. It was, however, an absolute prerequisite.

Problems with the 'volume and diversity' strategy in the new international context and the need to gain market share in the industrialized countries: 1974–84

The abolition of the gold standard in 1971 and the birth in 1973 of a system based on floating currencies engendered, through a series of unexpected interconnections, a fourfold rise in the constant price of oil. In 1974, automobile demand fell in the main markets: −23.3% in the United States; −22% in Japan; and −14% in Europe. It would not return to its 1973 levels before 1976 in Europe, 1978 in the United States and 1979 in Japan. In addition, demand shifted towards bottom-of-the-range compact cars that were equipped with front-wheel drive and which were economical in fuel cosumption terms.

The main problem became the acceleration in inflation that followed the higher raw material costs (and the industrialized countries' habit of indexing incomes to the cost of living). The American Federal Reserve Bank raised interest rates as a counter-measure, leading to a stronger dollar, the constitution of safety stocks and Ayatollah Khomeini's revolution in Iran. In turn, this engendered a second oil shock, with a doubling in constant oil prices between 1979 and 1981. The effects on the automobile market were less brutal than the initial shock's, but they lasted longer. Those countries that had borrowed heavily since 1974, particularly raw-materials-producing countries and Eastern Europe, saw their debt levels go through the roof. The automobile market collapsed for the first group, and began to stagnate for the second.

For the first time since the Second World War, automakers understood from 1974 onwards that they were competing directly in the international markets. This is because domestic consumption in their respective national markets was no longer growing fast enough to attenuate or hide the effects of this competition. Furthermore, many industrialized countries lacked raw materials, and to pay for the oil they imported they had no choice but to increase export revenues. The international arena was no longer just a complement to domestic activities – it became the very core of corporate life.

However, the countries and automobile manufacturing firms that participated in this battle did not all start from the same position. Countries where growth was already being driven by the export of specialized goods (FRG and

Sweden) or of consumer goods in common use (Japan), and where national income distribution was already geared towards external competitiveness, found themselves in a favourable position. Inversely, countries where growth was driven by domestic consumption and where income distribution was geared towards developments in internal productivity (United States, France and Italy) were harmed by direct competition from the former group. In addition, automobile producers from countries with a 'co-ordinated and export orientated' mode of growth were pursuing profit strategies that were appropriate for this new environment, be it 'quality' strategy followed by the specialist German and Swedish automakers, Toyota's 'permanent cost reduction' strategy or Honda's 'innovation and flexibility' strategy. They therefore had no need of building a new company governance compromise.

The 'volume and diversity' strategy that most of the other automakers were pursuing, and the 'Sloanian' model they were applying were not rendered obsolete as such by the new environment, despite what many observers believed and affirmed. One proof of this is Volkswagen, which adopted the above strategy and model. When a market shifts into a product renewal mode, a 'volume and diversity' strategy does become feasible. Plus it is possible to implement a 'Sloanian' model as long as several interrelated conditions are satisfied: market share has to be taken from the other actors (either through direct competition or by absorbing rivals and immediately commonalizing the platforms used for their marques' vehicles) in those countries where national income distribution remains moderately hierarchized; and the company governance compromise has to be geared to external competitiveness and not to productivity. Volkswagen achieved this admirably – but what about Renault?

One opportunity for gaining rapid market share almost presented itself to Renault on a platter. The crisis was almost fatal to Citroën, whose recent innovative models did not fit the new environment. However, Michelin, which was Citroën's majority shareholder, preferred to sell it to Peugeot, with support from the government of the time. Not only did Renault lose an opportunity, but it also had to break up its association with Peugeot, even though this was of greater utility than it ever had been before. Nevertheless, it is not at all certain that this failure ultimately caused much damage to Renault. Back then, Citroën was characterized by its 'innovation and flexibility' strategy, something that was incompatible with 'volume and diversity'. Peugeot was the one to be hurt by this incompatibility, and almost went bankrupt.

Renault's initial performances following the first oil shock were illusory. Along with Honda, it was the only automaker whose world-wide output did not drop in 1974. The R5 was for Renault in Europe what the Civic was for Honda in the United States: a 'crisis car' that corresponded to the new expectations of a large portion of the clientele. Renault's global production rose from 1.41 million units in 1973 to 2 million in 1980, a level it kept up in 1982 and 1983. Its penetration of the domestic passenger car market jumped spectacularly from 30.1% to 40.5%. Average volumes per platform increased even further, ranging between 250,000 and 400,000 units. Having said this, Renault was also launching top-of-the-range models (the R20 and the R30) that were not very economical in fuel consumption and lacked sufficient quality. These models were an expensive commercial failure for the RNUR. Worse still was the undermining of its earlier labour compromise. Although Renault was making and selling more cars than ever, its total wage bill and investment outlays were greater than its value added, and it was unable to balance its books (with the exception of a few years during which it bene-fited from other sources of income, specifically from financial revenues, (see appendix Table A5.1). The main reasons were that Renault's work crisis had become an employment relationship crisis – and its productive and organizational difficulties had degenerated into being a product crisis (Freyssenet, 1998b).

For a time Renault thought that it should diversify into non-automobile activities, offering a great deal of potential for development. Then, like many others, it began to hope that the raw-materials-producing countries would become high-growth automobile markets and rekindle global demand. It therefore tried to set up (or re-launch) production in several of these countries, particularly Algeria, Venezuela, Mexico and Iran. It failed in Algeria, Venezuela and Mexico, and while in 1975 it signed a contract for a 100,000 vehicle/year manufacturing plant in Iran, the Khomeini revolution got in the way. Above all, these new markets turned out to be highly uncertain – and the Japanese automakers were already present in them. Moreover, Renault's product offer was not really adapted, and local political situations were too complex.

The year 1978 confirmed how durable the crisis had become. The only solution left involved taking market share in the industrialized countries away from the other automakers. An alliance between Renault and Volkswagen would have been one of the more viable and economical solu-tions in Europe, with Volkswagen committing to a 'volume and diversity' strategy and adopting a front-wheel-drive. It would have been easy to com-monalize the two marques' platforms within a short period of time. Their status as state sector firms would have facilitated their rapprochement – the geographic complementarity between their respective markets in Europe reduced the risks of direct competition. Unfortunately, nothing ever came of this possibility.

The American automakers were the hardest hit by the first oil shock, and by the ensuing chain reaction. Chrysler had to withdraw to its home North American market and sold its European subsidiaries. American Motors Corporation (AMC) sought an ally to finance the renewal of its product range. It contacted Peugeot-Citroën specifically, but this company preferred to acquire Chrysler's European subsidiaries rather than adventure into America.

Finally, in 1979, it was Renault who responded to AMC's offer. In allying itself with a local automaker, the RNUR thought it could avoid making the same mistakes as it had twenty years before. In its plant in Kenosha, AMC assembled Americanized versions of the R9, R11 and R21 models, renamed as the Alliance, Encore and Medallion. Renault also built an engine factory at Gomez Palacio in North Mexico, and its trucks subsidiary, RVI, took a stake in Mack Trucks (becoming the largest shareholder). In addition, and with a view towards making collaborative arrangements at the top end of the scale, Renault took a 15% stake in Volvo in 1980.

However, the collapse of the American market between 1980 and 1982 forced AMC to the brink of bankruptcy. Rather than simply lose its stake, Renault chose to up its ante from 22% to 46%; 'Before the Alliance was even launched, the cost of the AMC deal was already 50% higher than expected' (Charron, 1985). Rocketing interest rates increased the company's debt burden dramatically. By late 1984, Renault's cumulative losses had reached 17.6 billion French francs and its debt was equivalent to 46.1% of its yearly turnover. The RNUR was semi-bankrupt.

A second withdrawal to Europe and the adoption of a 'quality' strategy: 1985–92

Renault was saved by a sudden and rapid drop in its break-even point, by a recovery in the automobile market and by a commercially appropriate strategic reorientation that took into account the changes that were taking place in the demand structure.

Reagan's investment-driven recovery policies, tax cuts and lower interest rates led to renewed domestic demand in the USA (and therefore in world trade) after 1984. In many countries, factors such as the sharp drop in the dollar's value, the drilling of new oil platforms, energy saving and the break-up of the OPEC all had an effect that was akin to a reverse oil shock (with real oil prices being divided by a factor of 2.9 between 1982 and 1987). Inflation dropped, particularly in those countries (that is, the United States, France and Italy) that dispensed with earlier wage indexing policies to introduce more 'competitive' pay settlement rules. To amplify a growth phase that had already started but which was being hampered by a lack of savings, governments in the main industrialized countries decided on the deregulation of capital flows. The purpose of this was to attract hot capital resulting from trade surpluses in Japan, the FRG and in a few oil-producing countries. At the same time, they eased credit restrictions to enable companies to carry out their restructuring programmes and become competitive again (thus catalysing job creation, according to some observers).

The most immediate and significant consequence of these measures was the development of a first 'speculative bubble' in the Triad countries. The financial opportunities created by this turn of events strongly accentuated income heterogeneity – with differentiation being the outcome of a wage settlement mechanism that emphasized individual performances as well as people's relative bargaining position in the labour market. Demand began to grow again – but its structure began to change simultaneously. After a moderately hierarchized automobile market came one characterized by increased demand for top-of-the-range products, featuring the emergence of a demand for models that were conceptually innovative and which expressed the practical and symbolic expectations of those new segments of the general population that had been strengthened by the general 'deregulation' trend.

A new leadership team took over at the RNUR in 1985 and immediately acted to rationalize company finances and re-establish executive authority. The new management abandoned the existing volume policy, thus achieving a dramatic reduction in Renault's break-even point (which dropped to 1.2 million vehicles). It also decided not to negotiate lower staffing levels with unions; definitively rejected the earlier 'company governance compromise'; reduced the influence of the hard-left CGT labour union; refocused the RNUR on the automobile business and on the European market; reshuffled the command structure by eliminating double reporting lines that involved both Group and branch management units; and called upon the state to fulfil its role as shareholder and help Renault to cut its level of debt.

Renault's gross operating earnings were back in the black in 1986, reaching close to 7 billion French francs in 1988 and in 1989. The Group's net financial indebtedness was cut to the equivalent of 10.1% of yearly revenues in 1989, with French state aid accounting for a quarter of this improvement. By 1989, output had returned to 1983 levels of 2 million passenger cars and small commercial vehicles – but this time around Renault made a profit of 6.9 billion francs, whereas six years earlier it had lost 1.8 billion.

This rapid lowering of the 'break-even point' was primarily the result of massive job cuts. Renault re-focused its activity not only on the automobile product itself but also on everything that was considered at the time essential to being an automaker: model design; manufacturing of the main mechanical sub-systems and body; and assembly. Renault had to get rid of a few subsidiaries that were profitable and strategic, but this was because it no longer had the means to fund their development, and such sales provided it with much-needed capital.

Starting in 1985, Renault began to sell its 15% stake in Volvo back to the Swedish automaker's other shareholders, and to withdraw from all its joint ventures in Africa. The most significant sale of all was that of AMC. Although the American subsidiary had had its first year of profitability in 1984, sale volumes were lower because of the American market's umpteenth reversion to more powerful models (and also because the Group design centre was so slow in adapting the R21). The impossibility of finding a partner willing to help manage and finance AMC convinced Renault in 1987 to sell its holding to Chrysler, and to concentrate again entirely on Europe. This renewed focus on Renault's home region was accompanied by a withdrawal from South America in favour of European subsidiaries. Renault Argentina, in which the RNUR had had a majority stake since 1975, became the CIADEA in 1992, a company in which Renault had only a 25% stake. The same thing happened in Colombia in 1994, with Renault cutting its stake in SOFASA from 74.5% to 23.7%. On the other hand, in 1991 it did buy 54% of its Slovenian assembler, Revoz, and a year later took a 56% interest in its Turkish subsidiary, Oyak Renault. From 1990 onwards, Renault began steadily to acquire the 29% of its Spanish subsidiary that was still owned by the general public, achieving 100% control in 2000.

This re-focusing was accompanied by a complete reorganization of the RNUR production apparatus. Starting in 1987, the Group's European factories in Belgium, France, Spain, Portugal and Slovenia/Yugoslavia were integrated progressively into a single industrial complex that supplied the whole of the European market. Plant production and distribution plans were determined and adapted centrally in the light of each factory's workload and variations in demand. Models were assembled on at least two sites, except for top-of-the-range and 'niche' vehicles. This integration and homogenization was not achieved without a few problems, particularly at the FASA, which through its own initiative and management had previously made a strong contribution to Renault's bottom line (Charron, 1998).

However, had the market not started to grow again (and above all, had Renault's timely strategic reorientation not taken place), recovery would not have been as spectacular. Since RNUR was not able to make money with a volume-based strategy, it took the decision to emphasize quality (which implies higher margins) and to pay the price for the shift. Commercial policy was therefore reorientated towards the Northern European markets, since they are more sensitive to quality – and, more importantly, more able to pay for it.

The restoration of links with Volvo was a logical and well-planned part of this strategy. This process began in 1991, when the two groups exchanged participation in their automobile and truck activities.[13] In the passenger car market, the putative merger was meant to put the Group in a position where it could attempt to do the same thing as Mercedes and BMW are aiming for: to offer a complete range of models and take a position in the upper niche of each market segment. This would have made it possible for Renault to achieve a better penetration of the Northern European markets and to prepare for its return to the USA. The two automakers began to build up a base of common sub-systems; study a platform for two of their models; and share suppliers. Last, but not least, these crossed shareholdings were a means for Renault to privatize its ownership structure steadily (Lévy, 1994).[14]

The well-timed move towards an 'innovation and flexibility' strategy: 1993–8

The bursting of the financial bubble led to a new confrontation between firms and national economies. However, these new battle conditions were not the same as in 1974–84, as inter-firm discrepancies in competitiveness had diminished instead of growing. Modes of growth in the United States, France and Italy had shifted towards decentralized wage bargaining, so that factors related to external competitiveness could be taken into account. Income distribution, having become more inegalitarian and variable, caused automobile demand to change at both quantitative and qualitative levels.

At the same time, the 'Eastern' countries were going through economic transition, and the so-called developing countries were 'emerging' industrially. The disorganization that followed the Communist regimes' implosion led to lower automobile production in the countries affected (dropping from 3.56 million units in 1988 to 1.66 million in 1994). Several automakers were put up for sale and some were taken over by European or Korean manufacturers. The ostensible dynamism of South East Asia, China and several Latin American countries attracted both capital and industry.

The bursting of the speculative bubble and the restrictive budgetary policies which the European governments felt they needed in order to cope suddenly deprived Renault of a clientele that could pay for the 'quality' that was the basis of its new strategy. These difficulties reinforced the Volvo shareholders' lack of trust, and in the end they refused to ratify the merger between the two automakers. The divorce took place without too many financial consequences, given that the alliance had basically been built around a share swap. However, Renault's chances to pursue a quality strategy (and, as a corollary, to penetrate new markets) became increasingly remote.

Thankfully, Renault had twinned its 'quality' project with a 'living cars' concept that emphasized comfort and friendliness over aggressiveness and speed (Pointet, 1997). The launch of a 'different sort of vehicle' was particularly well-timed. Changes in Europe's growth modes, which were moving in a more 'competitive' direction, had led to the emergence (next to the traditionally hierarchized demand of wage earners with predictable incomes of a new type) of a new demand from those sectors of the population who were benefiting from the new forms of wage earning and of income, and who were looking for vehicles with varying practical and symbolic usages (Boyer and Freyssenet, 2000b). Comforted by the success of the Espace, Renault further innovated by building up a whole range of passenger vans (the 'monospaces'), with the Twingo (1993) as a bottom-of-the-range product, and the Scenic (1996) in the mid-range. Later came the Kangoo (1997), a half-commercial and half-passenger vehicle; the Grand Espace (1998); the off-road 4-by-4 Scenic (2000); the Avantime (2001), a top-of-the-range three-door coupé passenger van, and the Vel-Satis, an originally designed luxurious car.

These models did not suffer from the fact that Renault had withdrawn back to Europe. Quite the contrary, their success can be explained by the fact that they were appropriate for the new clienteles in this part of the world. They limited the losses that Renault was incurring in the saloon car segment (following a weakness in its 'traditional' demand) and ultimately became the

RNUR's main source of profit. For four years in a row (1993–6) the company's value added was less than its break-even point.[15] Yet the problems that Renault now faced were different from those that had brought it to the brink of bankruptcy in 1984. In 1996, net consolidated financial debt was equivalent to 5.1% of yearly revenues; cash flow was positive, and equivalent to 3.8% of the same measure. Renault carried out a vigorous cost-cutting programme, closing three small assembly plants: Creil in France (part of a joint venture with PSA); Setubal in Portugal; and Vilvorde in Belgium. The latter was the only one to cause any real protest in Europe. In any event, and thanks also to the market's recovery, Renault's earnings have been strong since 1997 (see appendix, Table 5A.1).

The 'innovation and flexibility' profit strategy to which Renault has been *de facto* committed since 1993 is only viable under certain conditions. The firm has to be able regularly to generate internal teams who are capable of innovative design. Its salespersons must be aware of customer expectations and able to communicate such desires, usefully and quickly, to the designers. It has to be responsive all the way down the value chain, from the design through the manufacturing to the marketing phase, so that it can respond rapidly to the expectations that are being expressed by the new segments in society, and in order to be able to reconvert production apparatus and employees in the aftermath of successes and failures whose magnitudes it cannot really predict beforehand. It must have a low break-even point, a low integration rate and enough financial independence to be able to survive the failures that this type of strategy inevitably entails. Finally, the employment relationship it builds must be such that the company can get its employees to demonstrate whatever level of creativity and flexibility is required in any particular circumstance (Boyer and Freyssenet, 2000a). Has Renault been able to fulfil the prerequisites for this profit strategy?

The RNUR has kept its traditional range of saloon cars alongside the range of innovative vehicles it has developed in recent years. Of course, until now, no automaker has had any long-term success in pursuing these two product policies simultaneously. After all, the two orientations are supposedly based on two 'profit strategies' that are incompatible (Boyer and Freyssenet, 2000a). Renault started out by creating an Industrial Design Centre in 1988 to strengthen its preparatory studies, a decision that seems to have been moderately successful in innovation terms. In addition, the Group has also organized and centralized its design function into a matrix-like structure (with cross-departmental studies of the sub-systems that are going to be used on the vehicles still in the planning stages being carried out 'perpendicularly' to the normal sub-system studies). This is more adapted to a 'volume and diversity' strategy than to one that is based on 'innovation and flexibility'. The same applies to Renault's manufacturing function. Operators are polyvalent; they work in UETs (*Unités Élémentaires de Travail*: elementary work units); and working times are flexible – all of which comprises more of a response to the requirements of a 'volume and diversity' strategy rather than to one based on 'innovation and flexibility'. Renault had not prepared itself to be responsive to the success or failure of a model – but it has had this experience with the Scenic. It took a long time before reconverting its manufacturing lines and employees so that they were able to respond to the unexpected demand for this model. Citroën and Opel put this delay to good use, launching rival models in the meantime.

On the other hand, Renault's integration rate plummeted providing it with a greater ability to survive future failures. This rate dropped from 24.8% in 1988 to 10.8% in 1996. Similarly, having the state as its main shareholder gave Renault the freedom to take risks, something that is indispensable in an 'innovation and flexibility' strategy.

It is true that it takes a long time to create coherency between a given socio-productive configuration and the profit strategy that a firm is pursuing. This means that the firm is going to have to develop its own 'company governance compromise'.

Another explanation for Renault's not having made a clear choice in this respect relates to its uncertainty regarding the way in which income distribution is going to develop in Europe. European countries have introduced rules that are more competitive in nature, but these new rules do not apply in all sectors of activity, and there is no intention of privatizing the benefits system. Hence, the trend towards an emergence of new social segments (as a result of the vagaries of inter-personal competition) is neither as significant nor as clear-cut in Europe as it is, for example, in the United States. Renault's strategic hesitation thus becomes more understandable – although the RNUR will ultimately have to make choices in this area, especially since it has decided to become a automaker of global proportions.

The 'Asian' crisis and the globalization drive: 1998–?

In the mid-1990s, many people felt that globalization was the new 'one best way' upon which future profitability would be predicated. Occasionally, two-digit growth in certain emerging countries seemed to augur well for the irreversible nature of their economic take-off, and many decision-makers felt that it was paramount not to miss the boat. A complete liberalization of capital flows was supposed eventually to lead to a totally globalized market. The Triad countries' economic cycles began to decouple, and this justified making immediate attempts to penetrate their markets in an effort to offset lower sales in one region by increases in another. The constitution of new regional units such as the Mercosur, the renewal of the ASEAN, the Central European countries' attempts to join the European Union – all of this augured well for the existence of markets that would be increasingly vast and solid. More and more people laid plans for setting up facilities in emerging countries – with many of these plans in fact materializing.

Renault was in tune with this movement but remained circumspect. In 1997 it retook control of its Argentinian subsidiary, and decided to create an assembly plant at Curitiba in Brazil, returning to that country after an absence of a quarter of a century. These operations were conducted via COFAL (Financial Company for Latin America, a 70% subsidiary) and through associations with local investors: small shareholders in Argentina (49%), and the state of Parana in Brazil (40%). The following year, Renault founded Avtoframos in Russia, in conjunction with the Municipality of Moscow, which placed at its disposal some of the facilities at Moskvitch, an auto manufacturer in which it was the majority shareholder.

In the end, however, the emerging country boom remained relatively speculative in nature. By mid-1997, investors and lenders had taken fright at the mountain of debt that was accumulating. Starting from Thailand, the crisis spread progressively like dominoes falling to countries in South East Asia and Korea, and then to South America, before finely reaching Russia. It plunged Japan back into the economic swamp from which it had been struggling to extract itself since the bursting of the first financial bubble. Hopes of a recovery in the world automobile market, this time thanks to the emerging markets, were dashed again.

This turnaround, which was bothersome but not particularly dramatic for Renault (because of its comparatively lower investment outlays), in fact turned into a significant opportunity for the company. Having accumulated some financial reserves and with renewed confidence in its products, Renault began to explore the possibility of acquiring a Korean firm. During this search it discovered that there were much greater opportunities in a country that up to recent times had been a source of terror – Japan. Firms that were considered to be emblematic of the so-called Japanese model – Nissan, Mitsubishi and Mazda – were, in fact, in serious danger.

In order, Renault acquired Nissan (taking a 36.8% stake in March 1999), the Romanian automaker Dacia (80.1% in July 1999) and the Korean Samsung (70.1% in September 2000).[16] In January 2001, it sold its trucks subsidiaries RVI and Mack Trucks to Volvo Global Trucks, taking a 20% share of the capital and of all voting rights, thus becoming the main shareholder.[17] In less than two years it had re-focused on passenger and small commercial vehicles[18] and 'on paper' at least had attained a global mass in this field while maintaining a foothold in the large commercial vehicle sector.[19] As a unit, Renault-Nissan accounted for 9.2% of the world market in 2000, making it the world's fifth largest automobile group.[20] Renault set itself a target of 4 million vehicles in 2010, including 50% of sales outside Western Europe.

Questions remain as to Renault's real motivations for its recent actions. Up to a short time ago, people had viewed Renault as potential prey in future take-over battles. Do these recent actions comprise a desperate flight into the future; an audacious but potentially highly successful taking of risks; or opportunistic behaviour that is the product of a carefully thought-out strategy?

Everything depends on the success or failure of Renault's alliance with Nissan. Ever since this agreement was signed, it has been easier to evaluate the risks (Nissan's high debt levels; potential social problems; and misunderstandings and incomprehension between the partners) as well as the potential upside (similar product ranges in certain segments enable a sharing of platforms and mechanical subsystems; co-ordinated and pooled purchasing; a marriage between Renault's stylistic competency and Nissan's mechanical excellence; complementary markets; the utilization of each firm's under-employed capacities; joint research efforts; the establishment of joint sales organizations in certain parts of the world and so on).

In two years, Renault spent 36.3 billion French francs (5.53 billion euros) on acquisitions.[21] Yet its debt in 2000 remained at an acceptable level, the equivalent of 11.9% of its yearly turnover. Nissan was able to cut its enormous debt more quickly than expected thanks to rapid asset sales and dramatic cost-cutting, to such an extent that it made a positive contribution to Renault' s earnings in 2001 despite a market that was relatively depressed. The financial risk seems to have faded away – but what has happened to the expected synergies?

Co-operative arrangements have been implemented actively and are starting to produce results. A first shared platform will be ready in 2002 for (entry-level) B segment vehicles. This will act as a basis for future models such as the Nissan Micra, March and Cube, and for Renault's Clio and Twingo models (1.7 million vehicles in total). A decision has been taken to develop a second shared platform for the C segment – that is, for models such as the Nissan Almera and the Renault Mégane (2 million vehicles in total). By 2010, the two marques' number of platforms will have been cut back to just ten. Mechanical sub-system exchanges have been decided, and the joint development of a small direct-injection diesel motor has begun.[22] There should be eight families of shared engines by 2010, and seven families of gearboxes. Purchasing co-ordination commenced in 2001, and should save US$1.4 billion by 2005 compared to 1999. Mexico saw the first Renault vehicle to roll off a Nissan line (a Scenic, in December 2000). Nissan's new pickup truck, the New Frontier, will be assembled in Renault's Brazilian plant during the course of 2002. Renault has already returned to the Australian, Japanese, Peruvian and Taiwanese markets thanks to the commercial support it is getting from Nissan. In addition, the acquisition of Samsung, which is steadily to build up a range of original Renault or Nissan models and adapt them to the Korean market, will allow Renault to be the first foreign automaker to penetrate this market, providing it with further opportunities for development in Asia.[23]

Dacia has been assigned a totally different target. By 2004, this firm must produce a 'reliable and modern' 5,000 euro vehicle that can target the markets in Eastern Europe and the 'emerging countries'. With this project, Renault has given itself entirely over to a conceptual innovation strategy that consists of responding to latent demand from the population segments in these countries that are in a position to be able to move from a 'two-wheel' to a 'four-wheel' vehicle – as long as they are offered something that is reliable, functional and inexpensive yet socially presentable. Chrysler spent some time thinking about this idea but gave up on it after the merger with Daimler. With its Dacia project, Renault is risking offering a car that is completely original and specific. Furthermore, it is declaring that it wants to pursue an innovative product policy in the name of its own marque, something that is confirmed by the types of models that it has been announcing.

Hence our two final questions: will the Renault-Dacia innovation strategy be compatible with a commonalization of Renault, Nissan and Samsung platforms; and will Renault's innovative models suit regions for which they were not designed? In other words, will the alliance with Nissan reinforce Renault's currently successful orientation, or will it harm it?

Conclusion: what profit strategy for the Renault-Nissan alliance?

Although Renault has up to now had a good deal of luck with its innovative models, and even though it has maintained *de facto* independence thanks to its majority shareholder (the French state), it remains that the RNUR has not developed enough responsiveness to keep competitors from copying it rapidly, and from eating away at the innovation rent that is the source of its profits. Opel and Citroën, with their Zafira and Picasso models, have already taken more than 50% of the European mid-size passenger van range that Renault in fact invented, and which it could have easily dominated had it saturated demand and got rid of its models' inevitable initial defects. Now, it is obvious that to improve and ensure the success of future commercial passenger vans, specific platforms will have to be used. What will happen when Renault vans have to share their platforms with traditional Nissan models?

Are the new population segments in South America, Russia or Asia really looking for innovative vehicles? The practical and symbolic expectations inherent in social differentiation are closely related to local or regional contexts, and to a particular social segment's own historical trajectory. They are expressed through codes that are very difficult to understand, and especially to invent, for designers who come from other parts of the world.

Thus there are only three hypotheses for Renault and Nissan. First of all, the two automakers can split their roles, with Nissan taking a traditional product range that has been rationalized severely to accommodate a reduced number of platforms, and which responds to demand from segments in the population that have remained stable and moderately hierarchized; and Renault in charge of innovative models for those new social segments that are fond of consumption-based differentiation. Between them the two companies would cover the two types of demand that comprise the lion's share of the market at the time of writing. The question remains, however, as to where we can find, in this hypothesis, those synergies that will justify an 'alliance' that is so costly in terms of the financial and human resources it requires.

The second hypothesis has the two manufacturers adopting one and the same strategy, meaning either that Nissan adopts Renault's 'innovation and flexibility' or Renault adopts Nissan's 'volume and diversity' strategy. In this hypothesis the alliance is fully justifiable. However, if Nissan rallies the 'innovation and flexibility' strategy, in its own markets it will be in direct competition with Honda, which has long been successful in this domain. If Renault reverts to the 'volume and diversity' strategy, it will again be in direct competition with Volkswagen and PSA, which are far ahead of it. It may also have to compete with Fiat-Opel, if their alliance pushes through.

There remains a third path, one that consists of overcoming any structural incompatibilities between the two firms' respective profit strategies. This would involve making it feasible at the product design level to commonalize those parts that are being used in both traditional and innovative models, and which are therefore destined for markets that are also far from homogeneous. At the production level it would involve creating a modicum of compatibility between the flows' regularity and the reconvertibility of tools and of personnel. All in all, this is no more nor less than the invention of a new automobile architecture, and of a new socio-productive model. The revolution to be fought is as important as the one that General Motors carried out during the 1920s and 1930s, when it created compatibility between volume and diversity by designing both shared platforms for car models that were economically and socially similar, as well as a production system that provided it with the polyvalency that its equipment and employees needed.

Translated by Alan Sitkin

Statistical appendix: Renault

Table A5.1 Renault, 1945–2000

Year	Production (passenger cars and light commercial vehicles)				Workforce[2]			Turnover[3]			Net income[3]		Investments[3]	
	Worldwide	Domestic	Of which exports[1]	Production abroad[1]	World Renault Group	World automobile branch	France automobile branch[4]	World Renault Group	World automobile branch	France automobile branch[4]	World Renault Group	France automobile branch[4]	World automobile branch	France automobile branch[4]
1945	12,036	12,036					23,250			36				1
1946	28,842	28,842	12,614				29,050			77				7
1947	44,484	44,484	26,059				36,471			123				21
1948	65,317	65,317	26,375				39,770			305				19
1949	106,079	106,079	37,658				44,233			474				30
1950	131,903	131,903	46,590				48,519			570				46
1951	163,944	163,944	48,316				52,470			959				85
1952	169,543	169,543	36,437				52,138			1,178				90
1953	160,102	160,102	39,830				50,337			1,151				41
1954	198,932	198,932	52,078				50,400			1,338				38
1955	219,622	219,622	64,887				52,235			1,424				87
1956	264,044	259,825	68,868	4,219			57,467			1,696				85
1957	317,443	313,425	112,744	4,018			58,981			2,162				133
1958	409,185	405,436	165,947	3,749			62,010			2,532				178
1959	494,160	487,044	297,287	7,116			65,657			3,131				198
1960	542,927	521,969	276,563	20,958			61,432			3,227				184
1961	393,163	353,218	183,970	39,945			58,313			2,962				237
1962	565,555	536,955	229,569	28,600			65,036			3,703				179
1963	668,867	639,797	219,514	29,070			63,575			4,438				158
1964	551,755	497,555	164,058	54,200			58,899			4,268				275
1965	590,431	551,904	226,305	38,527			62,902			4,536				240
1966	737,979	648,354	243,566	89,625			66,171			5,534				310
1967	777,468	695,148	295,586	82,050			66,882			5,886		22		552
1968	807,407	714,314	339,635	93,093			76,060			6,468		20		542
1969	1,009,372	898,486	415,211	110,886			86,348			8,539		151		899
1970	1,159,745	1,040,112	561,006	119,633			97,261			10,674		5		1,336
1971	1,174,314	1,040,321	527,181	133,993			98,091			10,078		–197		1,183
1972	1,318,327	1,155,507	549,777	162,820			100,001			12,087		74		964
1973	1,414,563	1,209,342	604,034	205,221	175,000		101,415	20,659		13,777		57		815
1974	1,487,528	1,291,196	649,044	196,332	185,436		100,478	25,674		16,173		36		1,223

Table A5.1 continued

Year	Production (passenger cars and light commercial vehicles)				Workforce[2]			Turnover[3]			Net income[3]		Investments[3]	
	Worldwide	Domestic	Of which exports[1]	Production abroad[1]	World Renault Group	World automobile branch	France automobile branch[4]	World Renault Group	World automobile branch	France automobile branch[4]	World Renault Group	France automobile branch[4]	World automobile branch	France automobile branch[4]
1975	1,391,948	1,128,972	562,707	262,976	222,436	156,846	103,614	33,539	31,286	18,264		−551		2,153
1976	1,659,973	1,365,442	640,905	294,531	241,259	163,663	110,406	44,351	34,321	25,778	579	610		1,763
1977	1,737,707	1,398,550	624,106	339,157	243,456	170,632	110,485	48,589	39,770	28,696	−111	12		2,373
1978	1,718,398	1,372,084	613,927	346,314	239,447	167,229	108,586	56,215	49,850	34,011	−102	158		2,286
1979	1,899,470	1,544,995	730,771	354,475	233,408	169,794	106,740	68,535	58,006	42,185	1,016	470		2,786
1980	1,999,591	1,659,099	760,879	340,492	223,450	164,461	105,319	80,118	63,669	49,864	638	303	5,442	4,733
1981	1,764,702	1,479,691	640,156	285,011	215,844	157,402	103,613	87,971	76,272	53,620	−690	−875	6,345	4,555
1982	1,921,307	1,674,416	757,954	246,891	217,269	152,202	103,759	104,145	82,071	65,752	−1,281	−2,563	6,331	3,524
1983	2,035,133	1,842,801	979,425	192,332	219,805	161,643	102,528	110,274	85,379	73,560	−1,576	−1,875	8,043	3,941
1984	1,740,737	1,607,441	887,177	138,264	213,725	157,696	98,153	117,584	89,634	72,105	−12,555	−11,324	7,872	3,938
1985	1,637,634	1,499,979	881,149	137,636	196,414	144,961	86,122	122,138		72,644	−10,897	−11,241	6,209	2,762
1986	1,754,332	1,537,123	809,867	217,210	196,731	139,313	79,191	131,060	101,824	82,992	−5,847	−7,355	4,141	1,786
1987	1,831,390	1,612,146	809,589	219,244	188,936	136,646	75,911	147,510	114,375	93,333	3,254	2,314	5,170	3,090
1988	1,850,667	1,630,786	807,739	219,876	178,665	135,010	71,898	161,438	123,495	99,802	8,834	7,316	6,197	4,002
1989	1,966,724	1,717,279	837,608	249,445	174,573	129,699	70,720	174,477	135,717	113,731	9,289	6,932	8,703	5,146
1990	1,776,717	1,571,264	784,112	205,184	157,378	114,516	68,713	163,620	129,230	110,694	1,210	1,223	8,847	6,013
1991	1,790,709	1,587,787	829,298	202,922	147,185	106,232	63,644	171,502	133,206	112,297	3,078	2,467	8,303	6,624
1992	2,041,829	1,777,401	987,932	264,428	146,604	106,912	61,075	184,252	143,387	129,972	5,680	3,251	10,347	5,540
1993	1,713,633	1,459,188	817,788	254,445	139,932	103,148	60,608	169,789	130,179	116,776	1,071	−5,225	9,173	5,378
1994	1,850,267	1,618,831	923,485	231,436	138,279	102,358	59,346	178,537	135,506	130,875	3,636	1,463	12,188	7,337
1995	1,761,643	1,610,216	900,077	151,427	139,950	102,213	59,264	184,065	136,444	132,050	2,139	944	12,610	7,900
1996	1,741,161	1,602,632	961,940	138,529	140,905	111,523	58,528	184,078	145,962	135,658	−5,266	−190	13,550	
1997	1,867,619	1,121,970		745,649	141,315	112,178	47,773	207,912	165,788	159,232	5,427	4,135	12,875	4,129
1998	2,197,395	1,373,936		823,459	138,321	109,409	45,758	243,934	195,077	182,096	8,847	5,990	12,366	4,408
1999	2,257,918	1,376,707		881,211	159,608	131,261	44,584	249,483	197,062	193,753	3,506	4,434	13,619	
2000	2,427,178	1,407,717		1,019,461	166,114	136,574	45,942	263,534	206,548	202,495	7,082	9,540	15,606	5,457

Notes

1. Exports include vehicles that have been entirely broken down into kits of parts (CKD basis) with the exception of 'small series' corresponding to vehicles 'manufactured abroad'. From 1997, Renault discontinued publishing its export statistics, providing only information on vehicles assembled in France or abroad, regardless of the parts' origin.
2. Staff numbers are as of 31 December of the year concerned, including employees on temporary contracts.
3. Turnover, net income and investments are in millions of French francs. Turnover is net of taxes from 1971 onwards.
4. Workforce, net income and turnover in France and investments are for the RNUR (*Régie Nationale des Usines Renault*) and then for Renault, SA.

Notes

1 Exports, which represented 58.6% of all sales in 1947, dropped back to 29.5% in 1951. On the other hand, output quadrupled over the same time span, and the French franc's devaluation between 1948 and 1950 lowered the surcharges from which French automakers had been suffering in comparison with their competitors on the overseas markets.

2 The RNUR had to deal with funding constraints that were even more stringent than those the private-sector manufacturers faced. Unlike its rivals, it was not eligible for long-term, below-market-rate 'Modernization and Equipment Fund' loans. Paradoxically, it had to turn to the banking sector for finance (Ramirez, 1994).

3 Pre-assembled vehicle imports were subject to quotas and import duties of 24% in Belgium and 35% in the United Kingdom. On the other hand, local assembly using detached parts or sub-systems was only taxed at 8% in Belgium, and was free in the UK from any duties at all (although it did go along with the obligation that the foreign firm must purchase 50% of all components domestically and export 75% of its output to former British colonies). Because of the Haren plant's capacity, its location close to France, the port of Antwerp and the markets of Northern Europe, its relatively low ratio of locally produced parts, and a workforce that at the time was relatively cheaper than elsewhere, Renault increased its Belgian production to 8,700 vehicles in 1954 (Wafellman and Quackels, 1983). In the UK, on the other hand, high (51%) local contents ratios, the Commonwealth export obligation, greater production costs and the general level of competition kept annual output below 1,000 vehicles (Lukes, 1979; Ramirez, 1994).

4 In Ireland and in Australia (1949) agreements were reached with local importers who took responsibility for assembling vehicles that were sent in CKD kit form. In South Africa and Mexico (1950) agreements were reached with assemblers who were already working with other marques of vehicles. In Spain (1953) a deal was done with a firm (the FASA) which itself had the ambition of becoming an automaker. In the same year, Renault began to work with a commercial vehicle manufacturer in Japan (Hino Diesel). Although the latter two agreements were concluded at a later date, they were the only ones to be even moderately successful (involving 1,900 and 2,700 vehicles, respectively, in 1954). The agreement that had been signed in India was not renewed.

5 The economic stabilization measures that René Mayer and Antoine Pinay implemented in 1952 are a clear demonstration of this. They put a brake on rising demand and affected exports as a result of the currency revaluation that went along with this policy. In 1953, Renault's sales in fact dropped slightly, both in France and abroad. As such, it either needed to re-launch its exports in order to offset a slower growing domestic demand – or else the latter aggregate had to be galvanized through the implementation of a nationally co-ordinated and moderately hierarchized distribution of income.

6 In 1957, six European countries (Belgian, France, Italy, Luxembourg, the Netherlands and the Federal Republic of Germany) signed the Treaty of Rome, setting up a Common Market among themselves. For passenger vehicles, customs duties were supposed to disappear within a decade and a common tariff of 17.6% was to be put on imports from third-party countries. In 1958, customs duties on passenger vehicles were 17% in the Federal Republic of Germany, 24% in Belgium, Luxembourg and the Netherlands, 30% in France and 45% in Italy (Volpato, 1983).

7   It also offered a complementary pension system; indemnities above and beyond normal Social Security payments in the case of industrial accidents or illness; and later (in 1958) partial payments in the event of a reduction in working hours or of an increase in the number of days off work.

8   A plan put forward by Paul Ramadier, France's Minister of Finance at the time, almost compromised Renault's overall strategy. The idea had been to increase taxes to pay for the cost of the Algerian war – but this would have broken the back of a domestic automobile market that was in full expansion. Pierre Dreyfus succeeded in convincing the Ministry that instead of raising taxes on the French population it could obtain much-needed foreign currency by forcing French automakers to increase their exports significantly in exchange for counter-measures that would be beneficial to them (devaluation, relaxation of exchange controls, reimbursement of VAT, continued export aid despite certain provisions in the recently signed Treaty of Rome, accelerated depreciation schedules and so on; see Loubet, 1995).

9   It is not impossible that the new political environment created with Charles de Gaulle's return to power in 1958 convinced Pierre Dreyfus to turn the RNUR into France's leading exporter, and thus into something to be reckoned with (Ramirez, 1994).

10   Volkswagen had taken the precaution of substantially increasing the Beetle's finished quality, equipping the car with a more powerful engine while maintaining its robustness and reliability and keeping it easy to drive. Conversely, other automakers were happy simply to add to their cars whatever features were required under American law, forgetting local climatic constraints and driving habits. VW had also been steadily building up a distribution network (and above all, an efficient after-sales service) for nearly a decade. Its European rivals simply improvised in this area, with the exception of Simca (benefiting from the networks that Chrysler, its new owner, had just given it) and, of course, the American automakers' own European subsidiaries.

11   Many of the production cuts that resulted from the unsuccessful American adventure were incurred by the Haren plant in Belgium, where output dropped from 51,400 units in 1960 to 27,200 in 1961.

12   Between 1958 and 1973, foreign marque passenger car penetration rates rose from 9.2% to 25.8% in the FRG, from 2.5% to 26.8% in Italy and from 1.5% to 17.3% in France. This indicator can be used as a means of apprehending interpenetration within the Common Market, inasmuch as Japanese and American imports were very low at the time.

13   Renault bought 25% of Volvo Car and 45% of Volvo Truck, with Volvo buying 20% of Renault and 45% of Renault Industrial Vehicles. RVI's market was more or less French-based and subject to wild fluctuations that caused the subsidiary repeatedly to spill red ink. The merger turned RVI-Volvo Trucks into the world's second largest group in this sector, behind Daimler-Benz.

14   The attempted take-over of Skoda can also be analysed as part of this strategy. Volkswagen ultimately paid over the odds during this battle, thus forcing Renault to throw in the towel.

15   Despite the fact the Renault SA's break-even point was higher than the added value it produced (meaning that it was losing money on every car it sold), net Group earnings were strong in 1993, 1994 and 1995, primarily because of good performances by RNUR financial and foreign subsidiaries. Total 1996 losses of 5.2 billion French francs would have been much smaller had Renault not tried to

build up reserves in one fell swoop to cover all the costs of closing the Vilvorde plant in Belgium (4 billion francs).

16 Renault also bought 22.5% of Nissan Diesel, the commercial vehicle subsidiary of Nissan, as well as 100% of Nissan's financial subsidiaries in Europe. It has an option to increase its stake in Nissan Motors to 39.9% within four years of the agreement's signature, and up to 44.4% in the fifth year, at a price of 400 yen per share. Nissan also has the possibility of later acquiring a stake in Renault.

17 These 20% correspond to 15% purchased in exchange for 100% of RVI and Mack Trucks and 5% bought in the market. Renault is committed to not exceeding a 20% stake, except in the event of a take-over or an attempted take-over of AB Volvo by a third party, or if one of the current shareholders' participations exceeds Renault's. AB Volvo, a minority shareholding of the Group, is currently the world's second largest truck manufacturer, behind Mercedes and far ahead of Paccar, Navistar, Scania, Man and Iveco. Nissan Diesel is not part of this agreement.

18 Renault signed an agreement with General Motors Europe in 1996 to market GM's Master (renamed the Movano), and above all jointly to develop a replacement for the Trafic, which was being sold in 2001 under the names Renault Trafic and Opel Vivaro.

19 The agreement between Renault and Volvo was acceptable to the European Commission, as long as Renault took back its Coaches business (which two years before it had put into a 50–50 joint venture called Irisbus, together with Fiat's Iveco). Renault preferred to sell its shares to Iveco.

20 In 2000, Renault-Nissan was behind General Motors (14.4%), Ford (12.8%), DaimlerChrysler-Mitsubishi (11.2%) and Toyota (10.4%); just in front of Volkswagen (9%); and far ahead of PSA (5.1%) and Fiat (4.7%).

21 32.3 billion francs for Nissan, nearly 450 million for Dacia, 1.7 billion for Samsung and 446 million for AB Volvo – to which we should add for 636 million for Bennetton's Formula One stable, 419 million as part of a capital issue for the Avtoframos Russian subsidiary and 308 for the same sort of operation in Turkey.

22 Renault will be using Nissan's 3.5 litre V6 engine for its top-of-the-range models, plus its four-wheel drive transmissions for future off-road vehicles. Nissan will be putting Renault stick shifts into its smaller models.

23 Samsung is producing a top-of-the-range saloon car, the SM5, that is derived from the Nissan Maxima. In 2002 it will come out with a model for the C segment, also originally a Nissan.

References

Automotive News (1996) 'American Automobile Centennial: 1896–1996. The 100 Years Almanac', *Automotive News*, vol. 1, April.

Badiche, M. (1992) 'Renault et le transfert de technologie dans les pays de l'est européen', *Culture Technique*, no. 25.

Bardou, J.-P., Chanaron, J.-J., Fridenson, P. and Laux, J. (1977) *La révolution automobile*, Paris: Albin Michel.

Bonnafos, G., Chanaron, J.-J. and Mautort, L. (1983) *L'industrie automobile*, Paris: La Découverte.

Boyer, R. and Freyssenet, M. (1999) 'Rewriting the Future. Profit Strategies, Forms of Internationalization and New Spaces in the Automobile Industry', in A. Eckardt, H.-D. Köhler and L. Pries (eds), *Global Players in Lokalen Bindungen: Unternehmensglobalisierung in soziologischer Perspektive*, Berlin: Sigma.

Boyer, R. and Freyssenet, M. (2000a, 2002) *Les modèles productifs*, Paris: La Découverte (Revised English edition: *The Productive Models: The Conditions of Profitability*, London/New York: Palgrave, 2002).

Boyer, R. and Freyssenet, M. (2000b) 'A New Approach of Productive Models. The World That Changed the Machine', *Industrielle Beziehungen*, 2000/4.

Charron, E. (1985) 'La stratégie internationale de Renault', *Annales de la Recherche Urbaine*, no. 29.

Charron, E. (1998) 'FASA-Renault: Innovation in Productive Flexibility and Job Security', in R. Boyer, E. Charron, U. Jürgens and S. Tolliday (eds), *Between Imitation and Innovation: The Transfer and Hybridization of Productive Models in the International Automobile Industry*, Oxford/New York: Oxford University Press.

Combes, L. (1994–5) 'Renault: 25 ans d'Amérique latine', *Renault-Histoire*, nos 5–6–7–8.

Dreyfus, P. (1977) *La liberté de réussir*, Paris: J.-C. Simoën.

El Hentati, A. (1980) 'Stratégies des firmes automobiles: le cas de la RNUR', *DES*, Paris 1.

Fornaguera, S. A. (1992) 'L'industrie automobile française en Amérique du Sud: bilan et perspectives', *Thèse*, Paris 1.

Fouriez, J. (1974) 'L'implantation de la RNUR au Mexique', *DES*, Paris 1.

Freyssenet, M. (1979) *Division du travail et mobilisation quotidienne de la main d'oeuvre. Les cas Renault et Fiat*, Paris: CSU.

Freyssenet, M. (1984) 'Les processus d'internationalisation de la production de Renault: 1898–1979', *Actes du GERPISA*, no. 1.

Freyssenet, M. (1998a) 'Intersecting Trajectories and Model Changes', in M. Freyssenet, A. Mair, K. Shimizu and G. Volpato (eds), *One Best Way? The Trajectories and Industrial Models of World Automobile Producers*, Oxford/New York: Oxford University Press.

Freyssenet, M. (1998b) 'Renault, from Diversified Mass Production to Innovative Flexible Production', ibid.

Freyssenet, M. and Lung, Y. (2000) 'Between Globalization and Regionalization: What Is the Future of the Motor Industry?', in J. Humphrey, Y. Lecler and M. Salerno (eds), *Global Strategies and Local Realities: The Auto industry in Emerging Markets*, London: Macmillan, and New York: St. Martin's Press.

Freyssenet, M. and Lung, Y. (forthcoming) 'Multinational Car Firms Regional Strategies', in J. Carillo, Y. Lung and R. Van Tulder, *Cars, Carriers of Regionalism*.

Fridenson, P. (1979) 'La bataille de la 4 CV', *L'Histoire*, no. 9.

Fridenson, P. (1993) 'Renault face au problème du franc et du risque devises', in M. Aglietta, C. de Boissieu, M. Lévy-Leboyer and A. Plessis (eds), *Du franc Poincaré à l'écu*, Paris: Comité pour l'histoire économique et financière de la France.

Gleize, G. (1988) 'La RNUR et l'Amérique Latine depuis 1945. Brésil, Argentine, Colombie', *Maîtrise d'Histoire*, Paris 10.

Gonzalez, F. (1964) 'L'évolution des problèmes de débouchés de l'industrie automobile française depuis 1945. L'expérience Renault', *DES*, Paris 1.

Lévy, R. (1994) *Le cas Renault*, Paris: Notes de la Fondation Saint Simon.

Loubet, J. L. (1995) *Citroën, Peugeot, Renault et les autres*, Paris: Le Monde Éditions.

Loubet, J. L. (1998) *Renault, cent ans d'histoire*, Paris: ETAI.

Lukes, H. O. (1979) 'Renault au Royaume-Uni', *Bulletin de la section d'histoire des usines Renault*, no. 18.

Maison, M. (1996) 'La longue marche de Renault en Espagne', *Renault-Histoire*, no. 8.

Montagne, E. (1983) 'La stratégie de Renault en Amérique latine', *DES*, Paris 1.

Picard, F. (1976) *L'épopée de Renault*, Paris: Albin Michel.

Pointet, J. M. (1997) 'Cohérence de la stratégie produit de Renault', *Gérer et Comprendre*, no. 48.

Rahiji, M. T. (1981) 'La stratégie internationale de Renault: les cas de l'Espagne et du Portugal', *DEA*, Paris 1.

Ramirez Perez, S. M. (1994) 'Le processus d'internationalisation de la Régie Nationale des Usines Renault, 1945–1975', *Maîtrise d'Histoire*, Lyon 3.

Da Silva Ribeiro, E. (1987) 'L'implantation de l'industrie automobile en Argentine: le cas Renault', *DEA d'économie internationale*, Paris 1.

Volpato, G. (1983) *L'industria automobilistica internazionale*, Padua: Cedam.

Wafellmann, D. and Quackels, E. (1983) 'Renault en Belgique', *Bulletin de la section d'histoire des usines Renault*, no. 27.

Wenhamar, M. (1981) 'Stratégies de l'industrie automobile: le cas de la RNUR en Amérique latine', *DES*, Paris 1.

Yombo, C. H. (1988) La stratégie d'internationalisation de Renault, *DEA*, Paris 1.

6
Fiat Auto: From 'Forced' Internationalization Towards Intentional Globalization

Giuseppe Volpato

In order to look at the internationalization process of Fiat using the correct perspective, one must start with the fact that the first and most important intuition of Giovanni Agnelli Senior was that the Italian automobile industry, on the supply side, necessarily had to adopt an international focus. In other words, no Italian automobile manufacturer (and the same was true for all European manufacturers) could think of growing and developing by looking just at the domestic market. As a consequence, Fiat was born with a marked international attitude which shaped all initial production and market choices: a considerable amount of investment, the acquisition of modern machinery, in large part from abroad, a high level of vertical integration, and a strong participation in international sports events in order to exploit marketing effects. Without a focus on the vast international market one could not launch truly industrial automobile production, able to exploit the advantages of economies of scale both in new product development and in production methods.

The 'forced' internationalization

Today that attitude could be taken for granted, but in the past it was not so. Contemporary people might look back at the automobile industry as an industrial activity limited to a few makes, but in reality this was not true. According to a *L'Auto d'Italia* review, in 1907 there were fifty-eight firms in Italy established to manufacture automobiles, forty-six of which had already started operating. Most of them were located in Northern regions (twenty-three in Piemonte, sixteen in Lombardia, six in Liguria), but also there were six firms in Naples.[1] Today we do not even remember the name of these automobile firms because the selection process towards an oligopolistic structure of supply took place very early, based upon the capability to make strong economies of scale. This meant that there was a strong imperative for all automobile firms, except the American ones, to structure themselves in order to supply many foreign markets besides the domestic one.[2]

Exports clearly also required a commercial network, and Fiat, like other European firms, started a gradual process of development of its own foreign branches. The first stage lay in the activation of foreign agents. In some cases these were independent operators who, lured by the sports successes of the Italian make, approached the Turin firm to make them representatives in prestigious cities such as Paris, London and New York. This process began very early, in 1902, with the appointment of import agents in France and the USA.

The process of development of foreign branches became systematic after the First World War. In 1919, Fiat Hispanian and Fiat France were established, and in the following years twenty other branches were added: in major markets such as Germany (1922) and Britain (1924); in markets where important developments were expected – for example, Argentina (1923) and Brazil (1927), and finally in markets where the possibilities of granting production licences or setting up companies for vehicle assembly were evaluated – for example, like Poland or Turkey. The outcome of these fervent initiatives emerged clearly in the growth of exports. Between the two world wars, Fiat was the automaker with the highest ratio of exports to production, with shares changing, year by year, but on average remaining above 60%.

The 'adversed' internationalization

After the Second World War, the reconstruction of Italian industry began a period of strong economic growth which favoured the expansion of the automobile industry. Fiat, through the management of Vittorio Valletta, headed this process, with a rapid reorganization of the plants and the launch of new models. However, the attitude was not immediately aimed at manufacturing vehicles for the mass market. Post-war production exceeded the pre-war record by 1949, with 70,800 units (against 52,978 in 1939), but without the launch of a popular model adjusted to the spending capability of the average Italian family. This behaviour was driven partly by a prudential choice by Valletta, who intended to take a leap towards true mass production only once he was certain that the domestic market was ready. But it was also the outcome of a short-sighted policy of the Italian government, which did not consider automobiles to be an essential element of the industrial and economic growth of the country, but rather as a wealthy consumption good to be taxed heavily.

This behaviour dated back to the Fascist period, which had applied extremely heavy fiscal pressure on both fuel and vehicle road tax, but it also continued after this period, and was increased. In 1958, the fuel price in Italy was clearly higher than that of other European countries, including those without a national automobile industry, which would have had more reason to operate a policy of restraint on motorization. The effect of the road tax was similar, which in Italy was highly progressive, based on engine size, while in other countries there was a regressive approach.

So when the motorization process took off in Italy, Fiat was forced to specialize more and more in the lower market segments than did other countries. The first popular auto for the Italian market was launched in 1955 with the Fiat 600 model, and was followed just two years later by a model even smaller in size and with a smaller engine, the Fiat 500.

The second half of the 1950s in Italy clearly shows the new attitude towards the Italian demand for automobiles. In 1951, vehicles below 750 cc exceeded those between 751 cc and 1200 cc by 25%. In 1960 this ratio had completely changed. The smallest segment was over twice as big as the second, and ten times larger than the third. In conclusion, the strong fiscal incidence applied to automobile usage has distorted the segmentation of the Italian market significantly compared to the European one, and has progressively reduced the possibility of Fiat competing in foreign markets on the higher segments of automobile production.[3]

The 'denied' internationalization

The growth of the Italian market and the forced specialization in lower market segments yielded a strong decrease in the degree of internationalization of commercial opportunities for Fiat. It was a weakness factor, which was very clear to the management of the company. Gianni Agnelli himself underlined this aspect:

> Along the whole talk so far I have tried to demonstrate that the frequent difficulty of trends in different markets, especially those with higher economic development, the progressive unreversible disappear of national economic protectionism, the growing diffusion of uniform models of consumption, plus other factors will determine that the company will not be able to base and guarantee its security and its development, at least in Europe, within a single market.
>
> It is the world marketplace – which will be more and more single and homogeneous – which will be the playground where the future of our companies will be determined.
>
> In this market the decisive role will be played by the share of presence that each car maker will be able to ensure and defend. It is just above a minimum size that sales results can give guarantee of stability over time and of further growth, by allowing on the one side the efficient utilization of modern distribution and promotion tools, and on the other side those high production volumes which are necessary in order to reach maximum cost competitiveness.
>
> This determines the absolute necessity for Fiat to increase its participation to the world market and this nost just by referring to most sophisticated

markets and with higher motorization rates…but also to 'new' markets, those of under-motorized countries.[4]

To the president of Fiat it was clear that the need to become a large-sized company, on an international basis, was not linked just to the issue of economies of manufacturing scale and cost compression – aspects that are undoubtedly important in automobile production but which, as the experience of Japanese firms has demonstrated, can be partly compensated by more advanced management and higher labour productivity. It generally relates to a need connected with the economics of the whole company, linked to all main operating areas: from R&D to purchasing, and from commercial distribution strategy to the politics of integration on the production line.

As seen from the comments above, the president of Fiat had focused on the challenge of the world automobile industry, underlining the key passages through which the international projection of the Italian automobile group had to be achieved. The attempt to acquire Citroën must be remembered. The company, founded by André Citroën in 1919, quickly gained a strong position in the French industrial scenario, but the technological breakthroughs of the products and the company's modern marketing style had not been matched by corresponding financial success. André Citroën's drive to grow and win led to a policy of a continuous launch of investments and renovation of machinery, which kept the company in a situation of permanent financial stress. In 1934, the company collapsed and André Citroën had to step down, leaving the company to Michelin, which had the most credit due to them for supply.[5]

Under the new management, Citroën distinguished itself with high-level products, such as the revolutionary model 'DS' introduced in 1955, but without taking off very much economically. After all the Michelin ownership, radicated in tyre production, could not move heavily in automobile activities by becoming a strong competitor of its most important customers: Renault and Peugeot.

In 1967 Fiat decided to sell its participation into Simca to Chrysler, and to enter Citroën's capital with a considerable share. In October 1968 the two car makers announced an agreement of close collaboration, first approved by the authorities of the two countries. A joint committee would be in charge of research activities, investments and production programmes, purchasing and sales; a financial company would be created, Pardevi, of French nationality, to which the majority of Citroën S.A. stocks would be given.

The initial sharing of Citroën's capital was 35% to Michelin, 15% to Fiat, 1.66% to Berliet. The rest was fragmented among a multiplicity of subjects. A major event occurred in February 1970. Citroën's capital was increased and Fiat participated with a heavy share. The new sharing was 28% to Michelin, 26.9% to Fiat, 7.1% to Berliet and the remaining 38% to the public. At this point some resistances on the French side began to appear. Fiat wished for a progressive integration of the two product lines, and a rationalization of the production capacity. On the contrary, Citroën tended to protect its identity of the French manufacturer and consequently the differences between the two makes, at least this was the official reason.

Knowing the following developments, it could be argued that most resistances came from the political side.[6] Not only General De Gaulle would have negatively considered Fiat's entrance in Citroën as an offence to French *grandeur*. Given the difference in size, the new agreement would be seen as an acquisition of Citroën by Fiat.[7] But also other French car makers would have opposed the entry of a foreign competitor, which was one of the leaders of the European scene at that time. The agreement was ended in 1973. In 1976 Michelin sold to Peugeot the control package of Citroën, demonstrating the preference of the political power towards an all-French solution.

In the strategy of *avvocato* Agnelli, presented in Parliament in 1969, the agreement with Citroën represented the most important step towards the development of the Turin firm. It was designed in a period of market growth, so in the best conditions for success. Citroën would have probably gained more from this agreement than it actually had by being absorbed by Peugeot. Product lines of Citroën and Fiat could integrate much better than those of the two French companies. Citroën would have been granted the mission to occupy the prestige market segments. The absorption by Peugeot occurred in parallel with that of Simca-Talbot, in a perturbed market. Peugeot partly cancelled some programmes of renovation of Citroën's models.

The 'missed' internationalization

It is well known of Fiat in general, and of *avvocato* Gianni Agnelli in particular, though that the survival and success for individual car makers depended on production volumes.[8] Therefore it is not surprising that in 1984, as soon as the signs of market recovery and especially of Fiat competitiveness became clear, Vittorio Ghidella, CEO of Fiat Auto, imagined to negotiate an agreement with another industrial company. Ford of Europe was considered the most encouraging among the manufacturers contacted. The first meetings confirmed the convergence of the viewpoints of the two potential partners. During the second half of 1984 Fiat Spa holding entered into negotiation with Ford Motor Co. of Detroit, concerning Fiat Auto Spa and Ford Europe.

Soon the parties agreed that the sharing of components did not present any specific problem.[9] And even the joint design of one or more vehicles showed an encouraging positive balance in the cost-benefit. However parts purchasing and vehicle design did not yet represent strong economies.

Joint production of a model could have allowed savings in manufacturing costs of 10–15%. But Ford Europe had many production sites located in Germany, England, Spain, and the individual national companies (like Ford UK and Ford Werke AG) controlled the company capital of each activity. Ford Europe was only an organization co-ordinating tasks, without actual power. As a consequence, the rationalization of production capacity and joint vehicle manufacturing represented a very complex operation.

In addition the product lines of the two makes presented a high degree of overlapping. If on the one side this would have allowed to considerably lower the design and manufacturing investments, on the other side this would have required the discontinuance of some car models, and the closure of less efficient plants. In other words the new company emerging from the merger would not have been a sum of the given activities (a solution which could have been viable if the product lines and the market positions of the two makes would have been complementary).[10] On the contrary, what was needed was a true integration process. Fiat Spa, industrial holding of the Fiat Group, and Ford Motor Co. of Dearborn, USA would have had to establish a new company into which to convey their own automobile activities.

The project would have represented a revolutionary event, not just for its outcome on the international competitive equilibrium, but also for the innovative nature of this agreement with no equals. The strongest proof of the 'idyllic' climate of the negotiation, as it was defined by the media, came at the Geneva auto show in February 1985. For the first time, both Bob Lutz (President of Ford Europe) and Vittorio Ghidella officially confirmed the negotiation in progress.

As a matter of fact a structure able to integrate on the industrial level the two companies, although they would have appeared in the market through individual nameplates and distribution networks, would have been very relevant. In 1984 European market shares of Fiat and Ford ranked at the top levels, with 12.8% and 12.7% respectively, followed by Volkswagen (12.1%), Peugeot (11.5%), General Motors (11.1%) and Renault (11%). Therefore the mere union would have allowed to establish a great competitor adjusted to a manufacturing capacity of over 3 million vehicles per year, and on a market share of a fourth of the European total. Starting mainly from the manufacturing the integration could continue in various areas. For example Ford would have had a privileged access to new state-of-the-art manufacturing technologies which Fiat was developing (like in the new Termoli plant), while Fiat would have benefited from the long experience accumulated by Ford in the manufacturing of low-pollution vehicles. Also Ford could have benefited, thanks to its Italian partner, of a revitalization in vehicle style, which had been for some time one of the weaknesses of the brand. On the contrary, Fiat could take advantage of the highly internationalized structure of Ford Europe.

Then, in a more remote time horizon, synergies could have been played through a triangular activity with the USA. Both through easier commercial access and through design of a world car, that is a vehicle which through minor adjustments could have been marketed in all main car markets. Gianni Agnelli himself, in an interview held in September 1985, mentioned this possibility. He even underlined that in the agreement being discussed by Fiat and Ford there were, besides the immediate effects on the automobile industry, also interesting prospects of future co-operation for many other industries in which the Fiat Group was operating.

However, this vastness (and complexity) itself of the project greatly enhanced the issue of control of the joint venture emerging from the merger. Formally one could also think of a solution, which did not relegate one of the two partners in a minority position. A clear agreement was needed, defining who and how would have exerted the final decision power in all cases in which different positions between the two partners would have emerged.[11] Undoubtedly problems of this kind would have come up, since the rationalization and the division of labour across different plants would have inevitably determined the closing of some plants, which consequent manpower reduction. By the way, during the spring of 1985 this kind of conflicts manifested also within Ford, for the allocation of manufacturing of a new engine which Ford Werke would have preferred to develop in Koln, and Ford UK at Dagenham, and it acquired the traits of an 'iron-arm' contest between the Bonn and London governments.

At that time the size of Fiat and Ford Europe appeared, for some reasons, basically equivalent. Fiat lightly prevailed over Ford Europe on the automobile side, it had completed its reorganization after the long stage of crisis in the 1970s, and Fiat management had a great image on the industrial side while that of *avvocato* Agnelli had no equals in Europe. But at the same time the Ford Europe could boast many merits and the connection with its parent company, that enjoyed the position of the second automobile world producer and an international network which was considered the absolutely most advanced.[12]

It was clear since the beginning that the issue of final control was a key point for the whole operation. But the different legal and tax regimes under which the activities of the different companies were managed added huge complexity to the merging procedures. In other words it was impossible to determine *ex ante* the size of the merger. Only *ex post*, once resolved all problems, a clear picture would have been possible. This was increasing the importance of the issue of final power.

According to the press, at the end Ford proposed to assign the management of the company being established to Fiat, but for a fixed period (5–7 years), probably until *avvocato* Agnelli retired. Later, control would have gone definitively to Ford. A solution which was not accepted by the Italian partner and which led to the interruption of the negotiation.

Undoubtedly all the other car makers enjoyed the news. According to information which came through, the agreement entailed in a decade the harmonization of components, the sharing of transmissions, the installation of the Fire engine in the Fiesta, the manufacturing of the 'Panda' in a specific version for Ford to be marketed in North European countries, the design of a vehicle replacing the 'Ritmo' and the 'Escort' and a new family of engines.

But clearly such perspectives were not enough to overcome resistances relative to such complex agreements, and also risky, related to redistribution of power: both at company and at managerial level.

It is important to underline that this stop was not without effects for future internationalization strategies. The most important was that Fiat tended to consider (not without good reasons) as scarcely viable any form of agreement in which the attribution of decision power between the parts was not clearly defined from the beginning.[13] As a consequence mainly options of acquisition of other car makers were considered, and during negotiations future outcomes were designed with modest room for autonomy of the acquired firm.[14]

The failure of Fiat–Ford negotiation favoured agreements with partners not only financially but also technologically weak. So it was natural that attention was being directed mainly towards Eastern European countries. It is clearly and interesting area: population in 1985 of about 400 million, annual production at about 2 million vehicles, and a quite modest motorization level, but due to grow.[15] In the mid 1980s even most prudent estimates suggested a strong expansion in consumption in these countries.

According to estimates by a reliable institute such as the Nomura Research Institute, sales of new cars in the USSR should have increased from 1.3 million in 1985 to 1.6 million in 1995, with a growth in vehicles per 1,000 population from 45 to 68. But it was a forecast based more upon the expansion of supply capacity programmed by Soviet planning, than on the actual expansion of demand. If we think that in 1985 Greece, the country in Western Europe with the lowest motorization level, had 188 vehicles per 1,000 people, one can easily understand the size of the potential market still unexpressed by the USSR and by the Eastern European countries, for which waiting times for a booked vehicle were measured by the years.[16]

During the second half of the 1980s the Soviet Government decided to exert a considerable acceleration in the motorization process. Many automobile firms were interested into the project. Among them there was Fiat, which had a long tradition of attention towards the USSR.[17] In fact the Italian company had demonstrated its technical and organizational capability during the development of the Togliattigrad plant. The agreement between the USSR government and Fiat was signed in November 1989, at the eve of the first visit by Head of State Mikhail Gorbaciov in Italy. The project initially entailed an investment of over 2,000 billion lire to develop a plant in Elabuga (about 500 km from Moscow) to manufacture a sub-compact car (segment 'B'), with 300,000 units per year. In the April of 1990 press releases announced that Fiat had also won the agreement to develop a citycar (segment 'A'), and was operating to get the project for a 'C' segment vehicle. With these increases the program should have reached an annual production volume of 900,000 vehicles, for an overall investment of about 5,000 billion lire. An important aspect lay in the organization of the agreement. Different from the development of Vaz of Togliattigrad, where Fiat participated as chief of order to develop the plant 'keys at hand' and to grant the production licenses, the Elabuga project was based upon a joint-venture which would have had Fiat participating for 30% of the equity, while the remaining 70% would have been controlled by Elaz, branch of the Soviet Ministry of the Automobile Industry.

Unfortunately the economic and political difficulties of the Soviet Union already in 1991 required a dramatic reduction in the project. The development of the 'A' and 'C' segment models was frozen, while the production of the 'B' segment model was moved to the Vaz plant. The further aggravation of economic conditions and the crisis of the Soviet regime led soon after to the final cancellation of the programme.[18]

So it vanishes one of the most important initiatives in Fiat internationalization strategy. Furthermore, the increase in production by about one million units, the project created the possibility to operate important decentralization in component manufacturing, with subsequent triangulation of supplies; the establishment of a considerable order portfolio for machine tools and production systems for Comau and for other Italian firms; and for the Soviet Union, a step towards other economic initiatives, such as industrial vehicle production and ground-moving machinery.

The list of vanished opportunities, for reasons independent from Fiat, includes also the Yugoslavian case. Also in this country the presence of Fiat dated back to years before, through the licensing to Zavodi Crvena Zastava for the manufacturing of some models (among which the '750', the '125', the '126', the '132') which had initiated in 1954. With a total population of 23 million in 1990, an internal production of 274,000 vehicles, a well developed technological level and a favourable logistics proximity, Yugoslavia had reawakened Fiat's interest, and of many others. For example SKF, the world leader in ball bearings manufacturing had acquired a plant in Yugoslavia to supply the probable automobile developments of that country. Fiat had initiated a negotiation to acquire a considerable share of Zastava, but even in that case the worsening of the political situation and the subsequent split of the country had blocked any programme of development.

Fiat Auto towards globalization: the 'Project 178'

Programme objectives

A very relevant step of the internationalization process took place in 1993 with the 'Project 178'. The reasons behind this project are the same as those theorised by the other automobile companies. The most part of the future motorization processes will involve developing countries located outside the 'Triad': Western Europe, North America and Japan. The motorization growth will not be given by exports as this can create insurmountable problems for the balance of trade. It becomes increasingly necessary to plan and produce vehicles specifically designed for these countries' end-user tastes and usage conditions in which vehicle will be operated.[19] The most part of future competitiveness of automobile makers will derive from the ability to build a 'matrix-type' manufacturing organization on a world-wide basis, able to match the advantages of better developed countries (high added value activities) with those of developing areas (high labour intensive activities).

The objectives Fiat Auto intended to achieve with 'Project 178' were numerous and interrelated:

- create a production process on world scale aiming not only at a single car, but at a family of models to suit the different needs of developing economies having a dynamic motorization process,[20]
- establish an organizational learning process so as to make a centralized product design in adherence to the market needs in various countries,
- take advantage of experience gained through establishing the green-field factory plant in Melfi (Italy) and its internal organization as a paradigm to apply to the various new plants made under 'Project 178' in a flexible and adaptive way,[21]
- ensure absolute standardization of each manufactured model version, even if planned for different markets, through a selection of suppliers and their involvement on international basis,
- to progressively organize a global procurement system which allows to use in a flexible way the manufacturing capacity installed in different plants within the '178' project and the suppliers' capability in order to feed with a *just-in-time* system the assembly lines located in different countries.

The Italian phase

The new model project came to its final stage with regards to style characteristics (internal and external), in the summer of 1993. At that point a 'platform-based' organizational structure, involving an external engineering company – IDEA Institute – was set up for style development. The platform was the result of the integrated expertise of every Fiat Auto departments involved in the development: Purchasing, Technology, Product Planning and Design, Administrative Control. Technicians were detached from production plants of Fiat Auto in order to report the specifics needs of product use and needs (Brazil, Argentina, Poland) and of all main suppliers.[22] In such way a simultaneous engineering process was started, involving over 200 people.

A characterizing aspect of this project was the fact that each component manufacturer was responsible for the supplies to all assembly plants: either through its own location, or, where the know-how and quality standards must be transferred and where a training for sub-contractors must be started, through a joint-venture with a company already operating in that particular country.[23] In the future there will be many warehouses supplying the different assembly plants world-wide through an optimization organized on many levels, co-ordinated by a satellite system[24] (a) the level of available production capacity, (b) the level of financial nature linked to currency fluctuations and different tariff barriers, (c) the level of co-ordination of parts of the logistics chain. This process of homogenization and integration on a world-wide basis will be completed with the suppliers' acquisition of ISO 9000 certification.

Some time later the platform has moved to the Fiat pilot-plant in Turin in the two South American countries. The specific feature of the '178' project lay also in the fact that the platform did not end its activity when production started (as it usually happens), but it will continue throughout the whole life-cycle of the product. The procedures of continuous improvement of product and operations management have to be absolutely homogeneous across all countries.

The Brazilian phase

In January 1996 at the Betim plant in the state of Minas Gerais (Brazil), production for Palio model started and its sales drive took off in April.[25] Production was co-ordinated by a computer processing system similar but more advanced than the one used in the Italian plant in Melfi. This system controls each phase of vehicle assembly, identifying all features for each car and synchronizes supplies to mass production stations by logistics flow from suppliers towards the plant and within the plant. The Palio is assembled by 140 modules which have been reduced to 100 with the pitch of the second version unveiled in 2000.

At Betim plant, a total of 38 robots were used from steel sheet stamping (presses are fed by robotic systems), to welding (almost totally automated), to painting (partially automated), to final assembly equipped with a system of body rotation in order to facilitate operations carried out behind the vehicle. Because of production increase tied to the Palio launch and exports, in 1996 a high rate of over 21,000 staff employment was recorded and a mass training programme by Fiat Automovéis was continued. This programme was oriented towards helping the application of 'Integrated Factory' system already applied in Italy, and called in Brazil as *'Fabrica Racionalizada'*.[26] It was based on improving of performances through work teams and suggestion systems.[27]

The launch of Palio had a great impact also in the upward and downward part of the *filière*.[28] Concerning distribution, further sales network increase was seen and moved from 297 dealers in 1989 to 435 in 1997. Sales expansion was even faster so the average dealer size (expressed in number of cars marketed) was considerably reinforced reaching over 1,100 units, which represents an interesting size.

For suppliers the picture looks more complex. On one hand there has seen a considerable reduction of direct suppliers to 200 for the complete model assembly line in Betim, but the suppliers located in the nearby Fiat plant have increased their capacity to supply the assembly lines with just-in-time techniques. Furthermore, with globalization programme in progress tied to 'Project 178' the rate of nationalization of component suppliers had sharply increased. For Palio it had exceeded 92%. Regarding this, the establishment of a strong group of component manufacturers located in the state of Minas Gerais, very close to the Fiat Auto plant in Betim, represented one of the most interesting aspects of the Brazilian Fiat introduction. In fact, Fiat Auto plant in Betim, over 500 km from Sao Paulo, the Brazilian automobile pole by tradition, was considered a mistake by most observers. Actually, Fiat Auto did not only attract an increasing nucleus of local suppliers, but they can now show to supply different automobile industries operating in Brazil or in South America. At the beginning the investments affected also Fiat operations in Venezuela where a new assembly line of Fiat Automoviles de Venezuela started since March 1997 with the target to assemble 20,000 units of the 'Palio' and 'Siena' models. Later this part of the programme has been cancelled in 1999 due to the economic crisis of the country.

The Argentinian phase

Fiat's decision to heavily invest in Argentina materialized in 1995.[29] A new plant in Cordoba for 'Palio' and 'Siena' was decided. This new plant imitates the Italian one in Melfi (but with a lower automated level) and was accomplished in only 18 months. In February 1996 installation of a new machinery took place and in December 1996 production started. The plant includes welding, painting and final assembly, whereas forging is outsourced. It deals with total product investment of total US$640 million of which US$500 million invested for product, with direct employment of 5,000 people and 15,000 indirect ones. The most mechanized areas are welding and painting.

Similarly to what was accomplished in Melfi, there is a 500,000 square metre plant for suppliers located next to the plant (1 km). A 130 million dollar investment is estimated for suppliers operating with supplies made with electronic *kanban* system as well as synchronous *kanban* controlled by a computer system.[30] Also, the plant is equipped with a 'distribution system' of components coming from far away plants from Brazil and other countries.

From an organizational point of view the Cordoba plant reflects the 'Integrated Factory' theory, based on a flat structure (5 hierarchy levels) and on employment of 'Elementary Technology Units' (UTE[31]), which brought a wide training programme of 40 million dollars,[32] the largest ever carried out in Argentina by a single enterprise.[33]

'Project 178': international integration

As it is widely known, the '178 Project' is sold in 32 countries and currently built in 7 countries: Brazil, Argentina, South Africa, Poland, Morocco, Turkey and India, while other initiatives have been defined in Russia, China and Egypt

(Table 6.1). In Poland production of models of the Palio family (Siena and Palio SW) has started in March 1997 in the Bielsko-Biala plant, but co-operation between Fiat and the Polish industry has been ongoing since 1921. The turning year has been 1993, when Fiat acquired 90% of FSM, and established Fiat Auto Poland.

In Morocco production of the Siena and the Palio started in autumn 1997 and June 1998 respectively, by the Moroccan company Somaca, that works as a façonist. Fiat won an international tender to manufacture and distribute a small segment car, launched by the Rabat Government in 1994. Fiat did win the tender against Renault, PSA and Daewoo, by proposing the production of two models of the 178 project, both with gasoline and diesel fuel.

In Turkey the Fiat initiative dates back to 1971, to the agreements between the Italian group and the Turkish Group Koç, which developed into the establishment of the Tofas company, operating in Bursa where many Fiat Auto models have been manufactured for a long time. Production of two versions of the Palio models started in March 1998.

In January 1998 Fiat Auto defined an agreement through Fiat Auto South Africa (FASA) with Nissan South Africa (NSA), which owns a plant in Rosslyn. The co-operation agreement provides that NSA will carry out the assembly of the Siena, Palio, Palio Weekend and Strada pick-up models. FASA is due to monitor quality levels, and to promote the development of the local component industry, of the distribution and after-sales chain and of logistics.

In India, Fiat Auto has already established Indauto, a joint-venture with Doshi, an Indian group owner of Premier Automotive Ltd with which the Italian group has had relationship for a long time to develop an assembly plant in Kurla for the Fiat Uno production. The Fiat Auto programme in India also envisages the incorporation of Fial, a company entirely controlled by Fiat Auto, which has a plant in Pune to produce Palio, Siena and Palio Weekend, with a product investment of $200 million. Production of 178 derived models has started in 1999 at the Kurla plant, and will then be transferred to the new Pune plant with an expected output of 85,000 cars a year in full regime.

In Russia, a joint-venture between Fiat Auto and the Russian Gaz was set up and called Zao Nizhe Gorod Motors, to establish a plant dedicated to production of Palio Weekend and Siena (besides Marea). Due to the Russian financial crisis, plans for reaching 14,000 units belonging to the 178 car family, originally programmed for 1999, have been frozen.

Fiat Auto is bringing its 178 project to China, Fiat Auto agreed in January 1999 to pay around $60 million for a 50% stake in a joint venture with Nanjing-based Yuejin Motor Corporation. The stake was previously owned by Malaysian investment group Lion Corporation. In this new joint-venture Fiat Auto initially provided technological expertise and than the partners have launch a commercial variation of the Palio world car (the Fiorino pick-up).

In Egypt Fiat established in 1998 a joint-venture with the Industrial Group Seoudi for the production of the Siena model. The operations started in 2000

Table 6.1 'Project 178': the international concept

Country	Interested enterprise	Production capacity	Models manufactured	Specific product investments (millions $)	Production start	Status
Brazil	Fiat Automovéis	391,000	Palio, Palio WE, Pick-up	560	Jan. 1996	In progress
Argentina	Fiat Argentina	127,000	Palio, Siena	180	Dec. 1996	In progress
Poland	Fiat Poland	46,000	Siena, Palio WE	70	May 1997	In progress
Morocco	Fiat Auto Maroc Somaca	24,000	Palio, Siena	30	Sept. 1997	In progress
Turkey	Joint-venture with Koç Group	114,000	Palio, Siena, Palio WE	165	Mar. 1998	In progess
India	Fiat Indauto (PAL)	85,000	Palio, Siena, Palio WE	200	Mar. 1999	In progress
Russia	Joint-venture with Gaz	110,000	Siena, Palio WE	205	To be decided	On standby
Egypt	Fiat Auto Egypt Seoudi Group	20,000	Siena	15	May 2000	In progress
South Africa	F.A.S.A. Nissan S.A.	33,000	Palio, Siena, Palio WE, Pick-up	50	Aug. 1999	In progress
China	Nanja Yuejin Motor	100,000	Palio CV	90	Mar. 2002	In progress

Source: Fiat Auto.

and at the end of 2001 the annual total production of this car was about 5,000 units.[34]

Fiat aimed at a cumulative production target of one million units of the Palio family cars in May 1999 but after the economic crisis occurred in South America and Turkey the cumulative figure has been reduced consistently.

The 178 Project encompasses five different models. Every model is manu-factured in an identical way in all plants, not just on the component stand-point, but also on the quality one, in order to obtain a production system able to allow flexibilization mechanism on a world-wide basis, through exchange of parts and finished vehicles

From a technical-engineering point of view, standardization started at the design level. In the pilot plant of Corso Orbassano in Turin there is a sort of 'Conservatory of weights and lengths' with the 'sample' parts. It dictates the product and manufacturing specifications to which all Fiat and supplier plants must conform to. Then there has been an intense effort of standard-isation on the suppliers' side. All suppliers of the '178 project' are world-scale suppliers which have committed to ensure total technical and qualitative consistency of components, irrespective of production sites.

Finally a key role is played by the organizational and cultural integration of employees. Besides a continuous exchange of personnel across the differ-ent areas, a video-conferencing system has been set up to discuss key devel-opment stages. It is one of the most relevant and complex aspects of the project. It is just worth noting the different time zones of the areas involved and the variety of the languages. With regards to recurrent technical com-munications a system of instant translation of electronic messages has been developed, so a supply order generated in Turkish language in Bursa (or in any other assembly centre) will be automatically translated and transmitted in the language of the receiving plant, be it Polish, Brazilian or Indian.

Accomplishment of this globalization strategy should get competitive results. First of all, strengthening of market penetration in the different interested areas. The importance of displaying a product specifically made for developing countries and availability of local output base have already given important market results.

A new relevant step: the alliance between Fiat and GM

General Motors is the largest automaker with an annual production (as of 2000) of over 8.5 million vehicles, equal to 15% of world production, with total employment of 386,000 units and turnover over $184 billion, 87% of which achieved in vehicle sales. Hence it stands out as the best positioned automaker from the international competitive perspective, to the point that its commer-cial presence is significant in all the main commercial areas, with market shares equal to: 26.7% in North America, 9.3% in Europe, 16.3% in the whole of Latin America, Africa and Middle East, and 3.7% in the Asia-Pacific zone.

However the General Motors giant seems to have lost part of its past dynamic attitude, and features some areas in which financial and economic results are not as brilliant as one would expect for such an automaker (for example in the USA) or they even record some losses (as Opel operating in Europe). From here the interest of Detroit managers to look for a partner in a new ambitious project of international reorganization.

The Fiat Group has undoubtedly even more important reasons to pursue an agreement capable of strengthening its competitive opportunities without resorting to more radical moves. After a few months of confidential contacts, the agreement has been made public, but still in the definition stage on 13 March 2000. The end of the juridical aspects of the agreement took place on 24 July of the same year and at that time priorities were set at the highest level, to be carried out as soon as the European Union authorized it, which took place on 16 August.[35] In such way already on 13 September it was possible to name the Board of Directors and the main Top Executives of two 50/50 joint companies between General Motors Corporation and Fiat Auto SpA.

These two companies in joint-venture, having a twin and mirror organization between the two mother companies, are GM-Fiat Worldwide Purchasing BV, with operational headquarters in Ruesselsheim, and Fiat-GM Powertrain BV with operational headquarters in Turin, whose structures started to officially operate on 1 January 2001. Such JVs play a role of considerable importance with respect to full manufacturing cost: in fact the weight of purchasing and manufacturing of the powertrain systems represents about 80 per cent of the whole vehicle manufacturing cost.

The alliance is geographically limited to South America and Europe. This is due to the fact that in North America there isn't presently any 'strategic room' for such initiatives, since GM does not suffer particular competitive pressures. Vice versa, South America represents a market which the industry competitors judge very relevant for its growth potential, while in Europe competition has become particularly strong and, in such sense, the alliance aims at achieving a cost leadership.

The main objective of the agreement, as for all the other mergers and acquisitions carried out in the automobile industry over recent years, is cost reduction: when such agreement operates at full pace it should allow the two companies to save on the whole $2 billion. In fact the motto of the agreement is: 'Allies in costs, competitors in the markets.'

The two partners highlight a significant saving deriving from the synergies in purchasing and in the convergence of engines and transmissions. It is significant that by adding Purchasing activities to Powertrain manufacturing one obtains on average 80 per cent of the total manufacturing cost of a vehicle, while the remaining 20 per cent corresponds to the activities of final assembly of the product.

This is the last step of Fiat towards globalization. According to the Italian Company the alliance is very rewarding for both partners, but of course a right assessment of the alliance' fruit requires more time. At the moment companies' declarations underlines that the alliance is paying off earlier and better than expected. For instance purchasing synergies produced savings of about 220 million euros during the 2001. These synergies are a key force in reducing product costs and are providing fresh momentum to the company's profitability improvement programmes.

Statistical appendix: Fiat Auto

Table A6.1   Fiat Auto production of cars, by countries, 1995–2000, 000s of units

Countries	1995	1996	1997	1998	1999	2000
Italy	1,531	1,430	1,674	1,528	1,534	1,530
Brazil	430	512	582	393	392	434
Poland	273	308	328	337	344	291
Argentina	–	–	96	93	43	34
Other countries	12	21	30	38	41	36
Total	2,246	2,271	2,710	2,389	2,354	2,325

Table A6.2   Fiat Auto sales by area, 1994–2000, percentages

Countries	1994	1997	2000
Italy	40.55	39.00	43.48
Rest of W. Europe	32.95	32.00	39.13
North America	0.06	0.01	0.01
South America	25.13	25.00	14.84
Rest of the world	1.31	3.99	2.54
Total	100.00	100.00	100.00

Table A6.3   Fiat Auto: selected data, 1996–2000

	1996	1997	1998	1999	2000
Net sales (millions of euros)	21,950	26,202	24,859	24,101	25,361
Net income (millions of euros)	39	402	−258	−493	−599
Investments (millions of euros)	1,677	1,341	1,373	1,464	1,412
R&D (millions of euros)	501	535	608	711	776
Cash flow (millions of euros)	1,469	2,068	1,146	855	732
Net assets (millions of euros)	6,244	5,992	5,863	5,021	4,220
Employees (units at end of the year)	116,144	118,109	93,514	82,553	74,292

Notes

1 See Volpato (1993).
2 Only the US market presented, at the beginning of the century, a size that allowed many firms to grow big enough to exploit economies of scale. See Federal Trade Commission (1939) and Rae (1972).
3 For more analytic elements, see Volpato (1993).
4 Agnelli (1971).
5 See Broustail and Greggio (2000).
6 Broustail and Greggio (2000) mention some organizational difficulties, but nothing insurmountable. Quite strangely, they completely ignore the political aspects of the *affaire*.
7 In 1972, Citroën manufactured 649,000 vehicles, compared to over 1.5 million for Fiat, to which other activities must be added.
8 Gianni Agnelli declared in 1978, during the annual Fiat meeting: 'Who manufactures 3 million vehicles per year is in an aggressive position. Who manufactures 2 million is fine. Who manufactures just one million survives'. A similar concept has been reported in many other interviews.
9 The most natural option for this kind of co-operation seemed to be the joint design and manufacturing of a family of transmissions with which to equip the vehicles of the two makes. Fiat and Ford had already co-operated previously to develop an automatic transmission ('Selecta').
10 During the same period there was talk of interest by Fiat towards BMW. In this case there would have been a problem of identity for the BMW brand, but on the design and manufacturing side the partnership would have basically been a 'sum' of the two companies.
11 One of the proposals examined entailed the distribution of the company capital as follows: 49% to Fiat, 49% to Ford, and the remaining 2% to the Paris merchant bank Lazard Frères. But, according to Ford, this outcome, seemingly neutral, would have in reality favoured Fiat, given the long-time relationship of the Agnelli family with the merchant bank.
12 Ford US had a participation in Mazda, a Japanese automaker that had financial and competitive difficulties stemming from its relatively modest size, but which had some interesting strengths (it was the only company to manufacture vehicles with rotary engines) it produces a sub-compact in Korea, a joint-venture between Ford and Kia.
13 Similar events occurring in important recent joint-venture initiatives have reaffirmed this issue. See the Renault–Volvo case, cancelled in its latest stages, and Rover–Honda, ended abruptly on the acquisition of Rover by BMW.
14 Among the reasons underlined by the specialized press at the time, in interpreting the failed acquisitions of Rover and Saab, there is also the concern about acquired companies losing their autonomy and identity. Interestingly, the acquisition of Rover by BMW appears to be marked by a willingness to maintain an absolute distinction between the two nameplates.
15 Eastern European countries in 1985 in which national automobiles were manufactured were the USSR with 1.2 million vehicles, followed by Poland and Yugoslavia with about 250,000 vehicles, the Democratic Republic of Germany with 200,000, and Czechoslovakia with 100,000.
16 According to what was declared by the minister for the Soviet automobile industry, Nikolai Pugin, in the mid-1980s, the waiting time for a car wholly paid for at the time of ordering, was between three and five years.

17   Fiat's strategy of attention towards the East began in 1912 (Russia) and continued in 1916 (Hungary) and in 1921 (Poland).

18   Russia has recently reopened negotiations to develop a sub-compact car. The most likely partner to develop an Opel model is General Motors.

19   In Brazil, for example, the road network covers approximately 1.8 million kilometres, but only 13% is paved.

20   Production concentrates on five models: a two-volume hatchback called the 'Palio'; an estate car, 'Palio Weekend'; a saloon, 'Siena'; a pick-up, 'Strada'; and a mini-van.

21   See Camuffo and Volpato (1998).

22   Some of these suppliers were responsible for producing custom-made components, and therefore worked in co-design.

23   Basically, every Project '178' supplier must become a 'global supplier'.

24   For example, three families of engines are expected, manufactured in Italy, Brazil and Argentina, respectively. Hence the engines will be supplied to all assembly plants, which in their turn will exchange body parts.

25   The first Betim plant was established in 1973. On Fiat's previous experience in Brazil, see Volpato (1996).

26   See Camuffo and Volpato (1998).

27   Between 1992 and 1996 over 80,000 ideas for improvement were presented, reaching an 85% rate of application.

28   See Balcet and Enrietti (1997).

29   Fiat's presence in Argentina goes back to the end of 1950s. Assembly slowed down with the 1973 oil crisis, and in 1982 stock control was handed over to the local Macri Group (Volpato, 1996).

30   Electronic *kanban* supply is a just-in-time supply system involving a particular quantity of identical components. Synchronous *kanban* is a supply system in which each component is specific (for example, seats of different colours) and despatched in an ordered way according to the specific sequence followed by the assembly line.

31   There are 18 UTEs, five in welding, four in painting, and nine in final assembly. For a detailed analysis of the UTE structure, see Camuffo and Volpato (1998).

32   Among other things, the investment has enabled the establishment of a permanent training centre for Fiat Auto Argentina staff as well as suppliers, distributors and service network as an important step to developing further forms of integration.

33   The economic crisis that hit Argetina at the end of 1998 seriously worsened in 2002. This is affecting Fiat operations in that country, and the company is considering stopping production in Córdoba in order to concentrate on assembly in Betim.

34   Fiat Auto held almost 20% of the Egyptian passenger-car market in 2001.

35   The European Commission release said: 'The Commission took the view that although Fiat and General Motors will coordinate on an exclusive basis their activities in the production of power-trains and in the purchasing of components and parts, the alliance should benefit consumers. The Commission noted components accounted for a large part of the cost of new cars, so any savings the two firm make should be passed on to the consumers.'

References

Agnelli, G. (1971) 'Relazione presentata alla XII Commissione Industria', in Camera dei Deputati, *Situazione e prospettive dell'industria automobilistica nazionale, Indagini conoscitive e documentazioni legislative*, no. 7, Rome.

Balcet, G. and Enrietti, A. (1997) 'Regionalization and Globalization in Europe: The Case of Fiat Auto Poland and Its Suppliers', *Actes du GERPISA*, no. 20, May.

Broustail, J. and Greggio, R. (2000) *Citroën. Essai sur 80 ans d'anti-stratégie*, Paris: Vuibert.

Camuffo, A. and Volpato, G. (1995) 'The Labor Relations Heritage and Lean Manufacturing at Fiat', *International Journal of Human Resource Management*, vol. 6, no. 4, December.

Camuffo, A. and Volpato, G. (1997) *Nuove forme di integrazione operativa: il caso della componentistica automobilistica*, Milan: F. Angeli.

Camuffo, A. and Volpato, G. (1998) 'Making Manufacturing Lean in the Italian Automobile Industry: The Fiat Trajectory', in M. Freyssenet, A. Mair, K. Shimizu and G. Volpato (eds), *One Best Way? Trajectories and Industrial Models of the World's Automobile Producers*. Oxford/New York: Oxford University Press.

Federal Trade Commission (1939) *Report on Motor Vehicle Industry*, 76th Congress, GPO, Washington.

Freyssenet, M., Mair, A., Shimizu, K. and Volpato, G. (eds) (1998) *One Best Way? Trajectories and Industrial Models of the World's Automobile Producers*, Oxford/New York: Oxford University Press.

Rae, D. G. (1972) *The American Automobile – A Brief History*, Chicago: University of Chicago Press.

Volpato, G. (1993) 'L'internazionalizzazione dell'industria automobilistica italiana', in *L'industria italiana nel mercato mondiale dalla fine dell'800 alla metà del '900*, Turin: Progetto Archivio Storico Fiat.

Volpato, G. (1996) *Il caso Fiat: una strategia di riorganizzazione e di rilancio*, Turin: Isedi.

Volpato, G. (1997) 'Nuove sfide di un settore in forte evoluzione', in A. Camuffo and G. Volpato (eds), *Nuove forme di integrazione operativa: il caso della componentistica automobilistica*, Milan: F. Angeli.

7
The Cautious and Progressive Internationalization of PSA Peugeot Citroën

Jean-Louis Loubet

'L'Afrique est Peugeot', 'Peugeot, King of Africa': these headlines, which appeared in the African press in 1975, did not just reflect an outstanding sports season, with Peugeot winning the African Triptyque, and the Bandama, Moroccan and Safari rallies.[1] They also saluted an automobile company, which at its height controlled almost a quarter of the African market. To achieve this, Peugeot first relied on its excellent reputation to build a second-hand market with international ramifications. But then there were powerful importers such as Kenya, state contracts signed with countries that had been thought to be closed, such as Algeria and especially Libya, assembly plants in South Africa where Peugeot has worked since 1950, another in Nigeria, and later in Ghana, Kenya and in the Maghreb. At the time all eyes were on Kaduna (Nigeria) where the workshops built in 1972 and 1975 constituted the first African automobile factory. With advertising slogans boasting that Peugeot manufactured 'the cars of Africa' or 'the Queens of the Track', it was more than just a brand image that was being created, rather the image of an international company that had become a multi-brand company in 1975. However, Peugeot Citroën had not waited until they were successful in Africa to think of the international market. The choices Peugeot and Citroën made in this regard go back further than that, and reveal almost a century of the foreign policy of French companies. With PSA Peugeot Citroën, a whole period of the internationalization of the French economy becomes clear.

The constraints of history

In the mid-1920s, the French financial world agreed that two of the three major automobile manufacturers had a policy of conquering foreign markets: Citroën and Peugeot.[2] While the slump faced by the French franc in 1926 saw Renault withdraw into the domestic market, Citroën and Peugeot continued their efforts abroad. For these two manufacturers, internationalization was firmly rooted in their culture. Armand Peugeot (1849–1915), an engineer from l'Ecole Centrale, finished his studies in Leeds at the height of the English Industrial Revolution, going on to learn the intricacies of the metallurgical industry. André Citroën (1878–1935), an engineer from l'Ecole Polytechnique, was open to Europe because of his Polish–Dutch roots, even though the continent showed no unity. He ignored borders as far back as the early 1900s, setting up subsidiaries for his gear company in Warsaw, Vienna, Berlin and Moscow. Peugeot also looked beyond borders because of its location at a crossroads between France, Switzerland and Germany. It took advantage of its privileged location at the heart of the Lotharangie Industrielle, which was already becoming a pivotal economic area for Europe. A pioneer of the automobile industry, Peugeot was one of those famous brands that could export its success. French pre-First World War cars were expensive and good quality, and found custom for the most part among the aristocracy and bourgeois business class, which was far more numerous in Germany, Great Britain or even in the United States than in France. The transition to mass production after 1918 changed nothing with regard to international outlook. Citroën, which negotiated financial aid from Ford, and later GM in 1919, was hoping to become the vital link for one of these two American companies in the whole European continent. And when Citroën went ahead on its own to organize the Javel factory to produce automobiles at a rate of first 300, then 500, a day it was still with the certitude of really penetrating the international market. In 1926, Peugeot was selling one in four automobiles abroad, and Citroën one in two.

This internationalization of the automobile relied first on exportation. For Citroën, the leading French manufacturer, the majority of its foreign sales were to ten European markets: Great Britain, Belgium, Italy, Spain, Switzerland, the Netherlands, Germany and the three Scandinavian countries. At the same time, they set up in the French colonies, notably in the Maghreb, where two subsidiaries were founded, one in Algiers (1925), and the other in Tunis (1927). Major exporting was slow to take off because of American competition. Nevertheless, Citroën reached South America, Australia and South Africa. For financial and fiscal reasons related to exporting, Citroën decided to switch to local assembly from 1925–6 onwards. In the space of five years, six assembly plants of varying sizes were founded. Slough (Great Britain) and Haren (Belgium) were the biggest, followed by Cologne (Germany) and Milan (Italy). They were relatively integrated with regard to the production of the body, but totally dependent on Javel for components and mechanical parts. In 1927, Citroën was assembling almost 16,000 cars abroad, representing 21% of its total production. Two workshops were set up, in Poland and Denmark, without any real success, however, the idea being to get around the protectionist measures enforced in 1930 and thereby appear to be a constructor and not a seller. This strategy was shared partly by Peugeot. Already present in European markets, Peugeot decided to embark on a policy of partnership in order to progress more quickly. In 1924, the company signed an agreement with Isotta

Fraschini to distribute automobiles and bicycles, with the aim of reaching 3,600 automobiles in 1926.[3] This agreement was largely responsible for the creation of a Peugeot subsidiary in Italy, and became a real strategy model, since one of its administrators negotiated agreements on a similar basis, for assembly in Great Britain, Germany and the United States. The USA, which gave so much to the French automobile industry, represented a market that Peugeot and Citroën imagined they could conquer. They had the same idea: to propose products that were not available in America. However, neither the Citroën Kégresse vehicles, nor the Peugeot Diesel engine, though sold to the Morgan Bank in 1922, succeeded in gaining a foothold in the market.[4] But Peugeot persisted, and in 1928 created the Peugeot American Corporation in Long Island, New York, to produce and sell 5CVs, a model then unknown in America. The American plant was intended to be an 'export platform' from which it was planned to break into the Canadian, Mexican and Cuban markets. In the same way, Peugeot toyed with two other projects for the new 201: an export platform for the Far East, in French Indo-China and another, bigger one, in South America. With this in mind, Peugeot set up a subsidiary in Buenos Aires to penetrate the markets in Argentina, Chili, Paraguay and Uruguay.

But the Great Depression of the 1930s could have called everything into question despite Citroën's unbounded optimism. In 1932, in the middle of the American Depression, it was affirmed at the Congress for Major Industries in New York that the future of the automobile industry lay in exporting: according to the experts, there were 107 countries in the world that could be considered big markets for automobiles if import taxes and other customs duties were not to curb trade. Citroën proposed that all its manufacturers set up an International Society for Automobile Exportation which would allow a million more vehicles a year to be sold and would at the same time reduce the price per vehicle by 2,000 French francs. This society would also commit itself to helping rich countries to dispose of their second-hand cars by selling them to poorer countries that would thus have access to automobiles. The creation of new markets would, in turn, feed consumption, as manufacturers would undertake to set up assembly plants as soon as a fleet of 100,000 cars was formed. But the reality proved to be totally different. Protectionist policies and the devaluation of the pound and the dollar made any international strategy impossible. Neither the first measures to promote exporting (1934), nor the devaluation of the franc (1936) changed things in France, all the more so since manufacturers agreed that an internationalization strategy would only be possible if the domestic market was solid and profitable.[5] However, the French depression was long and especially painful for Peugeot and Citroën. The former was saved by family solidarity (1930), and the latter thanks to the arrival of Michelin (1935). The strategies adopted by the two companies to ride the depression were quite similar: the new management teams formed during these difficult years believed that the company had to concentrate all its efforts on the domestic market, and to focus on that, even if it meant abandoning foreign projects.[6]

If initially management spoke of 'maintaining footholds in the principal world markets, but at a lesser cost', very soon exporting was no longer seen as 'a safety valve which allowed excess production to be sold'.[7] This development says a lot about projects that were in progress. Factories were closed down and sold one by one. Citroën kept two foreign workshops, in Slough and Haren, but with much reduced output: 2,334 automobiles manufactured in 1938, representing 3.4% of production. At the same time, the sales subsidiaries were frozen, which meant that all foreign activity had come to a halt by the end of the 1930s. The depression had got the better of internationalization strategies.

The contradictions of the thirty-year post-Second World War boom

With the new conditions that emerged with the period of Reconstruction, exporting once again became a major preoccupation. But, contrary to pre-war times when internationalization policies were the expression of company strategies, it was now decisions made by the public authorities that had more of an influence. Jean Monnet's *Plan de Modernisation de l'Equipement* (1946) envisaged a daring automobile exporting policy with the single aim of bring-ing currency into the country in order to contribute to the financing of the Reconstruction. Manufacturers did not have much choice in any case, as the domestic market was being held back by a range of fiscal and administrative measures and by a labour policy that was increasing the predominance of industry over consumption. Thanks to the fact that their industrial plant was intact after the war, and to their internationally recognized 11CV, Citroën became the leading French exporter, with 76.7% of its production being exported in 1946 and 89% in 1947. Handicapped by the ransacking of its fac-tories in 1944, Peugeot only resurfaced in 1947, but because of the reputation its 202 had for being a good solid car it was able to establish itself on the African and South American markets, exporting 50% to 60% of its production. However, success remained precarious: though cars sold very well in markets shaken by war, competition appeared after 1949 from English products, which though old were very cheap because of the devalued pound, and from German models that were also very attractive because of the underpaid labour force.

It seemed that exporting would be impossible to sustain in the long term: first, there were too many markets – Peugeot exported to seventy countries in 1947, which made investment in marketing very heavy to bear; and export-ing was so expensive that it was not profitable. Considering how slow it was for capital to be returned, difficulties with exchange, stocking of automobiles and parts, and the networks that needed to be financed, the marketing of a vehicle abroad needed four to five times more capital than for the sale of a vehicle in France. Worse again, to sell abroad, prices had to be slashed and profit margins given reduced. For Peugeot and Citroën, the competition between them and state-owned Renault became more pronounced. While a state company could take more financial risks, knowing that its shareholder would never fail it, a private firm could only increase exporting activities if its domestic market was solid and very profitable. It was profit made in France that allowed exporting to be financed. In 1948, as soon as the public authorities gave some breathing space to the domestic market, Peugeot and Citroën took their activities in hand again, starting by renewing links with the French networks that had been abandoned since 1939. Since profit, which was linked directly to the profitability and development of the domestic market, became their priority, and they inevitably turned their back on internationalization. This was all the more possible since domestic sales were booming, through the emergence of a mass market, and because consumption was growing much faster than production capacity. In 1955, a 403 Peugeot, which a French client had been waiting one year for brought in a profit of 15–20%. The same model, sold abroad, barely covered marketing costs. The fact that exporting was limited to 25% of production showed that the company was committed to making profit and willing to give up market shares that had recently been acquired.[8] The Pinay experience made manufacturers even more cautious because the absence of a devaluation crushed French competitiveness. Citroën and Peugeot only exported very small volumes to over 100 countries, to avoid the consequences of the collapse of one of the markets. Peugeot went even further, by banking on the complementary nature of the two hemispheres to compensate for seasonal sales. Between the caution displayed by Peugeot and Citroën on the one hand and the rashness of Renault on the other, which announced its intention in 1955 to export half of its vehicles, the opposition that separated the private and public sectors in France became apparent.

Nevertheless, the turning point came in 1957 with the signing of the Treaty of Rome. The creation of the EEC marked an irreversible change. Citroën remained in the rearguard, however, being the least in favour of the Europe that was formed by the politicians. The company would have preferred the EEC to be built around countries such as Spain, Portugal and Greece, which had few cars, rather than a zone dominated by manufacturing countries. Citroën's attitude could also be explained by the fact that its range of products was unsuited to the European specificity and to the constraints of exporting: the 2CV made no profit, while the DS was so expensive and so complex that it needed a very structured and costly after-sales service and could therefore only be profitable if impossibly large volumes were sold. For Peugeot, in contrast, European integration brought the opportunity to catch up on lost years by capturing neighbouring markets such as the Benelux countries, Switzerland and Germany, where its 403 had a good hold on the market.

The signing of the Ramadier Agreement, increased their efforts. The fact that manufacturers were obliged to export a maximum number of automobiles under the threat of being taxed more heavily, succeeded in stimulating exports. The short-lived success in the United States did not have the dramatic consequences that the collapse of Renault had, but helped the decision to build an international strategy steadily and without risk. At a time, between 1950 and 1960, when countries decided to ban importing in an effort to gain factories on their home ground, Peugeot and Citroën become involved. Very early on they both became interested in former British territories such as South Africa, Australia and New Zealand, where solid sales had encouraged them not to abandon these markets. But their industrial presence depended on their importers' money.

At the beginning of the 1960s, Europe was still a major preoccupation, often far from the official borders of the union: Citroën was in Spain (1958) and in Portugal (1963), Peugeot was in Belgium (1953) and in Ireland (1956). In the 1960s, Peugeot and Citroën, like all French manufacturers, was in Latin America, the most European of the distant continents. Both companies set up in Argentina, Chile, Mexico and Uruguay,[9] faring better than Simca but not as well as Renault, which built seven factories thanks to diplomatic[10] and financial[11] aid, which Pierre Bercot (1903–91), president of Citroën judged to be unfair. Unlike the state-owned company, which 'set up anywhere it found a roof',[12] Peugeot and Citroën were looking for trustworthy allies and local capital. Maurice Jordan (1899–1976), the director of Peugeot, was categorical: 'As long as I am present, we will never put a franc into a foreign factory...we are prepared to help all locals who defend themselves against their authorities'.[13] This explains the refusal to set up in Brazil, Spain, Israel and Japan. And even when the money was there, as was the case in Algeria following the Constantine Plan (1959), and public funds were flowing like water, Peugeot abstained from building a factory because 'quality standards' would not be met. A Peugeot, especially in Africa, was a car that must not go wrong. Ranging from the 203 (1948) to the 504 (1968), these models formed the backbone of automobile supply, whether they were imported from France by subsidiaries or introduced directly by their owners. It was at this time that Africa became the garden of Peugeot, the leading export market for spare parts, the kingdom of a product which was as much appreciated as a taxi as it was as an official car.

The internationalization of Peugeot and Citroën was clearly marked by the associative policies conducted by the two manufacturers. In April 1966, Peugeot and Renault formed an association involving purchases, manufacturing and R&D, an association that also later opened up partially to Volvo. Though commercial activity was forbidden in the Union, the two associates decided to join forces outside its borders. There was no question of joining commercial networks abroad, even if several examples of that existed, but more pressure to regroup and reorganize existing factories to render them complementary. Peugeot thus benefited from the experience of the state company at the level of international and banking relations. In the longer term, the two manufacturers answered all international calls for bids in the name of the Association Peugeot–Renault, especially in South Africa, Australia, Canada, Chile, Greece, Madagascar and Peru. In that case, each of the manufacturers was able to use its influence to support its partner.

That is what Peugeot did to defend the position of Renault in South Africa, and what Renault did for Peugeot in Algeria, and particularly in the Soviet Union, where their association was at the heart of the co-operation agreements of 1966. Overall, the result was positive, since they both managed to put down roots in markets that had been difficult before that time. In another co-operative venture, Citroën joined with Fiat in October 1966. It was a difficult step towards internationalization in the sense that Fiat wanted to make Citroën a satellite brand in the image of Autobianchi, while Michelin wanted equality between the two firms. Despite this tension, however, exchanges began to take place: on a commercial level, the Citroën and Autobianchi networks came together to help each other sell their cars. It was an opportunity for Citroën, which was too isolated in France and in Europe. On a technical level, studies were launched to build jointly a commercial vehicle and a small car, using the Fiat 127 as a platform. With one good year and one bad year, by the end of the thirty-year post-war boom, Peugeot and Citroën had managed to take on a less national dimension. While Renault was exporting 50% of its production by 1959, Citroën managed the same in 1970 thanks to the GS, its first medium-sized car, and Peugeot in 1974 thanks to a range which was completed in 1975. Although it came late, this evolution was fundamental to Peugeot: in 1973 the management sought to set up their third assembly plant, not in France, but in Asia – or to be more secure, in Brazil, to feed the local markets and re-import cheaper products to Europe. This project came to a halt with the first petrol crisis.

The upheavals wrought by the petrol crises

Between 1974 and 1978, the Peugeot Group experienced the most profound change in its history. With the recovery of Citroën, and then the purchase of Chrysler's European subsidiaries, PSA chose external growth to bring itself up to the level of the world's biggest automobile manufacturers. With this change of course, PSA for the first time displayed a real international outlook:

> Up against a very concentrated American automobile industry, a Japanese industry which adds particular socio-cultural assets to the dimension of its company, which benefits from a protected domestic market and an undervalued yen, the European industry appears dispersed and vulnerable with seven major manufacturers, little standardized production and an insufficiently concentrated industrial plant.

PSA aimed to become the leading European manufacturer, which was a prerequisite in their opinion for fighting world competition. At the head of PSA, but not an originator of this strategy, Jean-Paul Parayre, a graduate of L'Ecole Polytechnique and former top civil servant, organized the overall coherence. Citroën contributed little at the international level: besides two plants in Spain and Yugoslavia which offered Peugeot the possibility of avoiding local protectionism, they eventually had double factories in South America and South Africa, and the one in Belgium did not appear to be very useful. On the other hand, Chrysler Europe had great potential despite the outdated, indebted and unproductive British and Spanish factories. Chrysler bought 6% of the European market with well structured commercial plants and formidably efficient, financial logistics based in Geneva, similar to Renault's creation in Switzerland in 1963[14]. For the first time, PSA found itself at the head of a real international structure, gaining a foothold in Northern Europe, complementing its private African garden with a pole in Iran for major exportation, and with great hopes of the United States.

During the turning point of the years 1970–80, PSA organized its internationalization, attaching each automobile division to its own few regions: Peugeot obviously counted on exporting to the African and South African markets, but also to the United States. Citroën took on Eastern Europe, while keeping up its links with the Iberian peninsula. Chrysler Europe, which had become Talbot, became a real asset for PSA in Northern Europe, and the United Kingdom, Europe's second market, which had never been great for Peugeot or Citroën. Between 1976 and 1980, several agreements were made. In 1976, Citroën began to co-operate with a Romanian company called OLTCIT to set up a factory that was to produce 130,000 Axel models a year, half of which would be re-imported to the EEC. In 1978, Citroën started a joint venture to make constant-velocity universal joints (1.6 billion French francs per year), and then made links with PSA's Fiat. Several projects were launched: the joint use of factories to make commercial vehicles (Pomigliano d'Arco, 1980) and later to make monospaces (Valenciennes, 1994); joint research for a small car that could be mass produced at a very moderate price; and uniting the Peugeot and Fiat subsidiaries in Argentina in an effort to support Peugeot, whose reputation there was just as exceptional as it was in Africa.[15] In its favourite continent Africa, Peugeot continued with its large markets in Libya, while developing a factory in Nigeria (Kaduna) where 66,600 vehicles were manufactured in 1979. Growth was such that Kaduna had to supply Africa and the Middle East while waiting for the project in Iran to be completed (1977). Peugeot was preparing to produce 100,000, 305 models in addition to the 70,000 Talbots assembled in CKD.

Last of all there was America, where Peugeot finally hoped to fulfil its dream of becoming establish there. Since 1976, the sale of the Diesel had been going so well that several brands were showing an interest in Peugeot. In 1977, AMC proposed its distribution network in exchange for the sale of its Jeeps in Europe … and a few million dollars to absorb its debt. PSA allowed Renault to raise the bids, being well aware that it would be a bad move, and that, moreover, they had been conducting top-secret negotiations with Chrysler since 1976! Buying Chrysler's European subsidiaries was just the tip of the iceberg. This operation, which was financed with

US$230 million plus the transfer of 15.5% of PSA's capital, was organized with the aim of making Chrysler, along with the Peugeot and Michelin families, one of the group's stable shareholders.[16] This choice was accompanied by a major project between Chrysler and PSA to collaborate in the domains of industry, commerce and finance. We shall mention only the essential sixteen, that is to say, besides the hope of jointly developing a small car, there was the sale of Peugeot diesel engines to Chrysler, co-operation in the exchange of components, and before long Chrysler helped Peugeot to distribute up to 50,000 mid- and top range models per year.[17]

However, all Peugeot's hopes were dashed with the global crisis that marked the 1980s. PSA was not only hit badly by the failure of the Talbot brand, but its whole foreign strategy also encountered a series of setbacks which added to the difficulties of the group. This failure happened in two stages. At the beginning of the decade, it was the situations in Romania, Argentina and the United States that shook the group. In Romania, a country damaged by incompetent administration, the OLTCIT factory was brought into service one year late despite the 310 million French francs-worth of material which had been brought in. When the first vehicles were finally produced (November 1981), they no longer made any sense for the European market. From that point on, no matter how things developed, Peugeot viewed the Romanian experience as a failure.

In Argentina, the situation was much more serious, as it was costing much more: losses of one billion French francs because of a catastrophic economic situation which the directors did not hesitate to compare to 'Germany in 1923 with its relentless pursuit of the same monetary policy despite the evidence' (see Note 7). An urgent decision was made to close down in Argentina as quickly as possible, despite a cost of US$400 million.[18]

Finally, the last disappointment, were the American projects. Undermined by the crisis, Chrysler procrastinated, agreeing to order engines from Talbot and transmission joints from Citroën but excluding 'little' Peugeot, to the advantage of a project with Mitsubishi, which was much less costly. This proved to be the point at which the French automobile was not competitive, with the two groups descending one after the other into a spiral of difficulties. The decrease in sales added to financial losses and debt, causing PSA to announce 'the worst results of the whole history of the company' (see Note 7). Faced with this adversity, PSA was saved, however, by its exports. In fact, it was exports to Libya and the Gulf, as well as production in Nigeria and Iran, that brought in the saving dollars. By billing its cars in dollars, PSA benefited from the spectacular rise in the green note, which was worth more than 10 French francs in 1985. But nothing could ever be taken for granted. While the company started major restructuring thanks to Jacques Calvet, it was the very countries where exporting had been going well that in turn began to slump. Importing to Libya came to a halt in 1983. In Iran, the lack of currency saw Peugeot's production go from 87,900 cars (1983) to 6,900 (1987). In Nigeria, austere political measures which caused prices to triple almost brought about the closure of Kaduna: 61,300 vehicles in 1983; only 1,900 in 1987. In the three cases, the drop in the price of petrol was a determining factor, underlining the fragility of countries that had counted exclusively on this black gold, but also the vulnerability of companies whose international strategy was not sufficiently diversified.

The difficult revival of internationalization

Would internationalization be sacrificed with the restructuring of PSA? This is what one could have thought, with the sale of the Argentinian business to Fiat, but in particular with the closure of numerous factories, as in South Africa (Citroën and Peugeot), Belgium (Citroën), Scotland (Peugeot), Morocco (Citroën), Romania (Citroën) and Yugoslavia (Citroën). To enable Peugeot and Citroën to survive the crisis they were in, they focused on the French factories. They were supported directly by three complementary industrial centres, all located in the European Union – Spain (Vigo and Villaverde), Italy (Sevel) and Great Britain (Ryton). This European ensemble worked coherently for the European countries that became the basic markets for PSA from 1980 onwards. This withdrawal into the old Continent can be explained by the history of the time: the slump between 1980–4 almost saw PSA disappear, with accumulated debts of 8.5 billion FF. This inevitably left its mark. With the strengthening of financiers at the head of the business, PSA rejected any dangerous operations and balked at the idea of getting involved in a new internationalization policy, which was intrinsically a factor of risk.[19] This was all the more understandable in that the European markets remained buoyant until 1989. But was this satisfactory? With 88% of sales made inside Europe, PSA remained too focused on a market that represented only 32% of world potential.

With the globalization of the economy it was no longer enough to be a European manufacturer. PSA wondered if it should forget its doubts and go ahead with an international policy far from its home base, which remained inaccessible at the time. To sell in Nigeria or in Iran, PSA was confronted with almost insurmountable constraints: it had to organize clearing agreements, notably petrol barters with German, English or French companies in order to first convince the French banking pool and then the Nigerian and Iranian central banks, without which the COFACE and the ECGD would refuse any cover for exports.[20] Without breaking with their traditional markets, PSA decided, under the impetus of Jacques Calvet, to turn towards Asia, a continent the group had neglected before that time. With rich countries, such as Japan and Malaysia, others with considerable potential, such as China and India, Asia was a territory of contrast that would be difficult to conquer. Considering that some markets were protected and others so untouched that everything needed to be built up from scratch, it seemed that it would be attempting the impossible for Peugeot to break into these countries. In 1986, PSA picked up its activity in Malaysia again, with Peugeot and then Citroën, which linked up with Proton. In Japan, Peugeot signed distribution contracts with Suzuki (1988) and Inchcape (1989), and Citroën with Mazda and Seibi (1989), planning to reach annual volumes of 30,000 and 20,000 vehicles, respectively. What great optimism![21] In China, projects were more difficult because of the ever-present and incompetent administration. Unlike Japanese and American manufacturers (and Peugeot), Citroën did not choose to install old equipment to assemble outdated models. In 1985, it proposed to set up two factories in order to produce the ZX for 1992–4. In 1995, the project expanded, as the Chinese agreed to see the capacity increase from 40,000 to 150,000 vehicles per year, so long as the necessary capital could be found. However other problems remained: selling was difficult in a country without a sales network or consumer credit. As for Peugeot, its old 504 and 505 models were not popular. Having supplied the Arabic and African markets, these were stopped at the same time as the factory in Canton (1997) in which Chinese manufacturers showed little interest. Would projects in Asia work out for Peugeot? That same year, Peugeot closed the factory in India two years after its opening as it found that the Doshi family was not a solid financial partner, nor was it able to find good quality sub-contractors, or to come to terms with a staff that was buttressed by acquired social benefits, the remnants of British colonization.

The great leap forward

In just a few years, this situation full of contrasts has developed distinctly. Now ranked at sixth place among car manufacturers in the world, and second in Europe, PSA Peugeot Citroën is getting a taste of real success. Its sales rose by 11.7 % in the year 2000, giving 5% of the world's market to the two makes. It's a record and all the more so, since the group accomplished it alone at a time when all the competing makes were busy trying to find world consolidating strategies. Many reasons explain PSA's success: as well as the return of development and of growth markets which made Peugeot 206, Citroën Xsara Picasso[22] and HDI engines[23] a resounding success, a new international policy must also be mentioned, the aims of which became one of the main ideas in the strategy developed by Jean-Martin Folz in 1997. This consists of aiming at a strong industrial or commercial presence abroad in order to launch into a prolonged growth that Western Europe is no longer able to offer even at times of prosperity, because of glutted markets. The future of this group therefore lies in internationalization, which implies making room for industrial and commercial means, and not forgetting human and financial ones too (see Table 7.1). The latter point had been considered a secondary matter for a long time, but has recently been taken into account in the management, that targets the internationalization of carriers, whether those of the directors who are to run the new factories and branches in the world, or the carriers concerning transferred skills.

Table 7.1 PSA Peugeot Citroën: sales outside Western Europe, 1998–2000

	1998	1999	2000
Peugeot	227,500	240,000	324,000
Citroën	131,000	122,000	157,000
PSA Group	358,500	362,000	481,000

Note: Private and light commercial cars.

Source: PSA activity reports 1998, 1999 and 2000.

PSA is already present in more than 140 countries, and has chosen to favour international markets where European-style cars are sold. This choice can be explained by the desire to optimize the industrial platform policy at the same time as reinforcing the strategy of localized and committed co-operation of the group in different areas.[24] Following this double logic, PSA has launched itself vigorously into a conquest of two specific regions: the CEEC area (Central Europe and Eastern Countries), and the Mercosur area in Latin America.[25] The CEEC area represents enormous potential: in 1999, PSA made a 26% progress on markets, rising by 8%. In the year 2000 the penetration rate was at 6%, representing nearly 110,000 sales. For these kinds of achievements, Peugeot and Citroën rely on local partners who develop important commercial support. For example, they have worked hand in hand since the late 1990s in Eastern European countries such as Poland, with great success – and recently in Croatia, Slovenia (2000), Estonia, Russia and Ukraine (2001). This strategy helps to constitute very precise structured sales networks, and exclusive and sometimes wholly owned subsidiaries, in order to envisage commercial conquests, but also to build centres capable of resisting possible turnaround circumstances. This is proof that internationalization is considered to be a long-term phenomenon. By the beginning of the twenty-first century, Peugeot and Citroën already had a large commercial penetration (more than 5% everywhere), which has given the two makes international recognition, especially in the CEEC area. The short-term target is fixed at around 7% to 8% of these markets for the year 2003.

The investment achieved in Mercosur (the second main area of conquest), is at the same time similar and different. Although the commercial commitment, built on recent European models, is the same as in Central and Eastern Europe, different means have been used: the setting up in South America relies on many local production units, whereas the CEEC markets are only provided by French, English and Spanish companies. This choice is linked directly to the creation of Mercosur, which liberalizes South American commerce and taxes importation heavily. The PSA Peugeot Citroën's approach was made in two stages: in July 1997, it opened its capital factory in Buenos Aires (Sevel Argentina), with most of the action taking place in

1998, and becoming the owner of 99.6% of the factory with a take-over bid in December 1999. In 2001, Peugeot Citroën Argentina Ltd assembled a whole range of vehicles: Peugeot 206, 306, 405, Partner and Citroën Berlingo. The company became the first national automobile producer (70,000 vehicles in 2000), exporting 33% of the total to Mercosur, especially to Brazil, but also to South Europe (the Partner and Berlingo models). At the same time as this Argentinian conquest, in 1997 PSA started building a factory in Brazil – at Porto Real in the state of Rio de Janeiro. Ready for use in December 2000, the factory opened its doors in February 2001 with the launch of the Citroën Picasso, the Peugeot 206 (voted car of the year 2000 in Brazil) following in April. In December, production reached 300 vehicles per day. Once again, PSA is focusing on a range of co-operations. The group benefits from the local sub-contracting that already exists between Sao Paulo, Rio de Janeiro, Bello Horizonte and Ford, Fiat, GM and VAG. But it focuses more on a town with high-tech industrial research facilities, able to deliver 60% of supplies in strained or synchronized flows. Porto Real's high-tech facilities are unique: the grounds around the PSA factory were offered free of charge to the suppliers of the joint ownership. Each of these: Faurecia, Vallourec, Magnetto Eurostamp, Gefco and so on, is free to build a factory and even to work with the other idustrialists. The Porto Real factory is very productive: it benefits from the latest range of investments in the organiza-tion flow, the setting up of short, hierarchical lines of action, and a cheap workforce which works in two teams (three in 2004) over six days a week. As far as the financing of the project goes (US$600 million),[26] since its begin-ning PSA has been able to rely on local help and participation, especially from the state of Rio de Janeiro and the Monteiro Aranha group, who will eventually be able partly to control a business that is at present controlled 68% by the group and 32% by the state of Rio.[27] The Mercosur project is ambitious and already showing signs of success: PSA is ranked in first place among the automobile distributors in Argentina, covering 16.1% of the mar-ket, helped enormously, it is true, by the excellent reputation of Peugeot, firmly fixed in the national automobile landscape since 1965. In Brazil, a completely new market for PSA is making fast progress, covering 2.2% of sales in 2000 (30,600 vehicles). The aim is to reach 100,000 vehicles, based on the rate of growth of Porto Real and on the development of two Peugeot and Citroën networks, equipped with 200 and 90 sales outlets, respectively. With factories in Argentina, Brazil and a further one in Uruguay, PSA is hoping for an 8% penetration on the Mercosur markets around 2003–4. Obviously, South America represents, along with Central and East Europe, the two most promising areas of future business for the Group. However, they are not the only ones, as many other markets presenting opportunities are at hand.

Among future markets, Turkey and Iran are choices that have been considered in depth by Peugeot and Citroën. And once again we come across strategies mentioned earlier: a European range of recent products and a policy based on building partnerships with local industries. In Turkey, PSA works with the group Kiraça, a company that has been assembling Peugeot cars since 1979. The factory, which was purpose built to assemble the company vehicle J9, is now assembling Peugeot Boxers and Partners; it was being renovated in 2001 at a cost of US$75 million, in order to reach a capacity of 40,000 vehicles per year. Development prospects are good thanks to a national market that exceeded 600,000 units in the year 2000. This situation made it possible for Peugeot to import the 206, which represented 30% of its market segment in 2000. In this part of the world, PSA is relying on a second market of opportunities in Iran. This is a country where the company managed to keep a hold despite serious internal economic difficulties. PSA has been tied to two Iranian companies for sometime: Iran Khodro (Peugeot, 1977; Talbot, 1978) and Saipa (Citroën, 1968), and PSA is now on its way to collecting the benefits of its patience. The contracts for the assembly of the 205 and 405, signed after the withdrawal phase of the 1980s, remained consistent at a rate of 200 Peugeot 405s a day. Today, the figure is being doubled with the launch of the Citroën Xantia, and in particular the Peugeot 206, for which the agreement to assemble 120,000 units was confirmed in December 2000.[28] In 2002, PSA should be on its way to providing more than 40% of Iranian automobile production, through these two makes.

Only China remains, representing a major element in Citroën's international strategy. Citroën, with its two strong factories at Wuhan (assembly) and Xiangfan (instruments), has a powerful industrial instrument at its disposal, capable of reaching very competitive prices thanks to a rate of integration of around 90%. But in order to capture the remaining 10% (8.5% gained in 2000 compared to 7.8% in 1999), Citroën has had to expend a lot of effort. Concerning the offer, the ZX (renamed the Fukang), has been made into a three-bodied vehicle with a boot at the rear to meet the needs of the rising taxi market. In 2001, the factory started making the Picasso mini-van model. This is a real gamble considering the difficulty that products with a difference have of being accepted. However, Citroën has an advantage: 400 car distributors (in 241 towns) with one of their tasks being to participate in the development of consumer credit. This willingness to launch new ideas ensures the company's credibility at the same time as controlling an integrated factory (and therefore being logically autonomous) in which the group owns only 26% of the shares. This explains the need to participate in raising capital in 2001 in order to carry out the second part of the project: the release of new models stimulates the market and enables the company to manage a joint venture. It is with this same logic that PSA has already started preparing its comeback in India, with a new model and a strong partner. This is the price of assertion of the internationalization, and of its success.

Jean-Martin Folz clearly quantified this success when announcing the group's results for the year 2000. He also took advantage of this occasion to prepare the ground for the coming years: the aim is to reach 3 million by

2003, and 3.5 million by 2004. PSA Peugeot Citroën must gain at least 10% of sales in every EEC country (except Germany) and sell 800,000 vehicles outside West Europe. That means 25% of sales: 200,000 in the EEC countries, the same amount for the Mercosur area, and 80,000 in China.[29] The international relationship is more than just the key to success, it is also the condition for growth and the durability of the group.

Translated by Eunice Nyhan and Natalie Holding

Statistical appendix: PSA Peugeot Citroën

Table A7.1   PSA Peugeot Citroën, 1973–2000

Year	Production[1]	Exports[2]	Employees[3]	Turnover[4]	Profits[4]
1973	765,930	365,922	60,645	9,024	215
1974	730,770	401,264	58,735	9,920	52
1975	659,777	–	58,565	11,820	110
1976	1,437,800	670,000	176,500	35,066	1,428
1977	1,568,400	810,000	184,500	41,885	1,251
1978	1,665,300	843,100	190,170	47,810	1,382
1979	2,310,400	1,356,800	263,000	71,034	1,800
1980	1,961,000	1,160,300	245,000	71,103	−1,504
1981	1,716,000	1,003,000	218,000	72,389	−1,993
1982	1,602,600	895,700	206,000	75,263	−2,148
1983	1,680,600	933,100	203,000	85,207	−590
1984	1,600,000	877,700	187,500	91,111	−341
1985	1,630,800	902,000	176,800	100,295	543
1986	1,707,100	951,800	165,000	104,946	3,590
1987	1,901,100	1,037,100	160,600	118,167	6,709
1988	2,080,700	1,201,500	158,100	138,452	8,848
1999	2,232,500	1,251,200	159,100	152,955	10,301
1990	2,208,200	1,276,800	159,100	159,976	9,258
1991	2,062,900	1,283,700	156,800	160,171	5,526
1992	2,049,800	1,306,700	150,800	155,431	3,372
1993	1,751,600	1,186,700	143,900	145,431	−1,413
1994	1,989,800	1,255,200	139,800	166,195	3,102
1995	1,887,900	1,164,100	139,900	167,913	1,703
1996	1,979,000	1,267,900	139,100	178,858	734
1997	2,078,000	1,513,600	140,200	186,785	−2,768
1998	2,269,300	1,612,500	157,300	221,439	3,178
1999	2,496,000	1,747,300	165,800	247,999	4,780
2000	2,878,000	1,982,900	172,400	289,808	8,612

Notes: Growth through acquisition means that it is not possible to make precise comparisons for the period before 1979. From 1973 to 1975, the statistics refer to Peugeot, and from 1976 to 1978 to PSA Peugeot Citroën, including the Chrysler subsidiaries.

1. Passenger cars, commercial cars, and light trucks. World production.
2. Exporting, including foreign production.
3. World employees.
4. Turnover is pre-tax, and profits are net; in millions of French francs (at the time of writing, 1 franc = US$0.15).

Source: PSA annual management reports.

Notes

1 The victory of the racing drivers Mäkkinen (Bandama), Anderson (Safari) and Mikkola (Morocco).
2 Credit Lyonnais archives, from the Banque de l'Union Parisienne et de Lazard (Citroën archives).
3 1,200 cars and 5,000 bicycles in 1924; 2,400 cars and 10,000 bicycles in 1925; 3,600 cars and 15,000 bicycles in 1926 (Peugeot archives).
4 Citroën crawler track vehicles, Kégresse licence.
5 1.5 francs per kilo.
6 Peugeot: Jean-Pierre Peugeot and Maurice Jordan; Citroën: Pierre Michelin and Pierre Boulanger.
7 Peugeot archives: Board of Directors of Automobiles Peugeot or PSA.
8 20% for Citroën between 1953 and 1958.
9 Citroën: Chile (1959), Argentina (1960); Peugeot: Mexico (1960), Argentina (1961), Uruguay (1962) and Chile (1964).
10 Pierre Bercot (1977).
11 It was to manage its international policy efficiently that Renault received its first state grant in 1963.
12 Citroën Board of Directors.
13 Maurice Jordan, quoted by Jean-Louis Loubet (1990a).
14 Renault Holding and Renault Finance (Loubet, 2000).
15 After the closure of the Citroën plants.
16 For further details, see Loubet (2001).
17 Peugeot sold 1,800 vehicles in the United States in 1980.
18 Resale of Sevel Argentina to Fiat.
19 Jacques Calvet is the former President of BNP. Jean-Bernard Guillebert, Daniel Hua and Léopold Jeorger belong to Société Générale.
20 COFACE for French CKD; ECGD for CKD in Stoke (Great Britain).
21 The maximum was reached by Peugeot in 1989, with 7,800 vehicles imported to Japan.
22 Throughout the year 2000, sales of Peugeot 206 and Citroën Xsara progressed by 30% and 50%.
23 High pressure diesel engines.
24 The main short-term co-operations are with Renault (engine V6 and automatic transmissions), Fiat (company cars and minivans), Ford (range of diesel engines).
25 On 26 March 1991, Argentina, Brazil, Paraguay and Uruguay signed the Asunsión treaty, creating the common market of South Cone (or Mercosur) to which Chile and Bolivia joined.
26 This is the global cost of the setting up of PSA in Brazil which made the creation of a company necessary – Peugeot Citroën do Brasil. The high-tech developed town of Porto Real represents an investment of US$50 million.
27 PSA has a factory able to make 14,000 units a year, assembling Citroën Xsaras and Peugeot 306 estate cars.
28 The local integration rate is worth 50% the value of the 206 (the XR model with air-conditioning), including the elements of the gearbox, the engine and interior equipment.
29 In Germany, the group is aiming at 6.5% of the market by 2004, thanks to an offer which corresponds better with the demand and a reorganization of Peugeot and Citroën networks.

References

Bercot, P. (1977) *Mes années aux usines Citroën*, Paris: La pensée universelle.

Boyer, R. and Durand, J. P. (1993) *L'après-Fordisme*, Paris: Syros.

Bricnet, F. and Mangolte, P. A. (1990) *L'Europe automobile, virages d'une industrie en mutation*, Paris: Nathan.

Broustail, J. and Greggio, R. (2000) *Citroën. Essai sur 80 ans d'antistratégie*, Paris: Vuibert.

Caracalla, J. P. (1990) *L'aventure Peugeot*, Paris: Denoël.

Célérier, S. (1993) *La machine humaine, un flux de fabrication et ses gestionnaires*, Céreq, no published.

Ciavaldini, B. and Loubet, J. L. (1995) 'La diversité dans l'industrie automobile française. Hésitations et enjeux. Regards croisés de l'Historien et de l'Ingénieur', *Annales des Mines, Gérer et Comprendre*, December..

Coriat, B. (1991) *Penser à l'envers, travail et organisation dans l'entreprise japonaise*, Paris: Christian Bourgeois.

Dalle, F. (1984) *Rapport sur l'industrie automobile française*, Paris: Imprimerie Nationale.

Fontaine, P. (1980) *L'industrie automobile en France. Notes et études documentaires*, Paris: La Documentation française.

Freyssenet, M., Mair, A., Shimizu, K. and Volpato, G. (eds) (1998) *One Best Way? Trajectories and Industrial Models of the World's Automobile Producers*, Oxford/New York: Oxford University Press.

Gandillot, T. (1992) *La dernière bataille de l'automobile européenne*, Paris: Fayard.

Garçon, A. F. (ed.) (1998) *L'automobile, son monde et ses réseaux*, Rennes: Presses Universitaires de Rennes.

Jemain, A. (1982) *Michelin, un siècle de secrets*, Paris: Calmann-Lévy,

Jemain, A. (1987) *Les Peugeot. Vertiges et secrets d'une dynastie*, Paris: J.-C. Lattès.

Loubet, J. L. (1979) *La Société Anonyme André Citroën, étude historique, 1924–1968*, Thèse de Doctorat d'Histoire, University of Paris X Nanterre.

Loubet, J. L. (1988) 'Le modèle moyen chez Peugeot', *Histoire, économie et société*, no. 4, December.

Loubet, J. L. (1990a) *Automobiles Peugeot, une réussite industrielle, 1945–1974*, Paris: Économica.

Loubet, J. L. (1990b) 'Quand les constructeurs automobiles découvrent l'exportation', *Revue française de gestion*, no. 79, July–August.

Loubet, J. L. (1992) 'Le modèle automobile français. 1934–1973', *Culture technique*, no. 25, October.

Loubet, J. L. (1994) 'PSA Peugeot Citroën, 1973–1992. Histoire d'un groupe automobile dans les années de crise', *Actes du GERPISA*, no. 10, April.

Loubet, J. L. (1995, 2000) *Citroën, Peugeot, Renault et les autres. Soixante ans de stratégies*, Paris: Le Monde Éditions, 1995; new edition: *Citroën, Peugeot, Renault et les autres. Histoire de stratégies d'entreprises*, Boulogne: ETAI, 2000.

Loubet, J. L. (1996a) 'Les trois France de l'automobile', *Enjeux-Les Échos*, no. 118, October.

Loubet, J. L. (1996b) L'industrie automobile', française d'une crise à l'autre', *Vingtième siècle*, October–December.

Loubet, J. L. (1998a) 'Citroën et l'innovation', *XX ° siècle*, no. 57, January–March.

Loubet, J. L. (1998b) 'Peugeot meets Ford, Sloan and Toyota', in M. Freyssenet, A. Mair, K. Shimizu and G. Volpato (eds), *One Best Way? Trajectories and Industrial Models of the World's Automobile Producers*, Oxford/New York: Oxford University Press.

Loubet, J. L. (1998c) 'Automobile: un grand coup de volant', *Enjeux-Les Échos*, special edition. 1973–1998, no. 138, July–August.

Loubet, J. L. (1999a) *L'industrie automobile. 1905–1971. Archives économiques du Crédit Lyonnais*, Genève: Droz.

Loubet, J. L. (1999b) 'Restructuring in the Auto Industry: The Precedent of the 1930s, Changing for the Better: Approches to Restructuring Entreprise Groups', *Insee Méthodes*, no. 95–6, December.

Loubet, J. L. (2000) *Renault. Histoire d'une entreprise*, Boulogne: ETAI.

Loubet, J. L. (2001a) *Histoire de l'automobile française*, Paris: Le Seuil.

Loubet, J. L. (2001b) *Road Book, Renault 1898–2001*, Boulogne: ETAI.

Loubet, J. L. (2001c) 'Peugeot, un sacré numéro', *L'Histoire*, no. 252, March.

Loubet, J. L. and Hatzfeld, N. (2001) *Les 7 vies de Poissy*, Boulogne: ETAI.

Loubet, J. L. and Hatzfeld, N. (2002) *Poissy, une légende automobile*, Boulogne: ETAI.

Lung, Y., Chanaron, J. J., Fujimoto, T. and Raff, D. (eds) (1999) *Coping with Variety: Flexible Productive Systems for Product Variety in the Auto Industry*, Aldershot: Ashgate.

Masdeu-Arus, J. (1992) 'Rapport de la Commission d'enquête chargée d'étudier la situation actuelle et les perspectives de l'industrie automobile française', *Journal officiel*, 13 June.

Moustacchi, A. and Payan, J. J. (1999) *L'automobile: Avenir d'une centenaire*, Paris: Flammanion.

Sauvy, J. (1998) *Les organismes professionnels français de l'automobile et leurs acteurs, 1896–1979*, Paris: CCFA.

Shimizu, K. (1999) *Le Toyotisme*, Paris: La Découverte.

Womack, J., Jones, D. and Roos, D. (1990) *The Machine that Changed the World*, New York: MIT Press.

8
The Internationalization of a Premium Automobile Producer: The BMW Group and the Case of Rover

Andrea Eckardt and Matthias Klemm

For the automotive industry, the 1990s was a decade of internationalization. The world witnessed spectacular developments, such as the DaimlerChrysler merger, Renault's alliance with Nissan and so on – initiatives that were driven by companies' overriding desire to become a global player. The first firm to hit the headlines for this reason, early in the decade, was BMW, with its decision to take over Rover. And yet, before five years had gone by, BMW and Rover were preparing to divorce.

The events that led to this break-up provide a perspective that is new, and will allow analysts to rectify their earlier predictions concerning how the addition or integration of another company can help a firm that is trying to go global – that is, when profit strategies (Boyer and Freyssenet, 2000) meet and collide. The trajectory approach enables a comprehensive understanding of the way in which profit strategies are devised, as well as of the associated problems. For this reason, we shall first take a quick look at the initial and secondary phases of BMW's trajectory, before switching our attention to the history of the Rover group. We shall subsequently discuss the linkage between these two entities, and elucidate how BMW's various approaches to the two firms' intertwining reflects its management's efforts to overcome the Rover crisis. Finally, we shall discuss the problems that remain, as well as the outlook for the world's smallest independent automaker – the BMW group.

The making of BMW and Rover

The BMW company came into existence in 1916, as the Bayerische Flugzeugwerke AG. Back then, the company only produced aircraft turbines. In 1928, five years after it had begun to produce motorcycles, BMW purchased the Eisenach automobile factory in Eastern Germany. Its experience of manufacturing cars that it developed itself began one year later, in 1929.

In the aftermath of the Second World War, BMW's production facilities were dismantled. The company started to produce motorcycles again in 1948, and automobiles followed in 1951. The business activity of the decades that followed can be divided into three phases: the first period (the 1950s) was an era of hit-and-miss product strategies, characterized by chronic undercapitalization; the second (from the 1960s until 1992) was a time of consolidation, expansion and, most importantly, the shaping of modern profit, product and sales strategies; and the third and current phase at the time of writing, with its focus on the process of internationalization, revolved around the purchase of Rover, which became an important component in a new strategy of globalization.

BMW during the 1950s: a time of trial and error

Despite its success in the motorcycle business, BMW's initial automobile production phase led to a number of setbacks in terms of the company's product and profit strategies. Neither the strategy of producing premium-class type 501 motorway vehicles, 500 series sports cars, nor the production (from 1954 onwards) of Isetta small cars (under licence from Italy's Rivolta company), could help the car division to reach the profit zone (Bochum and Dörrenbaecher, 1997). There are a number of explanations for this failure.

First, BMW never reached the necessary volumes, particularly in the top-of-the-range segment – and the small profits it made on its Isetta sales could not close the gap (Lewandowski, 1998). Originally intended to help BMW improve its image in the motorcycle market, Isetta was supposed to be a mere supplement to the existing range of automobile models. However, the incorporation of this brand caused a loss of focus for BMW's image; the company was producing cars with too wide a range of segments (Rosellen, 1983).

The inability to implement coherent profit and product strategies, plus chronic undercapitalization, forced BMW's management into a hit-and-miss strategy, thereby driving the company into its first, and so far most severe financial crisis (the company lost at least 5.9 million DM per annum during this time, dissipating nearly 50% of its equity). In 1959, various competitors offered to take over the company. After refusing offers from General Electric, Ford, AMC and the Rootes Group, and despite the popularity of the 700-Series models it launched that same year, the board of directors and the top stakeholder, the powerful Deutsche Bank, wanted to accept Daimler-Benz's offer to set up a collaborative arrangement with BMW. Daimler set a dead-line, stating that a decision had to be made at its general assembly on 9 December 1959. However, BMW's small shareholders protested, and succeeded in forcing an adjournment that was justified by the mistakes that had been made during the calculations of that year's losses: for a period of twelve months at least, the new 700 model's development costs had been recorded in a way that contravened the law – resulting in an automatic rejection of Daimler's offer. As a result, BMW maintained its independence, with its financial problems remaining unresolved until the Quandt brothers (Harald and Herbert), who ran one of Germany's largest investment funds, bought the majority of the company's shares in March 1960, replacing the Deutsche Bank. The two brothers then began to play an active role in running the business. BMW subsequently sold its aircraft turbines divison (the Allach plant), and raised enough new capital to build and launch a new middle-of-the-range automobile in 1961/2 (Bochum and Wortmann, 1998; Rosellen, 1983). In 1963, dividends were paid to BMW's shareholders for the first time in twenty years (profit was 3.82 million DM – Rosellen, 1983).

The relationship between management and labour – that is, workers' representatives – also played an important role during this crisis. This relationship can be characterized as being based on trust and the establishment of close personal relationships ('co-management'). In those days, the Quandts' efforts to save BMW were heavily supported by the man who was at the time the head of the works council, Herr Golda. This relationship represented an important element in the firm's trajectory; and as recently as the Rover crisis (see below), it still played a decisive role.

The modern BMW takes shape, 1960–92

The Quandts' involvement meant that BMW was clearly changing its capital strategy, and beginning to focus on a long-term orientation. In the years that followed, the company forged a coherent image and model strategy – one that turned out to be highly successful, and which remains unchanged at the time of writing, at least in its core elements.

After half a decade of stabilization and expansion, in 1967 BMW purchased the Glaswerke, its former competitor in the small cars segment, adding two new plants (in Dingolfing and Landshut) to its main plant and headquarters in Munich.[1] Production volumes reached 144,704 units. In 1969, the former chairman, von Kuehnheim, as representative of the Industriewerke Karlsruhe (which had also been a part of the Quandt-Gruppe), became managing director of BMW, a role he kept until 1992. Under his leadership, the company more than tripled its production, reaching more than 500,000 units in 1989. This achievement was the result of a series of measures.

In terms of the company's product strategy, during the 1970s BMW established and sharpened its image as a producer of sporty, innovative and high-tech automobiles, with a presence in the premium market segments. The 5-Series was introduced in 1972, the 3-Series in 1975 and the 7-Series in 1977 – all cars that have maintained their fame, presenting both the profit strategy's traditionalist element, and the core element of the BMW success story. In addition, a certain number of niche products were launched, for example the 6-Series in 1977 (Lewandowski, 1998).

During the 1980s, in order to satisfy increased market demand, BMW expanded its business lines, setting up overtly national/regional industrial complexes in Bavaria (Southern Germany), near the company headquarters. In 1984, a new greenfield plant was added, in Regensburg, to Munich's Dingolfing and Landshut production and component facilities (motorcycle production having been shifted from these locations to Berlin during the 1960s), and a components and suppliers park was built in Wackersdorf (1989). After the reunification of Germany, an additional components plant was reopened on BMW's former East German Eisenach site (1990). In 1983, BMW established a new engine plant at Steyr in Austria, an entity that was geographically close to the company's Germany-based production network, and which therefore cannot be interpreted as a step towards internationalization. Last, but not least, in 1987 BMW opened the FIZ (Forschungs- und Ingenieurszentrum – 'Research and Engineering Centre') in Munich, with this becoming the 'brain' of the company's R&D activities. R&D, technical planning, production engineering, quality assurance, value analysis and control, purchase, logistics and human resource management were all brought together under one roof (see Table 8.1).

As pertains to sourcing, BMW was one of Europe's first automobile producers to reorganize its supplier relations, and follow a type of global and systemic sourcing (Casper, 1995). During the 1970s, BMW had already started to establish an international network of purchasing centres (opening its first international office for global sourcing in 1983). Also during this decade, the company began to adopt a long-term supplier relationship approach that led to the development of system suppliers and the systematic introduction of just-in-time principles in the mid- to late 1980s. At the time of writing, BMW and its system suppliers engineer new products and production processes simultaneously. In so doing, BMW sees itself as 'system integrator', and there has been a continuous decline in the percentage of its production being manufactured in-house.

Above and beyond the aforementioned efforts, BMW continued to restructure its production and working processes in response to the increasing demands for product complexity and flexible scheduling. In the early 1980s, the firm was already partially divided into cost and profit centres.

It should also be mentioned that BMW experienced some internationalization at this time. In order to avoid high import tariffs, a CKD-plant was built in Portugal in the late 1950s, and another in Rosslyn (South Africa) in 1973. Despite these activities, BMW continued to follow an export-orientated strategy up to 1992. Only in terms of sales and sourcing did the company make any effort to internationalize its business by setting up overseas sales representations in the major markets, that is, in the USA in 1975.

Before 1992, BMW can be characterized as a company pursuing a nationally/regionally-centred production strategy, with a strongly interlinked production network and a clear export-orientated sales strategy.[2] It made automobiles for premium car segments in all major car markets, with a distinct and long-term-orientated product philosophy. The overall profit strategy had also been geared towards the longer term ever since the company had become a family-owned business in the early 1960s. This turned out to be very successful for the product, for sales and production strategies, as it was a coherent approach, and supported by the fact that the Quandt family was pursuing an appropriate capital strategy.

We shall now take a short look at the history of Rover, keeping in mind BMW's successful trajectory after the major crisis of the late 1950s. We would like to point out that, until 1982 at least, Rover was developing in a direction that was quite different from BMW's. Even though it was able to survive the serious crises that it too experienced, Rover never really recovered from certain major internal and external problems, and thus went through a variety of rescue strategies, and even owners. From 1982 onwards, Rover was able to stabilize its output volumes as a result of its co-operation with Honda. However, this was as much as anything a consequence of the fact that the company, with the exception of Land Rover, was shifting away from car production, and towards car assembly (in high-volume markets).

Rover and the decline of the British car industry, 1968–82

'The Rover brand has been the heart of the British motor industry since 1904' (www.rovergroup.com). Although Rover's roots can be traced back to the very beginning of the British car industry, our analysis will start in 1968, at the end of a long process of concentration in this industrial branch (Mair, 1998).

Before BMW's take-over of Rover, the latter company had represented the last domestic British mass automobile producer. Its history from 1968 on, when its predecessor, the British Leyland Motor Corporation (BLMC), was forged out of various mergers between several smaller producers that were seeking to reach the critical mass necessary to be competitive internationally, is one of dramatic decline – both in production and staffing levels (Mair, 1994). From 1970 to 1982, during which time Honda (three years after its decision to pursue a collaborative arrangement) was making its presence known at Rover, both production and employment declined by nearly 50% (see Figure 8.1). What had gone wrong? The answer is: nearly everything. First, the huge company (the world's second largest automobile producer outside the USA, incorporating sixty manufacturing plants, and serving 40% of the British market) had failed to implement a coherent product range and/or strategy (Scarbrough, 1986). Additionally, the company, despite its size, suffered from permanent undercapitalization. As with BMW in the 1950s, this meant that BLMC's new automobile development was following a hit-or-miss trajectory.

Second, the BLMC system of industrial relations, marked by the strong bargaining power of the shop stewards, and because of the 'highly fragmented nature of collective bargaining within BL, blocked most of its management's attempts to rationalize production. By 1975, there were 246 separate bargaining units, and 17 recognised unions in the company'

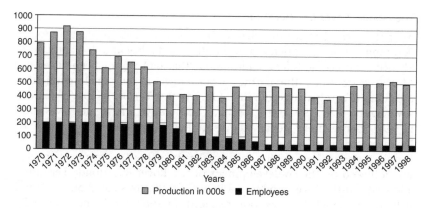

Figure 8.1 Rover production and employees, 1970–98
Sources: Mair, 1998; BMW annual report, 1998, interim 1999.

(Scarbrough, 1986). Official and unofficial strikes were quite normal at the time, and it was unusual if two weeks elapsed without any industrial action taking place (Mair, 1998).

In the absence of any major improvements in its production process, and given its well founded reputation for poor-quality cars, BLMC's market share declined – as did the entire world market after the oil crisis and recession of the early 1970s. After the UK became a member of the European Community, other car producers entered the British car market successfully. In 1975, BLMC experienced such a severe financial crisis that the government had to take the company over to prevent it from going bankrupt. To restore the company's fortunes, the National Enterprise Board, under the direction of Don Ryder, devised a ten-year plan (the Ryder plan). Its first provision was to merge all of the previously separated Austin-Morris and Rover-Triumph-Jaguar divisions. The ensuing rescue strategy incorporated rationalization, modernization, a stabilization of the production process (via the introduction of a new form of labour relations – that is, 'joint management committees'), the end of under-investment, and a consistent new model range (Scarbrough, 1986; Mair, 1998). The management projected a UK market share of 33%, leading the government to plan investments of £900 million, starting with an injection of £200 million at the Longbridge plant, where the first new model, the Metro, was to be produced. In 1978, however, the Group, now renamed British Leyland (BL), experienced a second collapse in sales and in its financial position, followed by a phase of massive workforce cuts, plant closures, and in the area of industrial relations, a reinforcement of the management's bargaining position.[3] By 1982, all the company's production facilities, with the exception of the Longbridge and Cowley sites, had been closed (Mair, 1998).

The Honda–Rover co-operation

After the second financial collapse there was no money available for the development of a proprietary new product, so BL began to look around for a partner who could offer an automobile that had already been developed. At the same time, the partner would have to be 'small enough' to preclude its being able to dominate BL (re: the fear of the loss of national sovereignty; Mair, 1994). As a result, a collaborative arrangement was struck in 1979 between BL (renamed Austin Rover, and later Rover) and the Japanese producer Honda. In 1981, BL started to assemble CKD kits of the Honda Ballade model, selling them under the name Triumph Acclaim. This was followed by the co-development of the Rover 800/Honda Legend. In addition, Austin Rover produced a Rover 200 that was based on the Honda Ballade – a model that was soon replaced (in 1987) by the new Rover 200 and the 400, cars that were based on the Honda Concerto. In 1989, a fifth model was jointly introduced, the Rover 600, this time using the Honda Accord as model.

According to Mair (1994), this was not a co-operation between equal partners: with the exception of the Rover 800/Honda Legend project, which had been a joint development and production project, Honda clearly dominated joint business activities. With Rover assembling Honda cars for the European market, Honda could circumvent import restrictions without any FDI, yet at the same time increase its financial profits by selling CKD kits and supplying parts (that is, engines) to Rover. Eventually, Honda was able to implement some structural control over Rover, especially with respect to the company's quality standards – it occasionally refused to accept some of the cars that were being produced by Rover because of their substandard quality. However, Rover also gained some advantage from this co-operation. With hindsight, the survival of the company was secured, and several improvements in terms of quality, working structures, human resource management, productivity and costs were achieved. In the meantime, Rover also changed ownership: British Aerospace bought Rover for a total of £192.6 million in 1988, with Honda also acquiring 20% of Rover's shares in 1989.

During the first years of this co-operation, BL still produced, in addition to the Honda-based Rover models, a second automobile range it had developed on its own (the Austin Maestro, Metro and Montego) – but it soon became clear that this range was another market failure.[4] From 1986 onwards, the company, now named the Rover Group, was restructured and strategically reorientated. Most of the vertical business activity was split up, and the Austin division abolished. Under the new chairman, Graham Day, the profit strategy was 'to develop a range of new Rover models of superior quality and design in the top niche of each size class. Interestingly Day's stated goal was the creation of a British BMW' (Mair, 1998).

Indeed, a couple of years later, Rover and BMW finally did get together, with the former being incorporated into the latter. This take-over was accompanied by various other internationalization steps, which were guided by the idea that BMW was to become a global player.

The 1990s – BMW's internationalization takes off

As we have seen, before 1992, BMW still was a national automobile producer. Over the 1990s, however, this has changed dramatically. The first step towards internationalization was marked by the announcement that the company was opening a completely new production site in the USA, the largest foreign sales market for BMW, in 1992 (see Figure 8.4 on p. 182). BMW was the first German automaker to decide to establish a new production plant in the American South East, far away from traditional automobile regions. One year later, its new CEO, Bernd Pischetsrieder, implemented a strategy that was explicitly global in its outlook: 'We will no longer be building any fully integrated production plants here in Germany, and Spartanburg is probably not the last plant that we will be establishing in a foreign country' (Wirtschaftswoche nos 1 + 2, 1995, p. 28; translated by the authors). At the same time as the Spartanburg plant was being built, BMW began both to upgrade and to integrate its older Rosslyn (South Africa) assembly facilities into its production network. This became the first plant to produce both BMW (3-Series) and Rover (Land Rover) cars under one roof. Additionally, BMW launched an overseas assembly offensive. In uncertain national markets such as Egypt, Indonesia, Malaysia, the Philippines, Thailand, Vietnam and Russia, BMW now assembles cars in co-operation with local partners.[5] The growing relevance of South East Asia for assembly operations may also indicate this region's importance in future global production plans. BMW has already announced its medium-term interest in opening production sites in this region. With respect to the South American markets, BMW – unlike other companies – has been acting cautiously because of the over-capacities that already mark this region. In order to satisfy local import restrictions, BMW has been assembling Rover automobiles in Brazil since 1998. In the long run, BMW wants to be producing vehicles in all its main sales markets (the Triad), and it wants to open new assembly sites in order to gain market access in those countries that are characterized by high import tariffs and local-content restrictions. Towards this end, the company has drawn up a so-called '*Weltbebauungsplan*', a plan for establishing facilities across the world. This is to be supported by a dual production strategy: every manufacturing facility will produce both a 'world automobile' (a model that can be sold in all the world's markets) and a region-specific model (Antrecht, 1995). This production philosophy is as follows: each plant is focused on the production of its own specific model, with this orientation being stabilized by the concomitant manufacturing of a so-called 'compensatory or supplemental model' (*'Ausgleichsmodelle'*).

The final point to be made is that BMW (together with Rover, after 1994) created the first truly international network of plants. For example, the company's Steyr plant in Austria produces for a number of destinations, including the US market, BMW's own South African plant and so on. It is BMW's largest engine plant, and as Bochum and Wortmann (1998) state, together with the UK and Brazilian plants, it may be the core of a truly globalized engine network. The Brazilian BMW-Chrysler joint venture plant will provide Rover plants with small engines.

This expansion in output has been accompanied by a number of other measures: new R&D subsidiaries were opened in the USA and Japan, and a new R&D centre was built in Gaydon (UK). Beyond this, BMW has tried to dynamize its global purchasing activities with its slogan, 'Purchase 2000', and at the same time reduced the number of suppliers that it uses (single sourcing). The purchasing centres in Spain, Italy, the UK, Australia, Japan, Canada and Mexico have been given a double mission: product management and supplier development. Only North America, Austria and South Africa still have their own purchasing organization.

Internal restructuring has also affected labour relations. BMW initiated a number of labour-related pilot schemes in 1991, resulting in a collective agreement (*'Betriebsvereinbarung'* – 'New Labour Structures') in 1995. The general aim is to increase flexibility, quality and long-term productivity (4% per year, against 2% under the old system). According to its management, BMW is trying to follow a middle road between the Swedish model, with its focus on employee satisfaction, and the Japanese model, with its emphasis on increased productivity (Bihl *et al.*, 1997). Work groups with between eight and fifteen members were introduced, who are entitled to make decisions about individual and group responsibilities, and about job rotation. BMW has for some time been a frontrunner in the disconnection of individual and company working hours; for example, it introduced the individual 36-hour, four-day work week, and at the same time increased total company working hours by about 33%. In 1996, a new working time credit account came into force for all production employees. It features a maximum annual range of 200 hours per employee, and about 10 million hours for the company. In this way, BMW is trying to balance seasonal fluctuations in customer demand and in model cycles so as to sustain staffing levels and a steady workforce. The new working time scheme, and the team work system, are supplemented by a new remuneration system that gradually replaces the traditional piece wage with a bonus-based remuneration scheme. Instead of the five former wage groups, there are nine at the time of writing. This new remuneration system is also regarded as an important precondition for the introduction of a common pay structure for blue-collar and white-collar workers in the future.

Additionally, the internationalization of production has been accompanied by a reorientation of product strategy. Since the early 1990s, BMW has been expanding its product range to become a full-line producer. Hence its development of niche models (the Z3 and Z8 roadsters, and the X5 sports-utility vehicles, which are to be produced in the US plant); it bought Rover (see below); and plans to take over Rolls-Royce in 2003. It has announced its intention to develop at least two new models each year.

BMW and its British adventure: the Rover take-over, 1994

In 1994, with a view towards attaining the critical mass required of any global player, BMW (somewhat surprisingly) acquired the oldest and largest British automaker, Rover Group Holdings plc (including Rover Group USA Inc.), paying £800 million for British Aerospace's 80% stake. Honda dissolved its four years of financial involvement with Rover by selling its 20% minority stake. At the same time, it agreed to further technical co-operation with Rover (BMW Annual Report, 1994).

Rover's take-over represented a novelty in the automotive industry, inasmuch that, until that point strategies of this sort had only been pursued by mass producers buying premium brands (Dolata, 1994). In this case, a premium producer was acquiring a generalist company. As such, the Rover take-over was regarded – and welcomed by the advertising sector – as both a quantitative and qualitative expansion, and/or as the internationalization of BMW, with the Rover model range providing an entry into the mid-range market without damaging the luxury BMW brand.

BMW/Rover: a couple that drifted apart (structural overview)

More than half a decade later, a structural overview reveals the existence of a certain polarity, with BMW being a high-selling and technologically highly innovative brand, and the Rover cars division being the problem child with low-selling models. This clearly does not correspond to earlier expectations and estimations of Rover as a BMW's British alter ego.

As mentioned above, this deal had been considered as an ideal, inasmuch the two companies were seen to be complementary, and because Rover was supposed to supplement the BMW model range. However, Rover turned out to be two businesses in one. Rover's car division have been losing market share – but Land Rover sales have been rising rapidly (Bochum and Wortmann, 1998). Unlike BMW, Rover, with its Rover 200 and 400 (facelifted and renamed R25 and R45 in 1999/2000) and its new R75 (the successor of the 600- and 800-Series – the former 100 was completely abandoned), is mainly positioned in the medium-price mass segment. It also covers niche markets with its famous Land Rovers and Range Rovers, and with the Mini and MGF sports cars. Previously, Honda had delivered parts, engines and so on for the Rover 200. Despite BMW often having being considered as a luxury car producer (the BMW 5- and 7-Series, and Rolls-Royce from 2003 onwards), its 'bread-and-butter car', the 3-Series (despite its high price), touches the middle-of-the range segment.

In terms of output, staff, sales and operating profits, BMW is the stronger partner, and its quantities are higher. BMW car production reached 755,547 units in 1999, with Rover production volumes at only 391,873 (see Figure 8.2). Out of 112,800 employees in total, in 1998, two-thirds (76,000) worked at BMW (see Figure 8.3).

Both figures show that the two companies have been moving in different directions since the take-over. BMW has constantly risen, while Rover is basically declining – both of them are perpetuating their historic trajectory!

With respect to the spatial distribution of BMW's and Rover's domestic production facilities, they are both situated in homogeneous national

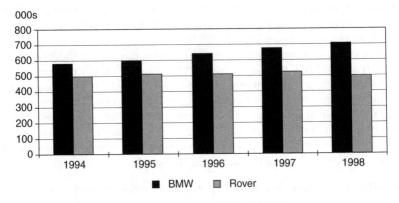

Figure 8.2   BMW and Rover car production, 1994–8 BMW Rover
Source: BMW annual report 1998.

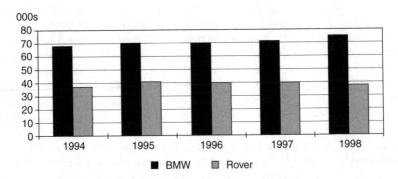

Figure 8.3   BMW and Rover employees, 1994–8 BMW Rover
Source: BMW annual report 1998.

regions, in Bavaria and the Midlands in England, respectively. These are tantamount to regional clusters. BMW has four major German plants – in Munich, Dingolfing, Regensburg and Landshut. Its three foreign plants are located in Steyr (Austria), Rosslyn (South Africa) and Spartanburg (USA). The four major Rover UK plants are located in Longbridge, Solihull, Cowley and Swindon. Except for its CKD facilities – mainly used in Land Rover assembly – in Malaysia, Kenya, Zimbabwe, Morocco, Turkey, Australia and Brazil, Rover has since 1998 not maintained any other foreign plants (see Table 8.1).

Table 8.1 BMW and Rover plants (incl. production models and workforce)

Plant/location	Country	Production range	Workforce
BMW Munich	Germany	3-Series saloon, compact version	24,1699[1]
BMW Dingolfing	Germany	3-Series saloon, 5-Series saloon, 5-Series touring, 7-Series saloon, 8-Series coupé	19,522
BMW Regensburg	Germany	3-Series saloon and coupé touring version and convertible	8,740[2]
BMW Berlin	Germany	BMW motorcycles	498[3]
BMW Spartanburg	USA	Z3 + Z8 roadster, Z3 coupé, X5,	2,217
BMW Rosslyn	South Africa	3-Series saloon, Land Rover Def.	3,201
Rover Longbridge	UK	Rover 200, 400, MGF, Mini	12,017
Rover Solihull	UK	Land Rover Defender, Discovery II, Range Rover, Freelander	12,414
Rover Oxford	UK	Rover 75	3,620

(Plus some further component and engine plants in Austria, Germany, UK and Brazil)

Notes
1. Incl. Head Office, BMW Research and Engineering Centre (FIZ).
2. Incl. Wackersdorf plant.
3. Excl. motorcycles.

Source: Annual report 1998, BMW, ww.bmw.com, 26.4.1999.

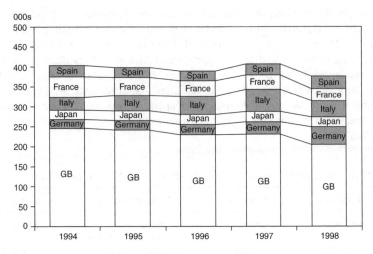

Figure 8.4   The principal markets for BMW and Rover, 1994–8
Source: Various annual reports.

The 'Anglo-Saxon internationalization' of BMW, as it might be called, occurred against a background of production hikes that were aimed at servicing the local British and American markets, and at selling into other national markets. In 1999, Rover's overall vehicle sales amounted to 429,157 units (Rover car division: 227,743; Land Rover: 178,000; MG: 11,719; Mini: 11,695), while BMW sold 751,272 vehicles. Figure 8.4 shows the main sales markets for each of these two firms. BMW sells its cars mainly in the UK and the USA, with the Italian and Japanese markets coming much further behind. These four countries represented 57% of BMW's total foreign sales. Rover shows a different picture; it sells its cars and Land Rovers mainly in Western Europe, above all in Italy, France, Spain, and lately in Germany (representing, in total, 60% of the firm's foreign sales). Moreover, the split between these countries is fairly even. Rover's home market, representing in 1998 42% (205,200 out of 487,700) of its total sales, has greater significance for the company than Germany has for BMW (which sells 33% of its output – that is, 232,500 units – in its domestic market). In other word, BMW's sales are more internationalized than Rover's, as its proportion of exports is 67%, against 58% for Rover.

These diverging sales profiles could be explained by the different buyer classes associated with each brand: primarily lower- and middle-class buyers for Rover, hence the firm's emphasis on the domestic market, versus a greater proportion of elite and upper-class buyers for BMW, explaining the international nature of the firm's sales. The fact that this domestically-orientated British mass producer is owned by a German company creates an additional challenge for BMW to deal with: the socio-cultural distance from British customers. This is somewhat comparable to the GM–Opel relationship in Germany. However, the issue is not particularly salient to the severe sales crisis that Rover has experienced (see below).

1999, Rover erupts in a crisis

Structural data on BMW and Rover gives an ambiguous picture of this coupling. Rover is clearly the somewhat smaller and weaker partner; however, the information available does not provide any great qualitative insight into the internal functioning of the relationship. In fact, the stability of Rover's numbers hides underlying problems that are so significant as to conceivably engender wholesale changes in the BMW Group's total make-up. It becomes possible to perceive Rover as the British BMW; the BMW–Honda connection comes to light (see Figure 8.5); and it is clear that BMW's strategic target of becoming a global player caused it to underestimate seriously the problems it was facing.

BMW acted initially in a very cautious manner towards the Rover management, and demonstrated a great deal of sensitivity towards the firm's different socio-cultural and national backgrounds, thus emphasizing Rover's autonomy as an independent sister company that was responsible for itself. A driving force behind this strategy stemmed from the desire not to mix the two brands, BMW and Rover, but to demonstrate that each had its own independent identity. Yet this strategy ultimately failed when, in early 1999, the previously latent Rover crisis came into the open for the first time.

In times of crisis, it is very easy to discern micro-politics. The disputes among BMW's leading managers and board members concerning Rover's future management and product policy reveal the underlying micro-political dimension that is often so well hidden from the public eye.

Since November 1998, a continuous slump in sales (especially the Rover 200 and 400 cars in the UK home market) culminated in a severe management crisis. At the time, the accounts were indicating tremendous losses, amounting to 1.9 billion DM, and cutting BMW's profits by nearly a third (27.5% – 903 million DM). One decisive reason for this was the CFO's inaccurate prediction of future exchange rates: Rover's domestic sales prices became too high, thus leading to the collapse of the home market and an automatic explosion in its investment costs. At the same time, BMW was achieving its highest profits ever, with an increase of 24% (3.9 billion DM). Rover's 1999 January–April Western European sales figures showed −20.6% compared to its sales over the same period in 1998, whereas BMW showed +17.9%. The BMW Group thereby faced an extraordinary polarization of its sales *vis-à-vis* Rover vehicles (Land Rover and the Mini excluded), with the latter very much in the role of a problem child. In fact, 1999's accounts showed an intensification of this polarization, with Rover increasing its losses to around 2.5 billion DM.

When this ongoing slump in sales became public knowledge in February 1999, earlier bones of contention re-emerged, and fights broke out concerning Rover's strategic aims. Decisions from the past, as well as the actors who had been responsible for them, were criticized openly. Four years previously, in 1995, the BMW chairman's major rival, Walter Reitzle (the vice-president for development and marketing) had already stated that he wanted Rover to be reduced to its Mini and Land Rover product lines – so as to supplement the BMW model range with niche vehicles, and not with cars aimed at the low- and medium-priced volume markets. He also wanted the closure of one plant. However, chairman Bernd Pischetsrieder won this argument, and Rover continued to produce its complete model range. BMW managers now admit that they failed, in the sense that they omitted to take certain drastic measures because of their fear of rekindling in certain British people the sort of latent resentment that BMW managers had experienced in the immediate aftermath of the Rover take-over.

Neither Reitzle nor the chairman remained in their positions after February 1999; chairman Pischetsrieder was ousted, and the VP resigned when he did not get a clear majority in the election for a new chairman. The new and surprising CEO of BMW was the former production and engineering VP, Prof. Joachim Milberg.

Milberg owes his appointment mainly to the collective block vote of the workers' representatives on the BMW supervisory board. According to German participation law, workers' representatives cast 50% of the votes on the supervisory board, with the vote of the board's chairman being decisive in the case of no majority. The British and German workers' representatives co-ordinated their actions at an earlier, secret, meeting, with the goal of preventing Reitzle from being elected (Taylor, 1999). This is an example of how transnationally co-operative workers' representatives are capable of affecting and co-determining the way in which an international company is steered at its highest level – that is, they can take advantage of their legal institutionalization. This is not to say that they have any say in any of the decisions that continue to be made in BMW's internationalization strategy – CEO Milberg will continue his predecessor's policy of developing successors for each car in the Rover model range; and of modernizing operations on a step-by-step basis. Depending on financial and personnel capacities, only one of the Rover plants has (and will continue to be) updated, in terms of its equipment, and with respect to the models that are to be produced there.

Forcing the integration of Rover: from a hands-off to a hands-on approach

While perpetuating this gradualistic approach, Milberg has also started to target management and working structures, and has started to implement a turnaround in the company's fortunes by means of two partial strategies: a short-term cost-cutting programme; and the integration and standardization of all Rover's processes into the BMW Group. Both strategies will affect and shape the way in which the production system is renewed and implemented.

Turning around Rover means cutting costs over the short term, and focusing on several areas of great expense, such as purchasing, production (a demand for productivity increases), distribution and marketing, R&D, logistics, administrative functions and personnel. The development of a premium quality will also be decisive. The managers of each area of recovery are supported by a core team that also reports to a lead team.

The recovery efforts are based on previous analyses that date from late 1998, which focused on Rover's competitive position. The defined turnaround tasks were then broken down into teams and measures referring either to organizational units or to functional tasks. The implementation phase is thought to need about a year and is to follow a defined timetable. A further measure of some significance will be the increased outsourcing – for example, of seats and other components.

In order to offset the cost explosion caused by the strength of the pound sterling, BMW is converting Rover's supplier accounting system to the euro, in an attempt to externalize exchange rate costs to local suppliers. The underlying argument – or threat – of BMW's management is that British suppliers could lose their contracts to competitors located on the Continent, and who can produce the same parts 10–15% cheaper.

Since this crisis first erupted, BMW has been steadfastly pursuing a course geared towards greater integration, involving a standardization of all core processes. Internal benchmarking studies have already attested to Rover's relatively poor production figures, mainly because the firm operates at low capacities, products require a great deal of reworking, and existing personnel regulations are stringent. Accordingly, current improvement efforts are aimed at bettering equipment uptime, and reducing the need for reworking.

A restructuring of BMW's board of directors; the fitting-out of the Birmingham plant so that it can handle new launches; face-to-face learning teams; the allocation of sister plants; an introduction of the BMW style of working structures; a transfer of BMW management culture and communications flows; and a combination of the labour relation systems – are all important measures that merit a lengthier description.

As mentioned above, the Rover crisis has also affected the BMW company's core structures. Nearly all of Rover's vice-presidents, who previously enjoyed the freedom to act independently, have had to resign, and their successors and area managers must now report directly to their respective BMW counterparts. The composition of executives, functions and tasks changed at the management board level. Only one VP has kept his position. The formerly autonomous Rover management that used to hold a seat on the board of directors has been abolished, and a new function – Financial Services and Shares – added to the existing ones (Development & Purchase, Finances, Distribution & Marketing, Production and Personnel and Economy & Policy). At the time of writing, all VPs are jointly responsible for each of the Group's brands. New collective functions and tasks will prevent the doubling-up of responsibilities. At one level below, area managers have been granted Group-wide responsibility, in their respective fields of expertise, for all the structures and processes, and for all the product lines. It is only in production, because of the importance of this function, that plant managers report directly to a VP. As for distribution and marketing activities, BMW has strengthened brand management against regional management. A brand or product manager has been assigned to each family of models.

All in all, the Rover crisis, with the ensuing integration drive, has led to increased (re)centralization, and thus towards a globalization of the BMW group – especially inasmuch as for BMW and Rover, productive activities have now become more and more interrelated.

The oldest Rover production site, Longbridge, plays a key role in all of this. It is the largest British car plant, and has been renamed 'Birmingham'. About 10,000 employees work there, making the Rover 25, 45, Mini, MGF, transmissions, pressparts and K-Series engines. The purchasing and group marketing department, as well as a transmission research and engineering centre, are also based there. In addition to the new R75, the launch of the new Mini in late 2000 is hoped to play a decisive role in the plant's future success, and in the organization of Rover cars. As long ago as 1997, BMW had already come to a decision regarding the new Mini model and, just as significantly, it had decided to integrate a model, for the first time, into the company's worldwide distribution network (with the exception of Japan and UK).

All this has created a certain pressure in favour of convergence. The measures being taken at the Birmingham factory, where the new Mini is to be produced, serve as an example of increased integration, and the same orientation should apply when the 25 and 45 Rover cars are replaced in 2002. The overall objective of the transformation – which has hitherto constituted the main factor of differentiation between the Rover and BMW organizations – is 'flexibilization', referring to an immense degree of product variability (the new Mini will be equipped with even more accessories than the Z3 Roadster), and to significant 'changeability' (and responsiveness) to customers' wishes. This puts a great deal of pressure on all the processes concerned (development, logistics, production and distribution).

The Birmingham plant has gone without substantial investment for almost thirty years, and its equipment can be compared to BMW's standard of almost twenty-five years ago. The plant received a huge £2 billion in investment, £152 million of which will come from public funds. BMW has already announced its intention of building a brand new lean factory for high-efficiency production on its Birmingham site, and has started to rebuild, expand and refurbish the finishing areas for the future Mini's assembly. A new press shop and body-in-white shop are to be built. In essence, the new configuration will involve a stand-alone facility for each model that will be worked on at this factory – huge as it is.

BMW views this transformation as a learning process that is to be executed by mixed teams comprised of both Rover and BMW employees. These teams are to operate at all organizational levels, with the launch teams being the most crucial at present. The groups are also mixed in so far as they ignore hierarchical and functional differences between participants. The programme is focused on training individuals who will be expected to impart their knowledge to their Rover colleagues, thus playing a key role in future launches bynegotiating objectives with teams and with their leaders (*'Zielvereinbarungsprozeß'* – management by objectives; the 'target agreement process').

BMW seems to be aware of existing cultural differences between its own employees and workers and Rover's, and appears to understand that bridging this gap will require time, a great deal of communication and training, and the creation of personal networks. Towards this end, a BMW shuttle has been installed, transporting BMW and Rover people by air between Germany and the UK three times a day. It is clear that there is little more that the personnel from the Munich headquarters can do in this regard.

These face-to-face learning processes, plus future Rover launches, are to be structurally supported by the sister-plant approach, in which specific BMW and Rover plants are to be twinned (Rover Birmingham/BMW Munich, Rover Oxford/BMW Regensburg, Rover Solihull/BMW Dingolfing). In the course of this restructurating, new equipment such as tools, robots and BMW quality IT programmes will also be installed. However, the Rover plants' standardization, integration and innovation processes will be hindered and partially interrupted – at least in its Birmingham factory – by the ongoing production of Rover 25 and 45 cars. Furthermore, the fact that the Birmingham plant has had to cope with more launches than its Munich sister plant will lead to some differences in its human resource organization.

All in all, the Rover personnel and labour organization is under pressure. In fact, this is the area that creates the greatest opposition to integration, given the 'single fighter' mood (as one manager called it) that prevails there – an attitude that had been reinforced by BMW's earlier hands-off-strategy. BMW's main principles with regard to personnel management, tenets that are going to be adapted but not copied at Rover, consist of individual and performance-related rewards; the flexiblization of working time and work attribution (Personal/*Arbeitseinsatz*); empowerment; a combination of team and performance orientations; overall performance assessments; and a shift of responsibilities to the shop-floor level. The aspects that are in most urgent need of a change are seen as working times and remuneration schemes. With overall guidelines that also provide a certain scope for adaptation, each plant will be able to install appropriate systems.

From BMW's point of view, managers are faced with very new tasks; they cannot fall back on whatever restructuring experience they have accumulated in the company's South African or US plants – facilites that could be steadily built up and expanded. In Rover's case, and for the first time, BMW's management has had to cut employment levels. By late 1999, BMW had laid off nearly 10,000 employees, and enforced the introduction of German working standards, such as working time credit accounts, the reduction of working time from 4.5 days/37 hours per week to 4 days/35 hours per week, no more extra pay for Saturday work, and increased equipment uptime for up to 100 hours a week. At Longbridge, job cuts and the diminution of working times are part of the so-called 'survival package' that has been in place since October 1998. Moreover, the wage system is also going to be changed, with a move towards greater differentiation. As recently as 1994, Rover management had reduced the number of grades in its overall wage system from six to three, and this without any interference from BMW.

To increase flexibility, indirect employees are to be transformed into direct production workers. There have also been problems with the standardization of teamwork, job enrichment and job enlargement structures. One of the greater challenges that BMW will have to cope with is the installation of a job rotation system, which has already failed three times at the Birmingham plant. A great number of BMW's personnel programmes are still unknown at Rover; for example, the management associate programme, the DRIVE trainee programme and several other services.

When identical German managerial structures (four levels of *Meister*; assembly process leader; team leader; manufacturing manager/area manager; and technical director/plant manager) are finally installed, Rover's structures will be comparable with those that prevailed at Munich seven years before, when the four-level system was first introduced there. In the meantime, a specific management problem has become evident at the Birmingham plant – compared to relationships in Germany, the communication flow between management and workers at the shop-floor level is poor, and a middle management hardly exists. German BMW workers and managers perceive Rover's management as behaving in a somewhat arrogant manner (for example, the predominance of written communication), and consider that this causes an inconsistency – and in the Germans' view, a superficiality – in the extrinsic motivational methods that are being used (BMW considers that its own personnel policy is value-orientated; Bihl, 1995). This will be changed now, mainly through the creation of new production leaders who can be compared with the German Meister, an individual who fulfils a basic but significant management function in the German production area. He or she controls, leads and motivates by showing an interest in each worker's behaviour and performance. Coaching or empowerment might be an appropriate characterization for this. Whether BMW will succeed in 'socializing' into this very new role the men and women who are affected by it – each with his/her own distinctive cultural and hierarchical background (for example, former shift managers, area managers, production group spokepersons) – remains to be seen. There is also the question as to whether each of these individuals will experience this socialization to the same extent.

All in all, the main differences between BMW and Rover can be found in such areas as quality control; the transparency and control of each worker's work (the existence of detailed job descriptions and job instructions); quality awareness; verbal problem-solving processes at BMW between management/Meisters and workers, versus written ones at Rover; intensive assessment talks; a flexibility enhancing system of rotation; and workers' representation. As the latter factor plays a decisive role in the way that working practices can be organized and reshaped, it is worth investigating.

Last, but not least, the ongoing BMW-Rover integration process also touches on an experiment that is perhaps the most radical of all – the linkage of two entirely different industrial and labour relations systems within a single company. In a European context, these two systems can in fact be construed as being diametrically opposed: 'British adversarial wilfulness meets German co-operative corporatism'. The four most important British unions at Rover (T&G, AEU, MSF, GMBE) have shop stewards whose bargaining power is unconditionally linked to workers' support. Nevertheless, these representatives will have to adapt their mode of expression to the standards of the German BMW works council, a legally institutionalized body that mainly represents Germany's IG Metall union. The Rover crisis has also led to shop stewards' reorientation. British shop stewards now face brand new representation and negotiation structures and cultures, ones based on co-operation ('co-management'), consultation and information.[6] BMW's workers' representatives do not need to have their negotiations with management legitimated by workers, and this provides them with a greater degree of independence in their actions and decision-making. The first event to bring the BMW works council and Rover shop stewards into a co-operative situation was the previously mentioned survival package. Here, and for the first time, British representatives moved closer to a German approach, accepting working time flexibility in exchange for job security.

All in all, the crisis made a few shop stewards change their fundamental attitude towards institutions such as the German works council. 'It's proving worthwhile, very worthwhile,' as one – habitually insular – Transport and General Workers' Union (TGWU) shop steward now admits. With respect to their co-operation with European works councils, German works councils are now having to deal with the presence of an 'external' British union representative. It is at this point that these two diverging information cultures may clash, as the relatively high information transparency between BMW management and its works council, which is usually accompanied by a modicum of confidentiality, contrasts markedly with the intense and direct information flows between Rover shop stewards and their workers. On the other hand, integrating the works council structure into the Rover representative system is also a challenge, one that the largest union on site (the T&G) has been trying to resolve through the establishment of a sort of dual practice strategy: some representatives act as in a works council, and others continue as shop stewards. This should also be a first step towards establishing and improving Rover's workers' relations with the all-important Munich head-quarters that now makes all the crucial decisions concerning the company.

Finally, we would like to turn to the correlation between international-ization and a company's production system. As a firm's production system stems from its shop-floor and management traditions, rooted in history and influenced by an untold number of restructuring initiatives and concomi-tant new management approaches, it would be interesting to discuss how internationalization or globalization introduces new dynamics via the addi-tion of new, foreign, 'sister' plants.

The German BMW production style can be characterized as involving the use of advanced skills and technology. Mair (1994) characterizes Rover as being on the wrong side of the various restructuring initiatives that have taken place since the late 1960s – most of the time aimed at introducing a Fordist logic against a dominant British craft model. A view of both compa-nies' internationalization trajectory now reveals a highly significant case in the guise of Honda. In the past, both firms have contacted Honda to discuss its production system, with the goal of learning from the Japanese firm (see Figure 8.5). Both have undertaken similar steps – but with opposite results.

Rover shared intensive platform production with Honda during the 1980s, with Honda holding a 20% stake in Rover after 1989. Yet Honda did not make any real commitment to the working and management practices and struc-tures on the shop-floor, despite having introduced a new teamwork structure, *kaizen* groups and workers' uniforms. Under Honda's guidance, the Longbridge plant made its best-selling cars ever (Acclaim, R8, R400), accompanied by the highest wages that have ever been paid to Rover workers. As Figure 8.5 shows, Rover entertained relations with Honda's US transplant in order to benefit from an information exchange. The Honda contact was a learning experience for Rover – as Andrew Mair puts it – 'to make cars again' (Mair, 1994).

BMW had a more indirect – albeit highly influential – contact with Honda when it recruited a surprisingly large number of managers from Honda's US transplant for its new Spartanburg subsidiary. One of these people became the first president of BMW's US plant. The company then tried to test American–Japanese transplant methods – that is, a lean production approach – in an environment that was not predominantly made up of a deeply-rooted European–German workforce, with all its labour institutions. In the end, however, and as far as learning is concerned, the main lesson for BMW was simply that it did not want to follow the same path as Honda – as this approach turned out to be incompatible with the company's American profit strategy of high flexibility and diversity, low volumes and high quality. For the moment, this initial plant concept is going to be revis-ited, and reliable production methods that have already been applied at

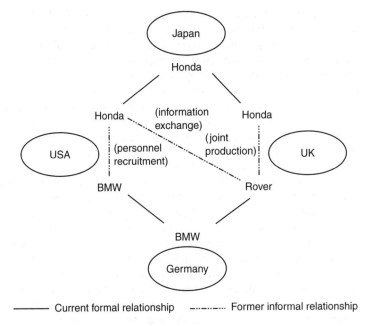

Current formal relationship ·—··—··· Former informal relationship

Figure 8.5 BMW and Rover and Honda input

BMW's Bavarian plants will be reinforced at the expense of the Honda philosophy (Eckardt *et al.*, 2000).

Conclusion

After having compiled a large amount of historical, structural and political information on BMW, eventually we have the following interpretation of the BMW Group, and the internationalization it experienced via its purchase of the Rover company during the 1990s.

The BMW Group, together with Rover, entered the twenty-first century with a view to creating a real convergence at all levels – that is, throughout its product, production, purchasing and sales activities. Its restructuring efforts have been enacted in a variety of different time frames. On the one hand, BMW's management has pursued a short-term restructuring programme in terms of the organization of work and production, and on the other, it undertook at the same time a long-term restructuring of its product, sales and profit strategies, essential components of the BMW trajectory.

1. With the short-term restructuring (that is, the drive towards integration), a critical question arises as to the measure's compatibility (that is, transferability). What sort of results will be achieved by Rover, newly

converted from Honda's to BMW's methods? How will BMW have to develop if it is to dominate the volume production segment? Will BMW succeed in finding a solution that combines its traditional profit strategy of high flexibility, high diversity and high quality for premium and niche cars – that is, the strategy that applies to most of its own range, but also to the Mini, MG and Land Rover – with the pursuit of a high-volume, medium-range car production strategy for its BMW 3-Series, and for the Rover cars? In the end, the attempt to run with two different production models, and to keep an autonomous Rover management structure within the BMW Group, has failed, and at the time of writing, the start-up of the R75 continues to be hampered by severe quality problems.

2. The long-term restructuring of the Rover product, sales and profit strategies (that is, the attempt to supplement BMW's profile in the small and medium-range segments) has been an ongoing strategy ever since the Rover take-over took place. The crisis raised serious questions about this orientation, yet the new senior management is holding on to it. A look at BMW's history shows that such an orientation is partly a product of BMW's trajectory – and yet, at the same time, it perpetuates this very same trajectory. In fact, it reflects the company's having created a coherent model range comprised of three basic models of high quality. As was the case with BMW, the modernization of the Rover product range, and the market introduction of this range, has occurred on a step-by-step basis. BMW therefore wants to acquire a full assortment producer, and offer six core models, plus other niche cars. It wants to establish models at the upper price levels in every market segment. Note that in the small and medium-range segments, the top price level has to be created by a premium car producer.

Rover is therefore a 'make-or-break marque' for the BMW group as a mass producer. It is essential that the company's small and medium-sized cars, and their old-fashioned image, are upgraded so that they become desirable, reliable and associated with high quality. The first BMW-developed Rover car, the R75, has a leading role to play here. In addition, the sales strategy of the hitherto domestically-orientated Rover cars is about to shift and become part of a world-wide distribution. The R75 and the new Mini are the first models that will be built with an eye towards the specifications and needs of foreign markets.

The problems that arise here concern the issues of timing and resources. Can BMW afford to wait two years before coming out with the models (the R30, which will be called the 35 or the 55) that are to be all-decisive in the small and medium-car segments? The recently facelifted R25 and R45, cars that were thought to have bridged the gap in the company's market timing, reflect both BMW's having taken a step towards a coherent product strategy and – given the slight recovery in sales figures in January 2000 – perhaps some light at the end of the tunnel. As such, Williams *et al.*'s (1994) doubts as to whether BMW is financially strong enough to pay for the developments that are required have not been refuted, and must be taken very seriously. A further indication of the significance of this financial aspect is BMW's retreat from its joint venture with Rolls-Royce in aircraft turbine production, a business that has turned out to be a loss-maker in recent years.

In addition to these financial and investment factors, the long-term and short-term restructuring efforts that have been made within the BMW Group – that is, the overall profit strategy – are connected by the micro-politics that are involved. This is because image, quality and flexibility – the core elements of the BMW profit strategy – depend first and foremost on workers' commitment to the company and to its managers.

3. Switching from an internal to a global perspective, BMW's management needs to take a certain number of important external actors and factors into consideration: the state; the European Commission; the shareholders; and the exchange rates.

As mentioned earlier, part of the enormous financial investment that is necessary to modernize the old Rover plant at Longbridge will be funded by the British government. However, the European Commission is currently scrutinizing this measure to see if it respects European competition law. If this funding is refused, BMW has announced that it might close the site, and open a new plant in Eastern Europe instead.

No less important than the issue of government aid is the disadvantageous exchange rate between the euro and the pound sterling. It is difficult to estimate the extent to which the strong pound has dramatized the Rover crisis by forcing up investment and production costs, and thus the price of Rover cars. All in all, future currency fluctuations will certainly influence Rover's chance to regain profitability in the year 2002.

As for Rover's overall strategic aims, these depend primarily on the main shareholder, the Quandt family, whose financial commitments have been the pillar of BMW ever since the firm's first real crisis. Given the power of this family, their vote will decide the future of both BMW and Rover – at a time when continued public criticism of BMW's management, combined with a strong pound and Rover's loss of market share, has again attracted competitors who would like to take over BMW. The question is whether the Quandt family will hold on to their long-term strategy involving the coexistence of two car branches under one roof ('*Mehrmarkenstrategie*'); whether they will they force the management to change its policies — for example, closing or selling the Rover cars division; or whether they will opt for some form of co-operation with another automaker? The next few meetings of the BMW board will surely shine some light on this topic.

Epilogue

At its meeting on 16 March 2000, the BMW board decided to break with the profit and internationalization strategies that it had been following up to that point. More than anyone else, it was the family owner, and the banks, who insisted on selling the Rover division – in all likelihood to Alchemy Partners Ltd, a British investment fund – and the Land Rover brand to Ford. Only the Mini brand, which is to be built at the Oxford plant, is to stay within the BMW group. According to BMW, all internal attempts at restructuring, however successful they may have been (cutting the inventory backlog by about 60,000 cars, the reduction of workers and capacities, quality and productivity improvement, and the shifting of the purchasing function to the Continent) were offset by external developments: the global decline in the demand for Rover cars, the product's weakness on its domestic market, the need to reduce prices by about £1,000 per car in Britain (because of the increased value of the currency), plus the aforementioned doubts over the provision of public funds.

With respect to BMW's management, the crisis had serious consequences. The sales, development and production vice-presidents Henrich Heitmann, Wolfgang Ziebart and Carl-Peter Forster – people who had voted against the decision to break up with Rover – were forced to resign. The new profit strategy now states that 'BMW is to become a full assortment producer by itself', especially through the development of a small 2-Series. The only exceptions now will be the two current extreme niche models: the Mini and the Rolls-Royce.

From a historical point of view, the BMW trajectory must now be rounded out by adding the Rover crisis of the late 1990s to the three preceding crises – in the 1950s, when was nearly taken over by Daimler-Benz; in the 1970s, during the oil crisis, when the public was opposed to its opening the new Dingolfing plant; and in the early 1990s, when BMW motorcycle production almost had to be closed down.

The surprising denouement of the crisis – and the crisis itself – offers new questions relating to the reconfiguration of the automobile industry's economic and political settings, and the way in which this context affects bargaining structures between workers, managers and shareholders (with the latter group exerting increasing pressure on management). Furthermore, the BMW/Rover case clearly raises a question mark over the management philosophy that is associated with the trend towards internationalization – the 'big is beautiful' orientation in which one company grows via the acquisition of another; an attitude that cropped up in many of the debates of the 1990s.

Statistical appendix: BMW and Rover

Table A8.1 BMW and Rover, 1985–99

Year	Total sales	Investment	Operating profit	Automobile sales					Workforce
				BMW Group	Rover	Germany	Great Britain	USA	
1985	18,078	1,376	301	440,732		148,200	33,500	87,900	53,925
1986	17,515	2,237	346	446,109		146,300	35,900	96,800	58,062
1987	19,460	2,112	376	459,502		147,000	37,500	87,800	62,794
1988	24,467	1,911	455	486,592		182,500	42,800	73,400	65,812
1989	26,515	1,820	558	526,462		190,400	48,900	64,900	66,267
1990	27,178	2,066	696	514,705		200,400	43,000	63,600	70,948
1991	29,839	2,123	783	552,103		222,300			74,385
1992	31,241	1,975	726	588,657					73,562
1993	29,016	2,214	516	534,397	357,930	202,900	40,900	78,00	71,034
1994	42,125	3,543	697	931,883	483,089	227,300	301,800	97,100	109,632
1995	46,144	3,477	692	1,073,161	507,254	228,200	304,300	113,300	115,763
1996	52,265	3,830	820	1,151,361	521,020	249,200	289,400	129,00	116,112
1997	60,137	4,520	1,246	1,196,096	487,737	258,800	294,100	143,900	117,624
1998	63,134	4,262	903	1,187,115	429,157	275,500	269,400	155,400	118,489
1999	67,100	4,218	903	1,180,429		*	*	*	114,952

Note: Total sales, operating investment and profit in millions of DM.
* Figures not available.

Sources: BMW Annual Reports; shareholders' letters.

Notes

1 The situation was quite different a few years previously: people had given serious consideration as to whether Glas should take over BMW, which was in a weakened state at the time. However, the Glaswerke had in the meantime failed in its attempt to upgrade its product range, as it lacked any real reputation in the upscale segments (Rossellen, 1983). The Glaswerke produced the Goggomobil, a car similar in size and shape to the Isetta.
2 In our interpretation and explanation of BMW's past export orientation, we are demonstrating a modicum of restraint in our references to the 'German export model'. Holisitic models are second-order constructs that represent the typical or average feature of a group of units at a meso- or macro-level (a country region, branch, industry and so on). They are therefore hardly usable as an *ex post* factor than can causally explain the behaviour of a given firm during a specific period in time. Rather, we need to focus on concrete factors such as product, production, market and country specificities, as well as economic and market policy. Other important factors include capitalization, the time orientation of management philosophies, and the constellation of bargaining power both inside and outside the firm. All of this influences a firm's profit strategy and the extent to which it fits in with different countries' market demand.
3 There is no doubt but that the Thatcher Government, which was elected around this time, with its introduction during the 1980s of a number of Employment Acts (1980, 1982, 1988, 1990, Trade Union Act 1984), was in favour of and supporting the undermining of the unions. This political interference in the field of labour relations reduced the possibility of disputes being worked out amicably – that is by restraining shop stewards' legal privileges (Cleff, 1997).
4 The two divisions made up a 'volume cars' division called Austin-Rover.
5 Land Rovers are also to be assembled in Thailand and Russia.
6 This verbal/discursive management culture seems to be something that many or most Rover workers and employees have also experienced at their place of work: 'We have no fear actually about the German management, we would welcome having more of that.'

References

Antrecht, C. (1995) 'BMW-Werk in SO-Asien: Der vertrauliche Weltbebauungsplan – und was dahiner steckt', *Capital*, December.
Bihl, G. (1995) *Wertorientierte Personalarbeit. Strategie und Umsetzung in einem neuen Automobilwerk*, Munich.
Bihl, G., Thanner, E. and Wächter, J. (1997) 'Anforderungen Neuer Arbeitsstrukturen an Führungskräfte und Mitarbeiter', *Zfo*, Heft.
BMW – various Annual Reports.
BMW AG (1993) *BMW – ein internationaler Konzern*.
Bochum, U. and Dörrenbaecher, Ch. (1997) 'Reactions to the Crisis: Job Losses, Shortened Working Week, Income Losses and Business Re-engineering in the German Auto Industry', in P. Steward (ed.), *Beyond Japanese Management: The End of Modern Times?*, London/Portland, Oreg.
Bochum, U. and Wortmann, M. (1998) *Internationale Mobilität in der Automobilindustrie – Fallstudien über BMW und zwei Automobilzulieferunternehmen*, Vortrag anläßlich des Workshops: WZB Berlin, 4–5 December.

Boyer, R. and Freyssenet, M. (2000, 2002) *Les modèles productifs*, Paris: La Découverte, 2000 (Revised English edition, *The Productive Models: The Condition of Profitability*, London/New York: Palgrave, 2002).

Casper, S. (1995) 'How Public Law Influences Decentralized Supplier Network Organizations in Germany: The Cases of BMW and Audi,' FS I 95-314 (WZB discussion paper).

Cleff, T. (1997) *Industrielle Beziehungen im kulturellen Zusammenhang*. Munich/Mering, International vergleichende Schriften zur Personalökonomie und Arbeitspolitik, Band 7.

Dolata, U. (1994) 'Der Rover-Deal von BMW', *Blätter für deutsche und internationale Politik*, Heft 3.

Eckardt, A. and Köhler, H.-D. (1999) 'The Internationalization of Premium Car Producers: The Case of BMW/Rover and Mercedes/DaimlerChrysler', in M. Freyssenet and Y. Lung (eds), *Internationalization: Confrontation of Firms Trajectories and Automobile Areas*, Proceeding of 7th International Colloquium of GERPISA (CD-ROM), Paris.

Eckardt, A., Köhler, H.-D. and Pries, L. (1998) 'The Internationalization Trajectories of the German Big Three', in M. Freyssenet and Y. Lung (eds), *The New Spaces of the World Automobile Industry*, Proceeding of 6th International Colloquium of GERPISA, Paris.

Eckardt, A., Köhler, H.-D. and Pries, L. (2000) *Auf dem Weg zu global operierenden Konzernen? Fallstudien zu den Internationalisierungsverläufen deutscher Automobilkonzerne in den 90er Jahren*, Final DFG report, Erlangen.

Lewandowski, J. (1998) *BMW. Typen und Geschichte*, Augsburg: Steiger Verlag.

Mair, A. (1994) *Honda's Global Local Cooperation*, London: Macmillan.

Mair, A. (1995) 'BMW, Honda and Rover: What Future for their Industrial Models?', *La Lettre du GERPISA*, no. 94, June.

Mair, A. (1998) 'From British Leyland Motor Corporation to Rover Group: The Search for a Viable British Model', in M. Freyssenet, A. Mair, K. Shimizu and G. Volpato (eds), *One Best Way? Trajectories and Industrial Models of the World's Automobile Producers*, Oxford/New York: Oxford University Press.

Rosellen, H.-P. (1983) *Das weiß-blaue Wunder. BMW – Geschichte und Typen*, Stuttgart: Seewald Verlag.

Scarbrough, H. (1986) 'The Politics of Technological Change at British Leyland', in O. Jacobi, B. Jessop, H. Kastendiek and M. Regini (eds), *Technological Change, Rationalization and Industrial Relations*, London and Sydney.

Taylor, R. (1999) 'Mitbestimmung rettet Rover', *Die Mitbestimmung*, Heft 5.

Williams, K., Haslam, C. and Johal, S. (1994) *Who's Responsible? BAE: BMW: Honda: Rover*, A public interest report from the University of Manchester, University of East London.

9
The Internationalization of the French Automobile Component Industry and the Case of Valeo

Lydie Laigle

Since the beginning of the 1980s, the automobile equipment sector has been concentrated and reorganized at the international level to assume a greater role in technological development and partial-chassis vehicle assembly, to co-ordinate with builders in their foreign set-ups, and face the intensification of world competition. The French automobile equipment-building sector, which at the start was greatly segmented, did not escape this process. However, it was only at the outset of the 1990s that most of the major French suppliers (Bertrand-Faure, Plastic Omnium, Labinal, ECIA and so on) developed their own globalization strategies. The Valeo Group is the only one to have been 'Europeanized' and internationalized progressively as early as 1980. Over ten years, France's share in Valeo's turnover went from 54% in 1986 to 32% in 1995 (compared to 58% for Reydel and 42% for Bertrand-Faure in 1996). At Valeo, only twenty-five out of a total of ninety-two sites remain in France at the time of writing.[1] This chapter deals with the understanding of the processes by which firms orientate their strategies of internationalization in relation to changes in their competitive, macro-economic, financial, labour and political environment. It is a question of speculating about the way that these firms profit from the opportunities created by such variations to alter their strategies and redeploy their activities on an international level.

Most of the internationalization trajectories can be divided into four phases:

(i) *export strategy*: based on the diversification of their clients (automobile builders);
(ii) *strategic alliances and shareholding investments*: numerous joint ventures and agreements between supplier companies;
(iii) *foreign direct investments*: realized in the framework of going beyond multi-domestic strategies, relayed from the 1980s by overall strategies

attempting to centralize advanced research means, organize logistics, as well as optimizing the international organization of industrial manufacturing processes (specialized and interconnected sites producing for several markets); and

(iv) *'globalization'*: characterized by a manufacturing process on a world-wide basis, a renewal of product ranges using common platforms and components, the international organization of R&D activities, and a world-wide organization of the supply network founded on 'global sourcing'.

In the first part, we shall present the changes in the French automobile equipment industry by focusing on factors supporting the internationalization of the main French suppliers. In the second part, we shall describe the trajectory of internationalization of Valeo, which is the biggest French supplier. Valeo's external growth and Europeanization from 1986 will be studied. We shall focus on Valeo's internal restructuring policy (the giving up of peripheral activities, regrouping and modernization of production sites and so on) which was carried out between 1989 and 1992, notably to gather the necessary financial resources for the globalization of the group's leading branches. In addition, we shall study the characteristics and stakes of these branches' internationalization, which, for some of them, meant setting up R&D centres abroad and strengthening their moves towards North and South America, Germany and the UK, but also meant creating new production sites in Eastern Europe and Asia.

The internationalization of the French automobile component industry

Characteristics of the French automobile component industry

Until the 1990s, the French automobile component industry was extremely fragmented and composed of medium- and small-sized companies. The purchasing policies of the French automakers were organized on a national basis: 80% of their purchasing stemmed from suppliers located in France (de Banville and Chanaron, 1999).

At the beginning of the 1990s, European car builders changed their purchasing policies by transferring part of the task of assembly to first-tier suppliers, who began to deliver complete segments of the vehicle (not just components); buying car components from suppliers located in the countries where automakers set up new plants; keeping in touch with French suppliers recently bought by American companies; and using suppliers organized on a world-wide basis. For example, in 1987, Renault purchased 70% of the total amount of its car components from French suppliers. By 1997, it was only 43.6% of car components that were bought from French suppliers, against 39.4% from other European suppliers (including 17% from German suppliers) and 17% from other foreign suppliers (including 13.5% from American and 3.5% from Japanese suppliers).

In the 1990s, three main factors had an impact on the reorganization and internationalization of the French automobile component industry: automakers' purchasing strategies reorganized on an European basis with 'global sourcing' policies and just-in-time production; the penetration of the French automobile component market by American and Japanese suppliers; the transfer of new tasks from automakers to suppliers, such as the manufacture of complete segments of the vehicle, and the R&D tasks dedicated to specific systems.[2] French suppliers regrouped and led industrial and technological redeployment following the impetus of the automakers.

The automobile equipment builder sector, in France (including the suppliers of components and the suppliers of complete segments of vehicles) employed 238,000 people and had a turnover of 195 billion French francs in 1996. The primary suppliers (who carried out technical development, manufacturing and assembly of vehicle operating systems) represented 52% of the total turnover of this industry. In 1996, the French network of these primary suppliers included 305 companies belonging to FIEV (the professional organization of auto industry suppliers) and employed 107,751 people with a turnover of 101 billion French francs. This network represented 30% of the employees and 21% of the turnover of the French auto industry.

Since the 1980s, the automobile equipment sector has been internationalized and reorganized progressively (concentration and hierarchical reorganization). In 1996, the ten biggest companies (with more than 2,000 employees) represented approximately a third of the people employed by the automobile equipment sector, while the 189 small-sized companies (fewer than 200 employees) included around 10% of the people employed by the sector.

Trajectories of the internationalization of French automobile component suppliers

The term 'trajectory' here includes focusing attention on the determining character of the firm's specificities inherited from the past, and of the economic and institutional contexts in which it developed, while at the same time considering the cumulative effects engendered by its strategic reorientations and its adaptive repositioning on different markets. The trajectories can only be evaluated and reconstituted *ex post*. They are the result of a conjunction of factors and cumulative events. This explains why one cannot consider that the trajectories followed by firms in the automobile industry converge towards similar situations. The problems encountered at each step of their internationalization and the paths chosen to overcome them were not the same.

Nevertheless, all the trajectories of internationalization include the following four main phases: external growth and export strategy; alliances and shareholding investments; foreign direct investments and the setting up of new plants; and globalization. Companies in the automobile industry can work through the four phases simultaneously and reasonably quickly.[3]

The first decisive phase in the internationalization of these firms is based on an increasing level of exports founded on the diversification among their clients (automobile builders). Since 1994, the increasing level of the production of French automobile equipment industry was a result of exports. The direct sales to French automakers increased by 3.9% (from 47,697 million French francs in 1995 to 49,454 in 1996), which is not a bad performance considering the saturation of the French automobile market: which showed an increase of only +3.3% during the same period of time. In addition, French automobile equipment suppliers increased sales, first orientated towards German manufacturers, then towards Japanese transplants located in Europe. Between 1986 and 1996, the share of exports in the total sales by suppliers located in France rose from 31% to 38%.

In 1998, more than 50% of the biggest European suppliers' turnover stemmed from exports. For example, Valeo's foreign sales represented 78% of its consolidated turnover in 1998 (including 37% to non-European countries). Nevertheless, the major part of the increase in component sales has been in the European Union – on the one hand, between the suppliers' manufacturing sites located close to constructors' plants and, on the other, between the suppliers' concentrated plants (which group together assembly lines of different products) and the various automakers' factories located across Europe.

In the 1990s, the geographical configuration of imports and exports was reorganized by the diversification of suppliers' customers (automakers), the numerous joint ventures and agreements between equipment manufacturers, and the concentration of the main suppliers' manufacturing sites in Europe. Over ten years, flows of exchange (exports–imports) of automobile parts and components have been positive. In 1996, this surplus was around 30 billion French francs, with a 162% rate of foreign trade (ratio of exports to imports) as Table 9.1 shows.[4] The rate between imports and exports was negative for three countries as indicated in the table: Italy (with a rate of 69% in 1996); Germany (with a rate rising from 87.3% in 1995 to 98.1% in 1996); and Japan (a rate of 29% in 1996). On the other hand, the rate was positive for Spain (cover rate of 202%); United Kingdom (258.7%); Belgium (350.3%); central and Eastern Europe (321%); and the USA (293%).

In 1997, the French automobile equipment industry recorded a foreign trade rate of 32.2 billion French francs (an increase of 10.2% over 1996, with the highest level of exports for ten years: 85 billion French francs). This bulk of sales were orientated towards nearby European countries. Exports increased by 32.7% to Italy; 15.4% to the UK; and 12.1% to Spain. They also increased to Eastern Europe (+31.1%) and Mercosur (+10.1% in 1997, against +18% in 1996). Sales to China increased more than 228% largely through the location of Citroën in that country.

Table 9.1 Commercial balance of French automobile equipment and component industry, 1996: exports, imports and rate (in millions of francs and percentages)

Countries	Exports		Imports		Rate
	Millions	%	Millions	%	%
Western Europe, including	59,413	77.7	41,281	85.0	143.9
Germany	17,318	22.6	17,648	37.3	98.1
Spain	15,455	20.2	7,646	16.2	202.1
United Kingdom	8,611	11.2	3,329	7.0	258.7
Belgium	6,267	8.2	1,789	3.8	350.3
Italy	4,711	6.1	6,833	14.5	68.9
Central and Eastern Europe	2,792	3.6	870	1.8	320.9
USA/Canada	5,180	6.8	1,697	3.5	289.4
South America	3,138	4.1	280	0.6	1120.0
Asia, including	2,534	3.3	1,888	3.9	135.4
Japan			1,421	2.9	
Other	3,433	4.5	1,137	2.3	301.9
Total	76,490	100.0	48,574	100.0	157.5

Source: Statistics from the FIEV.

Strategic alliances and shareholding investments: numerous joint ventures and agreements between supplier companies

The equipment manufacturing industry has been also internationalized thanks to numerous joint ventures and agreements between companies. The equipment manufacturers generally bought back or obtained participation in the financial capital of:

- other equipment manufacturers who controlled key technologies (electronics, air conditioning and so on) to be present in potentially profitable and growing niches in terms of market shares on a world-wide level;
- suppliers who manufactured complementary products, whose acquisition allowed them to become suppliers of complete systems (cooling systems, frontal blocks, and so on); and
- suppliers who already had their manufacturing sites located close to constructors' plants and/or who maintained business relationships with developing countries automobile builders.

French automobile component suppliers did not reinforce their internationalization just to follow their automaker customers abroad. The biggest French automobile supplier (Valeo) has been more internationalized than the three main automakers (Renault, PSA and Citroën). The internationalization of equipment suppliers was a result of economic and financial factors. Since the early 1990s, equipment suppliers have restructured their financial capital (financial acquisitions, joint ventures and so on) to increase their number of partners in order to have sufficient size and turnover (Amin and Sadler, 1995).

Up to 1990, the internationalization strategy of major equipment manufacturers consisted of increasing their presence on markets in the Triad: by strategic alliances with major German suppliers in order to benefit from the market generated by the reunification of the the two Germanys, East and West; and by technological trajectories that allowed them to control the design, production and marketing of complete operations with strong technological content.

Equipment suppliers such as Valeo, ECIA (a subsidiary of PSA) and BFA (Bertrand-Faure) reinforced their links with German suppliers. For example, in 1990, ECIA created a shared company in association with Leistritz (the German exhaust specialist).[5]

At the same time the technological partnership of the equipment manufacturers and their privileged-customer autobuilders has been developed. This technological partnership seems to have constituted, in many cases, a 'launch pad' towards the internationalization of equipment manufacturers. Major American suppliers bought European and French suppliers in order to diversify their range of automaker customers and to maintain their turnover in the face of the saturation of the American automobile market. The four American suppliers that obtained the highest number of financial participations were Magna, Textron, Lear and Exide (see Tables 9.2, 9.3).

Table 9.2 Transatlantic acquisitions by North American suppliers

Suppliers	Number of acquisitions	Turnover of acquisitions (millions $)
Exide	4	1,290
Textron	6	1,228
Magna	6	1,059
Lear	2	580
Federal Mogul	2	400

Source: Autobusiness, 1994–6.

Table 9.3 North American acquisitions in Europe by country, 1994–6

Countries	Number of acquisitions	Turnover of acquisitions (millions $)
Germany	22	4,025
France	9	1,832
Italy	13	1,096
UK	15	1,082
Spain	3	555
Poland	4	240

Source: UBS, Union des Banques Suisses (Swiss Bank Union), 1997.

Direct foreign investments and new plants set up by French suppliers

Direct foreign investments (DFIs) were carried out by equipment manufacturers, most of the time concurrently with their strategic alliances and joint ventures. In most cases, these DFIs were realised in the framework of going beyond multi-domestic strategies, continued from the 1980s by overall strategies attempting to centralize advanced research means, organize logistics and co-ordinate sales policy on a world-wide basis, as well as to optimize the international organization of industrial manufacturing processes (specialized and interconnected sites producing for several markets).

In addition, DFIs in developing countries were created in a process of economic integration of certain regional poles. Equipment manufacturers (as well as their DFIs in Europe) extended their internationalization towards the ASEAN (Association of South East Asian Nations) countries, China and Taiwan, instigating business flows between the countries in this area.

French equipment suppliers created manufacturing sites, in the first phase, in South of Europe (particularly Spain) and Central Europe (Belgium) to supply the French manufacturers located in these areas; in the second phase, in Great Britain and Eastern Europe, to deliver to the Japanese transplants and the German manufacturers; and in the third phase, in Asia to supply French automakers' new sites and to diversify their Asian automaker customers.

After the creation of new plants in Italy and Spain, followed by Germany and England, Valeo rationalized its manufacturing activities in Europe and reinforced its relations with Japanese, German and American manufacturers. BFA followed a similar trajectory of internationalization, but a little later and on a smaller scale. French plastics processing equipment suppliers based their internationalization on the Franco-German alliance. In 1990, Sommer-Allibert set up a factory in Peine, close to Hannover, near the Volkswagen site. Plastic Omnium also opened a new site specializing in the manufacturing of petrol tanks in Rottenburg, close to Munich. In addition, Sommer-Allibert set up a new site in Zwickau (in the south of the DRG), near Mosel, where Volkswagen created a factory to produce Golf models in 1991.

Globalization and interconnection of activities at the international level

Most internationalization trajectories lead to 'globalization', which is characterized by:

- a manufacturing process on a world-wide basis;
- an international division of work aiming as much as possible at locating heavily value-added production in countries with highly-skilled workers having a certain mastery of new technologies, and on the other, intensive work operations in countries with low labour costs generally using standard technology;

- regrouping differentiated product manufacturing adapted to the needs of local consumers and to export markets sometimes covering several continents (re-exporting subsidiaries);
- a renewal of product ranges using common platforms and components. Builders as well as equipment manufacturers use 'commonalization' and standardization practices for basic components to generate diversity from parts destined for variations of the same model marketed on different continents; and
- the international organization of R&D activities whose objective is to favour an adaptation of new product design for enlarged continental zones, while at the same time respecting local customer expectations and improving industrialization in emerging countries. This R&D organization is typified by: regrouping fundamental research centres in industrialized countries in the Triad, allowing for economies of scale in the design phase (through optimal concentration and use of experimentation and trial means, elimination of project duplication and so on), as well as economies of variety (through the re-use of research results for several development projects involving several countries and vehicle models, through dialogue between the different engineering departments and so on); moving centres of applied technical development to regions where the main international production sites are located; international data transmission networks between the different advanced applied R&D centres set up by autobuilders and major equipment manufacturers – a world-wide organization of the supply network founded on 'global sourcing', which allows for the flexible use of the industrial capabilities of suppliers located in different regions of the world.

This 'globalization' corresponds to a strategy by which major French equipment suppliers attempt to increase their profitability through an internationalization of their value-added chains and a change in their financial structure. Until 1990, the international deployment of French suppliers took place in continental Europe. They located their manufacturing activities in the South, North and East of Europe, and their R&D activities close to big cities. However, they located part of their applied development activities in their manufacturing sites in order to improve synergies between product development tasks and manufacturing processes. For this first stage of 'Europeanization', there was not a complete interconnection of their activities on an international level. Major French suppliers rationalized their sites in Europe to avoid the duplication of activities on the same territory, and grouped together the R&D centres specializing in complementary technologies.

Only since 1995, have French suppliers such as Valeo and Bertrand-Faure built an international chain of complementary activities, particularly to increase their number of customers, to respond to automakers' requests asking suppliers to participate in 'global sourcing' and be involved in technical partnership. On the one hand, automobile builders require their main equipment manufacturers to be able to deliver the types of components (destined for each vehicle for which they were selected) in all regions of the world where the vehicle is manufactured. In these conditions, the main equipment manufacturer is encouraged to increase its locations abroad. On the other hand, the technological partnership results in a selection and an involvement of the majors suppliers in the development of all the functions of the vehicle, at least three years before its commercial release. Under these conditions, equipment suppliers eventually manage 'satellite' systems co-ordinating three levels internationally: production capabilities, R&D activities and logistics flows.

Equipment suppliers, such as Valeo and BFA, set up R&D centres abroad only when there were niches for specific technologies in local markets. For example, Valeo opened a technical centre in Detroit concentrating on air conditioning in order to reinforce its expertise with American automakers. This suggests there is a need to create international data transmission networks between the different advanced applied research and development centres in order to re-use the results of development activities from several applied cases, and to select fields of research that might be exploited in the future.

Regarding manufacturing plants and logistic flows, the situation is extremely varied: particular sites, such as 'Valeo Safety Systems' in Blyth (North-East of England), provide components simultaneously for American manufacturers located in the United Kingdom and those situated in the USA itself. BFA plants which assemble seats are often located near the automakers' factories. The way in which the manufacturing activities are interconnected and located depends on various factors: delivery conditions (frequency, just-in-time and so on), characteristics of products (size, weight and quality of product and so on), manufacturing conditions (synchronized production, complete functions with many components, for example), sharing of capacity between several sites, human resources management (interconnected to many sites, competence required, for example), as we described in a detailed report for DATAR (Laigle, 1998).

In most cases, it is a question of finding a compromise between a great diversity in products marketed to a great number of countries and regions, but designed and manufactured (from common platforms and components) in specialized sites, allowing for economies of scale. In other words, how to manufacture a product in a particular region that has the maximum number of standard components (delivered by world-wide equipment manufacturers), but whose variety was designed to allow for it to be marketed in many regions of the world? New transnational organizations of industrial design and production adopted by different major suppliers are attempting to answer this question.

The equipment manufacturing industry is mobilized to make basic vehicle functions evolve on a technological level, to participate in their standardization/specification, and to deliver them in any region in the world, even if it means taking risks to innovate, to set up in developing countries and to organize logistics flows on a world-wide level. Consequently, globalization is conveyed by a transnationalization of the 'automobile system' in its entirety, including autobuilders and equipment manufacturers.

The internationalization of Valeo: trajectory and strategy

External growth and Europeanization of the Valeo Group from 1986

With the globalization of exchanges and competition came concentration (Amin and Sadler, 1995), hierarchical organization (de Banville and Chanaron, 1999), and growing globalization (Helper and Sako, 1999) of the world's leading automakers. In the case of France, this sector's globalization took place in two stages. At the beginning of the 1980s, penetration of the auto manufacturing market by foreign groups could be seen (in particular, German, British and American automakers), whereas French makers did not seem to take any notice of the importance of such a phenomenon (Laigle, 1996a). In the second half of the 1980s, French suppliers regrouped and led the industrial and technological deployment, under the impetus of autobuilders (PSA and Renault) who from then on were committed to changes in their relationships, as industrial and technological partners, with their equipment manufacturers (Laigle, 1996b).

In 1980, the French limited company Ferodo became Valeo. The group was strengthened at the beginning of the 1980s by external and sectorially diversified acquisitions.[6] In 1986, when Valeo was losing money, its financial capital was restructured with investments from an Italian businessman, Carlo de Benedetti (28% of its capital). The latter called in N. Goutard as CEO of Valeo and gave him the task of putting the firm back into its core industry as an auto equipment manufacturer, as well as carrying out its European deployment.

The CEO proceeded to get rid of subsidiaries belonging to other industrial sectors, merged and regrouped certain branches, and above all went ahead with acquisitions in more profitable domains of the automobile sector: lighting and signalling, motors and passenger temperature control, and electronics and passenger safety.

In 1990, the Valeo Group was thus made up of six divisions: lighting signalling (headlights and blinkers), electrical systems (alternators, starters and so on), wiping systems (wipers and their electric motors), passenger safety (locking and alarm systems and so on), clutches, friction materials (clutch boxes and automatic transmission boxes), passenger temperature control (air conditioning systems, electricity supply and so on) and distribution (commercial networks for spare parts).

The 1970s and 1980s were essentially characterized by a Europeanization of the Valeo Group. Its expansion into Italy dated from the beginning of the

1970s, where, after having launched the manufacturing of clutches, Valeo first bought firms specialized in lighting, and later in radiator cooling systems and heating systems.[7] Similarly, during the 1980s, Valeo continued to strengthen its presence among German autobuilders by buying, in 1988, the German firm Tibbe, and by opening new production sites at Reichenbach in Saxony to manufacture clutch systems, a site whose capacities were increased with the purchase of the clutch activities of Renak Werke three years later. Still in Germany, for its 'passenger safety' branch, Valeo created a research centre on the Erdweg site.[8]

The group also spread its activities to Spain before 1990, notably by taking control of the Spanish firm Clausor in 1988. However, unlike in Germany, it was mainly production sites that were opened in Spain, along with a few research centres.[9] In the UK, Valeo bought Delainair in 1989 a manufacturer of air conditioning and wiper systems.

The Group's globalization strategy was thus characterized in 1989 by European development which was carried out in different ways depending on the countries concerned (the exception being France): a majority of production sites in Southern European countries (Italy and Spain), a great many more technical and sales outlets compared to the production sites in Germany, and a low number of production sites supported by technical centres (a total of three) in Britain.[10]

1989 and 1992: Valeo's internal streamlining and globalization towards Japanese, German and American autobuilders

After having followed a strategy of external growth though the multiplication of acquisitions between 1986 and 1989, the Valeo Group began to privilege, starting in 1990, a streamlining of the production activities formerly acquired, while at the same time enlarging its international sites. It specialized and regrouped its production sites, notably to gain from economies of scale and variety (Chandler, 1990). This allowed it to free up financial resources that could help in its internationalization. The Group thus self-financed (from its cash flow) 3.5 billion French francs of investments in 1990, a figure representing 8% of its turnover, to replace or complete existing units.

Confronted with the slump in the automobile market at the end of the 1980s, Valeo drew up a streamlining plan including the closure of around fifteen sites in Europe and in the USA, which led to the loss of 4,000 jobs in 1990, around 10% of its personnel, from a total of 34,200 employees. This plan's goal was to improve productivity, cost price and product quality in order to increase its penetration of world automobile markets.[11] Valeo then undertook the restructuring of its leading activities (temperature control, friction materials, lighting and electronics) and gave up activities considered to be unprofitable because of their size, was considered to be insufficient to face competition from the world's major equipment suppliers (such as the brake systems bought by Allied Signal) or integral electronics, because of the specific technological know-how that this activity requires, skills already possessed by major international equipment manufacturers such as Sagem.

To sum up, between 1989 and 1992, Valeo's strategy was to streamline its activities while still continuing its internationalization in the context of a recession. This strategy was characterized by four complementary lines:

(i) abandoning 'peripheral' or unprofitable activities, with a view to finding the financial resources to support the growth and internationalization of leading activities;

(ii) streamlining its productive machinery through the regrouping of each of its branch's activities on to a reduced number of modernized manufacturing sites, each one adopting the Valeo production system applied on all of its foreign sites as well as in France to respond to autobuilders' demands for quality;[12]

(iii) the creation and setting up of new production sites along with investments in R&D (the creation of new R&D centres, changes in new product development procedures and so on). R&D's share of turnover rose from 3.9% in 1989 to 4.4% in 1991, an investment increase of 20.7% (from FRF717 million to FRF866 million), with R&D activities employing more than 2,000 people in 1990; and

(iv) internationalization which, in Europe, began to move away from Spain and Italy towards Germany and the UK, and grew as a result of sales to Japanese builders and the strengthening of its establishments in both North and South America.[13]

After the abandonment of four activities judged to be non-strategic – among which were the Hampton lighting unit in the USA and the Mitchell temperature control equipment factory in Spain – Valeo continued its re-centring policy during the 1990s.

These transactions were carried out to try to raise sufficient financial resources to reinforce leading divisions and to limit the group's debt in an unfavourable economic situation. Their objective was to finance the necessary investments for the development of leading activities from the Group's own self-financed margin to strengthen Valeo's position among the world's leading autobuilders. The 1990 sell-offs of the plastic injection firm, G. Cartier Industrie, Delanair Motors, Mitchell Temperature Control Equipment in Spain, the Hampton lighting unit in the USA, and the Sagem spark plug unit contributed to reducing Valeo's deficit by FRF700–800 million from the FRF4.3 billion of Valeo net debt at the end of 1989, and to provide for restructuring measures to the tune of FRF150 million.

Valeo's second line of strategy during this period of slower activity was to proceed with productive streamlining through the closing of smaller sites that were working beyond full capacity or in unattractive markets, and regrouping the sites with similar activities.

This regrouping, along with the sell-offs in the 1990s, caused a lowering of the Group's personnel. Valeo's 1991 balance sheet shows that there was a 21% drop in employees between the end of 1989 (34,200 employees) and the end of 1991 (27,000 employees), and that operating costs dropped sharply from FRF1415 billion to FRF878 million (with a further fall to FRF676 million in 1990). Of the three leading Valeo markets (Europe, the USA and Brazil), sales fell by 8% in the last quarter of 1990. Valeo reduced its temporary workforce by 50% in the second semester of 1990. It also cut 2,500 jobs starting in May 1991 (1,200 in France and the rest essentially in the USA and Brazil). The group's personnel was thus reduced to 26,500 employees at the beginning of 1992 (15,000 in France and 11,500 in the rest of the world). Some of these cuts included outright redundancies.

The third part of Valeo's streamlining strategy during the recession at the beginning of the 1990s was the development of its leading activities at international level by improving its sales and R&D efforts, and by creating new production and research sites. It is important to note that many of these creations took place via transfers of activity to the detriment of the group's older factories. In France, outright plant creations became very rare as of 1990, which corresponded to the strategy that the Group preferred, favouring its growth via production units located abroad.

Three R&D centres were created between 1990 and 1992: a clutch technical centre at Amiens on the production site of the Valeo Clutches factory, where a measurement laboratory, test tracks and prototype workshops were located, with the Advanced Research Centre being in St. Ouen; an electronics research centre (for electrical systems, passenger safety and electronics branches) in Créteil in the Greater Paris area, bringing together 200 people; and an electric motor research centre (CEREME) in St. Quentin en Yvelines in the Paris area.[14] The changes being made did not only involve France. During this period, Valeo redeployed its activities at the European level, notably working for Japanese transplants and German autobuilders, as well as at international level, by increasing its locations in both North and South America.

The fourth part of Valeo's strategy was more internationalization geared towards Japanese and American automakers, who suffered less from the shrinking European automobile market, while at the same time strengthening its market shares with German makers. Valeo made heavy investments in the UK between 1988 and 1992, to handle orders coming from Japanese transplants (Nissan, Honda and Toyota). In 1990, the heating and air conditioning activities inherited from the British firm, Delanair, were regrouped in a new plant at Gorseinon in Wales to meet heating, ventilation and air conditioning needs. Valeo Friction Materials concentrated on clutch pads. Moreover, this branch developed its international position, becoming a supplier to Japanese builders such as Nissan, Subaru and Isuzu, by consolidating its position as the world number one. In 1991, Valeo Lighting-Signalling implemented new technologies such as complex surface anti-fog headlights for Renault and Nissan, and lighting range correctors. The Alternator-Starter branch led to new and important markets in England with Honda thanks to its new lines of internally-ventilated alternators and reduction starters. The internationalization of Valeo Wipers also took place through setting up in the UK. Finally, at the beginning of 1992, Valeo Passenger signed an outline agreement with the Japanese equipment manufacturer Alpha Corporation – a major supplier of Nissan – whose turnover totalled FRF2 billion in anti-theft systems and auto locksmithing. To that can be added improved Valeo sales and technical presence in Japan, with the opening in 1989 of technical sales offices in Tokyo.

Thus, in 1991, equipment sales from the British sites represented around FRF2 billion, roughly 10% of the group's turnover.[15] In 1992, Valeo Lighting-Signalling was congratulated by Nissan for providing better quality, reactivity and development capacity performances during the launch of the new Micra and Primera models.

But Valeo did not intend to limit itself to supplying equipment for Japanese transplants in the UK. The group increased its investment in the USA, notably to profit from the Bush–Miyazawa accord on increasing American spare-parts exports to Japan. However, this internationalization towards Japanese and American builders did not go easily, as both countries had production systems related to their suppliers.

In Japan, builders work with their own equipment subsidiaries and rarely call upon foreign suppliers (Lecler, 1993). What is more, in most cases, Japanese equipment manufacturers follow their autobuilders abroad and acquire medium-sized firms, which explains the strengthening of their sales positions in Europe (Lagendijk *et al.*, 1996). Consequently, Japanese transplants only make use of foreign equipment suppliers when their own suppliers do not have local subsidiaries, or when their accredited suppliers are not able to give them the product they need.[16] In these conditions, Valeo's strategy was to offer products or systems that do not exist in Japan and are particularly adapted to meet European safety regulations and the requirements of insurance companies (mandatory anti-theft systems mounted on Japanese cars manufactured in England, for example). In 1995, Valeo was able to make 5% of its turnover from Japanese autobuilders.

The difficulties Valeo met in gaining a foothold in the American market are similar, since Ford and GM already have their own in-house suppliers. Moreover, the strength wielded by the UAW – the automobile industry union – concerning the choice of suppliers that manufacturers can make, is not to be underestimated in the obstacles that European suppliers meet in their attempted conquest of the American market. Still, Valeo obtained 15% of its turnover in North America, Chrysler being the Group's third-largest customer.

Between 1990 and 1992, Valeo launched itself in the construction of five plants (outside France and the UK).

1. In the former West Germany, in the area of passenger safety, Valeo regrouped three units on the Erdweg site.
2. In the former GDR, where Valeo took over the clutch activity of the German Renak Company and constructed a new factory on its Reichenbach site to carry out assembly of complete clutches from components furnished by European sites at Amiens (France), Fuenlabrada (Spain) and Mondovi (Italy). This new factory worked for Volkswagen[17] (Passat and Golf) and for Opel[18] (Astra and Vectra).
3. In the USA, the Valeo American subsidiary Blackstone (motor temperature control) invested in a new unit at Greensburg in Indiana to deliver new, complete motor cooling modules (for the Clio and the American market).
4. In Mexico, Valeo created a new plant in the motor temperature control branch at San Luis Potosi, stemming directly from the regrouping of the Valeo and Blackstone units (besides the temperature control factory created in Brazil two years earlier).
5. Finally, in Turkey, after having purchased 51% of Transturk Elektrik, Valeo built a plant to produce and distribute alternators and starters (which represented the third Valeo site in Turkey, after those created to deliver motor cooling systems and clutches for the Renault and Fiat factories).

1993–7: growth founded on the globalization of 'leader' branches

The economic recovery that occurred in the second half of 1993 and in 1994 allowed Valeo to strengthen its growth strategy through the internationalization of its leading branches (lighting-signalling, temperature control air conditioning, clutches and passenger safety), first orientated towards North America and Eastern Europe in the expansion of the early 1990s (but with new countries such as Poland), then towards Asia, in particular, emerging countries such as China and Korea.

Despite a 2% drop in turnover in 1993, Valeo's sales progressed by 38% in America and Asia, to represent 23% of its consolidated turnover, compared to 16% in 1992. However, sales slumped 10% in Europe, because of the 16% fall in European auto production. Thus, in 1993, it was the international growth outside of Europe, combined with the streamlining efforts made by the whole group, that contributed decisively to the consolidation of Valeo's results and allowed it to counter the decline in the automobile market. It then appeared – taking the recession in the European auto industry into account – that Valeo had every interest in pursuing its internationalization strategy, by developing its technological competitive advantage in leading branches.

In 1994, Valeo obtained a 14% improvement in its turnover in comparison with the preceding year (from FRF20 billion to FRF23 billion). Worldwide employment increased by 10%, from 25,400 to 28,100 employees. The number of engineers and R&D technicians grew by 15% in 1994, reaching 2,350 people by the end of the year. Annual R&D spending represented 5.5% of turnover in 1994, compared with 5.2% in 1993 and 4.7% in 1992. During this year, Valeo made 40% of its turnover in France (compared with 44% in 1991), 37% in the rest of Europe and 13% in North America. In first assembly equipment, sales progressed by 15% in North America (becoming the second largest market after France), 18% for all of Europe and South America, and 80% in Asia.

This trend for the development of sales in America, Asia and Europe (notably Eastern Europe) continued in 1996, when the Valeo Group recorded an increased turnover of 14.4%, at FRF28.9 billion.[19] Of this progress, 2.5 points is linked to the enlargement of the Group's world perimeter. International sales in 1996 represented 68% of the total of the Group's sales (compared with 63% in 1995, and 56% in 1991). These progressed as follows during 1996: +25% in Europe (apart from France), which represented in December 1996 46% of the Group's turnover; +23% in North America, which now represented 13% of turnover; and +16% in Asia and South America.

In fact, this internationalization happened differently for each of the Group's leading branches, as they were confronted with different environmental and technological situations. The lighting-signalling branch in 1994 opened a new factory in Pianezza, Italy, after the plant built in 1993 in Hirson in the Aisne département in France. In addition, an international research and development centre was created in Bobigny, near Paris.[20] In 1995, Valeo signed a contract with Honda in Japan to deliver headlights from French plants. In the first half of 1996, Valeo opened a new lighting factory in Canada. At the end of 1996, the company decided to close its rear-signalling plant in Evreux, France and transfer its manufacturing and blinker activities to French sites at Sens (600 people in the Yonne département) and Mazamet (400 people in the Tarn). According to the Group's management, this closure was justified by the necessity to 'safeguard the activity's competitiveness by strengthening plant specialization and reducing manufacturing costs'.

Competition in lighting and signalling was becoming more intense. For example, in the Mégane project (Renault), Valeo only supplied the headlights for the coupé model, while Amiclas won the market for the sedan and Scénic models. Present in France (Axo Scintex), Spain (Yorka) and Italy (Altissimo), Amiclas, which chalked up nearly FRF1 billion in turnover, at the time of writing employs nearly 350 people in France. The European signalling market appeared to be highly competitive: Valeo held 33% of this market in 1996, but Amiclas had conquered 25%, Hella 20% and Magneti Marelli 10%. What is more, the joint venture that the British firm Britax has signed with the Japanese Koito now allows it to offer overall lighting and signalling systems.

As of 1993, the passenger and motor heating branches went through major changes. These two branches were merged, with a view to offering a complete temperature control system to autobuilder customers.[21] The degree of internationalization of Valeo's temperature control activities grew sharply between 1993 and 1997. Valeo accelerated its internationalization with the acquisition in 1994 of the German electronics firm Borg Instruments and the creation of a joint venture with Siemens. Planned to compete with Japanese and American competitors in the air conditioning market, this joint venture with Siemens would allow Valeo to augment the number of passenger heating series (air conditioning and small electric motors) and, most important, to offer air conditioning systems for German autobuilders (Mercedes-Benz, BMW and Volkswagen). Moreover, the equipment manufacturer upgraded its Swedish site in Mjallby in 1996, which then became the Group's European centre for temperature control systems in heavy vehicles.

Valeo created new factories in North America in 1994, buying Lake Center Industries, a subsidiary of Atkinson, producing electronic equipment for heating and air conditioning control panels. This acquisition allowed it to develop its relations with Chrysler, GM and Ford. Valeo also strengthened its position in air conditioners in the USA by creating a new site in 1997 in Hamilton, Ohio that employed 300 people by 1998. This new set-up complemented that in Greensburg, Indiana specializing in the production of temperature control exchangers. To that was added in 1997 a motor and passenger temperature control research and development centre in Detroit, employing 300 people and representing a US$30 million investment.

In 1994, Valeo also went ahead with two joint ventures in Argentina with the industrial firm Casa Radiadores Argentina, which produces aluminium radiators for the Argentine and Brazilian markets, adding to the two plants created in Mexico and Brazil to supply passenger heating. In 1996, Valeo concluded an agreement to participate in Mirgor, the main manufacturer of air conditioners in Argentina.

The Valeo group began setting up in Poland in 1994 to serve the Korean Daewoo assembly units. In November 1995, Valeo acquired 80% of the clutch activity at FSO through the creation of a joint venture in which the Polish autobuilder will take 20% to manufacture and market clutches from the Kozuchow plant. In addition, Valeo created two subsidiaries in Poland in July 1996: one specializing in motor cooling systems, and the other in the marketing of the group's products on the Polish spare parts market. Valeo distribution Dystrybycja will also be present in Belarus and the Baltic countries. With these new sites, Valeo hopes to open the doors of new markets in Eastern Europe.

During the same period, Valeo increased joint ventures in China and Korea. In China, Valeo Wiper Systems signed a licensing contract in 1994 with the Wenling Auto Parts Factory. The contract covered the manufacturing of complete wiper systems. Wenling is the wiper supplier for most Chinese and European builders operating in China (Peugeot, Audi and Volkswagen). In the same year, Valeo committed to a joint venture in China – Valeo Automotive Air Conditioning – in Hubei. In December 1994, Valeo developed its third joint venture in China, with the Shanghai Automotive Industry Corporation (SAIC), to make alternators and starters especially for the Chinese car market.[22] In 1996, the Shanghai Valeo Automotive Electrical Systems Company took over the alternator and starter activities from SAEW, a Chinese industrial group, a subsidiary of Shanghai Automotive Industry Corporation (SAIC). In Korea, Valeo created a plant in Chochiwon specializing in motor temperature control, near the existing Taegu clutch plant. Asia thus appeared as the new territory for the Group to conquer. If Asia did not generate 5% of turnover in 1994, the 10% goal was almost reached at the beginning of 1997. This new form of internationalization towards Asia marked a turning point in the international strategy for the Valeo Group as well as for equipment suppliers in general (Lecler, 1996). It is no longer only about moving close to major autobuilder partners in their foreign premises, but also about generating new outlets with new autobuilder customers who are not part of the companies traditionally set up in industrialized countries.

In June 1996, Valeo bought Fist Spa, the Italian leader for car door handles and locks, based in Turin and employing 270 people. This acquisition allowed the passenger safety branch of Valeo to strengthen its position in the area of mechanical and electronic access and safety systems for passenger vehicles. Valeo reinforced its passenger safety branch by purchasing Lock Systems in November 1996 from the German firm Ymos, subsidiary of the Belgian steel company, Cockerill Sambre. Lock Systems, specialists in door locking and anti-theft systems, recorded FF1 billion in turnover and has five production sites, in Germany, France, the UK and Spain, employing 1,400 people.[23] With this operation, which came after the acquisition of the Italian Fist Spa, Valeo's passenger safety branch was now able to offer a complete range of systems covering door locking and mechanical and electronic anti-theft systems. This branch was to make a turnover of FF3 billion, which Valeo considers to be the critical size which will allow it to intensify technological development and internationalization.

The Group is aiming at reinforcing its R&D by pursuing the constitution of a number of specialized sites around Paris, near its decision-making centres and those of French autobuilders, but also abroad near its major customers to better meet their needs. Valeo has already set up three out of thirteen planned R&D centres outside France (in Germany, Sweden and the USA). In 1995, it created a fourth in the UK, specializing in passenger safety electronics. Valeo is also going to open an air conditioner and motor temperature control R&D centre in Detroit, USA, where 350 technicians will work. This centre is located near the premises of the three major American autobuilders, and close to Japanese builders. But the majority of the Group's

R&D centres will remain in the Paris area, where Valeo has regrouped six of its nine centres located in France.

1996: a troubled year for a change in Valeo's capital

Since the abandonment in November 1996 of the 27.4% of Valeo capital held by Cerus (a subsidiary of De Benedetti), the CGIP, which bought the greater part, has held 20.2%; the Caisse des Dépôts et Consignations, 6.8%; French institutional investors, 19.6%; American investors, 14.6%; British investors, 16.7%; and other foreign investors, 15.6%.

Beyond this division, discussions took place in 1996, the main question being asked was regarding the stakes and consequences of a future purchase of Valeo's shares by subsidiaries owned by direct competitors of French auto-builders, such as Delphi, a subsidiary of GM, the world's largest automaker. What resulted from these discussions is that the technological contents of the systems supplied has become such that constructors are now dependant on their suppliers for more than 50% of vehicle technical support. In fact, it is even greater than this, considering that equipment manufacturers can transfer a part of their technological advances to their autobuilder customers. It has also become practically impossible to reintegrate the innovation activities of these 'functional systems' into autobuilders' plants, as their research costs are now too high to be borne by a sole constructor.

In these conditions, the purchase of a supplier such as Valeo by a subsidiary of a foreign builder presents a risk – for French builders – of becoming a 'second-rate' customer. In other words, Valeo would have been encouraged to keep the 'first-hand status' of their discoveries from the subsidiary who had acquired it, and similarly from its main shareholder (a foreign builder), which could have aggravated the relative backwardness of French automakers in comparison to their international competitors. From this point of view, it is easy to understand why French autobuilders (but also public authorities) rose up against the take-over of Valeo by a competitor's subsidiary, something that would have given rise to a transfer of the group's R&D activities outside France, or at the least a transfer of numerous production sites, with dire consequences for employment in the automobile sector in France.

1997–8: pursuit of an internal and external growth regrouping strategy through internationalization

Valeo's internationalization strategy since the end of 1993, has been to reinforce its links with American, German and Japanese automakers (giving rise to new factories, but also to R&D centres in these countries), and to develop new relations with emerging countries' suppliers and autobuilders, such as those in India and China. During 1997–8, the group counted on pursuing its external growth and internal restructuring strategy.[24]

On the one hand, Valeo is considering continuing its industrial streamlining by reducing the number of medium-sized factories and regrouping its production on a reduced number of sites to obtain effects of volume, productivity gains and structure.[25] Valeo thus counts on meeting the autobuilders' requests for price decreases and financing a 14% increase in R&D from cash flow for 1997.[26] In the long term, it plans on developing sites specializing in a type of product that would be delivered to all the autobuilders on a given continent (North America, Europe and so on), in order to gain economies of scale and improve the competitiveness–price ratio. This is, in fact, already the case for alternators and starters, where the French factory supplies all the European autobuilders. It would seem to be moving towards the transnationalization of the Group's production sites, through the concentration of manufacturing sites and the homogenization of applied productive models (with the application of the Valeo Production System on all sites).

On the other hand, this strategy must be rationalized by decentralization (often of medium-sized concerns), through which the equipment maker has been led to conquer new car market shares. The group's strategy thus rests essentially on the expansion of market shares through external growth by developing new joint ventures with 'indigenous' suppliers to deliver components to builders located abroad. Valeo is planning to carrying out half of its activities outside Europe within five years, compared to 22% today, by intensifying the internationalization of its leading branches.[27]

Within this framework, Valeo is intent on continuing its efforts to enter the Asian market, by aiming to supply Japanese autobuilders in Japan (already the case for the Honda Civic), but most of all to profit from existing development potentials in South East Asia, India[28] and China. Concurrently, Valeo is considering carrying on its expansion in the USA, which represents the largest world market in terms of growth[29] (compared with the saturated European market), and towards South American countries such as Brazil, Argentina and Mexico.

Conclusion

Since the 1980s, Valeo has followed several internationalization strategies. The external growth and 'Europeanization' scheme was succeeded by a strategy of industrial restructuring and internationalization of its leading branches. First, the group orientated itself towards conquering market shares with Japanese, American and German autobuilders, then towards the strengthening of these relations – notably through the opening of R&D centres near these automakers – and finally through the setting up of new production sites in the emerging countries of Eastern Europe and Asia.

The Valeo Group's internationalization was thus carried out by a reconcentration on its leading activities, a continued and increased R&D effort, industrial restructuring, and the regrouping of its production activities. The tension between the concentration of production activities (sought out to obtain economies of scale in 'mature' markets) and decentralization (towards autobuilders' new sites) indicates the high stakes of the auto industry equipment suppliers' internationalization trajectory.

For the future, Valeo seems to favour a strategy of commonalization (the division of main organs and components for different range segments), by preferring the creation of continental production sites in markets such as Europe and the USA. At the same time, the Group intends to continue the conquest of new markets, which would require a certain adaptation of products and socio-productive models. The Group's internationalization strategy would therefore correspond to the regional diversification/world-wide commonalization scenario evoked by Freyssenet and Lung (1996, 2000).

Notes

1   All the turnover figures and facts cited (mergers, acquisitions, joint ventures, financial participation and creation of new sites) come from the annual results of the Group and the data issued by the Valeo Communications Department, as well as from the CCFA (French Chamber of Automobile Builders) Press Review. I have also re-used some of the data from my dissertation, for which I visited some ten Valeo production sites in France and four of its research centres (Laigle, 1996a).

2   Suppliers develop and manufacture essential functions of the vehicle such as lighting, signalling, braking, air conditioning, wiping, transmission and electrical systems. Among car components, two types of systems have been developed recently: exhaust (taking into account the sophistication of these systems) and electrical-electronic systems (which represented at the beginning of the 1980s less than 5% of the cost of a car, against 9% in 1996, and 20% in 2000).

3   The four phases of internationalization do not make up a sequential scheme that can be applied to all firms. These four phrases must be understood as constituent elements in internationalization trajectories, which can be experienced more or less simultaneously, according to the constraints and opportunities that the companies encounter (commercial barriers, price restrictions and so on). Moreover, these four phases are superimposed over time: the export phase, for example, continues at the same time as that of strategic alliances and foreign investments is developing.

4   However, the rate of imports (level of imports compared with the production of French suppliers) was high: rising from 48% in 1994 to 46.6% in 1996 (FRF47,246 million of imports in a total of FRF101,001 million of French automobile suppliers' production in 1996).

5   Before Leistritz joined ECIA in October 1989 to buy the French supplier Eli-exhaust (a subsidiary of group BFA).

6   The group attempted to diversify into sectors such as construction (Isba), foundries or steelmaking (Allevard steel springs).

7   Very quickly – from 1974 – the expansion of these production sites was accompanied by the opening of R&D and distribution centres. Since then, Valeo has not stopped strengthening its presence among Italian autobuilders by equipping a significant part of Italian Fiat models with clutches and radiators, and by expanding its distribution network. In 1985, Valeo Italy regrouped its administrative and national management activities in Santena, near one of these R&D centres.

8   It must be underlined that Valeo created five technical sales offices in Germany, of which the two largest are those in Stuttgart and Wolfsburg, each of which also

includes a technical centre working on the clutch, thermal and engine compartments, lighting-signalling and electric systems. Similarly, the Europeanization of the Group included the opening in Sweden of production sites and a technical centre, but only for thermal motors.

9   Thus, at the end of 1991, Valeo in Germany numbered five technical sales offices, two technical centres, an advanced research centre and two factories, and in Spain there were eight plants (of which five were associated with technical centres), but no advanced research centre and only one technical sales office, in Barcelona. All Valeo branches (apart from wiper and electronic systems) had at least one factory in Spain in 1991.

10 As will be seen, Valeo was subsequently to multiply its production sites in the UK to supply equipment to Japanese transplants.

11 One of the objectives of this restructuring by the Valeo Group's CEO was to increase the annual turnover per employee to FRF 700,000.

12 The production system (applied in the fifteen countries where Valeo is based) fits into the 'productive model' implemented by Valeo, organized around the five following main points:

   (i)   *Staff involvement*: ensuring the promotion of team spirit, simplifying hierarchies, favouring direct communication, expanding staff skills (5% of aggregate employee remuneration is devoted to training);

   (ii) *Valeo production system*: just-in-time organization with reduction of inventory, flexibility of production means and elimination of unproductive operations, permanent improvement through employee participation and responsibility, autonomous production teams, posting of performance indicators and so on;

   (iii) *Constant innovation*: increased research efforts to develop innovative, reliable, competitive products in terms of price, generalization of organization by project and simultaneous product/process engineering, optimization of development deadlines, notably through the elaboration of the Valeo Development Charter (based on those used by Toyota and Renault);

   (iv) *Supplier integration*: selection and reduction of the number of suppliers, quality audit and supplier conformity with Valeo quality norms, integration of suppliers in the research and development of products and systems; and

   (v)   *Total quality*: a systematic audit of each establishment, using as a reference the highest standards of international quality, a permanent update of the Group quality norm – Valeo 1000 – to meet automakers' demands.

13 Yet, in December 1991, Spain still represented 10% of the Group's turnover and Italy 9%, the latter now finding itself on the same level as Germany and North America, while the UK only represented 6% and Asia 4% (compared with 44% for France).

14 The R&D centre at St. Quentin en Yvelines (100 people) regroups the different technical centres the branches use (cabin safety, thermal motor and wiper systems) to adapt electric motors to their own needs. This new research centre brings together 100 people and will develop new electric motors to meet the needs of the three branches (production estimated to be 75,000 motors per day across the world).

15 The sites located in the UK are: the Gorseinon plant, for air conditioning device production, the Blyth factory for passenger safety, the Hengoed plant for wiper systems, and the Woodgate site for clutches. This latter site also includes a technical

centre and technical sales offices serving the four types of activity set up in the UK.

16 The possibilities are more open with a group like Honda, whose growth is turned towards areas outside Japan.

17 Volkswagen is alleged to have guaranteed Valeo sales volumes, or 25% of clutch supplies compared with 10% previously, so as to encourage it to open a new factory at Reichenbach.

18 It must be underlined also that the alternator-starter branch led to new and significant markets in Germany with Mercedes, Audi, BMW and Opel.

19 In December 1996, there were 16,300 employees in the group in France (compared with 15,400 in 1995), and 32,500 people across the world (against 29,600 in 1995).

20 This centre, which operates mainly in three areas (the design of optic systems, transformation of materials, and style) represented an investment of FRF300 million and consisted of 300 engineers and technicians, of which forty were dedicated to research and technological transfers. The centre has a rapid prototype workshop at its disposal, connected directly to computer simulation and imaging of research department projects: once a research result is validated, everything is done to streamline and automate its application in the project framework. Up to 80% of technical solutions used on a new major model come from standard libraries (300 projects in 1994), which allows for a reduction in development time of practically half. Lighting made up FRF3.6 billion at Valeo in 1994, or 15% of its turnover, 55% of which is directed towards exports.

21 As both 'hot and cold' thermal elements use the same technology and have connecting points in the vehicle (the air conditioning unit is linked to the motor's water circulation system), the stakes of regrouping are to benefit from research synergy and profit from very heavy investment (in climactic chambers and test grounds, for example). In the same vein, on the production side, it is now planned to produce parts destined for both engine and passenger temperature control on the same site. A passenger temperature workshop has been set up in the Italian motor temperature factory in Frosinine. By obtaining high volumes, the firm counts on better negotiating purchases of raw materials and aluminium tubes.

22 SAIC produced the Santana vehicle in association with Volkswagen.

23 Valeo sold its British windscreen wiper activity to the American supplier Textron in July 1996. This activity is located in Hengoed in the UK, represents a FRF100 million turnover (£12.7 million), and employs 180 people.

24 The group's management is hoping for favourable European markets for 1997, thanks to low interest rates, the end of the over-evaluation of the French franc and the DM, and contained inflation.

25 Valeo, for 1997–8, is considering industrial redeployment in Western Europe, from a FRF6 billion industrial investment scheme, including the modernization and enlargement of its European factories (sixty sites, of which twenty-seven are in France) in which it intends to concentrate its production.

26 Overcapacity in the world-wide auto industry puts enormous pressure on prices, to which, according to the Group's management, the Group must respond by 10% productivity gains for 1997–8 (against 5.8% in 1996).

27 The Group no longer plans to commit itself to diversification in sectors already occupied by major industry leaders, such as Bosch, for motor injection. It is more concerned with expanding market shares at the international level, into clutches, passenger safety and air conditioning, alternators and starters, while still keeping

abreast of the technological innovations that are going to concern these different branches in the coming years. Valeo expects to begin these innovations on small electric motors.

28 In 1996, Valeo signed a protocol agreement with the Indian clutch leader Amalgamations Ltd, and plans to continue this strategy in India to multiply its investments by 1999.

29 Valeo thus recognizes American autobuilders' competitiveness–price ratio is not linked to salary costs (similar to those in Europe, where plants are less union-dominated and, therefore, have a certain amount of salary competitiveness), but stemming from the high volumes that the American industry generates and its production costs, which are far below those in Europe.

References

Amin, A. and Sadler, S. (1995) 'Europeanisation in the Automotive Components Sector and its Implication for State and Locality', in Hudson and Schamp (eds), *Towards a New Map of Automobile Manufacturing in Europe?*, Berlin/Heidelberg: Springer-Verlag.

Asanuma, B. (1989) 'Manufacturer–Supplier Relationships in Japan and the Concept of Relation Specific Skill', *Journal of Japanese and International Economies*, no. 3.

de Banville, E. and Chanaron, J. J. (1999) 'Inter-Firm Relationships and Industrial Models', in Y. Lung, J. J. Chanaron, T. Fujimoto and D. Raff (eds), *Coping with Variety: Flexible Productive Systems for Product Variety in the Auto Industry*, Aldershot: Ashgate.

Chandler, A. (1990) *Scale and Scope, the Dynamics of Industrial Capitalism*, Cambridge, Mass.: Harvard University Press.

Freyssenet, M. and Lung, Y. (1996, 2000) 'Between Globalization and Regionalization: What Is the Future of the Automobile Industry?', *Actes of the GERPISA*, no. 18, November 1996; also in J. Humphrey, Y. Leclerc and M. S. Salerno (eds), *Global Strategies and Local Realities*, London: Macmillan/New York: St Martin's Press, 2000.

Helper, S. and Sako, M. (1999) 'Supplier Relations and Performance in Europe, Japan and the US. The Effect of the Voice/Exit Choice', in Y. Lung, J. J. Chanaron, T. Fujimoto and D. Raff (eds), *Coping with Variety: Flexible Productive Systems for Product Variety in the Auto Industry*, Aldershot: Ashgate.

Lagendijk, A., Laigle, L., Pike, A. and Vale, M. (1996) 'The Local Embedding of International Car Plants', EUNIT Seminar, Newcastle University, Draft paper for 'The Territorial Dimensions of Innovation', Conference, Dortmund, Germany, May.

Laigle, L. (1996a) 'Inter-Company Cooperation, Theoretical Approaches and Applications in the Case of Builder–Supplier Relations in the Automobile Manufacturing Industry', Doctoral Dissertation in Economics, University of Paris XIII, ENPC-LATTS, December.

Laigle, L. (1996b) 'New Relationships Between Suppliers and Car Makers: Towards Development Cooperation', EUNIT Discussion Paper No. 2, CURDS, University of Newcastle, March.

Laigle, L. (1998a) 'Le redéploiement productif et géographique des équipementiers de l'automobile en Europe' (Automobile component suppliers' changes in geographic location and production sites in Europe), LATTS Research Report, DATAR.

Laigle, L. (1998b) 'Co-operative Buyer–Supplier Relationships in Development Projects in the Car Industry', in R. A. Lundin and C. Midler (eds), *Projects as Arenas for Renewal and Learning Processes*, Kluwer Academic Publishers.

Laigle, L. (1998c) 'Stratégies d'internationalisation: l'industrie automobile montre l'exemple', *Problèmes Economiques*, no. 2591, 15–25 November.

Lecler, Y. (1993) *Partenariat industriel, la référence japonaise* (Industrial partnership: the Japanese reference), Lyon: L'Interdisciplinaire.

Lecler, Y. (1996) 'Stratégies de délocalization des fournisseurs de l'industrie automobile en Asie de l'Est et du Sud Est' (Strategies of supplier decentralization in the East and South East Asian auto industry), in M. Freyssenet and Y. Lung (eds), *The Automotive Industry: Between Homogenization and Hierarchy*, Proceedings of the Fourth GERPISA International Colloquium, Paris, 19–21 June.

10
European Automotive Distribution: The Battle for Selectivity and Exclusivity Is Not Over

Giuseppe Volpato and Leonardo Buzzavo

In Europe, the subject of car distribution, notwithstanding its importance, has been neglected by both scholars and the management boards of car manufacturers for a long time; therefore documentation and written material on this subject are quite limited. However, the information available shows that on a broad level its evolution has followed the approach adopted in the USA, but with some significant differences resulting from both the uniqueness of the European setting and the features of demand in the individual countries.[1] In a similar way to what happened in the USA, the first stage of the European motorization process, which developed at the turn of the nineteenth and twentieth centuries, featured the establishment of a mixed distribution structure which utilized: (i) direct sales from the automobile manufacturers through wholly-owned sites (branches); (ii) sales to distributors – wholesalers who channelled cars through retailers, which could be either owned by the distributor or independent operators (dealers); and (iii) sales through agents responsible for collecting orders from customers for the automobile manufacturer.

The structure of European car distribution in the early motorization process

Moving on to the specific traits of individual European markets, the presence of distributors – wholesalers were particularly strong in the UK, while in France, Germany and Italy this type of trade channel was less used, preferring a marked presence of branches directly owned by car manufacturers, located mainly in larger cities, and agents spread across the country in small centres.[2]

With the expansion of the European automobile market after the First World War, a second stage emerged during which some considerable changes arose in the distribution approach of automobile manufacturers. First, it is worthwhile pointing out that distributors gradually disappeared, apart from in the United Kingdom.[3] With the development of the automobile industry this commercial format was looked on unfavourably by car manufacturers, as it consisted in a partner who, given the large volumes sold and the wide market area covered, could exert a strong bargaining power, much larger than individual dealers could. Furthermore, the presence of distributors prevented manufacturers from having direct control over the final customers, and manufacturers wanted this control in order to carry out marketing policies without having to negotiate with other players. As a result of these changes, the number of agents increased significantly, and their legal status changed as well, as the manufacturers adopted a contractual scheme, similar to the one adopted in the USA, which defined the status of franchised dealer – an independent operator who is granted the mandate to sell vehicles manufactured by a automobile maker to the end customer. The dealer buys cars from the manufacturer, and sells them on a retail basis, while the agent operates in name and on behalf of the automobile maker. The dealer is granted an exclusive territory in which sales are carried out: this exclusivity is granted in exchange for the exclusivity which the car makers asks of the dealer, to sell only the products of that manufacturer.[4] The dealer's margin lies in the difference between the price at which vehicles are bought (equal to the sales price recommended by the manufacturer, commonly defined as the 'list price') reduced by a discount of about 20% off the list price, and the eventual sales price to the end customer. In other words, the dealer has a gross margin of about 20% of the turnover, from which, after covering all the costs of the commercial activity, there remains a profit. Finally, it must be pointed out that during this stage the franchise relationship has a fixed term, usually one year. When the contract expired, the parties could renew it for a further year, or cancel the agreement. But, with the increasing investment required by the automobile manufacturers to manage dealerships: larger and better equipped sales outlets, after-sales centres for repairs, stocks of spare parts and so on, the length of the franchising contract tended to increase to two or three years.

With the further commercial expansion triggered after the Second World War, a third stage emerged, in which the exclusive franchised dealer scheme became widespread in all the main European countries. Once again the changes were brought about by a strong expansion in automobile demand, which stimulated a mass market in Europe similar to the one that had developed in the USA since 1915. Inevitably, mass production also required mass distribution, with initiatives aimed at meeting the needs generated by the new situation. During this stage, the bulk of automobile distribution was carried out by a number of dealers whose relationships with car manufacturers were defined in detail by their exclusive franchising contract, which was imposed almost without exception by all the manufacturers. The specific features of this stage were determined by the breadth and specific details of the obligations towards the automobile makers that dealers undertook through the franchising contract, while the manufacturers in turn enjoyed maximum freedom of action, since they did not commit themselves either to volume, or to delivery times and prices.[5]

With the spread of sales through a network of exclusive dealers, a sort of vertical quasi-integration of automobile manufacturing and distribution was established. The dealer network was made up of independent operators, but their marketing policy was dictated by obligations entailed in the franchising contract, from which individual dealers could not diverge without risking losing their contracts. This represented a highly negative outcome for the dealers, as the franchising contract forced them into investment in tools and stocks of materials (mainly spare parts), representing sunk costs which could probably not be recovered if the relationship ceased, with a high risk of bankruptcy, and in any case with high entrepreneurial risks even if the dealers switched to another franchise.

Over time, the franchising contract proposed by the automobile manufacturers, and accepted by the dealers, evolved progressively, with the growth of restraints and obligations required by manufacturers before they would grant the franchise.

The sellers' market and the evolution of the distribution system based on exclusive franchised dealerships

As we have seen, the automobile distribution system based on a network of exclusive franchised dealerships has some negative aspects. However, it has developed in all markets with high levels of motorization. It is a rather strange phenomenon, which calls for some explanation. First, one could say that, since the automobile distribution system based on exclusive franchised dealerships was considered efficient by manufacturers, they were able, given their extraordinary bargaining power, to impose this desired distribution scheme on dealers. It is an interpretation that is only partly true, because dealers are independent entrepreneurs, and without their commitment the scheme could not have become widespread. The explanation for this lies in the fact that the automobile industry, from its earliest developments up to the 1970s enjoyed a trend of development that could be defined as 'astonishing', and which created a sellers' market, in which automobile demand was constantly higher than supply, with long delivery lead times and a low degree of competitiveness among car manufacturers.[6]

The outcome of this 'sellers' market' has created opportunities for high profits for auto manufacturers. These profits have partly been channelled to dealer networks, which in substance have accepted to give up their entrepreneurial independence, basically wiped out by the restraints entailed in the franchising contract, in exchange for high profitability levels, and low risk. This situation is summed up well in the words of one of the largest French Citroën dealers said to André Citroën in 1927, during a meeting with auto manufacturers' representatives and dealers, in which the dealer spoke about dissatisfaction caused by a temporary market difficulty:[7] 'Monsieur, vous avez fait nos situations. Grâce à vous, beaucoup d'entre nous ont pu mettre leur premier smoking. Grâce a vous, nous venons à Paris en wagon-lit. Vous ne voudriez pas nous voir reprendre nos bleus de travail et voyager en troisième classe!'

Consequently, the market situation the international automobile industry enjoyed for decades produced an agreement of sorts between car manufacturers and dealers. This pact also saw frequent friction in distribution networks because of the marketing policies adopted by automakers, which were highly variable and sometimes arbitrary, but it remained in place because it could preserve the economic interests of dealers. But this situation had some advantages for consumers as well. The interest among automobile makers to maintain their market share, even in a situation of 'restrained competition', as it was during the years of the sellers' market, did translate into a series of directives towards their respective distribution networks aimed at providing some services to end customers. For example, the dealer's obligation to establish a repair facility and a spare parts warehouse could underpin some services of primary importance to customers, but a structure that had eliminated any form of vertical quasi-integration could not have established these services in such a definite and methodical way (since offering such services would not have been attractive economically). Furthermore, this situation of restrained competition ensured a level of dealer turnover that was lower than the one that could have resulted in a situation without vertical quasi-integration, and this granted stability to the relationship between drivers and the operators of sales and service outlets. On the whole, this situation, although introducing some distortions into market mechanisms, had the merit of providing customers with warranties and protection, particularly for those customers who were less informed and less aware of their rights, who would have been less protected in a situation of lower profit margins and unbiased commercial conducts. Besides, one must not forget that if, on the one hand, it is not hard to envision some elements of inefficiency in this organizational module of auto distribution – and sometimes these are highly visible – on the other hand, auto distribution was in any case in a relative sense one of the most efficient distribution forms, because the gross margin granted to dealers could not exceed the discount operated by automobile manufacturers to dealers which, as noted earlier, was in the order of 20% of the list price – from which all dealer costs had to be deducted. In contrast, margins in the distribution of other consumer goods such as home appliances, furniture and clothing between manufacturer and distributor were much greater.[8]

The move from a sellers' to a buyers' market

From the 1970s onwards, a series of changes occurred in the European automobile market, which gradually led to it becoming a buyers' market.

Among the most relevant factors in this transformation, which matured in the middle of the 1980s, there are the oil crises, with the subsequent considerable inflationary push, the entry of Japanese competition to the international automobile market, and the gradual disappearance of first-time buyers. The latter aspect is well highlighted by some figures. In 1960, the level of motorization in the EEC was 76 vehicles per 1,000 inhabitants. The number increased to 203 in 1970, and 328 in 1980. This means that in 1980s almost every family unit had a car, and the now saturated market showed a flat demand trend for new cars. A direct consequence of this transformation was the appearance of excess capacity, and a strong increase in the level of competition among firms. All this determined the move from a sellers' to a buyers' market.

The final outcome of this great transformation appeared in the dramatic fall in profitability levels in the US and European automobile industries, which were forced to undertake a massive reorganization process. Initially, Western automobile manufacturers reorganized their parts supply, design and manufacturing systems. This stage, which took place from the end of the 1980s to the middle of the 1990s, ended with the development of a 'lean organization' system. It allowed the industry to recover much of its efficiency in the upward stages of the automobile supply chain. But it was evident that the full exploitation of the transformation also meant changes in the downward stages of physical vehicle distribution in the target markets, and of vehicle commercialization. As a consequence, a vast reorganization process between car manufacturers, dealers and drivers began, known as 'lean distribution'.

The complexity of the automobile supply chain

The move to a lean distribution system was not an easy task for car manufacturers, given the complexity associated with the whole distribution chain. As was pointed out previously, in each target market manufacturers distribute vehicles through a national sales company, which in turn manages relationships with a wide network of franchised dealers, authorized repairers, parts distributors, and the logistics companies involved in physical vehicle transport. The performance of the distribution system does not lie merely in the optimization of the individual sub-processes, but is strictly linked to the co-ordination of information and physical flows as well as relationships among actors at all levels. For example, the ability to change production at short notice is vital to lean distribution, so that supply can be maintained in line with demand. Strong examples can be found from the period of recession that affected most European markets in the early 1990s, when manufacturers with long programme change lead times built up huge stocks before downward adjustments could be made in volume.

In today's highly competitive automotive market, to manufacture attractively designed products of high quality at competitive prices is not enough, if the distribution chain is not capable of matching production efficiency and flexibility to customers' demand in an effective and efficient way. This means minimizing lead times, and avoiding 'pushing' vehicles with specifications that are different from what customers request, because clearing unwanted products implies costs. Lean distribution systems require a considerable reduction in stock levels, which are associated with a heavy economic burden. In order to fully understand the complexity of this process it is worthwhile underlining how the system works.[9]

Broadly speaking, dealers in a traditional supply system can satisfy customers' requests by sourcing vehicles through a basket of options: their own physical stock, transferring the vehicle from other dealers' stocks, locating an existing stock order within their portfolio to match the customer's requirements, or raising a brand-new order at the factory. Each option represents a trade-off between lead times and conformity with customers' requests. Selling from physical dealer stock, for example, allows short lead times, but it is highly unlikely that the vehicle being bought will fully match the individual customer's requirements. This happens because of the huge number of combinations of different vehicle specifications.[10] In other words, it is highly unlikely that the vehicles physically available at the dealership will match the customer's preferences from among the range of choices available.[11] In most cases, dealers with large stocks are eventually compelled financially to 'push' sales of these vehicles, giving discounts in order to clear the vehicles whose specifications differ from customers' original requirements. Hence, large stock volumes might yield two kinds of negative consequences. On the one hand, large vehicle stocks generate costs, mainly associated with interest costs and depreciation, plus the cost associated with space and the additional expenses involved (that is, maintenance, cleaning and management), plus any discount offered to customers. Second, they represent a filter to the real qualitative composition of demand, as most sales derive from what is available (what has been manufactured) rather from what the market demands, and the system loses an important chance to capture fully what real customer preferences are.

At the other end of the trade-off lies the possibility of raising a customer order from the factory, thus incurring in a long lead time. Customer orders involve a request for a fully specified vehicle matched to the needs of a specific customer. If this order has to go through the full cycle, lead times could easily take three months: this might lower customers' satisfaction or imply a lost sale, with consumers having a low willingness to wait.[12]

Within this stock–order continuum, there are other options such as transferring the desired vehicle from another dealership in the network (although this solution is rather inefficient), or perhaps trying to match as many customers as possible with existing stock orders in the dealer's portfolio. Stock orders basically represent 'blind' orders, which are meant to maximize future matching of customer demand. Dealers can try to match stock orders in their portfolios with customer demand, but understandably some of these orders will result in a vehicle being delivered to the dealer without having customer waiting for it, hence generating stocks.

The supply strategies of car manufacturers

The need to improve the degree of matching between production and demand, to reduce stocks, and the critical importance of lead times have pushed all automobile manufacturers to reorganize their distribution systems in order to become 'leaner'. For example, most manufacturers have developed an on-line link between dealers and the national sales companies (and with the factory), which makes the ordering process more efficient and reliable. Furthermore, most manufacturers are involved in developing better order amendment facilities: the possibility of amending an order closer to the time of production (for example, paint options) improves the ability to adjust vehicle specifications to meet customer preferences. However, the evolutionary trajectories show some differences in the paths that are unfolding.

Specialist manufacturers – for example, Mercedes-Benz, Volvo and Jaguar – aim to maximize sales by order, to have customers choose from among all potential vehicle specifications, and then wait for their vehicle to be delivered in due course. Specialist manufacturers have a very high product specification range available (with millions of specifications). Their overall stock level is relatively low, with most customers willing to wait to obtain their required specification.[13]

An example of a manufacturer where the drive towards a so-called 'build-to-order' situation has been particularly strong is Volvo, who have been working hard to minimize lead times, being able in some cases to deliver a vehicle to a full customer specification in little more than a month. Volvo was among the first manufacturers to move towards the implementation of a production policy based on the fact that no vehicle was going to be manufactured unless backed by a customer or dealer order. This approach translates into a very low level of physical stocks at the dealerships (mainly just showroom and demonstration stock), but it is clearly difficult to enforce this approach during market downturns.[14]

Asian manufacturers, on the other hand, tend to have very long order lead times, and a very limited degree of interaction with dealers, who have no access to the factory. This leads to a very small product specification being available (in the order of hundreds of specifications rather than millions), in order to maximize the possibility of matching existing physical stocks (generally in high quantities), with customers' demands. In order to keep lead times low, dealers often resort to national vehicle stocks as a way of satisfying customer demand. The growth of manufacturing plants for Asian makes in Europe (mainly in the UK), while being beneficial for a leaner distribution system, has not yet reached its full potential, since in many cases lead times still depend heavily on Asian production for some components. In other words, the European-based assembly plants have not yet been fully coupled with a lean component supply chain.

Volume manufacturers lie in an intermediate position between specialist and Asian manufacturers from a distribution standpoint: they have a medium product specification range (with thousands of specifications). They have medium order lead times, and generally high stock levels, with significant sales to customers from this source. Interestingly, volume manufacturers generally feature some differences in distribution performance within their own product lines. For example, models with a high demand feature low stock levels in the market and long lead times, while models that have not encountered satisfactory market success tend to build up large stocks, calling for special incentives and campaigns to push for sales from stock.

A very interesting development initiated by a volume manufacturer (Fiat) is the use of open order pipelines, and 'virtual stock' systems. With the 'virtual stock' approach, dealers can access (via an on-line information system) all the order portfolios of the other dealers in the network – that is, all the stock orders that have not yet been coupled to a specific customer. For example, Dealer A can locate in the system an order raised by Dealer B, consisting of a vehicle being delivered in two weeks' time, with the specifications required by Dealer A's customer. Dealer A can transfer this order automatically to his/her own order portfolio, and satisfy the customer within a reasonable lead time. The definition of 'virtual stock' refers to the fact that the object of the transfer is not a physical vehicle, but rather an order already placed in the system, which has not yet been coupled to a final customer.[15] This system (called 'Focus' in Fiat), has proved effective in the matching of supply and demand, and reducing stock levels, and has gradually been developed in similar ways by other manufacturers.

Recent research shows that the three manufacturer types are slowly converging, apart from in the product specification range, with the Asian manufacturers catching up with the other categories in reducing stock, order lead times and so on.[16] The UK-based factories are developing the discipline required to supply reliable, quality products, and they are thus developing the ability to be more flexible in relation to the marketplace.

Towards a lean distribution system

But as well as these different distribution approaches associated with different types of manufacturer (specialist, volume and Asian), there are significant elements of differentiation linked to regional/national diversity. Different national markets have featured varying evolutionary paths for their distribution systems, which play a role in the reconfiguration of the supply chain. In Germany, for example, there are about 17,000 main dealers with a rather low throughput (sales per dealer). In France and Italy there are roughly one-third of main dealers compared to Germany, although second-tier networks (sub-dealers) play a significant role. The UK market, in contrast, features a high degree of rationalization.

An interesting example of regional differentiation in the move towards lean distribution can be found in the UK, where most manufacturers have developed 'distribution centre' strategies. In most markets, manufacturers' stocks are held at relatively low levels (apart from Asian makes), and most stock is held at dealerships. In the UK, each manufacturer operates a few regional distribution centres, where vehicle stocks are pooled. In this way, franchised dealers are freed from the pressure to sell stock physically available at their site, and can encourage customers to source the vehicle they desire from a wider range of specifications (the vehicle can generally be delivered from the distribution centre to the dealer in a single day), or raise a new order from the factory. To a certain extent, the distribution centre approach resembles large-scale retailing practices, where individual store inventories are replenished via a set of regional warehouses. The debate over the efficiency of distribution centres is relatively intense. On the positive side, the wider adoption of distribution centres has generated an improvement in matching vehicles to customer requirements, and reducing lead times. On the negative side, however, it must be pointed out that distribution centres entail operating costs, and to some industry observers they are perceived as a natural response to specific features of the UK market.[17] On the whole, the UK market represents a testing ground for some manufacturers, who have declared that they are experimenting with one distribution centre in the UK before deciding to adopt them as an overall, European-wide policy.

While the distribution centre approach prevails in the UK market, in other markets the situation differs. In Germany, for example, the market dominance of domestic manufacturers has generated a context in which the build-to-order situation prevails, and customers are prepared to accept longer waiting times in order to achieve their preferred specification.

It must be said that the European context shows a marked difference from the US market. While in Europe, sales from dealer stock account on average for roughly a third of sales (although, with some variation, it is lower in Germany), in the USA they account for about 70% of sales. This 'stock push' attitude of the US market is consistent with a fairly traditional approach by domestic manufacturers towards supply systems, but it must also be explained through other factors, such as a different relative availability/cost of stocking space, and the fact that in the USA it is possible for a customer to close a deal and drive away with the desired vehicle (with temporary licence plates), while this is generally not possible in Europe. This possibility represents an incentive to 'close the sale' for each customer with vehicles which are available at the dealership.

It has been estimated that the losses associated with the inefficiency of the supply chain, when taking into account the effects of large stock volumes, amount to about 5% of revenue. In order to achieve a leaner distribution chain, manufacturers are triggering a set of important changes, relating to both the hardware and the software of processes.[18] The on-line information linkage between assembly plants, national sales companies and dealers allows for greater efficiency and speed in transactions, along with increased transparency. Leaner and more frequent ordering implies a lower intermediary role for national sales companies between assembly plants and dealers, where production can be fine-tuned more closely to market demand as perceived by dealer operators. On-line connections also affect logistics companies, whose role in distribution processes is becoming more and more integrated, with a higher degree of transparency, and a commonality of objectives, mainly through a uniform and shared target delivery date for each individual vehicle.

Another step towards leaner distribution has been the reduction or elimination of storage compounds (as previously stated, in the UK the situation is different), with an increase in direct distribution. Volvo vehicles being assembled in Belgium for customers of dealers in Northern Italy, for example, go via direct road transport from assembly to dealer. For dealers located in Central and Southern Italy, assembling truck loads at the national compound has been made far more efficient through a better integration with the logistics company, thereby reducing national stock down to a total of about one day's supply.

The drive towards lean distribution systems implies considerable changes also at the dealer end of the chain. For example, dealers must become familiar with new approaches (low stock levels and higher usage of information systems – for example, for amendments or order transfer facilities). The reduction of physical stock through a greater share of sales by order and 'virtual stock' systems implies a higher usage of customer-facing information systems, which are capable (using advanced multimedia techniques) of displaying to the customer the vehicle in all its required specifications. These systems are powerful marketing tools, as they can capture precious market information; in some cases they can also take into account customers' time requirements (willingness to wait), contributing to better production planning. Dealers play an important role in this whole process. As an example, potential benefits from the reduction in lead times achieved by the manufacturer through complex and expensive efforts can be completely wiped out if dealers are not fully committed to the system, and stick with old-fashion approaches.

The role of new information and communication technologies

New communication technologies such as the Internet and intranets play a critical role in the move towards lean distribution. On the one hand, they are capable of making traditional processes far more efficient, and the Internet allows a more effective relationship between the players in the distribution chain and the customer. On the other hand, however, besides offering opportunities these new technologies also represent a threat, as they empower customers by providing them with much more information, and allow the establishment of new forms of interaction. Customers become information-rich, as they have multiple access to information sources on vehicle specifications, prices, rebates and incentives, reliability and so on. In parallel, new players can aim to take advantage of the Internet and its pool of customer bases in order to promote new forms of interaction, by acting as providers of customer leads. In other words, customers looking for a vehicle of any make can access some Internet sites, select their best choice across a huge range of options, and then send it to a specific dealer. As well as brokers operating within this so-called 'referral system' (customers being referred to a specific dealer), there are also examples of brokers implementing a so-called 'fulfil-ment model' – that is, one in which they arrange for the complete transaction including delivery to the requested location. Clearly, manufacturers show resistance to these kind of developments, as they tend to take away some degree of control over customers, and can therefore infringe profitability. Most manufacturers are responding by developing their own Internet web-sites, making them more attractive and interactive for customers. In most cases, prospective customers are directed from the website to the franchised dealer in a specific location to close the sale. Some tentative experiments are unfolding where the Internet represents not just a channel for contact but also for fulfilment – that is, where the whole transaction cycle is dealt with on-line. Fiat, for example, carried out an early experiment in Internet selling, where consumers could go on-line and acquire information on a new special edition of the 'Barchetta' model.[19] The experiment did not produce good enough results in terms of sales, but represents one of the many 'laboratory' attempts made in order to acquire a better understanding of the processes involved in such contexts. While at the time of writing such developments are still at the experimental stage, there is a great deal of uncertainty on a variety of issues such as the evolution of customer attitudes towards electronic information channels, legislation, and relationships with existing dealer networks, which have perceived a threat of being by-passed by such approaches.

Although some industry observers had envisioned a massive resort to Internet-only brokers, it must be said that some of the most promising developments have come to existing players from the combination of new information and communication technologies (within a so called 'brick and click' perspective).

In this respect, it seems that one of the key areas of transformation will be the development of customer relationship management (CRM) systems, where the Internet channel is linked efficiently and effectively to dealers (and their dealer management systems) and manufacturers, and through support elements such as call centres.[20] Manufacturers have a strong interest in achieving a considerable degree of control over CRM systems, which are likely to represent one of the key battlegrounds over the years to come.

However, while it is likely that new information and communication technologies (ICTs) will play a major role in reshaping the format of the distribution system, the potential borne by ICTs cannot be grasped fully without a considerable shift in operating cultures and new processes.

Globalization and the competitive challenge

Towards the end of the 1990s, a new stage in the international automobile industry began, known as 'globalization'. This underlines how the main industralized poles – that is, the so-called 'Triad' of North America, Western Europe and Japan – feature saturated markets in which the demand trend, although representing the major share within the international market, will lose importance over the coming years against countries currently undergoing the industralization process in which, given their present modest level of motorization, there will be a significant growth in car registrations. Hence the need for automakers to move rapidly into the new markets by developing new plants located in the areas that feature the highest growth rates, and to achieve the managerial capabilities needed to co-ordinate the various critical variables in the industry (outsourcing, design, manufacture and distribution), with integrated forms on a world-wide scale. It is a long-range challenge, which requires the mobilizing of huge amounts of capital and great many skilled human resources, and which has recently led to a marked process of mergers and acquisitions between automakers, in order to carry out the globalization process in the fastest and most efficient way.

Therefore, after the stage of intense reorganization which took place in the 1990s, a new reorganization stage for car distribution has begun, where automakers and dealer networks face complex issues whose solutions are not yet clear.

More factors that are undermining current market equilibria among automakers and their relationships with distribution networks lie in the change in consumer attitudes and in the new opportunities generated by information technologies such as the 'electronic market'. These are broad themes, which can only be sketched in this section, with the aim of highlighting their key implications.

With respect to consumer attitudes and expectations, the most significant aspects lie in the full awareness of a strong bargaining position acquired with the move to a 'buyers' market', which translates into an active search for the most favourable contractual arrangements, forcing dealers offering the same make into competition among themselves, in a sort of game like an auction aiming at the lowest possible price. A considerable proportion of customers are now aware of incentive mechanisms that lead dealers' behaviour, and this knowledge is exploited in order to gain the maximum benefit. This behaviour has also been encouraged by the considerable increase in the level of attention given by the press (including the non-trade press) to aspects of the commercial relationship between dealers and end customers, and by the presence of Internet sites dedicated to vehicles and their distribution. This is an aspect that is going to play a growing role in auto distribution, not only for its strictly commercial aspects, but also for the operational conditions of the franchising relationship. For example, one of the features of the current contract lies in the prohibition imposed on the dealers in establishing sales and service points outside the contractual territory. Clearly, the diffusion of the Internet among potential buyers weakens this restraint greatly, and accelerates a process of looser customer loyalty towards a single dealership (store loyalty), or towards a specific make (brand loyalty), as it encourages 'shopping around' behaviour, in which a potential customer puts more dealerships in competition with each other, through an explicit request proposing a purchase of one or more vehicles. This aspect relates not just to new car sales, but also to used cars and financial services. In this case, the technological component considerably reinforces another need currently growing among customers, which is to receive a product or a service tailored individually to personal needs. The possibility a customer has of interacting via e-mail with a variety of commercial players in order to check if they have a vehicle readily available with a specific combination of options or a personalized finance package is increasing the number of commercial experiences that are boosting the level of customer expectations, thus posing new challenges to both automakers and dealers, which tend to show the limits of current relationships between manufacturers and networks.

Finally, we should consider the need to rethink the organizational and managerial forms of current franchising contracts, which could be wiped out by a possible decision by the European Union to abolish the current block exemption regime, upon which exclusive and selective distribution is based. As is widely known, consumers' associations (mainly in Britain) have been exerting strong pressure for many years towards the elimination of the exemption regime, considered to be the mechanism which allows price discrimination for vehicles in the different markets of the EU, and in particular with respect to the British market, where prices are much higher than those for similar vehicles in other countries. The European Commission is evaluating the possibility of a renewal (with some modifications) of the exemption regime for car distribution from the norms of the art. 85 of the Treaty of Rome, and the possibility of an elimination of the block exemption, thus defining the regime which would be applied from 2002 onwards (2002 is the year in which the current regulation expires). Clearly, automakers and distribution networks are against the elimination (although with different emphases), but on the other side they do not yet seem capable either to eliminate the extent of price discrimination in place in the different markets, or to elaborate a proposal to modify the selective distribution which, preserving the useful elements within it, could move towards the legitimate claims of consumers and operators interested in managing the cross-border trade of cars and commercial vehicles within the EU. Therefore, the possibility that in 2002 the Commission will decide to abolish the block exemption cannot be ruled out, and it seems likely that regulations for cars will be brought somewhat closer to regulations for vertical restraints in other industries.

At the time of writing, automakers, having acknowledged the contradictory effects deriving from the previous strategy of managing networks, are generally moving towards a dramatic reduction in the number of intermediaries, aiming at three main objectives: to reduce intra-brand competition among dealers in the same franchise; in such a way, to make it easier for dealers to achieve economies of scale; and to regain the share of 'dealer discount' which presently dealers are forced by the competitive game to give away to customers in order to close the sale.

With the acceleration in the merger and acquisition processes, in many cases manufacturers are aiming at establishing stronger relationships with fewer intermediaries, who will be granted representation for the different brands of the group within a given territory. This means that in most cases a franchising contract for the Fiat brand is tied in with Alfa Romeo and Lancia, while similar processes happen with other manufacturers, such as Ford (with Mazda and Jaguar), General Motors (with Saab), Renault (with Nissan) and Mercedes-Benz (with Chrysler). This rationalization translates into a reduction in dealer numbers. In the case of Fiat Auto, for example, the number of dealers in Europe has halved since the mid-1990s.[21]

Eventually, the process should yield some savings on the costs of distribution for automobile makers, equal to the lower discount granted to dealers, and with an improvement in profitability of dealers, which in recent years have experienced troubled operating conditions. If the profitability gain that dealers could obtain were equal on average to the economies of scale generated by the new situation (and not be associated with oligopolistic practices) it would not determine higher costs for end customers. In such a way, a new equilibrium would be reached, which could be satisfactory for everyone. But does this sort of 'squaring the circle' represent a hypothesis within reach? Doubts over this possibility are more than legitimate, for two main reasons. Looking at the recovery of efficiency, the experience of various decades in managing dealer networks has shown that large size (that is, a large number of vehicle sales per year) does not automatically translate into economies of scale and therefore into efficient management. As in any other industry, large size is a necessary but not sufficient condition in order to achieve adequate economies. Only with adequate managerial practices can a large-scale dealership achieve high profitability levels, as many cases of failure of large and very large dealers in Europe have proved. Consequently, it would be necessary for automakers to engage in a learning process driven in part by the dealers in order to achieve high managerial standards. A result which automakers have not been able to achieve so far, either with respect to dealers, or with their own branches (owned outlets), some of which have been shut down and others have been sold to dealers because of unsatisfactory results.

Another crucial aspect lies in the managerial skills and processes needed to cope with the new transformation. When a few traditional dealerships traditionally managed with a marked entrepreneurial attitude with specific managerial styles, are merged into a larger company, a marked shift in the degree of professionalism, specialization and management control is needed, which in many cases implies a burdensome and complex process of reorganization, whose scope is far from being fully grasped.

In any case, even if automakers could manage this kind of transformation, this strategy looks heavily endanged by 'the sword of Damocles' threatening the block exemption's elimination. If this were to take place, we might witness a fragmentation in vehicle distribution, as an outcome of the elimination of the relationship of vertical quasi-integration. Many new 'free' players would arise, interested in taking part in car distribution, but only in some of the aspects that fall within the complex dealer–customer relationship, and particularly in those activities that are believed to be profitable. On the whole, customers would use specialist operators for the products and services they could supply at a price that was lower than that of the 'generalist' dealer that is currently available. The outcome would be a fast disappearance of the generalist dealership as it would be contacted by customers only to carry out non-profitabile activities. The likelihood of a straight renewal is infringed by the alleged misconduct of some automakers, and the alleged anti-competitive nature of some of the vertical restraints entailed in current franchising contracts. However, it must also be said that a radical elimination of the block exemption is unlikely, as this would create a legal vacuum. In practice, the current movement is towards a new regulation, intended to evaluate the need to revisit some of the foundations of the current arrangements. One of these is the selectivity and exclusivity tie, which is believed by many to place too much control in the hands of manufacturers.[22] Another element being intensely debated is the link between sales and service – that is, the right of manufacturers to impose servicing tasks on their dealers – which must be rethought, taking into account the decrease in aftersales demand because of the higher reliability of new vehicles. Brand exclusivity is also an important item: the current degree of considerable restraint over the dealer's ability to represent other makes in the same facility might be eased. In parallel, there are also important changes stemming from technological developments affecting the traditional notion of 'territories' (hence with some effect over the 'exclusivity' dimension). In fact, franchising contracts at the time of writing prevent dealers from seeking active customer contact outside their mandated territories. But if it was possible in the past to discriminate between customers' locations by list of addresses and telephone numbers, it becomes impossible to do so with e-mail, and any regulatory framework has to cope with this reality.

On the whole, current automakers' strategies are moving in a direction that entails some risks for themselves and even higher risks for dealers, who are asked to carry out huge investments to achieve the desired consolidation process, whose benefits and critical aspects are yet to be fully explored.

Notes

1 For an analysis of the specificity and the evolution of car distribution in the USA, see Epstein (1928), Federal Trade Commission (1939), Hewitt (1956).

2 The use of branches was widespread in Germany, mainly by Daimler, later merged with Benz (in 1926). In 1930, the Daimler-Benz make had forty branches, which increased to forty-nine in 1938. At that time, the total number of branches operated by German manufacturers amounted to 166. See also Blaich (1981).

3 See Church (1981).

4 The first European automaker to impose as a necessary condition the clause of the exclusive franchise was André Citroën in 1919. In the United Kingdom, Ford also tried, during that same year, to impose this restraint, but the strong opposition manifested by dealers compelled the manufacturer to accept for several more years a significant number of exceptions.

5 In the US market, franchising contracts are thoroughly analysed in Federal Trade Commission (1939). In Europe, there are no similar analyses, but it is known that European makers did imitate US makers, both on manufacturing and on commercial practices. In France, it was mainly André Citroën who introduced an 'American-style' commercial policy, by using the advertising services of a US company who opened a subsidiary in Paris. See also Church (1981), Fridenson (1981), Sabatés and Schweitzer (1980).

6 Clearly, the industry has seen periods of sales reduction – for example, during the great US crisis of 1929 – and its effects in Europe. All industry observers agree on the fact that, up to the 1970s, production capacity was lower than the demand expressed by the market. See Federal Trade Commission (1939), Fridenson (1972), Volpato (1983).

7 Frerejan (1998).

8 Another service included in the specific organization of the distribution network lies in the financing of the purchase, promoted through a finance company owned by the vehicle manufacturer itself. In the USA, the first manufacturer to institute this service was General Motors in 1919, followed by Ford in 1923. In Europe, Citroën promoted it in 1919, followed two years later by Renault. In Italy, the establishment of a finance company by Fiat specializing in financing vehicle purchase (SAVA) dates back to 1925. See Volpato (1986).

9 For a more thorough examination of the move towards lean distribution, see Buzzavo (1997), Williams *et al.* (1998).

10 If we consider a single product line, when multiplying the number of trim levels, engine types, body types, options and paint/trim combinations, one can see that the number of potential combinations for one product are frequently in the order of hundreds of thousands, exceeding millions for some specialist producers.

11 In 1997, the percentage of European customers who bought a vehicle with specifications that differed from their original requirement was 30% for volume makes, 24% for specialist makes, and 11% for Asian makes.

12 The total order lead time for a vehicle is generally in five segments: order bank, manufacturing, shipping, delivery to dealer, handover to customer: (i) *order bank*: the orders entered into the system are not converted immediately into vehicles being assembled, as manufacturers define the sequence of vehicles to be assembled by taking into account a complex set of techno-economic factors, such as saturation levels of plants and of the workforce, labour schedules and component availability; (ii) *manufacturing*: it relates to the physical manufacturing and assembly of the vehicle, generally within a total of two days; (iii) *shipping*: this refers to the transport of vehicles from the plants to the destination market. This lead time can be affected negatively by the build-up of end-of-line stocks; (iv) *delivery to dealer*: this refers to the transport within the destination market to specific dealers, including both transit time and waiting time in distribution centres; (v) *handover to customer*: this lead time, which can be substantial in some cases, relates to any dealers' delay in making the vehicle available for handover (this is because of final preparation – pre-delivery operations), although in most cases the customers themselves might delay the pick-up of the vehicle for their own reasons – for example, sorting out payment.

13 In most cases, specialist manufacturers, particularly for prestige products, pursue a policy of careful under-supply, maintaining a controlled production volume in order to sustain their brand image.

14 During market downturns a manufacturer tends to require dealers to sustain the production volume by raising more stock orders, generally offering incentives (such as rebates, finance aid and so on).

15 For this system to work, dealers raise orders which are either 'blocked' (they cannot be accessed by other dealers), or 'available'. The latter are potentially accessible, and can be redirected electronically to a dealer requesting them. Dealers are invited to adjust their mix between 'blocked' and 'available' orders with different finance conditions ('blocked' orders, which are not accessible by the system, will feature shorter payment terms).

16 ICDP (International Car Distribution Programme) carries out a periodic investigation into the performance of the distribution chain of vehicle manufacturers in Europe.

17 The UK market, unlike most European markets, features a remarkable degree of seasonality. Because of licence plate change in August, and the attitudes consumers developed towards this, about 25% of annual sales were normally concentrated in that month. Distribution centres were looked at as a way to handle this huge sales peak, allowing for a sufficient supply to cope with this degree of strain to the system. The licence-plate system has now been modified, introducing a twice-a year change which has partially smoothened this high seasonality.

18 A more detailed calculation can be found in Williams *et al.* (1998).

19 The model was specially produced for this Internet experiment – and was not available through dealers. Customers interested in a test drive were required to deposit a modest sum (about 50 euro), and could go in to one of the fifty sites nationwide where a test drive was possible (the sites were not franchised dealers, but vehicle rental locations of a major company). If a customer wanted to buy a car, the vehicle was invoiced by the Fiat manufacturer-owned outlets (Succursali) and delivered to the customer's home, unless requested otherwise by the customer.

20 Some studies have shown that a great many consumers visiting automotive websites would like to make a telephone call to get more information – some form of interaction.

21 In the domestic market the number of dealers reduced from 1,407 in 1992 to less than 700 in 2000, while the total number of dealers in the other European markets decreased from 2,976 in 1992 to less than 1,500 in 1999, with a target of about 1,000. The objective is to achieve an average throughput of 1,000 units sold per dealership in Western Europe.

22 Selectivity allows automobile manufacturers to stipulate standards for their distributors (dealers), limiting their total number, and at the same time to oblige them to sell only to end customers or other members of the network. Exclusivity allows auto manufacturers to award dealers with sales territories on a subjective basis (in practical terms, manufacturers can 'pick' dealers at their discretion).

References

Blaich, F. (1981) 'The Development of the Distribution Sector in the German Car Industry', in A. Okochi and K. Shimokawa (eds), *Development of Mass Marketing*, Tokyo: University of Tokyo Press.

Buzzavo, L. (1997) 'La distribuzione snella nella commercializzazione automobilistica', *Economia & Management*, no. 1.

Church, R. (1981) 'The Marketing of Automobiles in Britain and the United States before 1939', in A. Okochi and K. Shimokawa (eds), *Development of Mass Marketing*, Tokyo: University of Tokyo Press.

Epstein, R. C. (1928) *The Automobile Industry – Its Economic and Commercial Development*, Chicago: A. W. Shaw.

Federal Trade Commission (1939) *Report on the Motor Vehicle Industry*, Washington: US GPO.

Frerejan, A. (1998) *André Citroën et Louis Renault – Un duel sans merci*, Paris: Albin Michel.

Fridenson, P. (1972) *Histoire des usines Renault*, Paris: Seuil.

Fridenson, P. (1981) 'French Automobile Marketing 1890–1979', in A. Okochi and K. Shimokawa (eds), *Development of Mass Marketing*, Tokyo: University of Tokyo Press.

Hewitt, C. M. (1956) *Automobile Franchise Agreements*, Homewood, Ill.: R. D. Irwin.

Okochi, A. and Shimokawa, K. (eds) (1981) *Development of Mass Marketing*, Tokyo: University of Tokyo Press.

Sabatés, F. and Schweitzer, S. (1980) *André Citroën – Les chevrons de la gloire*, Paris: Epa.

Volpato, G. (1983) *L'industria automobilistica internazionale*, Padua: Cedam.

Volpato, G. (1986) 'L'evoluzione delle strategie di marketing nell'industria automobilistica', in *Annali di storia dell'impresa n.2*, ASSI, Milano: F. Angeli.

Williams, G., Henderson, J. and Brown, J. (1998) *European New Car Supply and Stocking Systems*, ICDP Research Paper n. 2/98, Solihull, UK.

Wright, H. E. (1927) *The Financing of Automobile Installment Sales*, Chicago: A. W. Shaw.

11
Conclusion: Regionalization of the European Automobile Industry, More Than Globalization

Michel Freyssenet, Koichi Shimizu and Giuseppe Volpato

The automobile sector is often presented as the archetypal global industry. In this view, the auto business is one of the main drivers behind the homogenization of the world, both because of firms' internationalization strategies (mergers–acquisitions, the establishment of facilities in emerging countries, world autos, the international division of labour and so on) as well as a result of the social practices such firms enact via their organization of work and at the lifestyle (automobile civilization) level.

This chapter is an attempt to deconstruct a representation that neglects, as we have seen in the previous chapters, the heterogeneity of firms and spaces, the great diversity of the strategies being pursued, and the inherent contradictions of the competitive process. We shall use and test the analytical approach of productive and geographical trajectories of auto industry firms, which we have elaborated from the first and second international programmes of GERPISA (Boyer and Freyssenet, 2000b, 2002; Freyssenet and Lung, 2000).[1]

Growth modes, profit strategies and productive models

An analysis of automakers' trajectories and performances over the course of the twentieth century has allowed us to renew our understanding of the two essential conditions that are a prerequisite for profitability. The first is the relevancy of the 'profit strategy' to the 'growth mode' that typifies the countries in which firms deploy their activities. The second is the 'company government compromise' that exists between a firm's principal protagonists, a meeting of the minds that enables players to implement means that are coherent with the profit strategy being pursued – in other words, to invent or adopt a 'productive model' (Freyssenet *et al.*, 1998; Boyer and Freyssenet, 2000b, 2002).

Profit strategies are combinations of profit sources in compatible proportions. Basically, there are six sources of profit: economies of scale, diverse offerings, quality, innovation, productive flexibility, and permanent cost reduction. Until now, there have been no examples of firms exploiting all these profit sources simultaneously and with the same level of intensity. This is because of the contradictory nature of the sources' preconditions and means of implementation. For this reason, firms must choose among possible combinations of profit sources, unless they can invent ways of overcoming contradictions, as General Motors was able to do during the inter-war period when it created compatibility between volume and diversity. At the time of writing, five different profit strategies can be observed in the automobile sector: 'volume', 'volume and diversity', 'quality', 'permanent cost reduction', and 'innovation and flexibility'.

Profit strategies do not all possess the same degree of relevancy in time and space. Their appropriateness depends on the market and labour factor structures that characterize the different national modes of growth. These growth modes are not infinite in number, and several countries may at any point in time be applying the same one (Boyer and Saillard, 1995, 2001). They are divided into three main categories: growth modes with a national income distribution that is 'nationally co-ordinated and moderately hierarchized'; growth modes with a 'competitive' type of distribution; and growth modes with an 'inegalitarian' type of distribution. These categories are subsequently sub-divided according to the main driver of the growth: investment, consumption or export. The success of an internationalization policy is therefore predicated first and foremost on the relevancy of the firm's profit strategy to the growth mode(s) of the new countries it is entering (Boyer and Freyssenet, 1999; Freyssenet and Lung, 2000).

Profit strategies cannot be implemented with just any available means. Each has certain requirements that the firm's players must satisfy through a product policy, productive organization and employment relationship that are coherent and acceptable to them. The creation of an acceptable type of coherency between these various means infers the building of a 'company government compromise' between the firm's main players (executives, shareholders, banks, employees, labour unions, suppliers and so on). The means used to implement one and the same profit strategy can therefore differ from one another if this is needed to satisfy the requirements mentioned earlier. As such, the firm's protagonists do possess some room for manoeuvre during the development of their own compromise. In the case of an internationalized company, it is possible to have a variety of compromises, depending on the host country. Nevertheless, the firm's subsidiaries must each be in control and in charge of their own production systems and markets. This is not the case when they are part of one and the same regional or global industrial complex and deliver their output to markets that change depending on the current economic situation.

The liberalization of capital international movements and the deregulation of the labour market

The two main changes in the turning point of the 1990s were the liberalization of capital international movements and the deregulation of the labour market in some countries.

The liberalization of capital movements was one of the key elements of American economic growth during the 1990s. It was the origin of the destabilization of the previously best performing countries (Japan, Germany and Sweden) and of the temporary increase of the so-called emerging countries. American economic growth enabled the American automakers to again become profitable. The destabilizing of the countries characterized by a 'co-ordinated and export-orientated' growth mode (Japan, Germany and Sweden) made their automobile firms less competitive. The sudden increase of the emerging countries created the hope of a new development of the world automobile market. The free movement of capitals also engendered two speculative bubbles: the first concerning the emerging countries alone, and the second the so-called 'new economy', mainly in the USA. The bursting of the bubbles of the emerging countries in 1997, and of the new economy in 2000, stopped world growth and revealed the weakness of some Korean, Japanese and European automakers. This situation caused a new wave of mergers and alliances in the car industry.

With the deregulation of the labour market, the second main change mentioned above occurred in that, national income distribution became more 'competitive'. But this type of distribution was not developed to the same degree and extent in all countries of the Triad. 'Competitive' distributions of income, through the economic and social disparities they engendered, also led to a second automobile market for pick-up trucks, minivans, recreational vehicles and other conceptually innovative means of transport. This second market has become as large as the market for saloon cars in the USA.

It is in this context that the rearrangement of a world space that had been split up into several tendencies began: the generalization of trade liberalization; the constitution of regional spaces; and the affirmation or reaffirmation of nations, whether 'emerging' or not.

None of the scenarios of global space reshaping will be exclusive of the others, except through an accident of history. In order to avoid economic and political instability, generalized free trade presupposes world-wide rules and means to make them respected. However, it could be thought that these rules would take many years before being accepted as part of a sufficient and satisfactory agreement for all parties. Neither are there enough countries powerful enough to impose them on others in the foreseeable future.

This is why the countries that already maintain major trade exchanges seek (mainly or by default) to make up free trade zones, the rules of which are less difficult to work out and the immediate benefits easier to spread on a limited territorial scale. In this case, either a satellitization of emerging countries by the powerful industrialized countries, as is already the case in NAFTA, or accords between emerging countries who give up a certain autonomy will be seen, as the Mercosur countries are attempting to do. These free trade zones will either be steps to world-wide free trade, or if the latter is revealed to be utopian or impossible, towards the formation of regional economic and political poles. The scenario of a multi-polar world made up of countries grouped together according to region, whose economic growth would once again be self-centred and regulated, would also only be possible partially in the best of cases. The formation of such political and economic poles is a long and winding path with many potholes, as the experience of European Union construction has shown. In the medium term, one or two of these poles are possible.

In the end, these trends will not stop the fact that independent nations last and expand either because they make up regions on their own, or continents through the size of their population and natural resources; or because of their very independence they fill the role in the international economic system that other countries do not wish to see disappear.

Under these conditions, what are the chances of different profit strategies being possible for automobile firms?

A utopian globalization as the core volume strategy

The 'volume' strategy emphasizes a single source of profit: economies of scale – that is, mass production for as long as possible in constantly growing markets, with a reduced number of models that are specific to each major market segment. It can only be completely relevant under two conditions: the market must be in an extension mode (either because it is in an initial equipment phase or because it is homogenizing) and comprised of two or three homogeneous segments; the labour factor must be copious and capable of being mobilized for repetitive production.

These conditions presuppose a growth mode that is consumption-based as well as a type of income distribution that is either nationally co-ordinated and highly egalitarian or clearly stratified into two or three stable and numerically equivalent sections. As one can see, these conditions are very restrictive. No growth mode that has ever been seen in a capitalist economy has ever satisfied them completely. For these reasons, up to now the volume strategy has only been profitable during relatively short-lived initial automobile equipment phases – that is, before the demand has diversified. This was the case for Henry Ford with the Model T during the 1910s, and for Volkswagen with the Beetle (Jürgens, 1998).

The policy of world automobiles, one per major market sector, with each having its own platform, would regain pertinence in a world where the parties are converging toward similar forms of competition and similar modes of income redistribution. This being improbable, as seen from the comments above, does it necessarily mean that it is totally unthinkable? In fact, it can be viable under two conditions. The first is sufficient freedom of exchanges between main countries so that customs duties and exchange rate variations do not prevent world-wide concentration and specialization of production sites, an essential element of a strategy of economies of scale. The second is that a fraction of the customers on the main markets privilege low sales prices and only average quality.

The last automaker to do so, Volkswagen renounced the 'volume' strategy just before 1974. From the mid-1980s Ford tried again with its world automobiles policy, but was unsuccessful. During the 1990s, the Korean automakers seemed surprisingly to succeed, with one or two entry-level vehicles to target both emerging and industrialized countries. But their running into debt and the Asiatic crisis obliged them to accept a take-over by other automobile firms: Samsung by Renault, Hyundai by DaimlerChrysler, and Daewoo by GM (Freyssenet *et al.*, 2002).

'Volume and diversity' strategy: a global commonalization of platforms and a regional differentiation of models, under certain conditions

Following GM, Ford and Nissan (Freyssenet *et al.*, 2002) three European automobile firms (Volkswagen, PSA and Fiat) are pursuing the profit strategy we called 'volume and diversity'. Since 1974, only one has succeeded in building a 'productive model' to implement this strategy strongly in a profitable way: Volkswagen. More recently, PSA succeeded by choosing the same method. Internationalization and commonalization are the two indispensable conditions for the volume and diversity strategy, when the market increases slightly. But internationalization can involve only the countries where commonalization is commercially acceptable. The change in the structure of several markets at the time of writing limits this acceptability.

Characteristics, conditions and requirements

This strategy combines two sources of profits that would at first glance appear to be contradictory – volume and diversity. What General Motors invented during the inter-war period was a way of overcoming this contradiction by designing different marques' auto models on the basis of a single platform (at the time, the chassis) and by setting up a productive organization and employment relationship that made it possible to manage ostensible diversity (body, internal fittings and equipment) in an economic manner. During the 1940s GM succeeded in designing a productive model – the Sloanian model – that became for many managers the 'one best way' until the 1970s. The volume and diversity strategy thus precludes specific models as well as models that are conceptually innovative and are not compatible with many parts being commonalized with models from the traditional product range.

This requires a growing and moderately hierarchized market as well as a copious, polyvalent and promotable workforce. In fact, if the potential clientele is to accept this superficial differentiation and deep-seated commonalization, there cannot be any excessive economic and social differentiation between the various social categories, and social and professional mobility must have attained a certain level. Growth modes featuring a national income distribution that is 'nationally co-ordinated and moderately hierarchized' are the ones that best fulfil such conditions. This is why a volume and diversity strategy was the most pervasive (albeit not the only) strategy during the post-war boom years. It ran into difficulties when the market entered a product renewal phase in the countries where firms were pursuing this strategy, and the indispensable economies of scale could no longer be obtained because of an extension of the market.

However, they could be achieved by penetrating those markets that found themselves in an initial equipment phase, or through mergers and alliances with other firms. Still, certain preconditions had to be fulfilled for this to occur. Internationalization, for example, had to involve moving into countries that possessed the same types of growth mode, and designing local models that shared the same platforms, as those that could be found in the country of origin. The 'volume and diversity' strategy would thus be fully pertinent in the framework of a world where car owners would have basically common expectations globally, and would only differentiate regionally on secondary aspects. Mergers and alliances had to lead quickly to a commonalization of the relevant marques' platforms. Automakers who had developed a volume and diversity strategy during the post-war boom years found it difficult to make this change (Freyssenet *et al.*, 1998).

Lastcomer in the group of automakers beginning to pursue a 'volume and diversity' strategy, Volkswagen is the only one to have succeeded in finding a profitable way to implement it durably after 1974, and to implement the Sloanian model under these new conditions. But this automaker achieved this only in Europe. More recently, PSA followed a similar route. As in the cases of GM, Ford and Nissan, Fiat also failed in the rebuilding the new firm governance compromise required to implement the volume and diversity strategy in a coherent manner. In the 1990s, these firms tried unsuccessfully to commonalize their platforms on a global level and to differentiate them at a regional level.

Volkswagen, external growth and European commonalization

Volkswagen resolutely and immediately commonalized the platforms used for the auto models being made by the marques (Audi, Seat and Skoda) that it successively acquired in Europe (Jurgens, 1998). The four generalist marques (Audi, Seat, Skoda and Volkswagen) have built up model ranges with shared platforms. To achieve this, each marque has been associated with a specific brand image and broadened its individual range: Audi has moved downscale towards the A2 small-car market, whereas, inversely, the Volkswagen (VW) marque will soon be marketing a de luxe model. These ranges are being completed by niche vehicles that have been developed on high-volume platforms: the New Beetle and the Audi TT, for example (see Pries, ch. 3 in this volume).

It emphasized job preservation and reduced working times rather than wage increases. By so doing, and because of the appropriateness of the choices it made, Volkswagen's employees were able to have the best of both worlds. This success was facilitated largely by the export-orientated growth mode of the FRG. Wages had long been linked to external competitiveness rather than to internal productivity. By combining economies of scale with a product variety adapted to the specific offering to be made, this strategy would appear to be highly coherent. We can, however, discuss the various ways in which it could go wrong, as well as its limitations.

The volume and diversity strategy became less relevant when national income distribution began to operate according to modalities that were more competitive in nature – more individualized, based on 'merit', with a local and category-specific balance of power and an emphasis on financial opportunism. However, the growing demand for distinctive products rendered the product policy less commercially palatable. Internationalization and/or mergers/alliances became all the more essential in capturing this moderately hierarchized demand wherever it was found (Boyer and Freyssenet, 2000a). But since the end of the 1990s, VW also seems to want to make all types of vehicle, especially top-of-the-range and de luxe cars. For that, VW has bought prestigious marques: Lamborghini, Bentley and Bugatti. As we shall see in the next section, there are doubts whether this choice is relevant for a firm pursuing a volume and diversity strategy.

Past implementations of a volume and a variety strategy shows also that there is a permanent risk of cannibalism between marques, because of an excessive coverage of markets, and an insufficient differentiation of products. In addition, a solution that consists of compiling a local offering reflecting a product portfolio a firm has already developed elsewhere may turn out ultimately to be poorly adapted to the needs of a particular local market. The absence of a light truck market in North America is a long-standing weakness – and there is no guarantee that people will want to continue for much longer marketing standardized vehicles to the emerging markets.

The Brazilian example also contains significant lessons: there, VW was unable to benefit from an automobile policy aimed at encouraging the development of '*carros populares*', 'popular cars' (Norberto, 2000) – vehicles with motors of less than one litre that had caused the great expansion of the Brazilian market during the 1990s. This inability to adapt explains the decline in VW's market share and profitability in Brazil (see Jetin, ch. 2 in this volume). This market's specificity ultimately convinced Volkswagen to preserve a specifically Brazilian model. VW's success in China and South America is also based on models adapted to each of these markets: the Santana and the Golf.

PSA, internal growth and punctual co-operation

After a difficult fifteen-year period, Peugeot succeeded in obtaining from Citroën, its subsidiairy, the use of the same platforms (see Loubet, ch. 7 in this volume). Now PSA is implementing a volume and diversity product strategy systematically. After the painful experience of the absorbing of Citroën and Chrysler Europe, it is also convinced that internal growth and timely co-operation with others automakers is the cautious way to develop economies of scale and scope. PSA has signed a number of *ad hoc* co-operative arrangements: with Fiat for the production of passenger vans aimed at the upper market segments; with Toyota for the production of a small car; and with Renault and Ford for engine production. PSA is now one of the most profitable automobile producers. For the moment, its European-centred policy is more a strength than a weakness.

Fiat: emerging markets were not enough

Fiat has long been the most nationally orientated of all the European automakers, having broadened its brand portfolio on its domestic market (Fiat, Alfa Romeo, Lancia, Maserati and Ferrari) without setting up operations in the European Union's other countries (except for a brief experience in Spain, following an association with SEAT). However, there have long been links with countries now deemed to be 'emerging': the former USSR, Turkey, Yugoslavia, Brazil (Camuffo and Volpato, 1999).

At the beginning of the 1990s, Fiat sought enduring new volumes in the emerging markets and has designed a specific model that targets these new markets: the Fiat 178, which at the time of writing is still at the project stage (see Volpato, ch. 6 in this volume). This product offers good value for money, and will in all likelihood be able to conquer the first-time-buyers' market in the emerging countries. The production of this vehicle (known as the Palio) has been organized using a division of labour among the main protagonists (Turkey, Brazil, Poland and Morocco) in a components (that is, body parts) trade that has become widespread, and which feeds assembly and kitting plants spread around the world to the tune of 400,000 to 500,000 units per annum. The Palio model and its variants are to replace Fiat models that had mainly been targeted at the European market (the Italian automaker being almost entirely absent from North America and Japan). Without a doubt, Fiat has scored a few points, first with its adaptation to the emerging countries, and more specifically as a result of the multiple successes it has known: with the Palio; with its small city cars (the Cinquecento, to be followed by the Seicento, automobiles assembled in Poland and partially re-imported to the rest of Europe); and with the breakthrough of the Uno in Brazil where, unlike VW, Fiat has been able to take advantage of its 'popular car' policy.

However, this focus on penetrating the emerging markets, where high levels of market volatility have added to firms' vulnerability, has been offset by a slump in Fiat's fortunes in its domestic market, and more generally throughout Europe. Here, the Italian firm has lost a great deal of its market share as a result of an ageing product range (this despite major efforts that it has made to increase its process's competitiveness). Fiat's alliance with GM, which effectively paves the way for a take-over of the Italian firm by the American giant, suggests to a certain extent a failure – but it also opens new directions. Opel and Fiat share a range of products, and they can commonalize their platforms. Fiat's history isn't finished.

The dilemma for the 'volume and diversity' firms

The introduction of 'competitive' modalities of national income distribution has generated a second market. Fiat, PSA and Volkswagen, unsurprisingly, copied (as per the tenets of the 'volume and diversity' strategy they still pursue) the conceptually innovative models that Renault launched once they felt secure that these models would be a continuing success. Ford, GM and Nissan also copied the innovative models, pursuing an 'innovation and flexibility' strategy in their regional area: Honda and Chrysler (Freyssenet *et al.*, 2002).

But the 'volume and diversity' automakers are still faced with a dilemma. The models they have copied have become mundane, and will no longer offer the same kinds of profit margins in the future. Moreover, such models do not create economies of scale that are significant enough to compensate for the fact that their profit margins are lower than is usual with a novelty product – a consequence of the firms' difficulties in commonalizing their platforms with the platforms of traditionally hierarchized vehicles.

Is it now the turn of the 'volume and diversity' automakers to take up the gauntlet of conceptual innovation, to benefit from the considerable rent it offers for a while? Some of these manufacturers seem to be interested in this possibility, and have been allocating the task to one of their marques. However, it remains that, since the birth of the automobile industry, no one has ever succeeded in carrying out two different profit strategies for a significant period of time; the requirements are far too contradictory.

Still we should envisage the possibility that the current coexistence between the 'competitive and decentralized' distribution of income that tends to dominate in the private sector, and the 'co-ordinated and moderately hierarchized' distribution mainly preserved in the state sector might last. Are automakers now facing the challenge of having to create compatibility between sources of profit that would on the surface appear to be incompatible (that is, 'volume and diversity' versus 'innovation and flexibility')? Has the time come for a major new strategic invention? Is it possible that modular vehicle design will enable economies of scale while allowing for the design of new vehicle types involving varying combinations of basic modules? The other path is to develop again a general 'co-ordinated and moderatly hierarchized' income distribution at regional level and to adopt consumption as the source of growth.

The 'quality' profit strategy: nationally-based production and globalized distribution

For a long time, one of the important characteristics of the European car industry has been the presence of independant top-of-the-range and luxury carmakers, called 'specialist' manufacturers as opposed to 'generalist' manufacturers who target a wider market. Their profit strategy was to embrace the 'quality' strategy. They were located only in the country of origin and exported a large proportion of their cars. Since the end of 1990s, many of them, paradoxically, decided to integrate into large automobile groups, when the international market of top-of-the-range vehicles increased dramatically.

Characteristics, conditions and requirements

Here, the word 'quality' means not only reliability and finish, but also and above all the social distinctiveness that the product's style, utilization of certain materials, emphasis on finish and marque-related prestige offers, in the opinion of a privileged clientele that looks for such factors and is in a position to pay for them. This strategy induces those firms that have adopted it to specialize in the 'top-of-the-range', or in recent times in the upper part of each market segment. Earnings basically stem from the profit margins that the product and the top-of-the-range customers allow – the high price also acts as a means of distinction and social tiering, above and beyond any material justification.

A quality strategy is the one that features the greatest relevancy in time and space. There are very few societies in which a small, well-off section of the population is not ready to pay a high price to possess those products that can symbolize their economic and social position. For this reason, the top-of-the-range market has from the very outset been international in nature, and the specialist carmakers the most commercially internationalized over a long period (see Köhler, ch. 4; Eckardt and Klemm, ch. 8, in this volume).

Futhermore, a 'quality' strategy suggests the availability of a workforce that is for the most part highly skilled (and which has a reputation as such). Certain aspects of quality can in fact only be obtained by using the services of traditional professional workers (or, inversely, of technicians and even engineers who are graduates of the top universities) to manufacture parts in small series on highly sophisticated machinery. The reputation of a top-of-the-range brand is often related to the renown of its country of origin or of the region in which it is established, when this is famed for the seriousness and professionalism of the employees. In general, a 'quality' strategy is enhanced when the workforce is forced to maintain the national output's international specialization, notably to be able to continue benefiting from the high salary levels, social protection systems and stable employment perspectives that are enabled by the production of unrivalled specialized products.

For these reasons, regarding the market or labour, the 'co-ordinated and specialized export-orientated' growth mode (Germany and Sweden) is the one that affords the greatest visibility to the 'quality' strategy.

In growth modes that feature a co-ordinated and moderately hierarchized national income distribution, the top-of-the-range clientele is not totally cut off from other types of customers. So the specialist carmakers have found it difficult since the Second World War to put together a 'productive model' that is durable – meaning one that can continually find the right balance between large-series production methods and others that emphasize the product's 'hand finish' and customized qualities (Ellegard, 1995; Freyssenet, 1998).

Competitive distribution modes do not stand in the way of this strategy. It allows many actors to seek their fortune, yet at the same time it is less stable. It relies on the availability of workers who can be skilled but less attached to their firm. In the modes that feature a highly inegalitarian type of distribution, top-of-the-range clients are basically the only customers for new vehicles, and they are very devoted to the marque's international renown and to demonstrations of their own wealth.

A sea change in the international top-of-the-range market since the 1990s

With income distribution having become more 'competitive', the top-of-the-range segment has tended to become more heterogeneous. Demand for extreme top-of-the-range saloon cars (which had become marginal products) rose again. Above all, 'top-of-the-range' demand has arisen for small and medium-sized cars and for recreational vehicles.

These developments have presented the 'specialist' manufacturers with a new situation. On the one hand, if they are to cover the new top-of-the-range sub-segments they must make substantial increases in their design-related spending, productive capacities and distribution network. But on the other, they must fight off ambitious 'generalists' who also want to benefit from the new situation. To cope, they have adopted a variety of different paths, and now their trajectories are diverging completely.

Saab, Aston Martin, Jaguar, Volvo, Land Rover, Bentley and Lamborghini have ultimately opted to be integrated into a large automobile group pursuing the volume and diversity strategy: General Motors for the first (Saab), Ford for the four next brands, and Volkswagen for the latter two. By so doing, they hope to avail themselves of the resources they need. For these prestigious marques, which automobile groups are ready to spend considerable amounts of money upon, the market remains a global one. In fact, it is precisely because of this homogeneity of the market, and of the brand's image, that firms feel they can justify the investments they have been making (the good-will they have been paying). GM's global platform, with its code name 'Epsilon', should help with its development of one Saab model, two Opels, and several American models (ranging from Chevrolet to Saturn) arriving on the market from 2001. However, the logic of this 'volume and diversity' strategy that General Motors has been pursuing runs the risk that these top-of-the-range cars will lose their essential 'quality' – that is, their specificity (see Bordenave and Lung, 2002). Fiat, which was forced to take over Lancia in the 1970s and Alfa Romeo in the 1980s, lost these marques a large part of their prestige when it decided to launch, in their name, models whose platforms were being shared with Fiat's own models (see Volpato, ch. 12 in this volume). Ford grouped in a separate entity (called 'Premier Automotive') all the marques involved in its corporate 'quality' strategy: Lincoln, Aston Martin, Jaguar, Volvo and Land Rover. The objectives are the rationalized purchasing of components, shared R&D investments (that is, Volvo's safety competency) and the 'commonalization' of a certain number of electronic or mechanical components, and even the sharing of platforms. Although the commonalization seems to be limited to top-range cars, the risk isn't so different from the risk taken by GM. The consumers of top-range cars require very specific vehicles which include (and perhaps even have the greatest importance to them) platforms. Finally, the decision of Volkswagen to be present in the very highest top-range segment (Bentley, Lamborghini and Bugatti) is so strange that we must wait a little to see whether this orientation will last.

A second path for which a number of firms have opted is that of external growth. This involves acquiring other automakers who already cover, or else who are likely to cover, the new sub-markets of the top-of-the-range category. This was BMW's path when it purchased Rover in 1994 and Rolls-Royce in 1999. Rolls-Royce's new models have yet to appear. Land Rover's recreational vehicles were already positioned at the top of the range. With a few design modifications and a handful of vigorous actions aimed at improving manufacturing quality, Rover's small and medium-sized cars could have been integrated into a product range for well-to-do customers. However, for this to succeed, the policy would have had to have been carried out energetically and without wasting time, especially since the continued rise in the value of the pound sterling was cutting the company off from a significant chunk of its potential export market. To avoid a catastrophe, in 2000 BMW had to sell Rover to an English consortium for a token sum. On the other hand, it was able to sell Land Rover to Ford at a good price. All that BMW has retained from this adventure is the world-famous Mini, which it has turned into a small top-of-the-range urban vehicle (Freyssenet and Mair, 2000b; Eckardt and Klemm, ch. 8 in this volume).

Daimler (Mercedes) has chosen yet another path. In truth, its trajectory is relatively opaque and may even turn out to be full of danger (see Köhler, ch. 4 in this volume). In successively creating the Smart and the Maybach, in acquiring Chrysler and Mitsubishi, and in taking a stake in Hyundai, Daimler has embarked on two possible trajectories. Either it can become an automobile giant, turning out all kinds of vehicles for all sorts of clients, or else it can remain a top-of-the-range automaker, but for all types of vehicle. The difficulty is that neither Chrysler nor Mitsubishi are 'generalist' manufacturers, even though they have tried regularly to achieve this status. Nor are they top-of-the-range automakers. The only times that either has made a profit is when they have reverted to their original strategy – that is, to a strategy based on 'innovation and flexibility'. Yet the requirements of this strategy are such that it is almost totally incompatible with any other.

Finally, some top-of-the-range automakers prefer to remain small and independent, as, for example, Porsche and Pininfarina. They only co-operate with 'generalist' automakers for some products. And they always are profitable.

Industrial history is full of paradoxes. The paradox that we are focusing on at present is that the main 'specialist' automakers have either been losing their independence, or thinking that they must change their strategy at the very moment that the international market for top-of-the-range products is most likely to launch them on a new phase of expansion. But history isn't finished yet; some brands may yet become independent again.

Permanent cost reduction strategy: very restrictive conditions needed to succeed

Characteristics, conditions and requirements

In this strategy, costs are to be cut in all circumstances and at all times. To a certain extent, the other profit sources are no more than a complement, and even then only when they are feasible, useful and compatible. Cost reduction will always remain the prime objective when a firm envisages any situation, as no outcome is ever taken for granted. The strategy consists of lowering return costs by constant savings drives, both internally and through suppliers. It demands strict production planning and the avoidance of taking risks, such as running into debt, producing conceptually innovative products, volatile markets, mergers or acquisitions, productive internationalization and so on.

It is particularly well-suited when national growth is driven by the export of day-to-day products and when the redistribution of competitiveness gains is done in a co-ordinated and moderately hierarchized manner. Employees are subject to external competitiveness constraints, and the volume and structure of national demand is sufficiently predictable to avoid any unforeseen and costly variations in production.

For these same reasons, this strategy, which Toyota has been pursuing since the 1950s, is not as robust as it would appear, because it is so demanding. The strategy struggles when sudden changes occur (related, for example, to shfits in demand levels or in currency parities) – changes that can in one fell swoop ruin the patient and continual efforts required by employees and suppliers, who might then be inclined to curtail their participation in the cost-reduction drive, as was the case at Toyota in the early 1990s (Shimizu, 1999; Fujimoto, 1999).

PSA was the only European automaker to pursue a 'permanent cost reduction' strategy, but only until the mid-1960s. Since the 1990s, Toyota has attempted to implement this strategy in Europe. But since the beginning its British subsidiary has not succeeded in being profitable because of insufficiently attractive products, labour instability and large exchange-rate variation. With the opening of a new assembly plant in France in 2001 and the planned creation of a joint venture with PSA in the Czech Republic in 2005, Toyota is trying to offer products more adapted. It will also have the advantage of monetary stability in the euro zone.

Innovation and flexibility strategy: a necessary specific regional policy

Automakers who arrive late in the automobile sector and are trying to carve out a space for themselves among firms with already established market positions often choose to pursue an 'innovation and flexibility' strategy. This was the case of Honda in the 1960s. The relevancy of the 'innovation and flexibility' strategy has been reinforced by certain countries' recent tendency to develop a 'competitive' distribution of national income. This explains the extremely rapid renaissance of Renault in the 1990s, similar to the renaissance of Chrysler in the 1980s in the USA.

Characteristics, conditions and requirements

This strategy consists of designing products that respond to new expectations and/or emerging demands; manufacturing them massively and immediately if actual orders match forecasts; or, inversely, abandoning them rapidly and for as little cost as possible if they fail commercially. Profits actually stem from an innovation rent derived from commercial relevancy – as long as this innovation is not copied. The best way of delaying this outcome is to be able to satisfy the market segment that has been created in as short a period of time as possible.

An innovation and flexibility strategy is reinforced when the needs or lifestyles of the social categories that are being targeted change periodically, or when new categories emerge, with people who are distinct at an economic and social level. This is generally what occurs in those growth modes that are marked by a 'competitive' type of national income distribution. It is the reason why this strategy, which had become the bane of many automakers during the post-war boom years, has again become a winner, as witnessed by the good performances of Honda, Chrysler (before its merger with Daimler) and Renault (Boyer and Freyssenet, 2000b, 2002).

The firms pursuing this strategy must be financially independent. They must be entirely free to assume the risks that are inherent in conceptual innovation. They must also be free of any medium/long-term commitment to their suppliers, to enable them to change production rapidly if necessary. They must have at their disposal an easily re-convertible production tool and a workforce that enables innovativeness, at both product and production process levels. Last, they must also possess an extremely in-depth knowledge of which customer expectations are unsatisfied and unexpressed, to be able to offer innovative vehicles that are commercially appropriate.

For this strategy to succeed, the regionalization and heterogenization of demand would have to prevail over globalization and homogenization. This hypothesis may suit the producers that remain concentrated on a single region, taking advantage of their detailed knowledge of their markets, just as producers that internationalize ensure that they have the means to understand consumer expectations in the regions in which they invest. In these cases, regional design offices do more than simply restyle base models; they modify them in response to local desires, and they may even design specific models. Regional subsidiaries have a broad autonomy because they have to detect emerging local requirements. To do so, they rely heavily on local managers, designers, engineers and distributors. The function of the company at the global level is to take responsibility for financial control, the distribution of investments, particularly to new regions, and to ensure that knowledge drawn from experience is circulated.

Chrysler, an inconstant innovation and flexibility strategy

Since its creation, Chrysler has been characterized by flourishing periods during which it develops an innovation and flexibility strategy, followed immediately by difficult periods when it believes it can become an automaker like the others. In particular, its attempts to become an internationalized company in the 1960s and 1970s, through the purchase of European automakers and through its alliance with Mitsubishi, was a failure. In the 1980s, Chrysler revived because the invention of SUVs – products that accounted by 1999 for a third of the American market (Belzovski, 1998). However, it has not been able so far to procure means that are coherent, and which will enable them to pursue, profitably and durably an 'innovation and flexibility' strategy. Chrysler in particular was not quick enough to acquire an indispensable financial independence – that is, it could not lock up its shareholder structure. An attempted take-over in which Chrysler was a target for Kirk Kerkorian, a financier associated with one of the firm's former CEOs (Lee Iacocca), induced the firm's executives to agree to a merger with Daimler. However, the expected complementarities between the two firms turned out to be incompatibilities – stemming from the fact that they had been pursuing different profit strategies. For the time being, not only has Chrysler gained nothing from what has, purely and simply, turned into a take-over, but also many projects involving innovative models have been abandoned and the company's main innovators, in a weakened position, have left. By early 2001, Chrysler's strategy had lost all visibility (see Köhler, ch. 4 in this volume).

The regional renewal of Renault, endangered by the global alliance with Nissan?

After the failure of its attempt to enter the American market through its control of American Motors in 1980s, Renault adopted an innovation and flexibility strategy in the 1990s, launching a complete range of passenger vans after noting the success of its initial top-of-the-range van. These models did not suffer from the fact that Renault had withdrawn itself back to Europe. Quite the contrary, in fact, and their success can be explained by the fact that they were appropriate for the new clienteles in this part of the world. They limited the losses that Renault was incurring in its saloon car segment (following a weakness in its 'traditional' demand) and ultimately became Renault's main source of profit.

The company, somewhat surprised by the success of its innovative models (which in the end accounted for most of its profits, even though they should only have been the icing on the cake), preferred to prioritize productive and commercial internationalization, taking over Nissan, Dacia and Samsung instead of confirming its strategy and devising suitable models. Is Renault's present orientation compatible with that of Nissan? Indeed, Nissan has a totally different profit strategy: of volume and diversity. Until now, no single automobile group has been able to make a success of this type of cohabitation. In fact, the challenge Renault has embarked upon is nothing less than of inventing and establishing the means to surpass the structural incompatibilities of both strategy and production systems.

For the time being, Renault and Nissan appear to be moving towards a regionalization scheme: a division of roles among the world's various regions according to the competencies and advantages that each has acquired. Renault is to be the leader in Europe (absorbing the Japanese firm's activities there) and in the emerging countries (outside of Asia); and it will find shelter behind its partner in the Asia-Pacific region and in North America. Potential conflicts with Renault's other partners are being kept under wraps for the moment, with the Korean firm Samsung relying on Nissan's technologies, and Dacia in Romania undergoing a thorough restructuring. The new configuration might allow the Group finally to complete a project it had first announced in the early 1990s, with Nissan's attempt to offer a specific product range in each of the Triad's three poles. This product range is based on variants of three basic models, and on the development of a specific model in the emerging markets. For Nissan, as for the two major Americans, a 'volume and diversity' strategy, when extended to the international level, has had problems taking root.

The regional future of innovation and flexibility strategy

The most competitive redistribution of income in many countries today may favour the emergence of new strata or the modification of demand in existing categories. It must, however, not lead to social instability through excess competition, preventing truly new expectations from forming. The 'innovation and flexibility' strategy thus implies very fine attention to qualitative changes in the different markets, but also markets vast enough so that new demand represents sufficient volume. The scenario of the making up of regional poles adopting a competitive mode of income redistribution is favourable to this profit strategy, as it offers both innovative demand and the necessary volume. With this hypothesis, an autobuilder implementing the 'innovation and flexibility' strategy would not necessarily need to spread itself on a world-wide basis and be perfectly profitable on a regional scale. This could be the case for Honda, Chrysler and Renault, each being the 'innovation and flexibility' firm in its region of the world. A global firm pursuing this strategy is nevertheless conceivable, but it would be necessary for it to be able to design and produce innovative vehicles adapted to the new social strata that appear in the different areas, as Honda succeeded in doing in the USA in the 1970s and 1980s, and not to content itself with trying to sell innovative models elsewhere that have been designed in its home zone.

Conclusion

Although a logic of production (economies of scale) has induced automobile manufacturers to extend their area of commercialization on a global scale, it is in their articulation with a market, and synchronizing with demand, that they have incorporated the regional tier as a level at which they can achieve a certain coherence. Apart from the prestige automobiles, there are limits to the homogenization of global demand, and the failure of Ford's attempt to integrate its activities globally shows that automobile firms should be looking for more appropriate strategies – and, above all, for models or innovative forms of organization that are better adapted to a particular region. It is not at all certain that the real challenge is to be the first to globalize mono-regional strategies (such as the one that PSA has pursued) – biregional, multiregional, and even transregional strategies can all be relevant at a certain time, and in a given place.

Notes

1 This chapter draws on the findings of GERPISA's first and second research programmes (Boyer and Freyssenet, 2000b, 2002; Freyssenet and Lung, 2000), both of which were co-directed by Michel Freyssenet, working with Robert Boyer and Yannick Lung, respectively. The authors have benefited greatly from the discussions that have taken place within the GERPISA international network, but accept full responsibility for any errors that may have persisted in the present text.

References

Belzowski, B. M. (1998) 'Reinventing Chrysler', in M. Freyssenet, A. Mair, K. Shimizu and G. Volpato (eds) *One Best Way? The Trajectories and Industrial Models of World Automobile Producers*, Oxford/New York: Oxford University Press.

Bordenave, G. (1998) 'Le premier demi-siècle de Ford en Europe: la résistance opiniâtre d'un espace à l'universalisme proclamé d'un modèle d'organization productive', *Le mouvement social*, no. 185.

Bordenave, G. (2000) 'La globalisation au coeur du changement organisationnel: crise et redressement de Ford Motor Company', in M. Freyssenet, A. Mair, K. Shimizu and G. Volpato (eds), *Quel modèle productif? Trajectoires et modèles industriels des constructeurs automobiles mondiaux*, Paris: La Découverte.

Bordenave, G. and Lung, Y. (2002) 'Concurrence oligopolistique et mimétisme des stratégies d'internationalisation dans l'industrie automobile: Ford et General Motors', in H. Bonin *et al.* (eds), *Transnational Companies*, Paris: PLAGE.

Bordenave, G., Bélis-Bergouignan, M. C. and Lung Y. (2000) 'Global Strategies in the Automobile Industry', *Regional Studies*, vol. 34.

Boyer, R. (1999) 'La politique à l'ère de la mondialisation et de la finance: le point sur quelques recherches régulationnistes', *L'année de la régulation*, vol. 3.

Boyer, R. and Freyssenet, M. (1999) 'L'avenir est à nouveau ouvert. Stratégies de profit, formes d'internationalisation et nouveaux espaces de l'industrie automobile', *Gérer et Comprendre, Annales des Mines*, June.

Boyer, R. and Freyssenet, M. (2000a) 'Fusions-acquisitions et stratégies de profit: une nouvelle approche', *Revue française de gestion*, no. 131, November–December.

Boyer, R. and Freyssenet, M. (2000b, 2002) *Les modèles productifs*, Paris: La Découverte, 2000; English revised edition: *The Productive Models: The Conditions of Profitability*, London/New York: Palgrave, 2002.

Boyer, R. and Freyssenet, M. (forthcoming) *The World that Changed the Machine*.

Boyer, R. and Saillard, Y. (eds) (1995, 2001) *Théorie de la régulation. Etats des savoirs*, Paris: La Découverte; English edition: *Regulation Theory: The State of the Art*, London: Routledge, 2001.

Boyer, R., Charron, E., Jürgens, U. and Tolliday, S. (eds) (1998) *Between Imitation and Innovation: The Transfer and Hybridization of Productive Models in the International Automobile Industry*, Oxford/New York: Oxford University Press.

Camuffo, A. and Volpato, G. (1999) 'From Lean to Modular Manufacturing? The Case of the Fiat "178" World Car', IMVP-MIT Globalization Research.

Carrillo, J. and Hinojosa, R. (forthcoming) 'An Uncertain Trajectory in Regional Integration: The Future of Motor Vehicle Production in the NAFTA', in J. Carrillo, Y. Lung and R. van Tulder (eds), *Cars, Carriers of Regionalism*.

Carrillo, J., Lung, Y. and van Tulder, R. (eds) (forthcoming) *Cars, Carriers of Regionalism*.

Chanaron, J. J. and Lung, Y. (1995) *Economie de l'automobile*, Paris: La Découverte.

Durand, J. P., Stewart, P. and Castillo, J. J. (eds) (1998) *L'avenir du travail à la chaîne. Une comparaison internationale dans l'industrie automobile*, Paris: La Découverte.

Ellegard, K. (1995) 'The Creation of a New Production System at the Volvo Automobile Assembly Plant in Uddevalla, Sweden', in A. Sandberg (ed.), *Enriching Production*, Aldershot: Avebury.

Freyssenet, M. (1998a) 'Reflective Production: An Alternative to Mass-Production and to Lean Production?', *Economic and Industrial Democracy*, vol. 19, no. 1, February.

Freyssenet, M. (1998b) 'Intersecting Trajectories and Model Change', in M. Freyssenet, A. Mair, K. Shimizu and G. Volpato (eds), *One Best Way? The Trajectories and Industrial Models of World Automobile Producers*, Oxford/New York: Oxford University Press.

Freyssenet, M. and Lung, Y. (2000) 'Between Regionalization and Globalization: What Future for the Automobile Industry?', in J. Humphrey, Y. Lecler and M. S. Salerno (eds), *Global Strategies and Local Realities: The Auto Industry in Emerging Market*, London: Macmillan.

Freyssenet, M. and Mair, A. (2000a) 'Le modèle industriel inventé par Honda', in M. Freyssenet, A. Mair, K. Shimizu and G. Volpato (eds), *Quel modèle productif? Trajectoires et modèles industriels des constructeurs automobiles mondiaux*, Paris: La Découverte.

Freyssenet, M. and Mair, A. (2000b) 'De British Leyland à Rover: la recherche d'une stratégie de profit pertinente', in M. Freyssenet, A. Mair, K. Shimizu and G. Volpato (eds), *Quel modèle productif? Trajectoires et modèles industriels des constructeurs automobiles mondiaux*, Paris: La Découverte.

Freyssenet, M., Shimizu, K. and Volpato, G. (eds) (2002) *Globalization or Regionalization of the American and Asian Car Industry?* London/New York: Palgrave.

Freyssenet, M., Mair, A., Shimizu, K. and Volpato, G. (eds) (1998) *One Best Way? The Trajectories and Industrial Models of World Automobile Producers*, Oxford/New York: Oxford University Press.

Froud, J., Haslam, C., Johal, S. and Williams, K. (2000) 'Ford's New Policy: A Business Analysis of Financialisation', in M. Freyssenet and Y. Lung (eds), *The World that Changed the Machine: The Future of the Auto Industry for the 21st Century*, Proceedings of the Eighth GERPISA International Colloquium, Paris, June 8–10.

Fujimoto, T. (1999) *The Evolution of a Manufacturing System at Toyota*, Oxford/New York: Oxford University Press.

Guiheux, G. and Lecler, Y. (2000) 'Japanese Car Manufacturers and Component Makers in the ASEAN Region: A Case of Expatriation under Duress – or a Strategy of Regionally Integrated Production?', in J. Humphrey, Y. Lecler and M. S. Salerno (eds), *Global Strategies and Local Realities: The Auto Industry in Emerging Markets*, London: Macmillan.

Hanada, M. (1998) 'Restructuring to Regain Competitiveness', in M. Freyssenet, A. Mair, K. Shimizu and G. Volpato (eds), *One Best Way? The Trajectories and Industrial Models of World Automobile Producers*, Oxford/New York: Oxford University Press.

Humphrey, J., Lecler, Y. and Salerno, M. S. (eds) *Global Strategies and Local Realities: The Auto Industry in Emerging Market*, London: Macmillan/New York: St. Martin's Press.

Jetin, B. (1999) 'The Historical Evolution of Supply Variety: An International Comparative Study', in Y. Lung et al. (eds), *Coping with Variety: Flexible Productive Systems for Product Variety in the Auto Industry*, Aldershot: Ashgate.

Jürgens, U. (1998) 'The Development of Volkswagen's Industrial Model, 1967–1995', in M. Freyssenet, A. Mair, K. Shimizu and G. Volpato (eds), *One Best Way? The Trajectories and Industrial Models of World Automobile Producers*, Oxford/New York: Oxford University Press.

Layan, J. B. and Lung, Y. (forthcoming) 'European Regional Integration and Relocation of Productive Activities in the Car Industry', in J. Carrillo, Y. Lung and R. van Tulder (eds), *Cars, Carriers of Regionalism*.

Lung, Y. (2000) 'Is the Rise of Emerging Countries as Automobile Producers an Irreversible Phenomenon?', in J. Humphrey, Y. Lecler and M. S. Salerno (eds) *Global*

Strategies and Local Realities: The Auto Industry in Emerging Markets, London: Macmillan/New York: St. Martin's Press.

Lung, Y. (2001) 'The Coordination of Competencies and Knowledge: A Critical Issue for Regional Automotive Systems', *International Journal of Automotive Technology Management*, vol. 1, no. 1.

Lung, Y., Chanaron, J. J., Fujimoto, T. and Raff, D. (eds) (1999) *Coping with Variety: Flexible Productive Systems for Product Variety in the Auto Industry*, Aldershot: Ashgate.

Mair, A. (1994) *Honda's Global Local Corporation*, London: Macmillan.

Norberto, E. and Uri, D. (2000) 'La révolution des petites cylindrées Le marché nouveau des "voitures populaires" au Brésil', *Actes du GERPISA*, no. 29.

Shimizu, K. (1999) *Le Toyotisme*, Paris: La Découverte.

Volpato, G. (2000) 'La filière automobile italienne: vers la globalisation', in F. Bost and G. Dupuy (eds), *'L'automobile et son monde*, Paris: Editions de l'Aube.

Womack, J. P., Jones, D. T. and Roos, D. (1990) *The Machine That Changed the World*, New York: Rawson Associates.

Appendix: Presentation of the GERPISA International Network

GERPISA (the Permanent Group for the Study of and Research into the Automobile Industry and its Employees) started out as a network of French economists, and management, history and sociology researchers who were interested in the automobile industry. Founded by Michel Freyssenet (CNRS, sociologist) and Patrick Fridenson (EHESS, historian), it was transformed into an international network in 1992 in order to carry out a research programme on the 'Emergence of new industrial models'.

With Robert Boyer (CEPREMAP, CNRS, EHESS, economist) and Michel Freyssenet supervising its scientific orientations and under the management of an international committee, the programme (which lasted from 1993 to 1996) made it possible, thanks to its study of the automobile firms' (and their transplants') trajectories, productive organization and employment relationships, to demonstrate that *lean production*, which, according to the authors of *The Machine that Changed the World* was supposed to become the industrial model for the twenty-first century, was in fact an inaccurate amalgamation of two completely different productive models – the 'Toyotian' and the 'Hondian'. Moreover, it showed that there are, have always been, and probably always will be several productive models that are capable of performing well at any given time. Shareholders, executives and employees are not only not obliged to adopt a *one best way*; they have to devise a 'company governance compromise' covering the means that will allow them to implement one of the several profit strategies that are relevant to the economic and social environment in which they find themselves.

A second programme (running from 1997 to 1999) entitled 'The automobile industry, between globalization and regionalization', supervised by Michel Freyssenet and by Yannick Lung (Bordeaux IV, economist), tested the analytical framework that had been developed during the first programme in an attempt to better understand the new wave of automobile manufacturers' and component makers' internationalization that had been observed over the previous decade. The outcome was that the viability of the choices being made depends primarily on the chosen profit strategies' compatibility with the growth modes in the areas being invested.

The third programme (2000–2) was developed under Yannick Lung's supervision with the support of the European Union (COCKEAS project, thematic network 5th Framework, Key Action 4: HPSE–CT–1999–00022). It focuses on the issues at stake in the 'Co-ordination of knowledge and competencies in the regional automotive systems'. Supplementing existing studies of forms of regionalization in the automobile industry, the programme analyses the sector's new contours as well as the development of new relational and co-operative modes among its actors.

In 2002, GERPISA comprised 350 members from twenty-seven different countries. Affiliated with the Centre de Recherches Historiques (CRH) of the Ecole des Hautes Etudes en Sciences Sociales (EHESS), and acknowledged as a host structure by the French Ministry of National Education, its administrative offices are located in the Université d'Evry. It receives additional financial and material support from the French automobile companies, from their professional association (the CCFA), and from the European Union.

The international management committee is made up of twenty-four members: Annie Beretti (Innovation Department, PSA); Robert Boyer (CNRS-EHESS, Paris); Juan José Castillo (Universidad Complutense, Madrid); Jorge Carrillo (Colegio de la

Frontera Norte, Mexico); Jean-Jacques Chanaron (CNRS, Lyon); Elsie Charron (CNRS, Paris), Jean-Pierre Durand (Université d'Evry); Michel Freyssenet (CNRS, Paris); Patrick Fridenson (EHESS, Paris); Takahiro Fujimoto (University of Tokyo); John Humphrey (University of Sussex, UK); Bruno Jetin (Université Paris XIII); Ulrich Jürgens (WZB, Berlin); Yveline Lecler (MRASH/IAO, Lyon); Yannick Lung (Université de Bordeaux IV); Jean-Claude Monnet (Research Department, Renault); Mario Sergio Salerno (University of São Paolo); Koichi Shimizu (University of Okayama, Japan); Koichi Shimokawa (Hosei University, Tokyo); Paul Stewart (University of Bristol); Steve Tolliday (University of Leeds); Rob Van Tulder (Erasmus University, Rotterdam); Giuseppe Volpato (Ca'Foscari University, Venice); and Karel Williams (Victoria University, Manchester).

GERPISA publications

GERPISA edits in both English and French a quarterly review entitled *Actes du GERPISA* and a monthly newsletter called *La Lettre du GERPISA*. The review combines the writings the network's members have presented on a specific topic in various work meetings. The newsletter comments on news from the automotive world and provides up-to-date information on what is happening in the network. Findings from the first and second programmes have been published in a series of books, listed below.

First Programme: 'Emergence of new industrial models'

Boyer, R. and Freyssenet, M. (2002, 2000) *The Productive Models*, London/New York: Palgrave, 2002; First edition in French: *Les modèles productifs*, Paris: La Découverte, 2000.

Boyer, R. and Freyssenet, M. (forthcoming) *The World that Changed the Machine*.

Boyer, R., Charron, E., Jürgens, U. and Tolliday, S. (eds) (1998) *Between Imitation and Innovation: The Transfer and Hybridization of Productive Models in the International Automobile Industry*, Oxford/New York: Oxford University Press.

Durand, J. P., Stewart, P. and Castillo, J. J. (eds) (1999, 1998) *Teamwork in the Automobile Industry: Radical Change or Passing Fashion*, London: Macmillan, 1999; First edition in French: *L'avenir du travail à la chaîne*, Paris: La Découverte, 1998.

Freyssenet, M., Mair, A., Shimizu, K. and Volpato, G. (eds) (1998, 2000) *One Best Way? Trajectories and Industrial Models of the World's Automobile Producers*, Oxford/New York: Oxford University Press, 1998; French translation: *Quel modèle productif? Trajectoires et modèles industriels des constructeurs automobiles mondiaux*, Paris: La Découverte, 2000.

Lung, Y., Chanaron, J. J., Fujimoto, T. and Raff, D. (eds) (1999) *Coping with Variety: Flexible Productive Systems for Product Variety in the Auto Industry*, Aldershot: Ashgate.

Shimizu, K. (1999) *Le Toyotisme*, Paris: La Découverte.

Second Programme: 'The automobile industry between globalization and regionalization'

Carillo, J., Lung, Y. and van Tulder, R. (eds) (forthcoming) *Cars, Carriers of Regionalism*.

Charron, E. and Stewart, P. (eds) (2003) *Work and Employment Relations in the Automobile Industry*, London/New York: Palgrave.

Freyssenet, M., Shimizu, K. and Volpato, G. (eds) (2003) *Globalization or Regionalization of the European Car Industry?*, London/New York: Palgrave.

Freyssenet, M., Shimizu, K. and Volpato, G. (eds) (2003) *Globalization or Regionalization of the American and Asian Car Industry?*, London/New York: Palgrave.

Humphrey, J., Leclere, Y. and Salerno, M. (eds) (2000) *Global Strategies and Local Realities: The Auto Industry in Emerging Markets*, London: Macmillan/New York: St. Martin's Press.

Third Programme: 'Co-ordination of knowledge and competencies in the regional automotive systems'

Lung, Y. (ed.) (2002) 'The Changing Geography of the Automobile Industry, Symposium', *International Journal of Urban and Regional Research*, no. 4.

Lung, Y. and Volpato, G. (eds) (2002) 'Reconfuring the Auto Industry', *International Journal of Automotive Technology and Management*, vol. 2, no. 1.

Williams, K. (ed.) (2002) 'The Tyranny of Finance? New Agendas for Auto Research', *Competition and Change*, vol. 6, (double issue) nos. 1 and 2.

Information on GERPISA's activities can be obtained by contacting
GERPISA réseau international. Université d'Evry-Val d'Essonne,
rue du Facteur Cheval, 91025 Evry cedex, France.
Telephone: 33 (1) 69.47.78.95   Fax 33 (1) 69.47.78.99
E-mail: contact@gerpisa.univ-evry.fr
Website: http//www.gerpisa.univ-evry.fr

Index